Reaction Times

Reaction Times

Edited by
A. T. Welford
Professor Emeritus of Psychology, University of Adelaide,
Adelaide, Australia

With contributions by
J. M. T. Brebner, N. Kirby, D. McNicol,
T. Nettelbeck, G. A. Smith, G. W. Stewart
and D. Vickers

1980

ACADEMIC PRESS

A Subsidiary of Harcourt Brace Jovanovich, Publishers

London · New York · Toronto · Sydney · San Francisco

ACADEMIC PRESS INC. (LONDON) LTD.
24/28 Oval Road,
London NW1

United States Edition published by
ACADEMIC PRESS INC.
111 Fifth Avenue,
New York, New York 10003

British Library Cataloguing in Publication Data
Reaction times
1. Reaction-times
I. Welford, Alan Traviss
152.8′3   BF317   80-40646
ISBN 0-12-742880-1

Filmset in 'Monophoto' by Eta Services (Typesetters) Ltd., Beccles, Suffolk
Printed in Great Britain by Galliard (Printers) Ltd, Great Yarmouth

Contributors

J. M. T. Brebner *Department of Psychology, University of Adelaide, G.P.O. Box 498, Adelaide, South Australia 5001.*

N. Kirby *Department of Psychology, University of Adelaide, G.P.O. Box 498, Adelaide, South Australia 5001.*

D. McNicol *School of Psychology, University of New South Wales, P.O. Box 1, Kensington, New South Wales, Australia 2033.*

T. Nettelbeck *Department of Psychology, University of Adelaide, G.P.O. Box 498, Adelaide, South Australia 5001.*

G. A. Smith *Department of Psychology, University of Melbourne, Parkeville, Victoria, Australia 3052.*

G. W. Stewart *School of Psychology, University of New South Wales, P.O. Box 1, Kensington, New South Wales, Australia 2033.*

D. Vickers *Department of Psychology, University of Adelaide, G.P.O. Box 498, Adelaide, South Australia 5001.*

A. T. Welford *581 Kamoku Street, Apt. 506, Honolulu, Hawaii 96826, U.S.A.*

Preface

During the early days of experimental psychology in the nineteenth century, reaction times were one of the main areas of study, but by the middle of the present century they had become neglected to the extent that they are hardly mentioned in some leading textbooks of the time. From the 1950s onwards interest rapidly revived as it became recognized that the measurement of reaction times was an important psychophysical method, able to account with remarkable precision for various mediating processes between stimuli and responses, and providing a powerful means of making psychology a truly quantitative science.

Between 1969 and 1979 several of us in the Adelaide University Department of Psychology were actively engaged in research on reaction times. We became acutely aware of the lack of a comprehensive treatment of them in book form, and it occurred to us that we should attempt jointly to remedy the deficiency. Our first intention was to produce an exhaustive survey of research covering the whole area. However, it quickly became obvious that this was far too vast an undertaking to be practical. We therefore lowered our sights to trying each to summarize findings from our own research and field of special interest and to setting these in context. In doing so we hope to have provided the reader with at least a substantial base from which to extend his or her studies, and that the contexts of the various specialities provide a coverage, however sketchy in places, of the area as a whole.

Two points of presentation need brief mention. First, it has often been necessary to refer to the same work in more than one chapter. Attempts have been made in these cases to avoid repetition by means of cross-referencing, but this has not always been possible since the chapters have sometimes drawn on different aspects or interpretations of the work. Second, although we had a large measure of agreement among ourselves,

vii

there were also some divergences. Such is inevitable at the present stage of knowledge, and we have felt it better to let the differences appear than attempt to force ourselves to a single, unified view.

Our sincere thanks are due to those who helped us in the preparation of our scripts, especially Mrs M. Blaber, Mrs J. Fallon, Miss B. V. C. Batts, Miss V. Clark and Miss B. Persson.

May 1980   A.T.W.

Contents

Chapter 1

Introduction: An Historical Background Sketch

J. M. T. BREBNER and A. T. WELFORD

Reaction time, that is the time from the onset of a stimulus or signal to the initiation of response, has been recognized since the mid-nineteenth century as a potentially powerful means of relating mental events to physical measures. The many studies made during the latter part of the century and the theories which were built on them are now known to be too simple, although more recent developments have enhanced the value of reaction time as a measure rather than diminished it. It is still now, as it was then, a very relevant question to ask, if reaction time is longer in one set of circumstances than another, what is being done in the additional time? Although the means of answering the question are now much more sophisticated than they were a century ago, the insights gained by the pioneers, like their contemporaries in other fields of science, are impressive and provide a base we still build on to-day.

We may, therefore, properly begin by looking back to the earliest researches in this field of study. As so often happens, scientific interest was not aroused until a practical problem arose which needed to be solved. The search for lawful relationships between changes in the environment and the time to respond may be said to have begun in 1820 with the investigations of one man—F. W. Bessel, astronomer at Könisberg. The problem to which he applied himself was the accuracy with which he and his colleagues recorded the times of stellar transits. Astronomers of the early nineteenth century estimated the exact time at which a star passed the hairline of their telescopes, by listening to the ticking of a metronome and judging the point of time between the one second beats as precisely as they could. Differences between astronomers in their timings had been noted in the past and this led Bessel to undertake the acid test by comparing his own times with those of an astronomer visiting his observatory. Large discrepancies were obvious in the readings of the two men, with Bessel always judging the transit earlier

1

than his visitor did. This finding was published, and many astronomers proceeded to compare their own timing with that of their assistants and visitors from other observatories. The difference between two observers, which was shown in the form

Walbeck–Bessel = 1.041 seconds,

was referred to as the "personal equation", meaning the difference between two people. This term persisted for many years, but in 1888 Sanford distinguished the absolute personal equation from the original relative personal equation, and in time a person's speed or slowness of response came to be commonly attributed to his "personal equation" meaning the sum of that person's various characteristics.

After Bessel's first enquiry various astronomers went on to devise methods of overcoming the differences between individuals in their recordings. It was in this way that the earliest studies of reaction time began.

Ribot (1900) notes that it was Helmholtz (1850), himself following an earlier suggestion of Dubois-Reymond, who first designed a reaction time task in an attempt to measure the speed of neural transmission. The method consisted of holding constant the response to be made while varying the part of the body which was stimulated so that impulses had to be transmitted along longer or shorter lengths of nerve fibre. From the times taken over different measured lengths of fibre the velocity of neural transmission could be calculated. Speed of nerve conduction does not really concern us here because, as Helmholtz found, it forms only a small part of the total reaction time: the major part is taken up by central processes, and it is to these that most subsequent studies have been addressed.

Many of the early studies have been surveyed by Boring (1929) and by Woodworth (1938), see also Woodworth and Schlosberg (1954) and need not be gone over again in detail here. For our present purpose it is sufficient to note that, broadly, early studies dealt with five classes of problem, each of which is still very much with us to-day.

1. Sensory factors

(A) STRENGTH OF STIMULUS

Several early studies found that reaction time tended to shorten as the intensity of the stimulus increased up to a certain level, but thereafter was little affected by stimulus strength. Attempts were made later to fit formulae to the relationship. In particular, Piéron (1920) proposed several equations for different sets of results, of the general type

$$RT = \frac{a}{i^n} + k \tag{1.1}$$

to describe the relationship between reaction time and intensity, where i is a measure of intensity, a is a reducible time value, k is an irreducible time constant and n is an exponent which differs with various senses and conditions. This formulation allows that reaction time will decrease as a function of intensity down to the value of the constant k. This notion of an irreducible lower limit, a "physiological" limit to reaction time, was applied in so-called *simple RT* settings where there is only one signal and response, and depends on the assumption that the only information processed is that which indicates a signal has occurred. Any hypothetical k, however, could be assumed to vary across reaction time tasks according to various conditions.

Effective stimulus level appears to be relative rather than absolute. It depends essentially upon some difference or ratio between the stimulus and a pre-existing background state. An example is seen in an experiment by Hovland (1936) studying the reaction time to a stimulus in relation to previous adaptation level. He used a stimulus intensity of 250 foot candles and a series of adapting stimuli of 1, 50, 100, 150 and 200 foot candles, and found that mean reaction time decreased as the adaptation level diverged from the test stimulus level of illumination, changing from 154 milliseconds at 200 foot candles to 131 milliseconds at 0 foot candles.

Increasing the amount of stimulation in ways other than raising the relative intensity also affects reaction time. For instance, it varies with the area and duration of stimulation. These effects parallel similar improvements in perceptual performance with increased area (spatial summation) or duration (temporal summation).

The *area* of a stimulus has been shown to affect reaction time to taste stimuli (Elsberg and Spotnitz, 1938) and to visual stimuli (Froeberg, 1907; Ferrée and Rand, 1927). Longer *durations* of a stimulus also give slightly faster reaction times for visual stimuli (Froeberg, 1907) and auditory stimuli (Wells, 1913). With either area of duration, however, the change of reaction time is small and tends to be observed only over a narrow range of stimuli the extent of which varies with the relative sensitivity of the receptor mechanisms. Indeed, increasing either area or duration may lengthen reaction time rather than make it faster by providing the subject with an opportunity to take a *longer* sample of sensory information than is necessary (Gregg and Brogden, 1950; Birren and Botwinick, 1955; Botwinick *et al.*, 1958). Possibly reflecting this, reaction time is generally faster to the offset of a stimulus than to its onset (Jenkins, 1926; Kleint, 1928; Essen, 1937) a fact which accords with the idea that the "sample" period over which sensory information is integrated may increase with longer stimulus durations. From the distributions of reaction times obtained for stimuli of longer durations it should be possible to find whether the whole distribution shifted, or if rather there was a longer tail of slow responses indicating only occasional lengthening of the perceptual sample. If this second interpretation were correct, one might expect that sample length would be affected by instructions, as well as duration.

Not all experimenters have reported offset to give faster reaction times. Woodrow (1915), for example, obtained almost identical times to onset and offset with either visual or auditory stimuli, a point which is taken up again below. Nor does reaction time always vary with duration, and Raab *et al.* (1961) concluded that it was independent of duration over the range 10–500 milliseconds. On the basis of this study, these authors suggested that 10 milliseconds or less must be a critical duration above which there will be no effect on reaction time. The levels of illumination used in their study were 3000, 30 and 0.3 foot lamberts. A further investigation by Raab and Fehrer (1962) pinpointed the critical duration for five different intensities as shown in Table 1.1. Their data are consistent with an effect of intensity on reaction time, but stimulus duration appears to play little part and this finding is in apparent contradiction to the earlier reports (e.g. Froeberg, 1907).

Table 1.1. Critical durations of stimulus intensity, from Raab and Fehrer, 1962

Stimulus luminance (foot lamberts)	Critical duration (msec)
0.3	10–20
3.0	2–5
30.0	2–5
300.0	Less than 0.5
3000.0	Less than 0.5

However, this conflict exists in the interpretation of the data obtained rather than in the data themselves. Figure 1.1 shows selected results from Froeberg's and Raab and his associates' studies, and the extent of the correspondence in the results is plain. Equally clear is the very small effect of durations over 5 milliseconds, at least if reasonably high illumination levels are presented.

Vickers *et al.* (1972), using a computer-controlled oscilloscope display of relatively *low* intensity, have shown an inverse relationship between reaction time and accuracy as the duration of the display increases up to around 80 milliseconds. The work is discussed more fully by Vickers in the next chapter. Here it may be noted that the task in this study differs from those above in that the response required of the subjects was a choice reaction, involving pressing one of two keys to indicate which of two lines was the

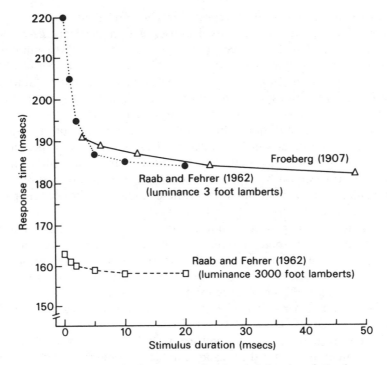

Fig. 1.1. Relationships between reaction time and duration of stimulus.

longer, and in that immediately after exposure the lines were both extended to a greater and equal length so that the original difference was masked. In this situation reaction time decreased from around 650 milliseconds to between 500–550 milliseconds as the duration of the stimulus lengthened to about 80 milliseconds. This shift is much greater than was observed in the previous studies.

A different aspect of duration is that studied by Grier (1966) who varied the *rise time* of an auditory signal. With fast rise times around 0.5 msecs, stimulus intensity had no effect upon reaction time, but with slower rise times reaction time did shorten as intensity increased.

It seems that we should view the effect of duration as a function of the information conveyed by the stimulus. For simple "change of state" judgements, the evidence from Froeberg (1907) and Raab and Fehrer (1962) indicates that there is no gain in speed if the subject is allowed to integrate information over anything more than a few milliseconds, but that this critical duration is a function of intensity (see also Grossberg, 1968). With more complex tasks, such as choice reactions or differential discriminations, the time over which integration can usefully take place is much longer.

Earlier work by Bates (1947) reported in Hick and Bates (1950) supports this kind of interpretation. Bates used a series of asymmetrical crosses which subtended around half a degree at the eye, and in which the amount of misalignment of the horizontal arm varied between 1 and 16 per cent. The easier discrimination (16 per cent misalignment) gave virtual certainty of a correct response with exposure duration of less than half a second, but for all other values maximum acuity was not achieved in less than 1.5–2 seconds. Critical durations, then, reflect the amount of information needed, and the rate at which it is derived from the effects of the stimulus display. It might be added that, with sufficiently precise measurement, the critical duration would be expected to be a range of durations over which performance improved. In this way all these studies can be seen as part of the same general pattern.

Summation or integration of information may occur temporally in any receptor, spatially in some or statistically when two or more receptors are stimulated at the same time. In all cases the speed of performance is facilitated if more relevant information is presented in the same, or less time. Thus, for example, the simple reaction time is shorter with binocular rather than monocular viewing (Poffenberger, 1912), and with binaural rather than monaural listening (Bliss, 1893). Paired visual and auditory stimuli simultaneously presented to the subject would not be expected to allow temporal integration since the sensory conduction time for auditory stimuli of about 10 msec (Kemp et al., 1937) is around 20–30 msec faster than visual sensory conduction time (Marshall et al., 1943). In line with this, Dunlap and Wells (1910) and Todd (1912) found reaction time to simultaneous visual and auditory stimuli approximated that to auditory stimuli alone. Todd did find that a combination of auditory stimuli and electric shock gave rise to faster reaction times than to either of these stimuli separately. This result seems capable of two explanations. First, the *possibility* of shock may have aroused or alerted Todd's subjects in such a manner as to decrease their usual auditory reaction time. This might perhaps be due to their using the shortest possible signal duration before responding, or the shocks may have aroused the subjects generally; if so, however, it would be expected that they would make many anticipatory responses. Second, this finding might be evidence of statistical summation. Consider Fig. 1.2 which shows the distributions of reaction time to two hypothetical signals *A* and *B*. *A* normally gives faster responses than *B* but it does not always do so. Therefore, if a subject is prepared to respond to either signal regardless of which is received first, then on some occasions what would have been a long reaction time in the *A* distribution will be replaced by a short reaction time from the *B* distribution. The effect of the joint stimuli will be to curtail the *A* distribution, giving a shorter mean reaction time than is obtained if the *A*

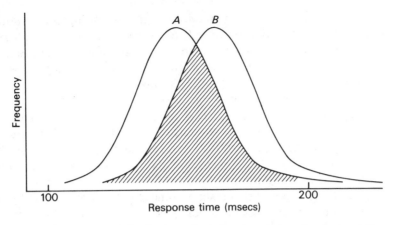

Fig. 1.2. Hypothetical distributions of reaction times to two signals *A* and *B*.

stimulus is presented alone. This explanation was offered by Raab and Fehrer (1962) to deal with the shortening of reaction time with asynchronous combinations of light followed by sound reported by Hershenson (1962). Reaction time to the paired stimuli was shorter than to the visual signal alone when the sound arrived over a range of intervals up to about 40 milliseconds after the light, but in no case was the reaction time to light and sound faster than to sound alone. This finding accords with a statistical summation point of view. Preceding the auditory component by the visual signal, or delivering both together, might produce some reduction of reaction time below that to the auditory signal alone.

In practice, any effect upon reaction time of the intensity, area or duration of a signal will result from the interaction of these factors. However, the preceding discussion shows that it is only with weak stimulation or under difficult conditions that appreciable effects are observed. Only at the low extremes of discriminability do these factors seem to come into play.

Evidence on whether other factors enter into the interaction is interesting but often indecisive. Piéron (1936) found that the effect of intensity on reaction time was *modulated* by the frequency of a vibratory signal within the range 64–1024 c.p.s. Fessard and Kucharski (1934), using auditory signals, observed no effect of pitch, at least with higher intensities of signal, and parallel results for vision had been obtained by Buccola and Bordoni-Uffreduzzi (1884) and Holmes (1926), who concluded that the visual reaction time was not a function of the wavelength of the light. More recently, however, it has been suggested that different colour mechanisms function at different rates (Mollon and Krauskopf, 1973).

Some other specific characteristics of signals are undoubtedly relevant.

Given the structure of the human eye with its decreasing proportion of cones and increasing proportion of rods from the fovea to the periphery of the retina, we should expect reaction time to depend upon the nature of the signal as well as the part of the retina stimulated. Fine grain patterns will be discriminated more rapidly if they fall within foveal vision in the light adapted eye, and moving stimuli or signals of low intensity will be dealt with faster if they fall on the periphery where the rod proportion is greater. It is also relevant to the speed of response that the activation of rods produces a strong message to the higher centres when several are stimulated together, whereas the cones act more independently producing a more faithful representation of the pattern of light falling on the central zone. Poffenberger (1912) showed that reaction time closely followed visual acuity at different points along the horizontal meridian increasing by some 18–26 msec at 45° from the fovea, and Hall and von Kries (1879) demonstrated that reaction time was faster if stimuli were delivered to those positions on the retina where acuity was relatively high—that is in the upper and nasal hemi-retinae as opposed to the lower and temporal portions. More recently, Kobrick (1965) found significant increases in reaction time to a flash stimulus in certain portions of the periphery, although he suggests that no significant increases occur along the horizontal midline even at the periphery. This result holds good for a flash stimulus, but would not be reproduced for more complex stimuli. Hackman (1940) demonstrated that, for practised subjects, the time to move the eye was affected by the position of a peripheral stimulus even when that position was known in advance by the subject. The increases in response latency found by Hackman were of the same order as those observed by Poffenberger. More recently, Bandzejova (1965) reported that reaction time increased as the distance between the stimulus and the point of fixation increased, being more noticeable between 50°–70° displacement.

All manner of stimuli and ambient conditions have been employed in the course of studying the simple reaction time, such as painful stimulation (Luca, 1928; Eichler, 1930) and passive rotation of the body (Baxter and Travis, 1938), and Schilling (1937) demonstrated that visual reaction time increased with increasing air pressure up to the equivalent of 300 ft below sea level. Looked at together, studies like those illustrate the degree to which highly specific features of the stimulus conditions determine the results obtained.

Why should increasing the intensity, area, duration or other features of a stimulus affect reaction time? Most attempts to formulate quantitative models of reaction time start with two assumptions: first, that the frequency of sensory impulses generated is related to the intensity of stimulation and, second, that the speed of decision varies with the rate of the impulses generated (Restle, 1961; McGill, 1961, 1963; Grice, 1968; Luce and Green, 1972). The first assumption accords well with physiological evidence on the effects of intensity (e.g. Galambos and Davis, 1943). In its simplest form the second appears as the time taken to accumulate some minimum amount of sensory information which will allow a decision that a stimulus has occurred. An alternative possibility which has not been canvassed is that stimulus intensity is directly related to the rate of neural firing which, in turn, is inversely related to the rise time for muscular activity in the effectors. This possibility gains support from results of physiological researches which show that the time between first electrical muscle activity and the onset of effector movement is longer for a choice response than a simple reaction (Wiesendanger *et al.*, 1969). No direct study of the effect of stimulus intensity upon rise times for simple reactions is known to the writers, but it seems credible that rise times should reflect stimulus intensities at least at the low end of the scale. This possibility might also fit the fact, often ignored in stochastic models of reaction time, that the *strength* of the response evoked, as well as its latency, varies with the intensity of the stimulus which is applied (Hovland, 1937; Mischenko, 1938; Hull, 1949; Razran, 1957).

Broadly speaking, the evidence is consistent with the fact that neural impulses resulting from sensory stimulation have, in order to be perceived, to be distinguished from a background of random neural activity—*neural noise*—in the sense organs, pathways and brain. If the neural impulses arising from sensory stimulation are weak, it will be necessary to accumulate them over an appreciable period of time before they can be reliably distinguished from the neural noise. As they become stronger, the signal-to-noise ratio increases and the amount of accumulation needed becomes less, until with high stimulus levels it approaches an asymptote so that reaction time changes little with strength of stimulus.

(B) SENSORY MODALITY

Reaction time is found to vary across the sensory modalities, but these variations seem to be due mainly to differences in the peripheral mechanisms rather than in the central processes. Sensory systems differ in three ways which manifest themselves in reaction time studies. First, there are differences in afferent conduction times. The time taken by an auditory signal to reach the central mechanisms is 8–10 msec (Kemp *et al.*, 1937) in comparison with the 20–40 msec taken by visual stimulation (Marshall *et al.*, 1943). Second, some sensory systems change state only slowly while others do so almost instantaneously. The vestibular system which controls the perception of position in space, for example, alters much less quickly than the auditory system. Third and last, it is convenient to regard some sensory systems as more sensitive than others. By this we mean that more discriminations are possible within the total operating range of the sensory apparatus. This leads to the situation where, in some cases, relatively small energy variations are readily detectable, while in others only large changes are discernible. Put briefly, it is difficult to control the strength of the effects of signals in different sensory modalities.

For these reasons, while it is possible to draw up tables showing the average reaction times to above threshold stimuli in various modalities, comparing reaction times across modalities is of doubtful value. Curiously enough, while standard works have always taken the line that a reaction time is composed of a series of internal processes (e.g. Woodworth and Marquis, 1947) there has been little attempt to compare the central decision time component across modalities, although Woodworth and Schlosberg (1954) note that differences in sensory conduction times between auditory and visual stimuli are sufficient to produce the difference between the generally accepted mean reaction times of 140 msec to auditory signals and 180 msec to visual. Other approaches have compared reaction times in different modalities with threshold level stimuli yielding essentially the same reaction time for vision and hearing of around 330 msec (Wundt, 1874), and have tried to account for anticipation ("guessing") in an attempt to estimate "true" decision times (Ollman, 1966). It is still not possible, however, to point to any systematic body of evidence that shows, other things being equal, that the central decision time component of a reaction time is similar across all modalities.

Bearing all these strictures in mind we may inspect in Table 1.2 typical values of a simple reaction time to reasonably intense stimulation in different sensory modalities. A much longer list could be compiled but it would serve little purpose to enumerate examples of the fact that stimulating different senses gives rise to different reaction times. Moreover, as we have tried to indicate, reaction time in any modality will be affected by specific factors like the locus of retinal stimulation and the type of stimulus presented.

(C) COMPLEXITY OF THE STIMULUS

This refers to the ways in which stimulus information is processed. As the Gestalt psychologists often stressed, although we can arbitrarily break a perceived figure or object into more specific features—as a triangle has three straight sides—what we perceive is the triangle and not three separate straight lines. Our central organization of stimulation does not necessarily work by adding together the smallest definable elements like sides and

Table 1.2. Some values of the simple reaction time for different sensory modalities

Study	Stimulus	Reaction time (msec)	Comments
From Woodworth and Schlosberg (1954)	Light	180	
From Woodworth and Schlosberg (1954)	Sound	140	
Robinson (1934)	Touch	155	
Kiesow (1903)	Salt on tip of tongue	308	One subject
Kiesow (1903)	Sugar on tip of tongue	446	One subject
Baxter and Travis (1938)	Rotation of the person	520	
Baxter and Travis (1938)	Change in the direction of rotation of the person	720	
Wright (1951)	Intense radiant heat	330	An approximation

angles, rather it seems to function in larger units even attributing "wholeness" or figure where some minor elements are missing. The main point may be made simply. The central organization of sensory activity is completed more rapidly where fewer different decoding processes are necessary. The Gestalt principles of perceptual organization are examples of this. If identification of the signal takes place before the reponse is emitted, the discrimination time will be included in the reaction time. In practice, because subjects could simply respond to *any* change in the environment before identification occurs, the simple reaction situation has been little used to study the complexity of stimulus patterns. Instead more consideration has been given to the choice reaction time setting where there are two or more different signals and responses.

2. Response characteristics

A number of fairly specific factors are known to influence the speed with which an effector can be brought into action in typical reaction time tasks. For instance, the extended finger shows a tremor of around 8–12 per second. There appears to be a tendency for the human operator to "phase in" his required movement with the tremor direction rather than interrupt the tremor activity. Travis (1929), using a reaction time task involving depressing a key with the finger, found that on 75 per cent of occasions his subjects' responses occurred as continuations of the tremor down-phase rather than breaking into the up-phase of the tremor. He concluded that reaction time depends in part upon the relation in time of the signal to respond and the tremor phase. This finding would, as Travis pointed out, mean that the maximum rate for repeated movements would be limited by the tremor rate. It could also tend to introduce a periodicity into the distribution of reaction times. The periodicity would fluctuate around 50 msec if immediate continuation of the direction of tremor was possible, or around some multiple of 50 msec if time was needed to phase in the required movement with the tremor cycle. Data from Tiffin and Westhafer (1940) indicate that reaction time is shorter and less variable if stimuli occur at the top or bottom points of the tremor cycle rather than randomly throughout the cycle, and this may give some support to the view that immediate continuation is not possible.

While some data support a periodicity in reaction time with a modal period as short as 25 msec (Harter and White, 1968) most of the evidence for periodicity in simple reaction time distributions points to around 100 msec as the cycle time (Jowett, 1955; Augenstine, 1955; Venables, 1960). This periodicity has, however, usually been ascribed to more central factors than muscle tremor and, in the case of Venables' study, has been observed for a voiced response to a visual stimulus rather than a finger movement. Moreover, a general tendency for regular fluctuations to occur in response output (Freeman and Wonderlic, 1935) has been observed. It seems likely, therefore, that the phasing of movement with tremor is only one example of a more general tendency.

A second specific factor is anticipatory muscle tension. There is considerable evidence that reaction is facilitated by a reasonable degree of initial muscle tension (Lange, 1888; Freeman, 1931, 1933, 1937; Freeman and Kendall, 1940; Davis, 1940). Currently, muscle tension tends to be regarded as an index of the level of cortical arousal. If so, it means that reaction time is facilitated not only by the state of the effector, but also by the general level of activation of the central mechanisms which affect both muscular tension and decisional activities. If the level of arousal is low, the organism tends to be inert, so that any incoming stimulation is slow to have an effect. If, however, the level is very high, neural noise may be increased and the signal-to-noise ratio be impaired. It is probably this arousal that is affected by such incentives as electric shocks for slow reactions. These have been found to shorten both reaction time and the speed of responding muscular action to approximately the same proportional extents, implying that they affected both central and peripheral mechanisms about equally (Weiss, 1965).

Some other factors may be briefly mentioned. First, an experiment by Gaskill (1928) showed that simple auditory or visual reaction time is slower if a signal to respond occurs at the beginning of inspiration or expiration in the breathing cycle than if it occurs during these activities. More recent evidence (Buchsbaum and Callaway, 1965) confirms that reaction time is faster for expiration.

Second, the early history of studies of motor coordination has been recorded by Meistring (1930), and some of the parallels between the organization of sensory input and of motor acts, can be drawn from this study. Many other workers have noted that, just as a perceived figure is seen as a whole and not as a summation of its parts, so voluntary movements are coherent units which cannot be analyzed into independent elements (Buytendijk, 1931; Cheng, 1937). Voigt (1933) has stressed that the Gestalt principles operate for motor behaviour as well as for perception of the world, and Barnes and Mundel (1938), studying the performance of factory operatives, demonstrated that particular units of behaviour such as "search", "select", "grasp", do not take standard times to perform, but rather vary according to the context in which they occur; that is, they are affected by the task as a whole.

Third, reaction times can be profoundly affected by the relationships between stimuli or signals and responses. If there is an easily recognizable, uniform and straightforward relationship, reaction time is shorter than if some more or less elaborate recoding is required to translate from signal to response. Especially is this so in a task involving several different signals and responses when the relationships differ between the several signal-response pairs. These relationships will be considered more fully in Chapter 3.

3. Preparation

It was early recognized that reaction time is usually shortened if a *warning* signal is given before the signal to respond. Since at the time the business of psychology was considered to be the analysis of the content of consciousness rather than the measurement of performance, the shortening was attributed to "expectancy" and this term is still in use although its conscious reference has been largely forgotten.

With simple reactions, the degree of shortening depends on the lengths of intervals between the warning and the signal to respond—the *foreperiods*— in a series of trials. If the foreperiods remain constant over a series, reaction time is usually at a minimum with foreperiods of about 0.3 sec and increases

as they become longer. The increase has been shown to continue up to at
least 320 sec (Bevan *et al.*, 1965). If several different lengths of foreperiod are
presented with equal frequencies in random order, reaction times tend to be
greater with foreperiods shorter than the mean of the series. With
foreperiods longer than the mean, reaction times are sometimes less still but
sometimes increase again (Woodrow, 1914; Klemmer, 1956; Karlin, 1959;
Botwinick and Brinley, 1962a,b; Aiken and Lichtenstein, 1964). With
foreperiods less than about 0.3 sec, whether uniform or varied in a series,
reaction may be delayed because processing of the warning has not been
completed by the time the signal to respond arrives. This type of delay is
discussed in detail in Chapter 6. It cannot, however, be the whole
explanation of longer reaction times following foreperiods shorter than the
mean of a varied series, because the same pattern is found when the shortest
foreperiods in the series are for longer than about 0.3 sec. The effect of short
foreperiods seems to be a function of the *relative* as well as the absolute
length of those in the series, as indicated in Fig. 1.3 (Drazin, 1961). Further
evidence of relativity is contained in the finding that reaction times are
affected not only by whether foreperiods are short or long in relation to the
series as a whole, but especially by their relation to the two or three
immediately preceding the trial concerned, as if subjective estimates of the
series were under constant review. Similar results have been obtained for
choice reactions (Bertelson and Boons, 1960) and for simple reactions when,
instead of a series of warnings followed at varying intervals by a signal to
respond, a series of signals to respond only has been given at varying
intervals from each to the next (e.g. Mowrer, 1940).

   A difficulty with foreperiods which vary in the way considered so far is

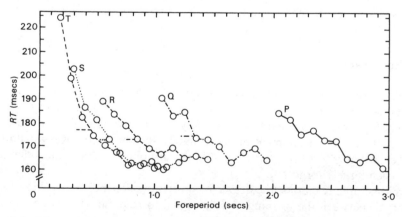

Fig. 1.3. Reaction times with different ranges of variable foreperiod. Data from Drazin
(1961).

that the probability of a signal occurring rises with the interval that has elapsed since the warning was given. A quite different pattern of reaction times is obtained if, instead of equal frequencies of different durations, the series of foreperiods is such that there is an equal probability at any moment of the signal appearing, given that it has not already done so. With these so-called *non-ageing* foreperiods, reaction times again fall as foreperiods increase up to about 0.3 sec, but thereafter they rise steadily and substantially (Nickerson and Burnham, 1969). The initial fall is probably again due to effects discussed in Chapter 6. To account for the later rise, consideration needs to be given to the nature of expectancy effects.

Subjective expectancy, if it is to affect performance, must imply that some kind of preparation to react is made before the signal arrives. This view is strengthened by the finding that, with simple reactions and a block of trials all having the same length of foreperiod, reactions often occur prematurely: the subject does not respond to the signal but to the warning after an estimated time interval. Such premature responses can be largely prevented by using a choice reaction task or by giving some "catch" trials in which the warning is given but the signal to respond is omitted—a situation which converts a simple reaction to one in which there is a choice between responding or not doing so. The results with varying foreperiods imply that subjects tend to prepare for the average length of foreperiod in a series of trials, and that their ability to hold their preparation is not perfect. If, therefore, the foreperiod is shorter than average, preparation will not be complete, but if the foreperiod is longer than average preparation may have been partly lost by the time the signal arrives. Further indication of the inability to hold a state of preparation is the increase of reaction time with length of foreperiod when this is kept constant over a series of trials, since the longer the foreperiod the less accurately subjects can estimate the time at which their preparation should be at a maximum (Klemmer, 1957). In line with this, reaction time has been found to be shortened with relatively long foreperiods (5 sec) if the warning is repeated a short time before the signal to respond is due, thus allowing preparation to be more accurately timed (Sanders, 1972).

Preparation in reaction time tasks has historically been divided into two classes: "sensorial" and "muscular" (Lange, 1888). The terms come from the days in which they referred to conscious attention, either to the stimulus about to arrive or to the response to be made. There was some controversy about whether reaction times achieved with a sensorial "set" were longer than or equal to those achieved with a muscular set. Certainly the latter in a simple reaction situation can have the dramatic effect that almost any fairly strong stimulus, such as the experimenter clapping his hands, can trigger the response.

The modern counterpart of sensorial set is selective attention to particular stimuli or giving close attention to the point at which a signal is known or expected to appear, thus ensuring that it is dealt with at once when it comes. As regards muscular set, the obvious possibility that the muscles concerned are to some extent preactivated received some, but not unequivocal, support during the early days (see Woodworth, 1938). More recent evidence from cortical-evoked potentials and electromyograms suggests that warning signals to some extent preactivate *responses* without necessarily activating the *muscles* concerned (Besrest and Requin, 1973; Karlin and Martz, 1973). Rather, there seems to be an inhibition of any reflex activity in these muscles which might interfere with the response, indicating that the preparation for response is essentially central (Requin, 1969; Requin et al., 1977). At the same time there may be a general increase of tone in muscles other than those directly concerned with the responding movement. This appears to imply some general activation or arousal of the organism which as mentioned previously would be expected to affect all the processes concerned, both perceptual and motor and both central and peripheral.

Any preparation of specific responses must obviously be less complete with choice reactions than with simple, but it is noteworthy that with choice reactions when the frequencies of the alternatives are unequal, the more frequent response—the one which more nearly approaches a simple reaction and is therefore more likely to be worth preparing for—has been found to be more affected by warnings than the less frequent (Bertelson and Barzeele, 1965).

4. Choice

It was early recognized that reaction times are longer if there are several possible signals and responses—*choice reaction times*—than simple reaction times in which there is only one signal and corresponding response. It was also known that the lengthening increases with the number of choices. To some extent this may be due to choice reactions both providing weaker signals and permitting less preparation than simple. For example, Vickers (1979) has argued that the several signals used in a choice reaction task have all to be fitted into a "dimension" of discrimination which is of limited size, so that the more signals there are, the less space is available to each. As regards preparation, Nickerson and Burnham (1969) whose results have already been mentioned, suggested that the lengthening they found of reaction time with foreperiod could be at least a partial explanation of the effects of choice: the greater the degree of choice the longer the interval between similar signals or, in other words, the less the probability of any given signal at any moment. Their own results are, in fact, well fitted by the equation

$$\text{Reaction time} = a + b \log\left(\frac{1}{p}\right)$$

where a and b are constants and p is the probability of a signal appearing at any moment of time. The equation is essentially the same as Equation 3.5 in Chapter 3.

Historically, the most important early study in this area was the comparison by Donders (1868) of simple and choice reactions—a and b reactions as he termed them—and the comparison of both with a c-reaction which used several stimuli, only one of which had to be responded to. Donders argued that the b condition required the subject to discriminate which stimulus had occurred in order to choose the appropriate response, while in the c condition the subject still needed to discriminate between the stimuli, but did not need to choose between different responses. He reasoned that, if the c-reaction involved discrimination but the a-reaction did not, subtracting the a- from the c-reaction time should give the time for discrimination. Similarly, subtracting the c- from the b-reaction time should give the time spent in choosing a response. His experimental ingenuity had broken a hitherto impregnable barrier and had provided a means of measuring mental processes, a psychological breakthrough of great importance. Soon his approach was being widely used and extended in an effort to analyze different types of decision processes into their various elements.

The subtractive method introduced by Donders survived for around 25 years. Gradually, however, it became clear that Donders' approach was too simple in that different processes may overlap in time and complex processes cannot always be analyzed into simple elements. In particular, Cattell (1886), following Wundt, had questioned Donders' logic, pointing out that responding only to one of two stimuli still required the decision to respond or not, as well as the discrimination of which stimulus had occurred. Wundt attempted to overcome the difficulty by introducing what he termed the d-reaction using two stimuli but only one response which was made on every trial regardless of which stimulus occurred, but only after the stimulus had been identified. This d-reaction proved unmanageable to many subjects, most of whom tended to perform the task as fast as a simple reaction: there seemed to be no additional time needed for identification of the stimulus. More modern research which has not required *subjective* identification but has used several stimuli and a single response to them all, has shown some rise of reaction time with number of stimuli, although the increase has been small (Teichner and Krebs, 1974). Modern developments of Donders' approach are discussed in Chapter 3.

Meanwhile, a further choice task introduced by Wundt deserves to be noted briefly. It is what he termed the *association reaction* in which time is measured to produce a verbal association to a stimulus, verbal or pictorial, presented under the instruction to respond as quickly as possible. This task can be seen as the forerunner of studies of cognition in which times to classify items or to state superordinates or examples of a class are measured, and of association time tests used for some clinical purposes and for "lie detection".

5. Conscious accompaniments

It has already been emphasized that most studies of reaction time in the nineteenth and early twentieth centuries were conducted with the assumption that the essential task of psychology was analysis of the content of consciousness. Many investigators, especially Wundt, Külpe and their associates, used reaction time procedures with the primary aim of having their subjects describe the conscious sensations accompanying their performances. There was therefore interest in, for example, feelings of tension and relaxation before and after the making of a reaction, and in what was at the time the highly provocative finding that there was seldom anything conscious to report during the actual reaction time itself. Under the influence of behaviouristic trends of thought from the 1920s onwards, interest in conscious accompaniments of reaction have largely disappeared and given way to the study of reaction *times* as such. One notable exception, which has continued to be studied, is feelings of *confidence* in judgements and decisions made. Recent research has shown that ratings of confidence can be closely related to facets of overt performance including reaction time. The matter is discussed more fully by Vickers (1979) and in Chapter 2 where confidence is an important parameter in his model of discrimination.

Despite the wide and intense early interest in reaction times, interest in them flagged during the middle years of the present century. For example, they are hardly mentioned in the "Handbook of Experimental Psychology" edited by Stevens (1951) or by Munn (1946) or even by Munn et al. (1969) in their introductory texts. Interest increased again, however, following the application of information theory to choice reaction times by Hick (1952) and Hyman (1953). Now they are again central to much of experimental psychology, providing what bids fair to be one of the most precise, sensitive and sophisticated means of realizing, in the highly complex context of modern psychological knowledge, the aims of the pioneers to achieve a physical measure of mental processes.

References

Aiken, L. R. and Lichtenstein, M. (1964). Reaction times to regularly recurring visual stimuli. *Perceptual and Motor Skills* **18**, 713–720.

Augenstine, L. G. (1955). Evidences of periodicities in human task performance. *In* "Information Theory in Psychology" (H. Quastler, ed.). Free Press, Illinois.

Bandzejova, M. (1965). *RT* as a function of the position of a stimulus in the visual field. *Psychologica* **16**, 179–212.

Barnes, R. M. and Mundel, M. E. (1938). Studies of hand motions and rhythm appearing in factory work. *Univ. Iowa Stud. Eng.*, Bull. 12.

Bates, J. A. V. (1947). Design and performance of the human servo. Paper read at I.E.E. Convention, May, 1947.

Baxter, B. and Travis, R. C. (1938). The reaction time to vestibular stimuli. *Journal of Experimental Psychology* **22**, 287–282.

Bertelson, P. and Barzeele, J. (1965). Interaction of time-uncertainty and relative signal frequency in determining choice reaction time. *Journal of Experimental Psychology* **70**, 448–451.

Bertelson, P. and Boons, J. P. (1960). Time uncertainty and choice reaction time. *Nature* **187**, 531–532.

Besrest, Annie and Requin, J. (1973). Development of expectancy wave and time course of preparatory set in a simple reaction-time task: preliminary results. *In* "Attention and Performance IV" (S. Kornblum, ed.), pp. 209–219. Academic Press, New York.

Bessel, F. W. (1823). *Astronomische Beobachtungen in Königsberg* **8**, 3–8.

Bevan, W., Hardesty, D. L. and Avant, L. L. (1965). Response latency with constant and variable interval schedules. *Perceptual and Motor Skills* **20**, 969–972.

Birren, J. E. and Botwinick, J. (1955). Speed of response as a function of perceptual difficulty and age. *Journal of Gerontology* **10**, 433–436.

Bliss, C. C. (1893). *Yale Studies in Psychology* **1**, 1–55.

Boring, E. G. (1929). "A History of Experimental Psychology." Appleton-Century, New York.

Botwinick, J. and Brinley, J. F. (1962a). Aspects of *RT* set during brief intervals in relation to age and sex. *Journal of Gerontology* **17**, 295–301.

Botwinick, J. and Brinley, J. F. (1962b). An analysis of set in relation to reaction time. *Journal of Experimental Psychology* **63**, 568–574.

Botwinick, J., Brinley, J. F. and Robbin, J. S. (1958). The interaction effects of perceptual difficulty and stimulus exposure time on age differences in speed and accuracy of response. *Gerontologia* **2**, 1–10.

Buccola, G. and Bordoni-Uffreduzzi, G. (1884). Sul Tempo di Percezione dei Colori. *Rivista di Filosofia scientifica*, **5**.

Buchsbaum, M. and Callaway, E. (1965). Influence of respiratory cycle on simple *RT*. *Perceptual and Motor Skills* **20**, 961–966.

Buytendijk, F. J. J. (1931). *Reaktionszeit und Schlagfertigkeit*. Rudolph and Meister, Kassell.

Cattell, J. McK. (1886). The time taken up by cerebral operations. *Mind* **11**, 220–242, 377–392, 524–538.

Cheng, P. L. (1937). Pattern cutting, pattern tracing, and ball rolling as complex eye-hand coordination tests. *Clinical Journal of Psychology* **1**, 230–251.

Davis, R. C. (1940). Set and muscular tension. Ind. Univ. Publ. Sci. Ser., No. 10.

Donders, F. C. (1868). Over de snelheid van psychische processen. *Onderzoekingen gedaan in het Physiologisch Laboratorium der Utrechtsche Hoogeschool*, 1868–1869, *Tweede reeks*, II, 92–120. Translated by W. G. Koster, 1969, On the speed of mental processes. *Acta Psychologica* 30, 412–431.

Drazin, D. H. (1961). Effects of foreperiod, foreperiod variability, and probability of stimulus occurrence on simple reaction time. *Journal of Experimental Psychology* 62, 43–50.

Dunlap, K. and Wells, G. R. (1910). Reactions to visual and auditory stimuli. *Psychological Review* 17, 319–335.

Eichler, W. (1930). Über die reaktionszeiten bei schmergreizen. *Z. Sinnesphysiol* 60, 325–333.

Elsberg, C. A. and Spotnitz, H. (1938). The sense of taste. *Bull. Neural Inst., N.Y.* 7, 174–177.

Essen, J. V. (1937). Time and reaction. *American Journal of Psychology* 50, 414–428.

Ferrée, C. E. and Rand, G. (1927). Intensity of light and speed of vision studied with special reference to industrial situations. *Trans. illum. eng. Soc.* 22, 79–110.

Fessard, A. and Kucharski, P. (1934). Recherches sur les temps de réaction aux sans de hauteurs et d'intensités différentes. I. *Année Psychol.* 35, 103–117.

Freeman, G. L. (1931). *Journal of General Psychology* 5, 479–494.

Freeman, G. L. (1933). The facilitative and inhibitory effects of muscular tension upon performance. *American Journal of Psychology* 45, 17–52.

Freeman, G. L. (1937). The optimal locus of "anticipatory tensions" in muscular work. *Journal of Experimental Psychology* 21, 554–564.

Freeman, G. L. and Kendall, W. E. (1940). The effect upon reaction time of muscular tension induced at various preparatory intervals. *Journal of Experimental Psychology* 27, 136–148.

Freeman, G. L. and Wonderlic, E. F. (1935). Periodicity of performance. *American Journal of Psychology* 47, 149–151.

Froeberg, S. (1907). The relation between the magnitude of stimulus and the time of reaction. *Archives of Psychology*, No. 8.

Galambos, R. and Davis, H. (1943). The response of single auditory nerve fibres to acoustic stimulation. *Journal Neurophysiology* 6, 39–57.

Gaskill, H. V. (1928). The relation of *RT* to phase of breathing. *Journal of Experimental Psychology* 11, 364–369.

Gregg, L. W. and Brogden, W. J. (1950). The relation between duration and reaction time difference to fixed duration and response terminated stimuli. *Journal of Comparative and Physiological Psychology* 43, 329–337.

Grice, G. R. (1968). Stimulus intensity and response evocation. *Psychological Review* 75, 359–373.

Grier, J. B. (1966). Auditory *RT* as a function of stimulus intensity and rise time. *Psychonomic Science* 6, 307–308.

Grossberg, M. (1968). The latency of response in relation to Bloch's Law at threshold. *Perception and Psychophysics* 4, 229–232.

Hackman, R. B. (1940). An experimental study of variability in ocular latency. *Journal of Experimental Psychology* 27, 546–558.

Hall, G. S. and Von Kries, J. (1879). *Archives für Anatomie and Physiologie*, 1–10.

Harter, R. M. and White, C. T. (1968). Periodicity within *RT* distribution and electromyograms. *Quarterly Journal of Experimental Psychology* 20, 157–166.

Helmholtz, H. L. F. (1850). Messingen über den zeitlichen Verlanf der Zucking animalischer. Muskeln und die Fortpflanzungsgeschwindigkeit der Reizung in den Nerven. *Arch. Anat. Physiol.*, 276–364.

Hershenson, M. (1962). Reaction time as a measure of intersensory facilitation. *Journal of Experimental Psychology* **63**, 289–293.

Hick, W. E. (1952). On the rate of gain of information. *Quarterly Journal of Experimental Psychology* **4**, 11–26.

Hick, W. E. and Bates, J. A. V. (1950). The human operator of control mechanisms. *Perm. Records of Res. and Devel.*, Monogr. No. 17–204, Min. of Supply.

Holmes, J. L. (1926). *RT* to photometrically equal chromatic stimuli. *American Journal of Psychology* **37**, 414–417.

Hovland, C. I. (1936). The influence of adaptation illumination upon visual reaction time. *Journal of General Psychology* **14**, 346–359.

Hovland, C. I. (1937). The generalization of conditioned responses. II. The sensory generalization of conditioned responses with varying intensities of tone. *Journal of Genetic Psychology* **51**, 279–290.

Hull, C. L. (1949). Stimulus intensity dynamism (V) and stimulus generalization. *Psychological Review* **56**, 67–76.

Hyman, R. (1953). Stimulus information as a determinant of reaction time. *Journal of Experimental Psychology* **45**, 188–196.

Jenkins, T. N. (1926). Facilitation and inhibition. *Archives Psychology*, No. 86.

Jowett, G. H. (1955). The comparison of means of industrial time series. *Applied Statistics* **4**, 32–46.

Karlin, L. (1959). Reaction time as a function of foreperiod duration and variability. *Journal of Experimental Psychology* **58**, 185–191.

Karlin, L. and Martz, M. J. (1973). Response probability and sensory-evoked potentials. *In* "Attention and Performance IV" (S. Kornblum, ed.), pp. 175–184. Academic Press, New York.

Kemp, E. H., Coppée, G. E. and Robinson, E. H. (1937). Electric responses of the brain stem to unilateral auditory stimulation. *American Journal of Physiology* **120**, 304–322.

Kiesow, F. (1903). Zur Frage nach der Fortpflanzungsgeschwindigkeit der erregung im sensiblen Nerven des Menschen. *Z. f. Psych. und Phys.*, **33**, 444–452.

Kleint, H. (1928). Reaktionen auf erlöschende Fichter. *Indus. Psychotechn.* **5**, 28–29.

Klemmer, E. T. (1956). Time uncertainty in simple reaction time. *Journal of Experimental Psychology* **51**, 179–184.

Klemmer, E. T. (1957). Simple reaction time as a function of time uncertainty. *Journal of Experimental Psychology* **54**, 195–200.

Kobrick, J. L. (1965). Effects of physical location of visual stimuli on intentional response time. *Journal of Engineering Psychology* **4**, 1–8.

Lange, L. (1888). Neue Experimente über den Vorgang der einfachen Raction auf Sinneseindricke, *Philos. Stud.* **4**, 479–510.

Luca, G. (1928). Cerebral reaction and *RT* in relation to *painful* stimuli. La reazione cerebrale et il tempo di reazone in rapporto a stimuli delorosi. *Riv. di Psicol.*, **24**, 14–17.

Luce, R. D. and Green, D. M. (1972). A neural timing theory for response times and the psychophysics of intensity. *Psychological Review*, **79**, 14–57.

Marshall, W. H., Talbot, S. A. and Ades, H. W. (1943). Cortical response of the anaesthesized cat to gross photic and electrical afferent stimulation. *Journal of Neurophysiology* **6**, 1–15.

McGill, W. J. (1961). Loudness and *RT*. *Acta Psychologica* **15**, 193–199.

McGill, W. J. (1963). Stochastic latency mechanism. *In* "Handbook of Mathematical Psychology", Vol. 1 (R. D. Luce, R. R. Bush and E. Galanter, eds.). Wiley, New York.

Meistring, W. (1930). Beiträge zur Prüfungder Koordinations fähigkeit, Beihefte z. Zsch. f. angeur. Psychol., No. 49.

Mischenko, M. N. (1938). On the relationship between stimulus intensity and response intensity. *Trud. tcentral. psikhoneurol. Inst.*, Vol. 10, pp. 64–90.

Mollon, J. D. and Krauskopf, J. (1973). *RT* as a measure of the temporal response properties of individual colour mechanisms. *Vision Research* **13**, 27–40.

Mowrer, O. H. (1940). Preparatory set (expectancy)—some methods of measurement. *Psychological Monographs* **52**, No. 233.

Munn, N. L. (1946). "Psychology". Houghton Mifflin Co., Boston.

Munn, N. L., Fernald, L. D. and Fernald, P. S. (1969). "Introduction to Psychology". Houghton Mifflin Co., Boston.

Nickerson, R. S. and Burnham, D. W. (1969). Response times with nonaging foreperiods. *Journal of Experimental Psychology* **79**, 452–457.

Ollman, R. (1966). Fast guesses in *RT*. *Psychonomic Science* **6**, 155–156.

Piéron, H. (1920). Nouvelles recherches sur l'analyse du temps de latence sensorielle et sur la loi qui relie ce temps à l'intensité de l'excitation. *Année Psychologique* **22**, 58–142.

Piéron, H. (1927). L'influence de l'intensité sur le temps de réaction à la cessation du stimulus luminem. *C.R. Soc. Biol.* **97**, 1147–1149.

Piéron, H. (1936). Recherches experimentales sur la sensation vibratioire cutanée. *Année Psychol.* **36**, 88–102.

Poffenberger, A. T. (1912). *RT* to retinal stimulation with special reference to the time lost in conduction through nerve centres. *Arch. Psychol*, No. 23.

Raab, D. and Fehrer, E. (1962). The effect of stimulus duration and luminance on visual reaction time. *Journal of Experimental Psychology* **64**, 326–327.

Raab, D., Fehrer, E. and Hershenson, M. (1961). Visual reaction time and the Broca-Sulzer phenomenon. *Journal of Experimental Psychology* **61**, 193–199.

Razran, G. (1957). The dominance-contiguity theory of the acquisition of classical conditioning. *Psychological Bulletin* **54**, 1–46.

Restle, F. (1961). "Psychology of Judgement and Choice". Wiley, New York.

Requin, J. (1969). Some data on neurophysiological processes involved in the preparatory motor activity to reaction time performance. *Acta Psychologica* **30**, 358–367.

Requin, J., Bonnet, M. and Semjen, A. (1977). Is there a specificity in the supraspinal control of motor structures during preparation? *In* "Attention and Performance VI" (S. Dornic, ed.), pp. 139–174. Erlbaum, Hillsdale, New Jersey.

Ribot, T. (1900). La Psychologie de 1896 à 1900. *Proceedings 4th International Congress Psychology*, Paris, 1900, pp. 40–47.

Robinson, E. S. (1934). Work of the integrated organism. *In* "Handbook of General Experimental Psychology" (C. Murchison, ed.). Clark University Press, Worcester.

Sanders, A. F. (1972). Foreperiod duration and the timecourse of preparation. *Acta Psychologica* **36**, 60–71.

Sandford, E. C. (1888). Personal equation. *American Journal of Psychology* **2**, 3–38, 271–298, 403–430.

Schilling, C. W. (1937). Quantitative study of mental and neuromuscular reactions as influenced by increased air pressure. *Nov. Med. Bull. Wash.* **35**, 373–380.

Stevens, S. S. (1951). "Handbook of Experimental Psychology". John Wiley and Sons, New York.

Teichner, W. H. and Krebs, Marjorie J. (1974). Laws of visual choice reaction time. *Psychological Review* **81**, 75–98.

Tiffin, J. and Westhafer, F. L. (1940). The relation between reaction time and temporal location of the stimulus on the tremor cycle. *Journal of Experimental Psychology* **27**, 318–324.

Todd, J. W. (1912). Reaction to multiple stimuli. *Arch. Psychol.*, No. 25.

Travis, L. E. (1929). The relation of voluntary movements to tremors. *Journal of Experimental Psychology* **12**, 515–524.

Venables, P. H. (1960). The effect of auditory and visual stimulation on the skin potential response of schizophrenics. *Brain* **83**, 77–92.

Vickers, D., Nettelbeck, T. and Willson, R. J. (1972). Perceptual indices of performance: the measurement of "inspection time" and "noise" in the visual system. *Perception* **1**, 263–295.

Vickers, D. (1979). "Decision Processes in Visual Perception". Academic Press, London.

Voigt, E. (1933). Über den Aufbau von Bewegungsgestalten. *Neue psychol. Stud.* **9**, 1–32.

Weiss, A. D. (1965). The locus of reaction time change with set, motivation and age. *Journal of Gerontology* **20**, 60–64.

Wells, G. R. The influence of stimulus duration on *RT*. *Psychological Monographs*, 1913 **15**, 1066.

Wiesendanger, M., Schneider, P. and Villoz, J. P. (1969). Electromyographic analysis of a rapid volitional movement. *American Journal Phys. Med.* **48**, 17–24.

Woodrow, H. (1914). The measurement of attention. *Psychological Monographs* **17**, No. 76.

Woodrow, H. (1915). Reactions to the cessation of stimuli and their nervous mechanism. *Psychological Review* **22**, 423–452.

Woodworth, R. S. (1938). "Experimental Psychology". Henry Holt, New York.

Woodworth, R. S. and Marquis, D. G. (1947). "Psychology". Methuen, London.

Woodworth, R. S. and Schlosberg, H. (1954). "Experimental Psychology". Henry Holt, New York. Methuen, London.

Wright, G. W. (1951). The latency of sensations of warmth due to radiation. *Journal of Physiology* **112**, 344–358.

Wundt, W. (1874). "Grundzüge der physiologischen Psychologie", 6th edn. Engelmann, Leipzig.

Chapter 2

Discrimination*

DOUGLAS VICKERS

1. Introduction

One of the most fundamental capacities of any organism is the ability to respond to differences between aspects of its environment, as measured along some objective dimension. The dimension in question may be a simple physical quantity, such as length, weight or intensity, or a higher order variable, such as some variation in the probability of the joint occurrence of two particular features in the same object. On the human level, the number of dimensions along which some discrimination is possible is so great that particular interest attaches to those for which no differentiation normally occurs (e.g. Julesz, 1962, 1975; Caelli and Julesz, 1978; Caelli et al., 1978; Victor and Brodie, 1978; Julesz et al., 1978). At the same time, a parsimonious assumption tacitly underlies most research to the effect that, whenever differentiation does occur, it will prove to be mediated—in its later stages at least—by a single type of mechanism, operating in an essentially identical manner, irrespective of the precise nature of the variable which is discriminated.

Since the publication of Fechner's (1860, 1966) *Elements of Psychophysics*, human discriminative performance has been conventionally investigated by instructing an observer to compare a stimulus of variable magnitude v along some particular dimension with one of a constant or standard magnitude s, and to indicate (either verbally, or by some action, such as pressing one of the two keys) whether the variable appears to be greater or less than the standard with respect to the dimension in question. Occasionally, observers have been permitted to make a third intermediate response to indicate that v and s appear to be equal (e.g. Kellogg, 1930, 1931; Vickers, 1975), and a

* I am grateful to the publishers for their permission to include in this chapter some material which has recently been presented, albeit organized differently, by Vickers (1979).

detailed discussion of these three-category experiments has been presented by Vickers (1979). However, since we are not concerned here with the process of identification, we shall restrict attention to the more common type of task in which only two response categories are allowed.

Although discrimination has been studied by means of all three of the psychophysical procedures outlined by Fechner (e.g. Kellogg, 1929), most researchers have attempted to avoid the so-called "errors" of anticipation and habituation associated with the method of limits and the method of adjustment (Woodworth and Schlosberg, 1954; Corso, 1967) and have employed some form of the method of constant stimuli (Guilford 1954; Clark et al., 1967). A typical experiment is that by Festinger (1943a) in which five observers were asked to compare pairs of vertical lines, presented simultaneously in a tachistoscope for 0.5 sec, and to say "longer" or "shorter", according to whether the line on the right appeared longer or shorter than the one on the left. The left-hand line, or standard s, was a constant 190.5 mm, and the right-hand, or variable v, took one of 15 different values ranging from 165.1 up to 215.9 mm. Each value of v was presented an equal number of times in an order which was designed to be unpredictable, and which assured that the *a priori* probabilities of a "longer" or a "shorter" response were equal. A second type of experiment, involving successive rather than simultaneous comparison, is exemplified by the study of Pierrel and Murray (1963), in which observers were instructed to say whether the second of two sequentially lifted weights was heavier or lighter than the first (or standard) weight. In this type of task, it seems most straightforward to assume that the observer makes his judgement by comparing each value of the variable with some remembered representation of the standard.

Also within the framework of the method of constant stimuli, a third type of experiment is exemplified by the studies of Crossman (1955), in which observers were required to sort packs of well-shuffled playing card blanks into two piles, according to whether each card had a large or a small number of spots drawn on it. In experiments of this type it has often been assumed that the observer constructs his own mental standard, and that its value lies somewhere between the values of the two different stimuli (Hughes, 1964; Welford, 1968, p. 50; Link, 1975, 1978; Link and Heath, 1975). An alternative assumption, which may apply particularly to highly discriminable stimuli, is that the observer maintains a standard corresponding to each of the two possible stimulus values, and classifies each stimulus by means of an identification rather than a discrimination process (cf. Ryder et al., 1974). However, in the more usual situation, where the difference between stimuli is small, the general pattern of results closely resembles that for the discrimination of simultaneously presented stimuli, which suggests that both tasks may be executed by the same discrimination process (Shallice and Vickers, 1964; Vickers, 1979, pp. 61–62, 74–75, 93–96).

Whatever the precise form of the experiment, interest has focussed mainly on three dependent variables: the relative frequency with which the observer makes each alternative response, the time he takes, and the degree of confidence he expresses in his judgement. Other psychophysiological studies of EEG, heart rate and GSR have been carried out (e.g. Vaughan and Ritter, 1973; Buser and Rougeul-Buser, 1978; Picton *et al.*, 1978; Gaillard and Perdok, 1979). However, since psychophysiological studies have yet to play a major role in developing theoretical models of discrimination, and since the relationships between psychophysiological and behavioural measures remain unclear, these results will not be considered in this chapter. In a similar vein, some researchers, such as Audley (1964, 1970), have considered the force with which a response is made. However, since almost all experiments have been designed so that the occurrence of a response is an all-or-none affair, this aspect of performance will also be omitted.

Within this restricted field of enquiry, attention has been concentrated on the effects of manipulating three independent variables. The first— ostensibly objective—variable is that of discriminability, usually measured by the effective physical difference $(v - s)$ between the value of the variable v and that of some actual or inferred standard s. The second—more subjective—variable is that of response bias (or the comparative readiness of the observer to make each alternative response), and the third is the observer's degree of caution (or the overall care with which he makes his judgements). Most theories of discrimination can be construed as attempts to account for the correlated changes in response frequency, time and confidence which follow variation in one or more of these independent variables. This chapter is intended primarily as a summary of empirical work on the measurement of reaction time in discrimination tasks, and we shall first consider the effects of variations in discriminability, bias and caution on the first of these response measures, before going on to examine their effects on response time and confidence. We shall briefly discuss some of the theoretical accounts which have been put forward to account for the empirical relations which emerge at each successive stage. Finally, we shall compare three of the main types of mechanism which have been advanced to account for the general features of the discrimination process.

2. The relative frequency of alternative responses

(A) EFFECTS OF VARYING DISCRIMINABILITY

In an experiment, such as the one by Festinger (1943a) described above, in which values of the variable both greater and less than the standard are presented, one of the first aspects to be examined has been the relative frequency with which an observer makes a particular response. For example, attempts have been made to relate responses of the form "$V > S$" to the objective stimulus difference $(v - s)$, where V and S represent subjectively perceived magnitudes of v and s, respectively.

If an observer were capable of discriminating perfectly, then the *psychometric function* which results when the relative frequency of "$V > S$" responses is plotted against $(v - s)$ should resemble the step change illustrated in Fig. 2.1a. However, it has been generally found since Pierce and Jastrow (1885) that the psychometric function shows little evidence of the discontinuities implied by Fig. 2.1a, but tends to take the form of a continuous, sigmoid curve, as exemplified by the results of Brown (1910), shown in Fig. 2.1b (Urban, 1910; Guilford, 1954; Corso, 1967).

To account for the fact that discriminative performance is not error-free, it has been generally assumed since Jastrow (1888) that the sensory representation of a stimulus does not maintain a fixed value, bearing a constant relation to its objective, physical magnitude, but exhibits—over even a short time—a distribution of values. Numerous sources of this supposed variation have been suggested, including momentary fatigues (Jastrow, 1888), fluctuations in attention (Cattell, 1893), after-effects of cerebral activity (Welford, 1965, 1968), spontaneous neural activity (Barlow, 1956; Kuffler et al., 1957; Barlow and Levick, 1969a,b), as well as variability in the stimulus itself (Hecht et al., 1942, de Vries, 1956). However, on the basis that the combined effects arising from many independent sources of random variation should be closely approximated by a normal curve, most writers have agreed that the sensory representation of two stimuli (such as v and s) may be satisfactorily described by two normal distributions of sensory effect, as illustrated in Fig. 2.2 (e.g. Cattell, 1893; Boring, 1917; Tanner and Swets, 1954).

In order to account for the particular shape of the psychometric function, Thurstone (1927a,b) further assumed that such fluctuations occur from trial to trial, and that the observer's judgement on a particular trial is a function of the momentary "discriminal difference" $(V - S)$ between their sensory representations. If the distributions of sensory effect from v and s are normal, uncorrelated, and have equal variances, then it can be shown that, over a series of trials, the distributions of $(V - S)$ differences should also be normal, with a mean $\overline{(V - S)} = (\overline{V} - \overline{S})$, and a standard deviation $\sigma_{(V-S)} = \sqrt{2\sigma_V^2} = \sqrt{2\sigma_S^2}$ (cf. Hays, 1963, p. 315). When low values of v are considered (i.e. when $v \ll s$), the mean $\overline{(V - S)}$ will be negative, and the bulk of the distribution of $(V - S)$ differences will fall below zero. Conversely,

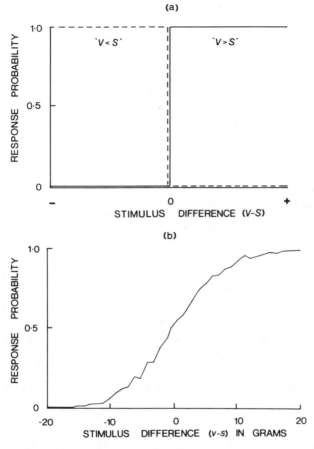

Fig. 2.1. Theoretical and empirical psychometric functions. (a) Illustrates the discontinuous function which would be expected if the observer were capable of perfect discrimination. (b) Shows a typical empirical function for responses of the form "$V > S$", obtained by Brown (1910). (The curve is redrawn, with permission, from Woodworth and Schlosberg, 1954, p. 216, Fig. 8.10.)

when high values of v are considered (i.e. when $v \gg s$), the distribution will be predominantly positive.

Hypothetical probability density distributions of discriminal differences arising from two stimuli v and s are shown in Fig. 2.3. The figure illustrates how the proportions of positive $(V - S)$ differences depends on the difference between $\bar{V}$ and $\bar{S}$ (and hence on the relative values of v and s), as well as on the value of $\sigma_V = \sigma_S$. More particularly, it can be seen from the figure that, for any particular combination of the values of $(\overline{V - S})$ and of

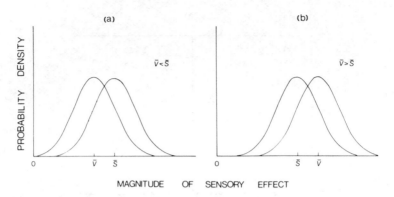

Fig. 2.2. Hypothetical probability density distributions of the sensory effect corresponding to two stimuli v and s. The distributions are normal with means $\bar{V}$ and $\bar{S}$ and $\sigma_V = \sigma_S$. (a) Shows the case where $\bar{V} < \bar{S}$ and (b) the case where $\bar{V} > \bar{S}$.

$\sigma_V = \sigma_S$, the probability p of a positive $(V - S)$ difference is given by the area under the normal curve between $(V - S) = 0$ and $(V - S) = +\infty$. If the value of $\sigma_V = \sigma_S$ is assumed to be constant, and successively high values of $(V - S)$ are considered, then this area will increase from a lower limit of 0 (when the entire distribution of discriminal differences falls below zero) up to a value of 1 (when the entire distribution is positive). In other words, the function relating p to $(V - S)$ is a cumulative normal ogive.

If it is further assumed that $\bar{V}$ and $\bar{S}$ (and hence $(\overline{V - S})$) are linearly

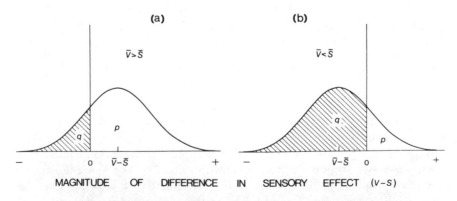

Fig. 2.3. Hypothetical probability density distributions of $(V - S)$ differences in the magnitude of sensory effect arising from two stimuli v and s. (a) Illustrates the case where $\bar{V} > \bar{S}$, and (b) the case where $\bar{V} < \bar{S}$. The probability of a positive stimulus difference corresponds to the area p, while that of a negative difference corresponds to the shaded portion q, with $p + q = 1$.

related to v and s, and that the probability P of making a response of the form "$V > S$" corresponds to the proportion p of positive $(V - S)$ differences, then the function relating P to the objective stimulus difference $(v - s)$ should also be a cumulative normal ogive. A proposal of this kind, termed the "phi-gamma hypothesis" was first put forward by Urban (1910) and Boring (1917). It implies that the making of a judgement of the form "$V > S$" depends upon the result of a single, infallible subtractive comparison between the momentary values of the sensory effects produced by the stimuli v and s.

In cases where the magnitude of the sensory effect is not linearly related to the objective value of the stimulus, and where the effective difference between stimuli may be relative rather than absolute, then Thurstone (1928) has suggested that empirical response frequencies should conform to a cumulative normal ogive when plotted against logarithmic values of the objective difference $(v - s)$. However, Thurstone also pointed out that the error in fitting a normal ogive is likely to become appreciable only when the Weber fraction is large, and would usually be negligible for the restricted range of stimulus values studied in the determination of a difference threshold. Indeed, apart from an informal comparison by Fritz (1930), most early results suggest that the normal ogive fits empirical data as well as any type of asymmetrical function (Pierce and Jastrow, 1885; Cattell, 1893; Urban, 1910; Brown, 1910; Boring, 1917; Cartwright and Festinger, 1943; Festinger, 1943b; Guilford, 1954).

More recently, the cumulative logistic function has also been suggested as a useful alternative description of response frequencies in discrimination (Berkson, 1944, 1953; Guilford, 1954; Luce, 1959; Bush, 1963; Ogilvie and Creelman, 1968; Bock and Jones, 1968). As Link (1978) points out, since empirical response probabilities are not themselves cumulative, some theoretical reason is needed to explain why they should appear to match the cumulative logistic, and two models which provide a rationale have been proposed by Link (1975, 1978) and by Vickers (1970, 1979). However, few (if any) empirical data would be capable of distinguishing between a normal ogive and the cumulative logistic. Apart from the close similarity in the shapes of the two theoretical functions, there is the added difficulty that the distributions of empirical response frequencies are highly skewed due to their truncation at zero or unity. Moreover, any additional sources of error may give rise to disproportionately large effects on the estimates of empirical frequencies, and obscure further the extent of agreement between empirical and theoretical functions. Indeed, if the study of discrimination had been restricted to relating response frequencies to some measure of discriminability, it seems likely that theoretical progress would have remained minimal.

(B) EFFECTS OF VARIATION IN BIAS

A second main focus of interest, which has stimulated a considerable amount of theorizing in this area, has been provided by the widespread recognition—even among the early psychophysicists—of the operation of subjective biassing factors predisposing an observer to favour one response rather than the other (e.g. Jastrow, 1888; Thurstone, 1948; Woodworth and Schlosberg, 1954). The objective stimulus difference $(v - s)$ at which an observer makes an equal proportion of "greater" and "lesser" responses is termed the "point of subjective equality" (PSE), and the distance between the PSE and an objective stimulus difference of zero is known as the "constant error". As its name implies, the constant error has traditionally been interpreted as a measure of subjective bias. For example, Festinger (1943b) showed that the PSE was shifted upwards when observers were instructed to guard against making "greater" responses incorrectly. Conversely, when observers were told to be careful not to make "lesser" responses incorrectly, the PSE was displaced in the opposite, negative direction.

Although the constant error was widely recognized as an indication of subjective bias, the absence of any theoretical counterpart for bias within the classical psychophysical model outlined above made it impossible to arrive at an unequivocal interpretation of the shape or position of the psychometric function. It was to meet this difficulty as it arose in the context of the measurement of absolute thresholds that Tanner and Swets (1954) developed the theory of signal detection, which permits a clear distinction between the degree of bias towards making one response rather than the other and the observer's sensitivity to a signal of a given intensity (or to a stimulus difference of a particular magnitude). Accounts of the application of signal detection theory to differential judgements are less common than for the case of detection (e.g. Green and Swets, 1966; McNicol, 1972; Egan, 1976). However, a clear exposition has been given by Treisman and Watts (1966), and the relations between signal detection and discrimination have recently been studied in these terms by Bonnel and Noizet (1979).

According to Treisman and Watts, the observer does not make a discriminative judgement on the basis of sampling a subjective difference $(V - S)$ which is greater or less than zero. Rather, he bases his decision on whether the momentary $(V - S)$ difference exceeds or falls below some arbitrary criterion or cutoff magnitude x_c. As illustrated in Fig. 2.4, if the cutoff lies below zero, there will be a bias in favour of responses of the form "$V > S$", and, if x_c lies above zero, there will be a converse bias in favour of responses of the form "$V < S$".

As in the case of simple detection, the outcomes of an observer's decisions

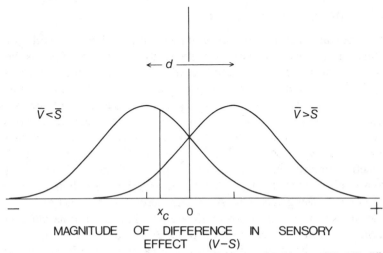

Fig. 2.4. Hypothetical probability density distributions of subjective $(V - S)$ differences consistent with a signal detection approach. The distribution with mean less than zero corresponds to the case where $\bar{V} < \bar{S}$, while that with a mean greater than zero corresponds to the case where $\bar{V} > \bar{S}$.

may be partitioned into four categories: (G/g), (G/l), (L/l), and (L/g), where (G/g) means making a response of the form "$V > S$" when v is objectively greater than s, (G/l) means making a "$V > S$" response when v is objectively less than s, (L/l) a response of the form "$V < S$" when v is objectively less than s, and (L/g) the same response when v is objectively greater than s. The position of the cutoff can then be characterized by the ratio y_g/y_l between the ordinates at x_c of the "greater" $(\bar{V} > \bar{S})$ and the "lesser" $(\bar{V} < \bar{S})$ distributions, as evaluated from the empirical probabilities of (G/g) and (G/l) responses. Meanwhile, the difference d between the means of the two distributions can be interpreted as a measure of the observer's discriminative ability, and can be evaluated by the algebraic difference between the z-scores for the two independent probabilities $P(G/g)$ and $P(G/l)$.

As shown by Treisman and Watts, any change in the position of the cutoff will shift only the *PSE*, leaving both the value of d and the precision (or "steepness") of the psychometric function unaltered. The consequent variation in the constant error can be interpreted on the classical, Thurstonian model as due to changes in the subjective bias of an observer towards one or the other response. Variations in the classical measure of the precision of the psychometric function, on the other hand, correspond to changes in d, i.e. to the basic sensitivity of the observer to a given stimulus difference. As such they would not be expected to occur simply as a result of some subjective change in attitude.

34 DOUGLAS VICKERS

(C) EFFECTS OF CHANGES IN CAUTION

A third important factor in the development of an adequate model of the discrimination process has been the recognition that, besides displaying variations in bias, observers seem capable of making judgements with varying degrees of *caution*. For example, in the experiment described in the Introduction, Festinger (1943a,b) investigated the effects of different sets of instructions on the number of errors made in a two-category task involving discrimination between the lengths of two simultaneously presented lines. In the case of all five observers, Festinger found that the precision of the psychometric function increased as the emphasis in instructions was changed from one of speed, through "usual" instructions (implying a compromise), to one stressing accuracy. A similar increase in the accuracy of both responses had been found earlier by Garrett (1922) as the time allowed for each discrimination was increased from 0.2 up to about 2.0 seconds.

More recently, the effects of variations in caution have been studied by Vickers and Packer (1980) in a task involving the discrimination of pairs of simultaneously presented line lengths. By means of appropriate instructions, set for speed or accuracy was manipulated in successive blocks of trials. Figure 2.5 shows the mean percentage of correct responses made in successive

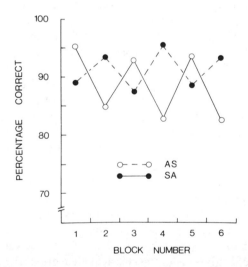

Fig. 2.5. Mean percentages of correct responses obtained by Vickers and Packer (1980) in successive blocks of trials alternating set for speed or accuracy. Filled circles denote data for the SA group which began with a set for speed; open circles those for the AS group which began with a set for accuracy. Each point represents an average based on 100 trials by each of 10 observers.

blocks by the ten observers in both the SA (speed then accuracy) and the AS (accuracy then speed) orders. As would be expected from the figure, set for accuracy was associated with a significantly higher percentage of correct responses, irrespective of the order in which the blocks were performed.

Such clear evidence for an overall improvement in accuracy implies a change in discriminative sensitivity (d), rather than a variation in bias (β). The fact that this improvement follows a simple change in instructions indicates the operation of a further, subjective or "attitudinal" factor, which may usefully be labelled "caution" to distinguish it from response bias. It appears that observers may improve their discriminative performance by adopting a more cautious attitude, albeit at the possible expense of taking more time over each decision.

Since the signal detection model outlined above assumes that the observer bases each decision upon a single observation of the current discriminal difference $(V - S)$, and since the time required for an observation is assumed to remain roughly constant, it is not possible on this version of the model to account for the possibility of trading speed for accuracy. However, a number of related models have been suggested which do incorporate such a feature (e.g. Crossman, 1955; Green *et al.*, 1957; Swets *et al.*, 1959; Hammerton, 1959; Schouten and Bekker, 1967; Taylor *et al.*, 1976). All are based on an important modification—originally suggested by Thomson (1920)—namely, that the distribution of $(V - S)$ differences should not be regarded as a distribution of values over a series of separate trials, but over successive instants within the duration of a single trial. Consequently, instead of basing his decision upon a single $(V - S)$ difference, the observer might base it upon the average of a "fixed sample" of n successively observed differences, each observation taking an equal amount of time. To account for variations in caution, it is then only necessary to suppose that the observer can choose to increase or decrease n so as to achieve a satisfactory balance between speed and accuracy. This modification to the signal detection model would account for the findings of Festinger, Garrett, and Vickers and Packer, which imply the operation of subjective variations in caution. However, for a more stringent evaluation of this type of fixed sample model, it is necessary to consider the second major dependent variable in discrimination tasks—that of response time.

3. Response time

(A) EFFECTS OF VARYING DISCRIMINABILITY

One of the most firmly established findings in the study of discrimination is that, as some measure of the difference between two stimuli is decreased, the time taken to discriminate between them increases (Henmon, 1906; Lemmon, 1927; Kellogg, 1931; Johnson, 1939; Festinger, 1943a,b; Crossman, 1955; Birren and Botwinick, 1955; Botwinick *et al.*, 1958; Thurmond and Alluisi, 1963; Pickett, 1964, 1967, 1968; Morgan and Alluisi, 1967; Pike, 1968, 1971; Vickers, 1970; Vickers *et al.*, 1971). Although Woodworth and Schlosberg gloss over its importance by pleading that "naturally it takes more time to distinguish two stimuli that are very similar than two which differ greatly" (1954, p. 33), the effect has long been regarded as a "second law of psychophysics" (Kellogg, 1931) and, over the last two decades, response times have constituted the main focus of interest in the study of discrimination. In this subsection we shall look first at the effects of varying discriminability on mean response times, before going on to consider the relation between the mean time for correct and incorrect responses, and to examine other features of the response time distributions.

1. *Discriminability and mean response times*
Although the inverse relation between discriminability and response time is well established, there has been comparatively little study of the precise nature of the function linking the physical difference between v and s to the time taken to discriminate between them. In an early study, Henmon (1906) suggested that as physical difference $(v - s)$ was decreased arithmetically, judgement time appeared to increase geometrically. On the other hand, in a later study, Crossman (1955) concluded that the rise in mean response time with reduced discriminability was best described by a "confusion function", according to which response time should be inversely proportional to the difference between the logarithmic values of the two stimulus magnitudes, and hence should depend on the ratio (v/s) rather than on the difference $(v - s)$.

As mentioned above, in connection with the relation between discriminability and response time, the assumption of a linear relation between objective stimulus difference and sensory effect seems to be a satisfactory approximation for the restricted range of values employed in most psychophysical studies of discrimination. Consistent with this, the effect of the ratio (v/s) on mean response time seems to be apparent only with highly discriminable stimuli (which tend to be discriminated without error), and to be overshadowed by that of the difference $(v - s)$ when discriminability is reduced and errors become more frequent (Birren and Botwinick, 1955; Botwinick *et al.*, 1958; Welford, 1968). However, when $(v - s)$ is severely reduced, and performance approaches chance level, the rate of increase in response time is reduced and the mean times (for correct responses) begin to level off (Kellogg, 1931; Pike, 1968; Vickers, 1970; Vickers *et al.*, 1971). As an example, Fig. 2.6 shows a typical pattern of mean response times obtained in two unpublished experiments described by Vickers (1979, pp. 61, 75).

It is of course difficult to suggest any general relation between discriminability and response time, since the exact feature of the stimulus upon which the discrimination process operates may often be uncertain. Again, what is regarded as the effective stimulus difference is at least partly determined by the initial assumptions which are made regarding the coding of stimulus intensity, and a succinct presentation of several of the main possibilities is given by Petrusic and Jamieson (1979). Finally, the interpretation of response time measures depends on the nature of the decision process which must be assumed to operate on the difference information in question—in whatever form it is coded.

So far as the fixed-sample models mentioned in the previous section are concerned, the inverse relationship (illustrated in Fig. 2.6) between objective stimulus difference and mean response time can be accounted for, provided

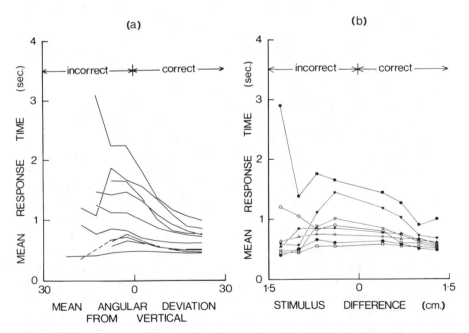

Fig. 2.6. Mean response times obtained in two unpublished experiments by the author with (a) R. J. Willson and (b) K. Domac. (a) Shows mean times to respond "clockwise" or "anticlockwise" to circular arrays of randomly oriented line segments similar to those shown by Vickers (1979, p. 76). The data represent means of the times for both judgements considered together, and classified only as correct or incorrect. (b) Shows similar results from an experiment in which observers classified a series of singly presented lines as "long" or "short". In both (a) and (b) individual curves represent data for individual observers.

that attention is confined to those experiments in which discriminability is varied only from one substantial block of trials to another. When dealing with a series of very easy discriminations, observers might plausibly be supposed to adopt a low value for n. On the other hand, when confronted with a series of more difficult discriminations, it seems reasonable to expect that observers would increase the size of the sample n, so as to decrease the chance of error, even at the cost of requiring more time for the additional observations. Indeed, it can be shown that the effective discriminability d (corresponding to the difference in units of $\sigma_{(V-S)}$ between the means of the two distributions in Fig. 2.4) should increase as the square root of n (or of time if it is assumed that observations are taken at a steady rate). In terms of a fixed-sample model, therefore, the inverse relationship between objective stimulus difference and mean response time can be seen as resulting from an attempt by the observer to maintain an acceptable error rate by increasing n when $(v - s)$ is reduced.

Unfortunately for this approach, when the size of $(v - s)$ is varied unpredictably from trial to trial, rather than from one series of trials to the next, the observer has no way of deciding in advance upon an appropriate value of n. Nevertheless, a large number of experiments in which $(v - s)$ has been varied from trial to trial, have shown that both mean response time and the proportion of incorrect responses are inversely related to the size of the objective stimulus difference (e.g. Henmon, 1906; Lemmon, 1927; Kellogg, 1931; Johnson, 1939; Festinger, 1943a,b; Thurmond and Alluisi, 1963; Pickett, 1964, 1967, 1968; Morgan and Alluisi, 1967; Vickers, 1970; Vickers et al., 1971; Swensson, 1972). As argued by Vickers (1970, 1979) and by Swensson (1972), this concomitant variation of time and errors is inconsistent with the notion that the observer predetermines a value for n so as to speed a time commensurate with the difficulty of each discrimination.

On the other hand, a slightly different type of process, which is capable of accounting for this feature, is exemplified by a so-called "optional stopping" model, first suggested by Cartwright and Festinger (1943), and later considered by Swets and Green (1961) in the context of signal detection. According to this approach, it is assumed that the observer adopts two independent cutoffs x_g and x_l, as illustrated in Fig. 2.7. If an observation falls above x_g, he responds "V is greater than S" and, if it falls below x_l, he responds "V is less than S". Otherwise, if the observation falls between x_g and x_l, he takes another observation, and continues to do so until he encounters one which falls outside this region of no-decision.

On this approach, bias in responding can be accounted for by supposing that the positions of k_g and k_l are asymmetrical about zero, while variations in caution can be accommodated by assuming that the absolute (unsigned) values of both k_g and k_l can be reduced by conditions which favour fast responding, or increased by those conducive to accuracy. Finally, since the chance of an observation falling within the region of no-decision is determined by the mean and variance of the inspected $(V - S)$ differences, both the mean number of observations required to elicit a response, and the eventual accuracy of that response, would be expected to vary from trial to trial as a function of the discriminability of the stimuli presented on each occasion. Indeed, an optional-stopping process of the type proposed by Cartwright and Festinger is capable of giving a good account of all of the features of discriminative performance touched on so far. Difficulties with the model only begin to appear when we consider the comparative times for correct and incorrect responses, to which we now turn.

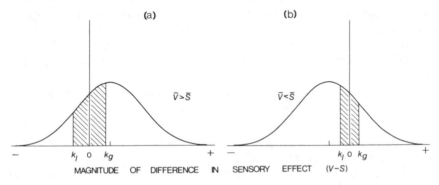

Fig. 2.7. Hypothetical probability density distributions of subjective $(V - S)$ differences in an optional-stopping model of the type proposed by Cartwright and Festinger (1943). (a) Shows the case where $\bar{V} > \bar{S}$, and (b) the case where $\bar{V} < \bar{S}$. The shaded area from k_l to k_g defines the region of no-decision.

2. Mean times for correct and incorrect responses

In an attempt to overcome the problem of the precise relationship between objective stimulus difference and mean response time, and to provide a common basis on which to compare the predictions of several theoretical models, Audley and Pike (1965) suggested that the mean time taken to make a particular response could be plotted against its probability of occurrence at various levels of discriminability to provide a latency-probability function which was characteristically different for a number of theoretical models. Since responses with a low probability of occurrence would normally correspond to errors, while those with a high probability of occurrence would usually be classified as correct, such latency-probability functions can provide a picture of changes in the relation between the mean times for correct and incorrect responses as discriminability is varied. However, the application and interpretation of statistical tests of the goodness of fit of alternative theoretical functions to a given set of empirical data is complicated by the fact that empirical response times are subject to variation by other (unevaluated) factors besides those which determine empirical response probabilities (Weatherburn, 1978). Accordingly, although it is perhaps reasonable to assume that these factors remain constant, most recent work has been concerned with more direct comparisons—at a fixed level of discriminability—of the times for correct and incorrect responses.

Where p, q and r are the respective probabilities that an observation will exceed x_g, be less than x_l, or fall in the region of no-decision, then Broadbent (1971, p. 291) has shown that, for a memoryless model of the type envisaged by Cartwright and Festinger, the mean number of observations required for a correct response is $r/1 - r$), and that this is identical to the number for an incorrect response. This suggests that a useful test of this variety of optional-stopping model would consist of comparing the times for correct and incorrect responses to stimuli of nominally constant discriminability.

While the prediction of identical times for correct and incorrect responses is quite straightforward, empirical results on this issue do not, however, conform to such a simple pattern. Discrimination experiments in which speed has been stressed have generally found times for incorrect responses to be the same—or, occasionally, less than—those for correct responses (e.g. Laming, 1968), while those with an emphasis on accuracy have found mean times for errors to be longer (e.g. Kellogg, 1931; La Berge, 1961; Cross and Lane, 1962; Pierrel and Murray, 1963; Pickett, 1967, 1968; Audley and Mercer, 1968; Pike, 1971). Meanwhile, among experiments in which instructions have implied some compromise between speed and accuracy, times for correct and incorrect responses by the faster observers show little or no difference, while incorrect responses by slower observers are clearly longer than their correct ones (e.g. Henmon, 1911; Wollen, 1963; Pike, 1968; Vickers, 1970, 1979, p. 62; Vickers et al., 1971).

As Broadbent (1971) has noted, the finding that times for incorrect responses are longer than those for correct when observers are slower and more careful is inconsistent with the prediction of a memoryless, optional-stopping process. At the same time, the complexity of the empirical results has given rise to a variety of alternative models. In the remainder of this subsection we shall examine in turn four of the main possibilities that have been proposed.

One of the first alternatives to be considered was a "runs" process suggested by Audley (1960), in which a response is made as soon as k successive momentary stimulus differences of the same sign are encountered: if k_g positive $(V - S)$ differences are sampled in succession, the observer responds "V is greater than S". Conversely, if a run of k_l negative differences is encountered first, he responds "V is less than S". The observer continues to take observations at a steady rate until one of these two criteria are satisfied. This model is thus a partial memory process, in the sense that the occurrence of observations is stored only for as long as the observations continue to be of the same sign.

If the observer takes observations from a distribution of subjective stimulus differences with mean $(\bar{V} - \bar{S})$ and standard deviation $\sigma_{(V-S)}$, then positive and negative differences will be sampled in an independent, random sequence, with probabilities p and $q = (1 - p)$, respectively. For any given values of p and q, and of the criteria k_g and k_p, the probability of making each alternative response can be calculated, along with the distribution of the number of observations required to make it (Audley, 1960; Audley and Pike, 1965; Vickers et al., 1971). As shown by these authors, when the values of k_g and k_l are equal, and low (e.g. 2), then the mean predicted time for a given response made incorrectly tends to be greater than that for the same response made correctly to a mean subjective stimulus difference of the same magnitude. However, when the values of k_g and k_l are equal, and high (e.g. 4 or 5), then predicted times for correct and incorrect responses are virtually identical.

Since this trend is the opposite to that just noted in the results of several experiments, the runs model has not been widely pursued as a model of the discrimination process (cf. Sanders and Ter Linden, 1967; Vickers et al., 1971; Vickers, 1979, pp. 56–64). Instead, two other models have been developed and considered: one predicting longer times for incorrect than for correct responses, the other predicting identical times for both.

In the simplest version of the first of these, the "recruitment" model proposed by La Berge (1962), the observer is conceived of as inspecting the stream of $(V - S)$ differences until he encounters a total of k_g positive or k_l negative differences, whereupon he responds "V is greater than S" or "V is less than S", respectively. Detailed predictions for this model have been presented by La Berge (1962), Audley and Pike (1965), Vickers et al. (1971) and Vickers (1979, p. 71). While its prediction of longer times for errors is consistent with the results of those experiments cited above in which observers have responded cautiously, it is contradicted by the results of studies in which observers have tended to trade accuracy for speed.

The second possibility, which has enjoyed a considerable vogue, is a "random walk" process, originally derived by Stone (1960) from Wald (1947), and subsequently developed by Edwards (1965), Laming (1968), Link (1975, 1978) and Link and Heath (1975). According to the simplest version of this model, as presented by Edwards (1965), the observer can be thought of as inspecting the stream of $(V - S)$ differences until the number of differences of one sign exceeds that of the other by a critical amount k_g (in the case of positive differences) or k_l (in the case of negative), whereupon he responds "V is greater than S" or "V is less than S", respectively. As shown by Edwards (1965, p. 314), when the prior odds in favour of each response are equal, this is equivalent to proposing that the observer responds when he has attained a predetermined likelihood ratio in favour of one alternative.

If the observer takes both the sign and the magnitude of the inspected differences into account, the criterion for a response can be construed as the attainment of a critical difference k_g in one direction between the accumulated magnitude of positive and negative differences, or of a (possibly different) value k_l in the other. As Swensson and Thomas (1974) point out, this criterion is analogous to the difference between the totals in Edwards' version. Detailed predictions for the two versions have been presented by Edwards (1965), Audley and Pike (1965), Laming (1968) and Vickers et al. (1971). Both versions predict that the distributions of times for correct and incorrect responses should be identical. This prediction is clearly contradicted by the bulk of studies of discrimination, in which the mean times for incorrect responses are longer than those for correct.

In an attempt to deal with this difficulty, Link (1975) and Link and Heath (1975) have shown that the prediction by the random walk model of identical times for correct and incorrect responses depends on assuming that the distributions of inspected differences are symmetrical about their means (as is the case with the normal distributions in Fig. 2.3). If the distributions are asymmetric, then errors may be faster or slower than correct responses, depending on the direction of the asymmetry (cf. Thomas, 1975). If it were assumed that the shape of the distribution of $(V - S)$ differences varied as a function of the degree of caution exercized by an observer, then this modification could perhaps encompass the various results cited at the beginning of this subsection. However, as Laming (1979) has commented, it introduces an additional, free stimulus, parameter, and there seem to be no independent grounds for assuming that the distribution of sampled differences should change from symmetrical to asymmetrical as the criteria employed by an observer are made more rigorous.

One further model, to which this last objection does not apply, is an "accumulator" process proposed by Vickers (1970, 1979). According to this hypothesis, the observer accumulates the magnitudes of the positive and negative $(V - S)$ differences in two separate stores until the accumulated amount of positive difference t_g reaches or exceeds a certain critical magnitude k_g, or until the accumulated amount of negative difference t_l reaches or exceeds a (possibly different) critical magnitude k_l. If the total t_g reaches k_g first, the observer responds "V is greater than S" and, if t_l reaches k_l first, he responds "V is less than S". Otherwise, he continues to take observations until one of these criteria is satisfied. As soon as a response is made, t_g and t_l are reset to zero, and the process is ready to begin anew. As illustrated in Fig. 2.8, the process may be thought of as a conditional random walk, in which a step to the right is taken if a positive $(V - S)$ difference is encountered, and a step to the left if the difference is negative. Within each observation interval, the magnitude of each step is determined by the magnitude of the sampled difference.

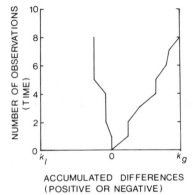

ACCUMULATED DIFFERENCES
(POSITIVE OR NEGATIVE)

Fig. 2.8. The accumulator model conceived as a conditional random walk. A response of the form "$V > S$" or "$V < S$" is made when either of the accumulated totals of positive or negative differences reaches or exceeds k_g or k_l, respectively.

Although this model is conceptually simple, an essential feature is that it operates on (asymmetrical) truncated distributions of positive and negative subjective stimulus differences. Since this makes its mathematical analysis extremely difficult, Vickers (1970, 1972, 1979) has explored its predictions by means of extensive computer simulations, some results of which are presented in Fig. 2.9. As can be seen from the figure, when the values of k_g and k_l are equal and low (e.g. around 1), the predicted number of observations is approximately the same for a response of the form "$V > S$", made correctly to a stimulus difference of x units, as it is for the same response, made incorrectly to a difference of $-x$ units. However, as the values of k_g and k_l are increased through $k_g = k_l = 3$, up to $k_g = k_l = 7$, the mean number of observations taken by the simulated model becomes progressively greater for incorrect than for correct responses. This feature corresponds well with the pattern of empirical data outlined at the beginning of this subsection, and has the advantage of being an inherent property of the model, requiring no additional, independently justified assumptions.

(B) CHARACTERISTICS OF THE RESPONSE TIME DISTRIBUTIONS

Each of the models outlined in the last subsection predicts certain systematic changes in the distributions of response times as a result of variations in

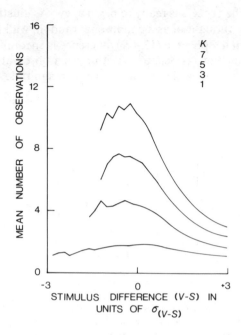

Fig. 2.9. The mean number of observations required by a computer simulation of the accumulator model to make a response of the form "$V > S$" for various values of $k_g = k_l$, represented by k.

discriminability, bias or caution. However, Taylor (1965) has remarked that papers in which such models are developed usually concentrate on theoretical issues, and do not attempt experimental verification. Conversely, the older studies of response times have been generally concerned with means, and have taken little account of other features of response time distributions. This is unfortunate, since, as Broadbent has commented, "there seem to be so many theoretical possibilities that some experimentation to narrow down the possibilities is badly needed" (1971, p. 322). Such studies seem to be particularly desirable, since there are quite striking differences between the shapes of the distributions predicted by some of the models.

So far as the empirical data are concerned, a detailed study of various aspects of response time distributions by Vickers (1970), Vickers et al. (1971) and by Wilding (1974, 1978) reveals an encouraging uniformity. Their findings concerning standard deviation, skew and kurtosis will be summarized briefly, together with those for two other unpublished experiments by Vickers and Domac and Vickers and Willson, details of which are given by Vickers (1979, pp. 61, 75).

1. *Standard deviation*

Figure 2.10 shows some empirical data from the two last experiments. As found by Vickers (1970), Vickers *et al.* (1971) and by Wilding (1974, 1978), the pattern of standard deviations typically follows that for mean response times in showing clear effects of discriminability and of the degree of caution exercized by an observer, as well as a tendency towards a maximum value for incorrect responses at small stimulus differences, where the proportion of errors is relatively high (around 0.4). As pointed out by Wilding (1978), this pattern is consistent only with the predictions of the accumulator model outlined above* (cf. Vickers *et al.*, 1971).

Further comparisons are possible if standard deviations are plotted against the corresponding mean response times. As can be seen from Fig. 2.11, the runs, random walk and accumulator models all predict an *approximately* linear relation between standard deviations and means. However, while the two former processes predict a slope near unity, the latter predicts a more gradual slope, with coefficients decreasing as values of $k_g = k_l$ increase. Figure 2.12 shows the best fitting straight lines obtained when the data of Fig. 2.10 were plotted against the corresponding mean response times shown in Fig. 2.6. The coefficients of slope range from 0.1 up to 1.0 in Fig. 2.12a, and from 0.3 up to 2.1 in Fig. 2.12b, with means of 0.5 and 0.8, respectively. The general trend of these results, and the average value of the coefficients, are not well accounted for by the runs, random walk or recruitment models, although they are consistent with those predicted by the accumulator.

2. *Skew*

Figure 2.13 shows some empirical data from the two experiments from which results are shown in Figs 2.6 and 2.10. As can be seen from Fig. 2.13, when empirical measures of skew are plotted against values of the objective stimulus difference $(v - s)$, they show a direct, roughly linear relationship over most of the range, with a steeper rise for correct responses at large stimulus differences (cf. Vickers, 1970; Vickers *et al.*, 1971; Wilding, 1974, 1978). Except in the case of errors at large stimulus differences, an overwhelming majority of empirical measures is positive (cf. Vickers, 1979, p. 75). Again, the trend and range of these values are consistent only with the predictions of an accumulator process (cf. Vickers, 1970, pp. 47–48; Vickers

---

* The relevant predictions for this model were presented by Vickers (1972). The model differs slightly from the version considered by Vickers *et al.* (1971) and by Wilding (1974). The differences are discussed by Wilding (1978, p. 237) and by Vickers (1979, pp. 80–82).

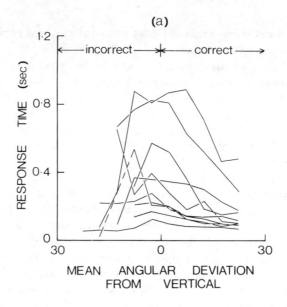

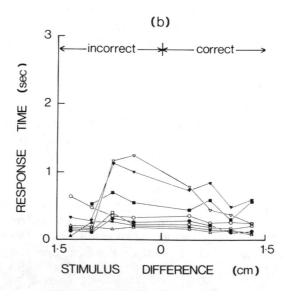

Fig. 2.10. Empirical standard deviations in response time obtained in unpublished experiments by the author with (a) R. J. Willson and (b) K. Domac. Data have been organized in the same way as the corresponding mean times shown in Fig. 2.6.

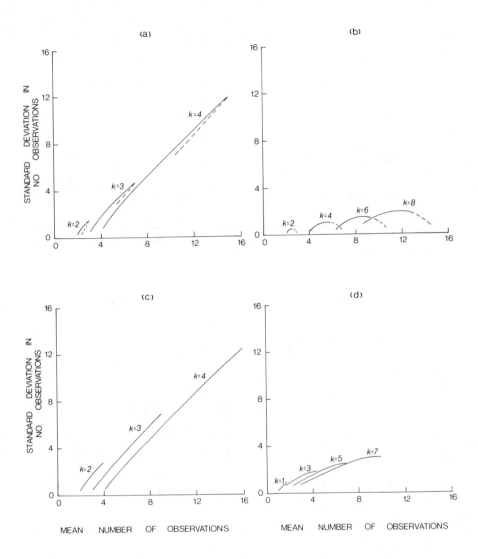

MEAN   NUMBER   OF   OBSERVATIONS   MEAN   NUMBER   OF   OBSERVATIONS

Fig. 2.11. The pattern of standard deviations in the times taken to make responses of the form "$V > S$", as predicted by (a) the runs, (b) the recruitment, (c) the random walk and (d) the accumulator models, plotted against the corresponding means for various values of $k_g = k_l$, represented by k. Where incorrect responses could be distinguished from correct, the former are shown by broken, and the latter by solid lines.

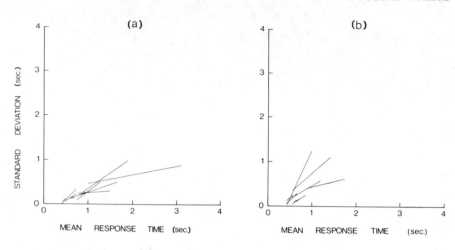

Fig. 2.12. The patterns of best fitting straight lines obtained when the empirical standard deviations in Figs 2.10(a) and (b) were plotted against the empirical mean times shown in Figs 2.6(a) and (b), respectively.

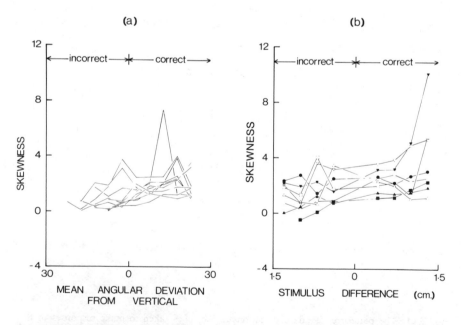

Fig. 2.13. Empirical skewness measures for the response time distributions obtained in two unpublished experiments by the author with (a) R. J. Willson and (b) K. Domac. Data have been organized in the same way as the corresponding mean times and standard deviations shown in Figs 2.6 and 2.10.

et al., 1971, pp. 159–160, 163–164; Wilding, 1974, pp. 488, 494–495; Wilding, 1978, pp. 236, 242; Vickers, 1979, pp. 67, 74–76, 93).*

3. *Kurtosis*

Figure 2.14 shows the empirical measures of kurtosis obtained in the same two experiments for which results are shown in Fig. 2.13. Again, these data are typical in showing a direct relationship between kurtosis and the objective stimulus difference ($v - s$). As with skew, the measures are predominantly positive, and tend towards high values in the case of correct responses to highly discriminable stimuli (cf. Vickers, 1970, pp. 47–48; Vickers *et al.*, 1971, pp. 161–165; Wilding, 1974, pp. 488, 494–495; Wilding, 1978, pp. 236–242; Vickers, 1979, pp. 67, 93). Both the trend and the range of values resemble those predicted by an accumulator process, but are not well accounted for by the other models considered in this section.

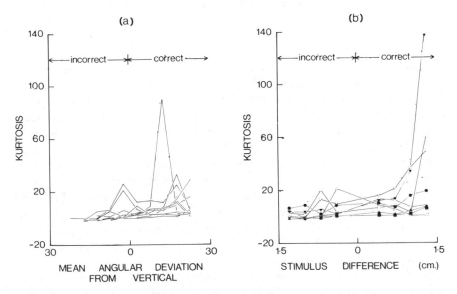

Fig. 2.14. Empirical measures of kurtosis for the response time distributions obtained in two unpublished experiments by the author with (a) R. J. Willson and (b) K. Domac. Data have been organized in the same way as the corresponding mean times, standard deviations and skewness measures shown in Figs 2.6, 2.10 and 2.13.

* Although Wilding (1978, p. 237) has commented that empirical values of skew and kurtosis sometimes exceed those presented as theoretical predictions for the accumulator (e.g. Vickers, 1979, p. 93), the latter rapidly accelerate for low values of $k_g = k_l$, particularly when slightly more discriminable stimuli are considered.

4. Classification of response time distributions

As demonstrated by Snodgrass et al. (1967, pp. 14–16), values of the second, third and fourth moments may be used to classify distributions of response times into various types, as distinguished by the Pearson classification outlined by Kendall and Stuart (1968). Following the example of Snodgrass et al., Vickers (1979, pp. 94–96) examined 878 response time distributions obtained in four different experiments, and found that 92 per cent of these were classified as Pearson Type IV, with a small proportion of Beta distributions (2 per cent and 6 per cent of the first and second kind, respectively) which appeared to be associated with very fast responding. These proportions were close to the corresponding values of 96 per cent, 1 per cent and 3 per cent observed in distributions generated during computer simulation of the accumulator process. Similarly, changes in the shapes of the empirical distributions as discriminability was varied were found to be closely matched by those obtained in simulations of the accumulator process, but were not well described by the other models (Vickers, 1979, pp. 94–95).

5. Possible restrictions and alternatives

Although the results summarized above are remarkably consistent, a number of writers have argued that the use of higher moments to characterize empirical response time distributions, and to legislate between alternative theories, may not be quite as straightforward as has been assumed. For example, Taylor (1965) and Wilding (1978) have drawn attention to the fact that empirical distributions are affected by factors other than a purely statistical variation in the number of observations necessary to reach some criterion. As a result, it may be inappropriate to make direct comparisons between empirical and theoretical measures. However, Wilding (1978) found that differences in time between "preferred" and "non-preferred" responses could be satisfactorily explained as being due to the adoption by an observer of unequal criteria rather than as indicating an additional response factor. Similarly, variation in stimulus-response compatibility was found to affect only the mean of the response time distributions, and was not associated with changes in their shape. While it is of course possible that these changes might be affected by other response factors, the apparent close relationship between empirical and theoretical measures may perhaps for the moment be taken at face value.

In a recent paper, Ratcliff (1979) has also pointed out that indices of the shape of response time distributions based on moments are very sensitive to extreme observations (which may arise from other, extraneous processes), and are limited by the considerable variance usually associated with estimates of these measures. Although measures of skew and kurtosis in the distributions of times for correct responses examined by Vickers (1979) are each based on substantial numbers of observations (250 to 600), these fall short of the ideal of several thousand suggested by Ratcliff. However, the regularity within the results for each observer, and the consistency across observers, both suggest that the problems raised by Ratcliff may not be as severe in simple discrimination studies as in more complex experimental tasks. Meanwhile, the technique of "Vincent averaging" across observers, proposed by Ratcliff, promises to be extremely useful for arriving at a general characterization of the complex changes in shape which occur in response time distributions as discriminability, caution and (possibly) bias are varied.

(C) EFFECTS OF VARIATION IN BIAS

While the effects of bias on response times have been studied in signal detection tasks (e.g. Carterette *et al.*, 1965; Pike *et al.*, 1974; Pike and Dalgleish, 1976; Vickers, 1978, 1979, pp. 149–151, 163–165), and in choice-reaction (e.g. Welford, 1971, 1973, 1975; Vickers, 1979, pp. 273–283), no published data are known in which these effects have been studied in a two-category discrimination task, in which both discriminanda have been presented simultaneously for comparison. However, Laming (1968, 1969) has performed two experiments in which observers were required to classify each of a series of vertical lines, presented one at a time, as "long" or "short". Observers in the first experiment were told about the *a priori* probability of each response, but were not so informed in the second. In both experiments, the *a priori* probability varied from one series of trials to the next, with this variation being quite systematic (gradually increasing or decreasing) in the second experiment.

Laming's (1968) results are shown in Fig. 2.15. They show that, as the *a priori* probability of one stimulus (e.g. stimulus *a*) increases, the probability of making the alternative response (B/a), given that stimulus, decreases. Conversely, the probability of making response *A* given the alternative stimulus (i.e. A/b), increases. Meanwhile, the time taken to make response *A* decreases, while that to make *B* increases.

These data can be given a straightforward interpretation in terms of any of the optional-stopping models discussed in the immediately previous subsection. Instructions emphasizing particular care with respect to one response, or indicating that it is less probable than the alternative, would both be expected to lead to a higher criterion value for that response and/or to a lower criterion for the alternative. Such a view ascribes the effects shown in Fig. 2.15 to a change in some parameter of the decision process (specifically, k_g and/or k_l), rather than to some priming or facilitation of the

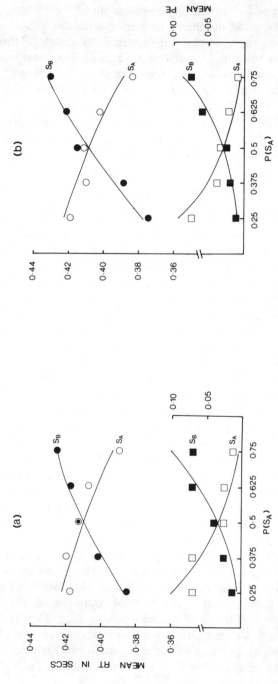

Fig. 2.15. Mean response times (averaged over both correct and incorrect responses) and the proportions of errors obtained by Laming (1968) in (a) Experiment I and (b) Experiment II. (Redrawn, with permission from Laming (1969, Figs 1 and 2).)

response mechanism, which is independent of the quality of the sampled information. On this view, therefore, we should expect that variations in bias and discriminability should show some evidence of interaction in their effects on response times. However, no published data are known which are relevant to this question.

(D) EFFECTS OF CHANGES IN CAUTION

As mentioned earlier, discrimination performance has been found to show an unbiased improvement when instructions emphasize accuracy, or when the time allowed for each judgement is increased (Garrett, 1922; Festinger, 1943a). Thurstone (1937) was one of the first to recognize that this improved accuracy seemed to be achieved at the expense of speed, and suggested that, for a constant stimulus difference, the relation between the time taken to make a judgement and its probability of being correct was approximately ogival. Some confirmation of this relation was obtained by Philip (1936, 1947) in a series of experiments in which observers were required to discriminate between two sets of rhomboid shapes presented at various speeds, or between the relative frequencies of differently coloured dots exposed for different durations. More recently, in a study of discrimination between the relative frequencies of sequentially presented red and blue light flashes, Vickers et al. (1971) found that when the percentage of errors, made by each observer in each session, was plotted against the corresponding mean response time, the data were fairly well described by a single function. As Vickers (1979, p. 43) argues, this suggests that, in this experiment at least (where the probability of sampling a particular stimulus event could be controlled), differences between the fast and slow sessions of an individual observer are analogous to those between a fast observer and another, slower one, and can be explained in terms of variations along a single underlying continuum constituting the compromise adopted between speed and accuracy.

While there seems to be considerable agreement about the general form of such a speed-accuracy trade-off function (cf. Pachella, 1974), many different possibilities have been considered concerning the precise relationship between accuracy and response time in discrimination (e.g. Swensson, 1972; Lappin and Disch, 1972a; Pachella, 1974). For example, Yellott (1971) has proposed that, over a series of trials, an observer's judgements are composed of two kinds of response. The first kind arises on occasions when he has taken a sufficient (more or less constant) time to make an errorless discrimination, and the second kind arises when he makes a fast guess. According to this view, changes in the speed-accuracy trade-off correspond to variations in the proportion of fast guesses within a series of reponses.

One difficulty with this approach is that (as we have seen above) errors generally take longer than correct responses. To accommodate this finding, Swensson (1972) has considered the possibility that, if the observer does not achieve a true discriminative response by a certain "deadline", he again resorts to chance responding. However, despite its complexity, this version too seems to be clearly ruled out by Wilding's (1974) results, which contain no evidence of the multimodality in response time distributions predicted by the deadline model.

Swensson (1972) and Lappin and Disch (1972a) have also considered a number of theoretical functions derived from the work of Pew (1969), Schouten and Bekker (1967), Taylor *et al.* (1967), Pachella *et al.* (1968), Pachella and Fisher (1969), Swanson and Briggs (1969) and Pew (1969). However, neither set of experimenters found any decisive superiority in the fit provided by any particular function to their data, and Pachella (1974) and Swensson and Thomas (1974) have discussed some of the considerable statistical difficulties involved in such comparisons. Meanwhile, Vickers (1979, p. 90) has drawn attention to a severe limitation of these formulations within the context of discrimination: namely, that, without additional assumptions, they fail to explain why empirical trade-off functions should vary either in slope or intercept (or both) as a function of the discriminability of the stimuli concerned (Philip, 1947; Swensson, 1972).

Figure 2.16 shows a clear example of the effect of different levels of discriminability on the trade-off functions relating the percentage of correct responses, made in the speed and accuracy blocks in Vickers and Packer's (1980) study, to the corresponding mean times for all responses (correct and incorrect). The systematic ordering over levels of discriminability is reminiscent of the changes in *ROC* curves predicted by signal detection theory as detectability is increased (Green and Swets, 1966; McNicol, 1972; Egan, 1976). Indeed, a number of writers have suggested that some form of "latency operating characteristic" might be useful in distinguishing between effects which are solely due to variations in the observer's degree of caution and those arising from some improvement or deterioration in the quality of the sensory information upon which his decision process operates (e.g. Lappin and Disch, 1972a, 1972b, 1973; Thomas and Myers, 1972). Meanwhile, unlike the other formulations considered by Swensson (1972) and by Lappin and Disch (1972a), models such as the random walk or accumulator necessarily predict that the trade-off function generated by variations in the criteria k_g and k_l is unique to each particular degree of discriminability (cf. Swensson and Thomas, 1974; Vickers, 1979, p. 89). In this respect, these models are also to be preferred to other approaches, such as Thomas's (1973) "expectancy" model, which require additional, explicit assumptions to that effect. On the other hand, although the use of trade-off functions has been suggested for the study of a variety of cognitive tasks (Wickelgren, 1977, 1978; Kantowitz, 1978), all the optional-stopping models considered in the previous subsection predict trade-off functions of the same general shape, and it seems unlikely that empirical data will serve to distinguish between them. At the same time, the practical usefulness of trade-off functions outside the restricted context of discrimination may be limited by the variety of sources of error which may operate in more complex tasks (Rabbitt and Vyas, 1970).

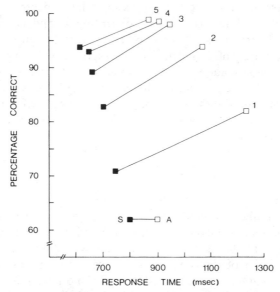

Fig. 2.16. Mean percentages of correct responses made obtained by Vickers and Packer (1980) at different levels of discriminability ranging from lowest (1) to highest (5), plotted against the mean times for all responses (correct or incorrect). Filled squares denote data obtained under a set for speed (S), and empty squares those obtained under a set for accuracy (A). Each point is based on 60 trials by each of 20 observers.

4. Confidence

A third dependent variable, to which response frequency and time are often related, is the confidence reported by an observer after making a particular judgement. Confidence reports have been expressed in a variety of ways, such as by a set of terms like "sure", "not quite sure" etc., by a set of categories, such as the letters *a* to *e*, or in terms of a percentage scale (Foley, 1959; Adams and Adams, 1961). Unlike response frequency and time, however, which are objective measures, taken by the experimenter, of aspects of the observer's overt response to some objective feature of the stimulus, each confidence rating represents an estimate by the observer of some subjective parameter associated with his own covert processing of stimulus information. As such, confidence measures are a common adjunct in studies of discrimination, though rarely investigated in their own right. Nevertheless, confidence measures constitute an interesting model for controlled introspection of the kind recently advocated by Liebermann (1979) and it seems likely that interest in this aspect of discriminative performance will increase.

In the meantime, several methodological aspects remain unexplored, such as the usefulness of ratio scales for expressing relative degrees of confidence (Torgerson, 1958). Little is known concerning confidence in incorrect responses, and instructions given to observers typically ignore the problem of assigning a rating of confidence to a response which is subsequently judged to have been made in error. Despite these difficulties, however, the general pattern of experimental results is remarkably consistent and clear. As with response frequency and time, we shall begin with the effects of discriminability, before going on to consider those associated with variations in bias and caution.

(A) EFFECTS OF VARYING DISCRIMINABILITY

In an early experiment on the discrimination of pairs of lifted weights, Garrett (1922) found that confidence, expressed as a percentage, appeared to be a monotonic, negatively accelerated function of stimulus difference. Similar results were obtained in two later studies by Johnson (1939) and by Festinger (1943a,b) of discrimination between the lengths of two lines. Further confirmation of this relationship has been obtained in a more recent study of lifted weights by Pierrel and Murray (1963).

In terms of the signal detection model proposed by Treisman and Watts (1966), this finding could be explained by supposing that the position of the observer's cutoff x_c remains fixed and that confidence is determined by the amount by which a given observation exceeds (or falls below) x_c. However, such an explanation is not possible within the framework of the more comprehensive random walk model. Indeed, since the observer in this view is conceived of as continuing to sample sensory information until some predetermined likelihood ratio criterion is achieved, the most natural expectation on this view is that, provided the criteria remain unchanged, all responses of the same type should be made with an equal degree of confidence, irrespective of the discriminability of the stimuli.

Audley (1960) has suggested an alternative hypothesis, which can account for the observed relationship between discriminability and confidence, and which can be applied to any of the optional-stopping models reviewed in the previous section. According to this view, confidence is an inverse function of the number of observations required to satisfy the decision criterion (irrespective of how this is specified). Because decisions at lower levels of discriminability will generally require more observations, this would explain why they tend to be made with lower confidence. Furthermore, this hypothesis is consistent with the finding that, for a given level of discriminability, observers are less confident when they take longer to reach a decision (Henmon, 1911; Audley, 1964).

(B) EFFECTS OF VARIATION IN BIAS

The hypothesis that confidence is somehow determined by the number of observations required to fulfil some preset criterion corresponds to the established empirical generalization that confidence in discrimination tasks is an inverse function of response time (e.g. Seward, 1928; Volkmann, 1934; Johnson, 1939). However, when this notion is used to extend any of the optional-stopping models discussed in the previous section, it leads to some unexpected—if not paradoxical—predictions.

To account for the effects of variation in bias, models such as the random walk assume that the observer sets appropriate relative values for k_g and k_l. For example, if particular care is to be exercized in making responses of the form "$V > S$" then the observer would plausibly be expected to increase the criterion k_g for that response, while maintaining the same value of k_l for the other. If he does so, then the mean time taken to make "$V > S$" responses should be longer—in comparison both with the time taken to make the alternative response, and with that previously taken to make the same response at the original (lower) value of k_g. In other words, if confidence is an inverse function of the number of observations (and hence of time), then instructions to be particularly careful in making a certain response should lead to decreased confidence in that response.

No published data are known concerning the effects on confidence of variations in bias. However, the results of an unpublished experiment, carried out in the author's laboratory by K. Calembakis, indicate that this prediction is not borne out. In alternate blocks of trials, observers in this experiment were instructed to exercize particular care in making responses of the form "$V > S$", and, in the remaining blocks, to exercise particular care in making the converse response. Contrary to the prediction, the "careful" responses, although taking longer, and being less frequently in error, were made with higher confidence. Similar—though less clear—results have also been obtained in another unpublished pilot experiment by J. Packer. It should be stressed that these studies need to be corroborated by further work. However, some other relevant evidence, also consistent with them, is to be found in the study of effects of changes in caution, to which we now turn.

(c) EFFECTS OF CHANGES IN CAUTION

As in the case of bias, Audley's "inverse function of time" hypothesis predicts that an increase in overall caution for both responses, which leads to slower, more accurate judgements, should also result in a decrease in confidence. However, the few experiments in which subjective caution appears to have been manipulated have found no change in confidence. For example, observers in Festinger's (1943a) experiment were required to indicate whether a vertical line of variable length was longer or shorter than a standard and, after each judgement, to express their confidence in its correctness in terms of a scale ranging from 0 to 100. The task was performed under "accuracy" instructions (in which observers were exhorted to avoid errors), "speed" instructions (in which they were encouraged to respond as quickly as possible) and "usual" instructions (which implied a compromise). Differences in instructional set were associated with the expected changes in response time and accuracy. However, no consistent change was found in the standard deviation of ogives fitted to the empirical plots of confidence against stimulus difference. Results resembling these have been obtained by Johnson (1939), who employed similar instructions, and also by Garrett (1922), who presented stimuli at varying rates.

These results are surprising and Vickers (1979, pp. 184–185) has suggested that they may be an artefact of the scaling strategy adopted by observers. Specifically, since instructions usually emphasize the need to employ the complete range of the confidence rating scale, observers may have adopted a relative rating strategy, according to which a rating of 100 was assigned to the most confident responses in each condition, and a rating of 0 to the least confident, irrespective of differences in the subjective impression experienced in the various conditions. This interpretation seems reasonable in view of the design of these experiments, in which the emphasis on speed or accuracy was varied only from one complete session to another (Garrett, 1922, p. 27; Johnson, 1939, p. 31; Festinger, 1943a, p. 292).

Support for this interpretation comes from the experiment by Vickers and Packer (1980), mentioned earlier, in which observers were asked to decide which of two vertical lines was the longer, and to indicate their confidence in each judgement by pressing the appropriate one of two sets of buttons arranged in a linear array ($L5$, $L4$, . . . , $R4$, $R5$) from left to right. Set for speed or accuracy was alternated over successive blocks of 100 trials within one continuous session of 600 trials. During four practice blocks, also performed with alternating set for speed or accuracy, observers were trained to adopt a single, uniform convention for scaling their subjective feelings of confidence.

As would be expected, observers in this experiment produced a higher percentage of correct responses (Fig. 2.5) and had longer response times during blocks performed under a set for accuracy. Less predictably, judgements under an accuracy set were more confident than those made under a set for speed (cf. Fig. 2.17). As shown in Fig. 2.18, this difference held over all five levels of discriminability. The greater confidence associated with an accuracy set in this experiment reinforces the view that the traditionally accepted findings of Garrett (1922), Johnson (1939) and Festinger (1943a) are artefactual. Of more immediate importance, the positive relationship, which emerges between confidence and response time when speed and accuracy blocks are compared, runs counter to the hypothesis that confidence is an inverse function of the number of observations required to reach a decision.

An alternative hypothesis, capable of accommodating these results, and of explaining some other recalcitrant data, has been suggested by Vickers (1972, 1978, 1979) in terms of the accumulator model of discrimination. According to the "balance of evidence" hypothesis proposed by Vickers, a basis for confidence is to be found in the difference c between the totals t_g and t_l in the two accumulators. In particular, as Figs 2.19(a) and (b) illustrate, if the criteria k_g and k_l in the accumulator process are both assumed to be equal to k, and k remains fixed, then the difference c between the totals t_g and t_l at the moment one reaches k depends upon the relative rates at which

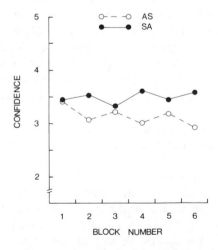

Fig. 2.17. Mean confidence ratings obtained by Vickers and Packer (1980) in successive blocks alternating set for speed or accuracy. Filled circles denote data for the SA (speed then accuracy), and open circles those for the AS group. Each point represents an average of the mean ratings made by each of ten observers.

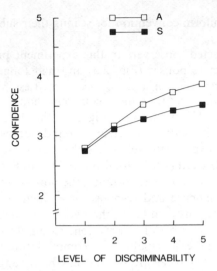

Fig. 2.18. Mean confidence ratings obtained by Vickers and Packer (1980) at each level of discriminability from lowest (1) to highest (5). Filled squares denote data obtained under a set for speed (S), and empty squares those obtained under a set for accuracy (A). Each point represents an average of the mean ratings made by each of 20 observers.

the totals increase. When the magnitude of the variable lies close to the standard, these rates will be similar, more observations will be required for one total to reach k, and the value of c at the moment of decision will be smaller. Conversely, as can be seen in Figs 2.19(b) and (c), when discriminability is held constant and the value of k increased then decisions will tend to be made with larger values of c. Thus the "balance of evidence" hypothesis shares with the "inverse function of time" interpretation the prediction that, provided an observer's degree of caution remains constant, decisions taking longer should be made with less confidence. However, if discriminability is held constant, and the observer induced to vary his criteria (e.g. by instructions emphasizing speed or accuracy), then the "balance of evidence" hypothesis predicts that decisions reached with more stringent criteria, though taking longer, should be made with greater confidence.

Vickers (1979) has shown in detail that the "balance of evidence" hypothesis gives a good account of the empirical relationships between confidence and both discriminability and response time found in the studies of Henmon (1911), Garrett (1922), Johnson (1939), Festinger (1943), Pierrel and Murray (1963) and Audley (1964). In addition, it has the advantage over the "inverse function of time" hypothesis in being consistent with the direct relation between confidence and number of observations found in the "expanded judgement" tasks of Irwin *et al.* (1956) and Geller and Pitz

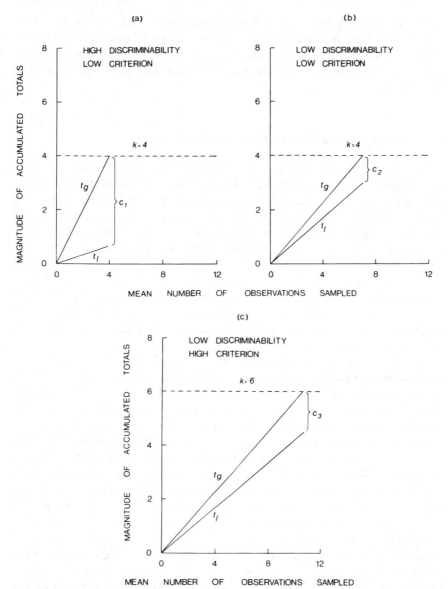

Fig. 2.19. Representation of the average states of the totals t_g and t_l of (randomly varying) positive and negative differences present in the two accumulators after varying numbers of observations. (a) Shows the discrepancy c_1 between the totals at the moment a low criterion ($k = 4$) is reached and observations consist predominantly of large positive differences. (b) Illustrates the smaller value of c_2, which results when the differences are more evenly balanced between positive and negative, and more observations are required to reach the criterion. (c) Illustrates the increased value c_3, which results when the need for more observations arises from an increase in criterion rather than a decrease in discriminability.

(1968), in which confidence is monitored continually, rather than only at the time of a single, final decision. As pointed out by Swensson and Thomas (1974, p. 230), this difference is the sole determinant of the likelihood ratio, and constitutes an efficient description of the statistical information sampled from the stimulus.

5. Summary, conclusions and further developments

In the course of our review of experimental findings on discrimination, certain general features of human discriminatory performance have emerged, and a number of theoretical conclusions may be drawn. In the first place, it appears that errors arise because the sensory representations of stimuli are subject to various sources of random disturbance, and that bias in responding may be exhibited by observers, who possess some capability for varying their relative readiness to make one response or the other. Both features are incorporated in the signal detection model, in which discriminatory judgements are not determined in an all-or-none fashion by a sensory threshold which remains stable for each individual, but by the selection of a criterion amount of difference which may vary from one situation to another.

The effects of variations in caution on the overall accuracy of discriminative performance suggest, however, that discrimination is not achieved by the application of a variable criterion to a single observation of the sensory input. It appears rather that observers also possess some capacity for counteracting the variability in the sensory representation of stimuli, albeit at a cost of taking more time to respond. On the other hand, the concomitant variation in response time and errors as discriminability is varied unpredictably from trial to trial, indicates that this additional time is not due to the observer taking a predetermined number of multiple observations of the momentary sensory differences between the variable and the standard. Instead, discrimination appears to be mediated by some kind of optional-stopping facility, whereby observers can tailor the number of observations to correspond with the discriminability of each stimulus pair. Meanwhile, the finding of longer times for incorrect than for correct responses suggests that the discrimination process is not memoryless, but probably involves some integration or accumulation of information over successive observations within a particular trial.

All of these features are embodied in a number of recent optional-stopping models, which differ mainly in the precise stopping-rule specified by each, and in their assumptions concerning the kind and amount of information remembered by the discrimination mechanism. Of those considered, models incorporating only partial memory, or in which the magnitude of sensory observations is ignored, seem less adquate and less plausible than a model such as the random walk, in which observations are taken continuously until one of two predetermined different criteria is reached. However, one disadvantage of this model is that it wrongly predicts equal times for correct and incorrect responses, and its parsimony is reduced if, in order to overcome this disadvantage, it is necessary to assume that the distributions of sampled differences become increasingly assymetric as a function of the stringency of the criteria adopted by an observer. A related difficulty is that, in its unmodified form, the random walk model does not give a good account of the changes in the shapes of empirical response time distributions as discriminability is varied.

These objections do not apply to the accumulator model, in which successive observations of the momentary stimulus differences, each varying in magnitude, and classified according to sign, are summed in two separate, unidirectional accumulators until the total accumulated in favour of one or the other decision outcome reaches a predetermined critical level k_g or k_l. This last model gives a good account of all the effects of discriminability touched on in this review. Bias is accounted for by assuming that the observer sets unequal values for k_g and k_l, while variations in caution are accommodated by supposing that the values of both criteria can be increased (or decreased) simultaneously. As required by the data, the mechanism embodies an optional-stopping facility and (as its name indicates) it depends upon the accumulation of information over successive observations.

The advantages of the accumulator become even more apparent when we consider the effects of discriminability, bias and caution on confidence. Since the difference criterion employed by the random walk is equivalent to a likelihood ratio, then, strictly, we should expect that, provided the criteria remain constant, all decisions by this process should be reached with an equal degree of confidence—a prediction which is clearly contradicted by the evidence. At the same time, while confidence measures at a fixed level of discriminability vary inversely with response time, increases in criterion levels are associated both with longer times and with increased confidence. These findings argue strongly against the extension of the random walk model by the addition of a hypothesis to the effect that confidence is an inverse function of the number of observations required to reach a decision. On the other hand, both these and several other findings can be economically explained in terms of a balance of evidence hypothesis, according to which confidence is determined by the difference between the totals reached in an accumulator process. This amounts to asserting that confidence is determined by a *post hoc* assessment of the likelihood ratio.

The three main theoretical models of discrimination may now be seen in a clear perspective. The signal detection model discounted the notion of an absolute threshold in favour of a variable criterion, or cutoff, applied to a single observation of the sensory input and expressible in terms of a likelihood ratio. The random walk model represents a development in which several observations are taken until a predetermined likelihood ratio is reached in favour of one alternative, or a (possibly different) ratio is reached in favour of the other. The accumulator model, on the other hand, employs a suboptimal criterion for a response, but effectively assesses the corresponding likelihood ratio after each decision. Such a procedure provides the observer with a maximally effective source of information for monitoring and adjusting his own discriminative performance. Indeed, Vickers (1978, 1979) has suggested that, while observers may not employ a predetermined likelihood ratio as a criterion, they may adopt some such quantity as a target or reference input for a self-regulating decision mechanism. According to this view, the varying likelihood ratios (or levels of confidence) achieved in individual decisions are compared with certain desired likelihood ratios (or target levels of confidence) and criterion levels are automatically adjusted so as to reduce any discrepancy.

Vickers (1979) has explored the properties of an adaptive accumulator process of this kind, in which the primary criteria k_g and k_l are increased or decreased, respectively, according to whether the confidence in the corresponding responses falls short of, or exceeds, the reference level. Such a self-regulating system performs in a stable manner and responds appropriately to a wide variety of constraints in the stimulus sequence to which the static version remains insensitive. In addition, a hypothesis of this kind also explains the conclusion by Laming (1979) that observers in Rabbitt's (1966) and in his own (1968) experiments usually appear to be aware that they have made an error, even when no explicit knowledge of results is provided.

Vickers (1979) has presented some results selected from a very extensive programme of computer simulations of this adaptive accumulator model. The general picture that emerges from these simulations is of an adaptive system which makes quite frequent, but relatively small reductions, and—less frequently—is "brought up short" by making a glaring error, which in turn occasions a large upward revision and a markedly longer response time. These properties of the theoretical process are well matched by Laming's recent interpretation of empirical findings, according to which

it is clear that, after he has made an error, the subject makes some adjustment to his decision process which results in a decreased probability of error and an increased response time on the following trial. . . . Since, however, one does not observe a continuing decrease in the incidence of errors and a continuing increase in response time throughout a block of choice-reaction trials, there must be, presumably, some small contrary adjustment to the decision process following a correct response; and the succession of adjustments . . . maintains the decision process in a dynamic equilibrium (1979, pp. 203–204).

Vickers (1978, 1979) has shown that a number of other simple judgements, including three-category decisions, judgements of sameness and difference and signal detection, may all be mediated by a general purpose adaptive decision process of the kind inferred from studies of discrimination, supplemented by an additional identification process based on the sum minus the modulus of the accumulated totals t_g and t_l. Vickers (1979) has gone on to show that a more complex task, such as choice-reaction may be mediated by a simple parallel arrangement of elementary, self-regulating decision modules of this kind. According to this view, any stimulus selected out of n possibilities, can be identified by making a series of comparisons in parallel between momentary values of the presented stimulus and each of a set of n stored standards, with the results being accumulated in the appropriate stores of each of a set of n three-category decision modules. Comparisons are assumed to continue until the value in the intermediate store of any one module reaches its criterion level, and triggers an identifying response. Although formulated independently, and based on quite separate data, this parallel eventuation model of identification bears very close affinities both to Ratcliff's (1978) and to McClelland's (1979) theories of memory retrieval. The most obvious differences lie in the choice of the decision process itself and in the fact that Vickers' parallel eventuation process is composed of self-regulating modules and is capable as it stands of showing adaptive or learning behaviour. This said, however, it is clear that the resemblances between these three approaches are sufficiently close to justify the hope that the psychology of perceptual discrimination, and of human information processing in general, may be entering upon an era of large-scale, integrative theorizing, in which the relations between a number of experimental paradigms and between diverse areas will become much clearer.

References

Adams, J. K. and Adams, P. A. (1961). Realism of confidence judgements. *Psychological Review* **68**, 33–45.
Audley, R. J. (1960). A stochastic model for individual choice behaviour. *Psychological Review* **67**, 1–15.
Audley, R. J. (1964). Decision-making. *British Medical Bulletin* **20**, 27–31.
Audley, R. J. (1970). Choosing. *Bulletin of the British Psychological Society* **23**, 177–191.

Audley, R. J. and Mercer, A. (1968). The relation between decision time and relative response frequency in a blue-green discrimination. *British Journal of Mathematical and Statistical Psychology* 21, 183–192.

Audley, R. J. and Pike, A. R. (1965). Some alternative stochastic models of choice. *British Journal of Mathematical and Statistical Psychology* 18, 207–225.

Barlow, H. B. (1956). Retinal noise and absolute threshold. *Journal of the Optical Society of America* 46, 634–639.

Barlow, H. B. and Levick, W. R. (1969a). Three factors limiting the reliable detection of light by retinal ganglion cells of the cat. *Journal of Physiology* 200, 1–24.

Barlow, H. B. and Levick, W. R. (1969b). Changes in the maintained discharge with adaptation level in the cat retina. *Journal of Physiology* 202, 699–718.

Berkson, J. A. (1944). Application of the logistic function to bio-assay. *Journal of the American Statistical Association* 39, 357–365.

Berkson, J. A. (1953). A statistically precise and relatively simple method of estimating the bio-assay with quantal response, based on the logistic function. *Journal of the American Statistical Association* 48, 565–599.

Birren, J. E. and Botwinick, J. (1955). Speed of response as a function of perceptual difficulty and age. *Journal of Gerontology* 10, 433–436.

Bock, D. R. and Jones, L. V. (1968). "The Measurement and Prediction of Judgement and Choice". Holden-Day, San Francisco.

Bonnell, A. M. and Noizet, G. (1979). Application of signal detection theory to perception of differences in line length. *Acta Psychologica* 43, 1–21.

Boring, E. G. (1917). A chart of the psychometric function. *American Journal of Psychology* 28, 465–470.

Botwinick, J., Brinley, J. F. and Robbin, J. S. (1958). The interaction effects of perceptual difficulty and stimulus exposure time on age differences in speed and accuracy of response. *Gerontologia* 2, 1–10.

Broadbent, D. E. (1971). "Decision and Stress". London: Academic Press.

Brown, W. (1910). The judgement of difference. *University of California Publications in Psychology* 1, 1–71.

Buser, P. A. and Rougeul-Buser, A. (1978). "Cerebral Correlates of Conscious Experience". North-Holland, Amsterdam.

Bush, R. R. (1963). Estimation and evaluation. In "Handbook of Mathematical Psychology" (R. R. Bush, E. Galanter and R. D. Luce, eds.), Vol. I, pp. 429–469. Wiley, New York.

Caelli, T. and Julesz, B. (1978). On perceptual analyzers underlying visual texture discrimination. Part I. *Biological Cybernetics* 28, 167–175.

Caelli, T., Julesz, B. and Gilbert, E. N. (1978). On perceptual analyzers underlying visual texture discrimination. Part II. *Biological Cybernetics* 29, 201–214.

Carterette, E. C., Friedman, M. P. and Cosmides, R. (1965). Reaction-time distributions in the detection of weak signals in noise. *Journal of the Acoustical Society of America* 38, 531–542.

Cartwright, D. and Festinger, L. (1943). A quantitative theory of decision. *Psychological Review* 50, 595–621.

Cattell, J. M. (1893). On errors of observation. *American Journal of Psychology* 5, 285–293.

Clark, W. C., Brown, J. C. and Rutschmann, J. (1967). Flicker sensitivity and response bias in psychiatric patients and normal subjects. *Journal of Abnormal and Social Psychology* 72, 35–42.

Corso, J. F. (1967). "The Experimental Psychology of Sensory Behaviour". Holt, Rinehart and Winston, New York.

Cross, D. V. and Lane, H. L. (1962). On the discriminative control of concurrent responses: the relations among response frequency, latency, and topography in auditory generalization. *Journal of the Experimental Analysis of Behaviour* **5**, 487–496.

Crossman, E. R. F. W. (1955). The measurement of discriminability. *Quarterly Journal of Experimental Psychology* **7**, 176–195.

de Vries, H. (1956). Physical aspects of the sense organs. *In* "Progress in Biophysics and Biophysical Chemistry" (J. A. V. Butler, ed.), pp. 256–258. Pergamon, London.

Edwards, W. (1965). Optimal strategies for seeking information: models for statistics, choice reaction times, and human information processing. *Journal of Mathematical Psychology* **2**, 312–329.

Egan, J. P. (1976). "ROC Analysis". Academic Press, New York.

Fechner, G. T. (1966). "Elements of Psychophysics" (Translated by H. E. Adler, originally published 1860), Vol. 1. Holt, Rinehart and Winston, New York.

Festinger, L. (1943a). Studies in decision: I. Decision time, relative frequency of judgement, and subjective confidence as related to physical stimulus difference. *Journal of Experimental Psychology* **32**, 291–306.

Festinger, L. (1943b). Studies in decision: II. An empirical test of a quantitative theory of decision. *Journal of Experimental Psychology* **32**, 411–423.

Foley, P. J. (1959). The expression of certainty. *American Journal of Psychology* **72**, 614–615.

Fritz, M. F. (1930). Experimental evidence in support of Professor Thurstone's criticism of the phi-gamma hypothesis. *Journal of General Psychology* **4**, 346–352.

Gaillard, A. W. K. and Perdok, J. (1979). Slow cortical and heart rate correlates of discrimination performance. *Acta Psychologica* **43**, 185–198.

Garrett, H. E. (1922). A study of the relation of accuracy to speed. *Archives of Psychology* **56**, 1–105.

Geller, E. S. and Pitz, G. F. (1968). Confidence and decision speed in the revision of opinion. *Organizational Behaviour and Human Performance* **3**, 190–201.

Green, D. M. and Swets, J. A. (1966). "Signal Detection Theory and Psychophysics". Wiley, New York.

Green, D. M., Birdsall, T. G. and Tanner, W. P. (1957). Signal detection as a function of signal intensity and duration. *Journal of the Acoustical Society of America* **29**, 523–531.

Guilford, J. P. (1954). *Psychometric Methods* (2nd Edn). McGraw Hill, New York.

Hammerton, M. (1959). A mathematical model for perception and a theoretical confusion function. *Nature* **184**, 1668–1669.

Hays, W. L. (1963). "Statistics for Psychologists". Holt, Rinehart and Winston, New York.

Hecht, S., Shlaer, S. and Pirenne, M. H. (1942). Energy quanta and vision. *Journal of General Physiology* **25**, 819–840.

Henmon, V. A. C. (1906). The time of perception as a measure of differences in sensation. *Archives of Philosophy, Psychology and Scientific Method*, No. 8, 1–75.

Henmon, V. A. C. (1911). The relation of the time of a judgement to its accuracy. *Psychological Review* **18**, 186–201.

Hughes, I. M. (1964). Crossman's confusion-function and multi-choice discrimination. *Quarterly Journal of Experimental Psychology* **16**, 177–180.

Irwin, F. W., Smith, W. A. S. and Mayfield, J. F. (1956). Tests of two theories of decision in an "expanded judgement" situation. *Journal of Experimental Psychology* **51**, 261–268.

Jastrow, J. (1888). A critique of psycho-physic methods. *American Journal of Psychology* **1**, 271–309.

Johnson, D. M. (1939). Confidence and speed in the two-category judgement. *Archives of Psychology* **34**, 1–53.

Julesz, B. (1962). Visual pattern discrimination. *Institute of Radio Engineers, Transactions on Information Theory, PGIT*, IT-8, 84–92.

Julesz, B. (1975). Experiments in the visual perception of textures. *Scientific American* **232**, 34–43.

Julesz, B., Gilbert, E. N. and Victor, J. D. (1978). Visual discrimination of textures with identical third-order statistics. *Biological Cybernetics* **31**, 137–149.

Kantowitz, B. H. (1978). On the accuracy of the speed-accuracy trade-off. *Acta Psychologica* **42**, 79–80.

Kellogg, W. N. (1929). An experimental comparison of psychophysical methods. *Archives of Psychology*, No. 106, pp. 1–86.

Kellogg, W. N. (1930). An experimental evaluation of equality judgements in psychophysics. *Archives of Psychology* **112**, 1–79.

Kellogg, W. N. (1931). Time of judgement in psychometric measures. *American Journal of Psychology* **43**, 65–86.

Kendall, M. G. and Stuart, A. (1968). "The Advanced Theory of Statistics", Vol. 1. Griffin, London.

Kuffler, S. W., Fitzhugh, R. and Barlow, H. B. (1957). Maintained activity in the cat's retina in light and darkness. *Journal of General Physiology* **40**, 683–702.

La Berge, D. (1961). Generalization gradients in a discrimination situation. *Journal of Experimental Psychology* **62**, 88–94.

La Berge, D. (1962). A recruitment theory of simple behavior. *Psychometrika* **27**, 375–396.

Laming, D. R. J. (1968). "Information-theory of Choice-reaction Times". Academic Press, London.

Laming, D. R. J. (1969). Subjective probability in choice-reaction experiments. *Journal of Mathematical Psychology* **6**, 81–120.

Laming, D. R. J. (1979). Choice reaction performance following an error. *Acta Psychologica* **43**, 199–224.

Lappin, J. S. and Disch, K. (1972a). The latency operating characteristic: I. Effects of stimulus probability on choice reaction time. *Journal of Experimental Psychology* **92**, 419–427.

Lappin, J. S. and Disch, K. (1972b). The latency operating characteristic: II. Effects of visual stimulus intensity on choice reaction time. *Journal of Experimental Psychology* **93**, 367–372.

Lappin, J. S. and Disch, K. (1973). Latency operating characteristic: III. Temporal uncertainty effects. *Journal of Experimental Psychology* **98**, 279–285.

Lemmon, V. W. (1927). The relation of reaction time to measures of intelligence, memory and learning. *Archives of Psychology*, No. 94.

Liebermann, D. A. (1979). Behaviourism and the mind: a (limited) call for a return to introspection. *American Psychologist* **34**, 319–333.

Link, S. W. (1975). The relative judgement theory of two choice response time. *Journal of Mathematical Psychology* **12**, 114–135.

Link, S. W. (1978). The relative judgement theory of the psychometric function. *In*

"Attention and Performance VII" (J. Requin, ed.), pp. 619–630. Lawrence Erlbaum, Hillsdale, N.J.

Link, S. W. and Heath, R. A. (1975). A sequential theory of psychological discrimination. *Psychometrika* **40**, 77–105.

Luce, R. D. (1959). "Individual Choice Behaviour". Wiley, New York.

McClelland, J. L. (1979). On the time relations of mental processes: an examination of systems of processes in cascade. *Psychological Review* **86**, 287–330.

McNicol, D. (1972). "A Primer of Signal Detection Theory". Allen and Unwin, London.

Morgan, B. B. and Alluisi, E. A. (1967). Effects of discriminability and irrelevant information on absolute judgement. *Perception and Psychophysics* **2**, 54–58.

Ogilvie, J. C. and Creelman, C. L. (1968). Maximum likelihood estimation of receiver operating characteristic curve parameters. *Journal of Mathematical Psychology* **5**, 377–391.

Pachella, R. G. (1974). The interpretation of reaction time in information-processing research. *In* "Human Information Processing: Tutorials in Performance and Cognition" (B. H. Kantowitz, ed.), pp. 41–82. Lawrence Erlbaum, Hillsdale, N.J.

Pachella, R. G. and Fisher, D. F. (1969). Effect of stimulus degradation and similarity on the trade-off between speed and accuracy in absolute judgements. *Journal of Experimental Psychology* **81**, 7–9.

Pachella, R. G., Fisher, D. F. and Karsh, R. (1968). Absolute judgements in speeded tasks: quantification of the trade-off between speed and accuracy. *Psychonomic Science* **12**, 225–226.

Petrusic, W. M. and Jamieson, D. G. (1979). Resolution time and the coding of arithmetic relations on supraliminally different visual extents. *Journal of Mathematical Psychology* **19**, 89–107.

Pew, R. W. (1969). The speed-accuracy operating characteristic. *In* W. G. Koster (Ed.), *Attention and Performance II*. *Acta Psychologica* **30**, 16–26.

Philip, B. R. (1936). The relationship between speed and accuracy in a motor task. *Journal of Experimental Psychology* **19**, 24–50.

Philip, B. R. (1947). The relationship of exposure time and accuracy in a perceptual task. *Journal of Experimental Psychology* **37**, 178–186.

Pickett, R. M. (1964). The perception of a visual texture. *Journal of Experimental Psychology* **68**, 13–20.

Pickett, R. M. (1967). Response latency in a pattern perception situation. *In* A. F. Sanders (Ed.). *Attention and Performance I*. *Acta Psychologica* **27**, 160–169.

Pickett, R. M. (1968). The visual perception of random line segment texture. *Paper read at Ninth Meeting of the Psychonomic Society*.

Picton, T., Campbell, K. B., Baribeau-Braun, J. and Proulx, G. B. (1978). The neurophysiology of human attention: a tutorial review. *In* "Attention and Performance VII" (J. Requin, ed.), pp. 429–467. Lawrence Erlbaum, Hillsdale, N.J.

Pierce, C. S. and Jastrow, J. (1885). On small differences in sensation. *Proceedings of the National Academy of Sciences* **3**, 75–83.

Pierrel, R. and Murray, C. S. (1963). Some relationships between comparative judgement, confidence and decision-time in weight lifting. *Ameican Journal of Psychology* **76**, 28–38.

Pike, A. R. (1968). Latency and relative frequency of response in psychophysical discrimination. *British Journal of Mathematical and Statistical Psychology* **21**, 161–182.

Pike, A. R. (1971). The latencies of correct and incorrect responses in discrimination and detection tasks: their interpretation in terms of a model based on simple counting. *Perception and Psychophysics* **9**, 455–460.

Pike, R. and Dalgleish, L. (1976). The components of latency of response in two models for auditory detection with deadlines. *Perception and Psychophysics* **19**, 231–239.

Pike, R., McFarland, K. and Dalgleish, L. (1974). Speed-accuracy trade-off models for auditory detection with deadlines. *Acta Psychologica* **38**, 379–399.

Rabbitt, P. M. A. (1966). Errors and error correction in choice-response tasks. *Journal of Experimental Psychology* **71**, 264–272.

Rabbitt, P. M. A. and Vyas, S. M. (1970). An elementary preliminary taxonomy for some errors in laboratory choice reaction time tasks. *In* "Attention and Performance III" (A. F. Sanders, ed.). pp. 56–76. North-Holland, Amsterdam.

Ratcliff, R. (1978). A theory of memory retrieval. *Psychological Review* **85**, 59–108.

Ratcliff, R. (1979). Group reaction time distributions and an analysis of distribution statistics. *Psychological Bulletin* **86**, 446–461.

Ryder, P., Pike, R. and Dalgleish, L. (1974). What is the signal in signal detection? *Perception and Psychophysics* **15**, 479–482.

Sanders, A. F. and Ter Linden, W. (1967). Decision making during paced arrival of probabilistic information. *In* A. F. Sanders (Ed.), *Attention and Performance I. Acta Psychologica* **27**, 170–177.

Schouten, J. F. and Bekker, J. A. M. (1967). Reaction time and accuracy. *In* A. F. Sanders (Ed.), *Attention and Performance I. Acta Psychologica* **27**, 143–153.

Seward, G. H. (1928). Recognition time as a measure of confidence. *Archives of Psychology*, No. 99, p. 59.

Shallice, T. and Vickers, D. (1964). Theories and experiments on discrimination times. *Ergonomics* **7**, 37–49.

Snodgrass, J. G., Luce, R. D. and Galanter, E. (1967). Some experiments on simple and choice reaction time. *Journal of Experimental Psychology* **75**, 1–17.

Stone, M. (1960). Models for reaction time. *Psychometrika* **25**, 251–260.

Swanson, J. M. and Briggs, G. E. (1969). Information processing as a function of speed versus accuracy. *Journal of Experimental Psychology* **81**, 223–229.

Swensson, R. G. (1972). The elusive tradeoff: speed versus accuracy in visual discrimination tasks. *Perception and Psychophysics* **12**, 16–32.

Swensson, R. G. and Thomas, R. E. (1974). Fixed and optional-stopping models for two-choice discrimination times. *Journal of Mathematical Psychology* **11**, 213–276.

Swets, J. A. and Green, D. M. (1961). Sequential observations by human observers of signals in noise. *In* "Information Theory: Proceedings of the Fourth London Symposium" (C. Cherry, ed.), pp. 177–195. Butterworths, London.

Swets, J. A., Shipley, E. F., McKey, M. J. and Green, D. M. (1959). Multiple observations of signals in noise. *Journal of the Acoustical Society of America* **31**, 514–521.

Tanner, W. P. and Swets, J. A. (1954). A decision-making theory of visual detection. *Psychological Review* **61**, 401–409.

Taylor, D. H. (1965). Latency models for reaction time distributions. *Psychometrika* **30**, 157–163.

Taylor, M. M., Lindsay, P. H. and Forbes, S. M. (1967). Quantification of shared capacity processing in auditory and visual discrimination. *In* A. F. Sanders (Ed.), *Attention and Performance I. Acta Psychologica* **27**, 223–229.

Thomas, E. A. C. (1973). On expectancy and the speed and accuracy of responses. *In*

"Attention and Performance IV" (S. Kornblum, ed.), pp. 613–626. Academic Press, London.

Thomas, E. A. C. (1975). A note on the sequential probability ratio test. *Psychometrika* **40**, 107–111.

Thomas, E. A. C. and Myers, J. L. (1972). Implications of latency data for threshold and nonthreshold models of signal detection. *Journal of Mathematical Psychology* **9**, 253–258.

Thomson, G. H. (1920). A new point of view in the interpretation of threshold measurements in psychophysics. *Psychological Review* **27**, 300–307.

Thurmond, J. B. and Alluisi, E. A. (1963). Choice time as a function of stimulus dissimilarity and discriminability. *Canadian Journal of Psychology* **17**, 326–337.

Thurstone, L. L. (1927a). Psychophysical analysis. *American Journal of Psychology* **38**, 368–389.

Thurstone, L. L. (1927b). A law of comparative judgement. *Psychological Review* **34**, 273–286.

Thurstone, L. L. (1928). The phi-gamma hypothesis. *Journal of Experimental Psychology* **11**, 293–305.

Thurstone, L. L. (1937). Ability, motivation and speed. *Psychometrika* **2**, 249–254.

Thurstone, L. L. (1948). Psychophysical methods. *In* "Methods of Psychology" (T. G. Andrews, ed.), pp. 124–157. Wiley, New York.

Torgerson, W. S. (1958). *Theory and Methods of Scaling*. New York.

Treisman, M. and Watts, T. R. (1966). Relation between signal detectability theory and the traditional procedures for measuring sensory thresholds: estimating d' from results given by the method of constant stimuli. *Psychological Bulletin* **66**, 438–454.

Urban, F. M. (1910). The method of constant stimuli and its generalizations. *Psychological Review* **17**, 229–259.

Vaughan, H. G. and Ritter, W. (1973). Physiologic approaches to the analysis of attention and performance: tutorial review. *In* "Attention and Performance IV" (S. Kornblum, ed.), pp. 129–154. Academic Press, London and New York.

Vickers, D. (1970). Evidence for an accumulator model of psychophysical discrimination. *In* A. T. Welford and L. Houssiadas (Eds.), *Current Problems in Perception. Ergonomics* **13**, 37–58.

Vickers, D. (1972). Some general features of perceptual discrimination. *In* E. A. Asmussen (Ed.), *Psychological Aspects of Driver Behaviour*. Institute of Road Safety Research, S.W.O.V., Voorburg, The Netherlands.

Vickers, D. (1975). Where Angell feared to tread: response time and frequency in three-category discrimination. *In* "Attention and Performance V" (P. M. A. Rabbitt and S. Dornic, eds.), pp. 455–469. Academic Press, London.

Vickers, D. (1978). An adaptive module for simple judgements. *In* "Attention and Performance VII" (J. Requin, ed.), pp. 599–618. Lawrence Erlbaum, Hillsdale, N.J.

Vickers, D. (1979). "Decision Processes in Visual Perception". Academic Press, London and New York.

Vickers, D. and Packer, J. S. (1980). Effects of alternating set for speed or accuracy on response time, probability and confidence in a unidimensional discrimination task. Unpublished research report.

Vickers, D., Caudrey, D. and Willson, R. J. (1971). Discriminating between the frequency of occurrence of two alternative events. *Acta Psychologica* **35**, 151–172.

Victor, J. D. and Brodie, S. E. (1978). Discriminable textures with identical Buffon needle statistics. *Biological Cybernetics* **31**, 231–234.

Volkmann, J. (1934). The relation of time of judgement to certainty of judgement. *Psychological Bulletin* **31**, 672–673.

Wald, A. (1947). "Sequential Analysis". Wiley, New York.

Weatherburn, D. (1978). Latency-probability functions as bases for evaluating competing accounts of the sensory decision process. *Psychological Bulletin* **85**, 1344–1347.

Welford, A. T. (1965). Performance, biological mechanisms and age: a theoretical sketch. *In* "Behaviour, Ageing and the Nervous System" (A. T. Welford and J. E. Birren, eds.), pp. 3–20. Charles C. Thomas, Springfield, Ill.

Welford, A. T. (1968). "Fundamentals of Skill". Methuen, London.

Welford, A. T. (1971). What is the basis of choice-reaction time? *Ergonomics* **14**, 679–693.

Welford, A. T. (1973). Attention, strategy and reaction time: a tentative metric. *In* "Attention and Performance IV" (S. Kornblum, ed.), pp. 37–53. Academic Press, London.

Welford, A. T. (1975). Display layout, strategy and reaction time: tests of a model. *In* "Attention and Performance V" (P. M. A. Rabbitt and S. Dornic, eds.), pp. 470–484. Academic Press, London.

Wickelgren, W. A. (1977). Speed-accuracy trade-off and information processing dynamics. *Acta Psychologica* **41**, 67–85.

Wickelgren, W. A. (1978). Wickelgren's neglect. *Acta Psychologica* **42**, 81–82.

Wilding, J. M. (1974). Effects of stimulus discriminability on the latency distribution of identification responses. *Acta Psychologica* **38**, 483–500.

Wilding, J. M. (1978). An investigation of possible response effects on the latency distribution of identification responses. *Acta Psychologica* **42**, 231–251.

Wollen, K. A. (1963). Relationship between choice time and frequency during discrimination training and generalization tests. *Journal of Experimental Psychology* **66**, 474–484.

Woodworth, R. and Schlosberg, H. (1954). "Experimental Psychology". Holt, New York.

Yellott, J. I. (1971). Correction for guessing and the speed-accuracy trade-off in choice reaction time. *Journal of Mathematical Psychology* **8**, 159–199.

Chapter 3

Choice Reaction Time: Basic Concepts

A. T. WELFORD

The time to react in a situation in which any one of several signals may occur, each calling for a different response, must include four processes: first, reception of the signal by a sense organ and conveyance of data by afferent nerves to the brain; second, identification of the signal; third, choice of the corresponding response; and fourth, initiation of the action that constitutes the response. The first of these processes is relatively short—a few milliseconds. The last of the four processes is also short for simple hand actions requiring little strength, such as pressing a morse key or microswitch. It tends, however, to be a little longer when a vocal response is required and may be substantial when the response is a more elaborate or powerful motor action such as jumping with the whole body (see, for example, Onishi, 1966).

The main part of choice reaction time, however, is taken up by the second and third processes, of identification and choice. There has been some controversy as to whether these can properly be separated, but it seems clear that they can be, at least for certain purposes. In particular it is possible to distinguish between studies in which the discriminability of signals has been varied while their number and the degree of choice of response have been kept constant, and studies in which discriminability has been constant, or roughly so, and the number of different signals and corresponding responses has varied. The first type of study has been discussed in Chapter 2, the second type will be considered here. It must be said at once that despite a great deal of careful experimental research and lively theoretical discussion, there are in this area still many conflicts, anomalies and unanswered questions. The comprehensive scheme which can embrace all the evidence has yet to be formulated. Meanwhile, some partial formulations appear to have sufficient heuristic value for them to be worth pursuing simultaneously, in the hope that they will eventually converge and that the present confusion will be overcome.

1. Hick's information-theory law

An important advance in treating this second type of situation was made by Hick (1952a) who proposed, on the basis of his own data and also those of Merkel (1885), that in making choice-reactions the subject gains "information", in the information-theory sense of the term, at a constant rate.

Merkel had presented his subjects with signals ranging, in different trials, from one to ten alternatives. The signals consisted of the arabic numerals 1–5 and roman numerals I–V, printed round the edge of a disc. The subject waited for each signal with his fingers pressed on ten keys and, when a number was illuminated, released the corresponding key. The arabic numerals corresponded in order to the fingers of the right hand and the roman to the left. When less than ten choices were required some of the numerals were omitted.

Hick's own experiments used as a display ten pea-lamps arranged in a "somewhat irregular circle". The subject reacted by pressing one of ten morse keys on which his fingers rested. Choices of less than ten were obtained by omitting some of the lights. The frequencies of the various signals for any given degree of choice were carefully balanced and presented in an irregular order so as to ensure as far as possible that the subject should not be able to predict what signal was coming next. Each light appeared 5 sec after the completion of the previous response—an interval too long for the subject to judge accurately when the signal would appear.

Hick found that if the number of possible signals is taken as n and reaction time is plotted against $\log(n+1)$, the observed reaction times for different numbers of signals lie on a straight line which also passes through the origin, as shown in Fig. 3.1. We can thus write

$$\text{Mean choice reaction time} = K \log(n + 1) \qquad (3.1)$$

where K is a constant. If we work in logarithms to the base 2, $\log_2(n + 1)$ = 1 when $m = 1$, so that K is the simple reaction time. The $\log_2$ unit is known in information theory as the *bit*, and has proved a convenient unit for describing and comparing a wide range of experimental conditions and performances.

The obvious question arises, why $(n + 1)$ and not n? Hick pointed out that when a signal appears, the subject must decide not only which signal it is, but also whether a signal has occurred at all. Failure to make the latter decision results either in reaction when there is no signal present or failure to react when there is one. The additional task of guarding against such errors can be conceived of as adding one to the number of possible conditions to be distinguished—instead of dealing with signals 1, 2, 3, . . ., n,

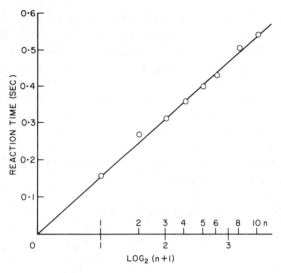

Fig. 3.1. Data from a choice-reaction experiment by Hick plotted in terms of equation (3.1).

the subject must deal with states corresponding to $0, 1, 2, 3, \ldots, n$. We may denote the sum of the possibilities including *no signal* as N, defining N as the equivalent total number of equally probable alternatives from which the subject has to choose, and then rewrite eqn 3.1 as

$$\text{Mean choice reaction time} = K \log N. \qquad (3.2)$$

This formulation has become known as *Hick's Law*. It should be understood that this is an "ideal" formula and that time lags in the apparatus or in the making of a response may add a constant to the time.

Hick's line of approach is supported by three further findings:

(**a**) The amount of information transmitted in a choice reaction task is reduced if the signals are not all of equal frequency. The amount of information due to uncertainty about which signal will occur can be worked out by summing the amounts of information conveyed by each signal weighted according to the probability of its occurrence. We can therefore write in place of $\log N$ in eqn 3.2

$$\sum_{i=0}^{n} p_i \log\left\{\frac{1}{p_i}\right\} \qquad (3.3)$$

where p_i is the probability of each possibility in the set taken in turn. This expression reduces to $\log N$ when all the probabilities are equal. Unequal probabilities reduce the amount of uncertainty and thus the magnitude of expression 3.3, and have been found to produce correspondingly shorter reaction times (Hyman, 1953).

(b) Information transmitted is also reduced when signals tend to follow one another in recognizable sequences or when any signal is followed by any other more often than expected by chance, even though the overall signal frequencies are equal. This is really an extension of the foregoing case. The probabilities of different signals are functions of previous signals, and are thus unequal at any given point in the series, although the inequalities even out over the series as a whole. Hyman found the expected shortening of average reaction times in these cases also.

(c) The amount of information gained is reduced if the subject makes errors. The amount gained when errors are present is, in information theory terms, given by the equation

$$\text{Information gained} = \sum p_s \log\left\{\frac{1}{p_s}\right\} + \sum p_r \log\left\{\frac{1}{p_r}\right\}$$

$$- \sum p_{sr} \log\left\{\frac{1}{p_{sr}}\right\} \tag{3.4}$$

where p_s is the probability of each signal, p_r the probability of each response and p_{sr} the probability of each signal-response pair. When there are no errors, so that each signal always leads to its corresponding response, eqn 3.4 reduces to eqn 3.3.

Hick found that the shortening of reaction times when substantial numbers of errors were made was by approximately the amounts expected. Howell and Kreidler (1963) and Fitts (1966), who compared groups of subjects performing choice reaction tasks with instructions for speed, for accuracy, or for both, confirmed that overall rates of information gain were not significantly different for the three types of instruction, although the balance between speed and accuracy was shifted as the instructions required.

Equation 3.4 provides a means of combining speed and accuracy into a single score, and emphasizes the important fact that times for different tasks are comparable only if errors are held constant. Conversely, error rates can be compared only if times are held constant.

The $+1$ in Hick's formulation has not always proved easy to understand, and an alternative equation proposed by Hyman (1953) has often been preferred. He proposed in place of eqn 3.1

$$\text{Choice reaction time} = a + b \log n \tag{3.5}$$

where a is the simple reaction time and $b \log n$ represents the increase over the simple reaction time due to the need for identification and choice.

On the whole, eqn 3.1 fits the facts better than eqn 3.5, but often there is little to choose between them and in some cases eqn 3.5 provides the better fit. The reason for the variability is indicated in a reformulation of the problem by Smith which is set out in Chapter 5. He argues that a subject has to build up a central state in favour of a particular response as opposed to others, to a criterion level, and that a response is made when this level is reached. The approach is analogous to Vickers' accumulator model outlined in Chapter 2. Smith assumes that

$$\text{Reaction time} = K \log\left(n\frac{C}{E} + 1\right) \tag{3.6}$$

where E is the strength of the incoming signal in terms of signal-to-noise ratio and C is a measure of the criterion level at which a response is initiated. C is low in conditions stressing speed rather than accuracy, and becomes higher as the requirement for accuracy rises. When $C = E$, eqn 3.6 is equivalent to Hick's eqn 3.1. The effect when C exceeds E can be seen if eqn 3.6 is rewritten

$$\text{Reaction time} = K\left[\log\left(n + \frac{E}{C}\right) + \log C - \log E\right] \tag{3.7}$$

As C becomes large or E small, the fraction E/C approaches zero. At the same time ($\log C - \log E$) introduces a constant increase regardless of n, so that if reaction time is plotted against $\log n$, the intercept is above zero. Equation 3.6 then approximates Hyman's eqn 3.5. It can reasonably be assumed that E was less in Hyman's experiment than in Hick's because the signal lights were less bright. Consistent with this, Hyman's reaction times were somewhat longer than Hick's for each degree of choice.

(A) FURTHER APPLICATION OF HICK'S LAW

Hick's law and its extensions seem capable of describing performance in a wide variety of sensory-motor performances. To take only one example, Fig. 3.2 shows results obtained by Crossman (1953) for sorting playing cards. The subject held a well-shuffled pack face down in one hand. With the other he turned up the cards one by one and sorted them into various classes as quickly as possible. The number of classes was varied in different trials from 2 up to 26. Additional trials were given in which the cards were in a prearranged order, such as alternate red and black, so as to provide a measure of the time taken to turn and place the cards when no identification or choice was required—in other words, a measure of movement time. The results are shown by the upper line in Fig. 3.2. Roughly speaking, time per card is the sum of movement time and $K \log n$, where n is the number of classes. The point that falls farthest away from the line is that for the 13

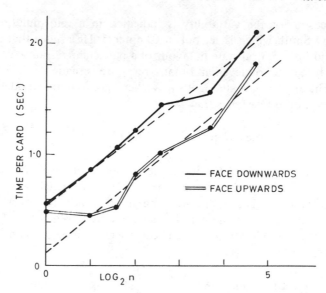

Fig. 3.2. Data from a card-sorting experiment by Crossman. The points along each line represent (from left to right): dealing cards in a prearranged order; sorting into—red/black; pictures/red plain/black plain; suits; red pictures/black pictures/plain in four suits; suits, dividing 6 and below from 7 and above; numbers; numbers, separating red and black.

numbers: these seem often to be easier to deal with than less familiar sets of signals. We shall return to this point later.

We may question whether it is sufficient to estimate movement time by dealing into only two piles. Should not the cards instead be dealt into as many piles as there are classes to give a different estimate of movement time for each number of classes? An indication that this elaboration is un-necessary is contained in the results Crossman obtained with the pack held face up so that the subject could see each card immediately after he had removed the previous one. The lower line of Fig. 3.2 shows that the time per card was either the movement time or roughly $K \log n$, whichever was the longer. It appears that identification and choice can overlap with movement, so that the two can develop together. Extra movement time required with large numbers of piles can thus be absorbed in the extra time needed for identification and choice.

2. Models of choice reaction

Hick recognized clearly that expressing choice reaction time in terms of information theory was only descriptive and not truly explanatory. He and others since have therefore attempted to go further by formulating models of the detailed process of identification and choice lying behind the logarithmic relationship between reaction time and degree of choice, and expressing these models in mathematical terms. The mathematical formulations, often of considerable sophistication, will be surveyed in Chapter 5. In the present chapter consideration will be given to the main types of process envisaged as constituting what may be termed the *microbehaviour* of identification and choice.

The theoretical models concerned fall into two main groups:

(A) SERIAL MODELS

These assume that subjects make a series of subdecisions, each of which excludes some of the possibilities, until a final identification of one signal and choice of its corresponding response are made. It is usually assumed that each subdecision takes the same amount of time. On this assumption, the simplest serial procedure, that of scanning possible signal sources and their corresponding responses in turn until the signal which has occurred and its corresponding response are found, would produce results which do not fit the facts. The average number of subdecisions required would be $(n + 1)/2$ so that reaction time would be *linearly* related to the number of possibilities instead of to the *logarithm* of the number.

Two other serial models do, however, yield an approximate logarithmic relationship:

(i) The subject identifies the signal and its corresponding response as lying within one half of the total possibilities, then within one half of this half, and so on. A two-choice task thus requires one decision, a four-choice two decisions, an eight-choice three decisions, and so on (Hick, 1952a). This is the most efficient procedure according to classical information theory (Shannon and Weaver, 1949).

(ii) A modification of (i) holds that the subject divides the total possibilities into two, or sometimes three or more classes and inspects each class in turn until the one containing the required signal and response is found. He then subdivides that class and again inspects until he finds the required subclass, and so on (Welford, 1960, 1968). Thus for each decision between two classes, the subject sometimes requires one inspection and sometimes two—an average of 1.5 if the signals are random and equiprobable. Similarly, for each decision between three classes a subject sometimes requires one, sometimes two and sometimes three inspections, resulting in an average of two. The model differs from (i) in assuming that if the required signal and response are not in the class inspected first, the subject does not simply assume that they lie elsewhere, but makes a further inspection or inspections to check positively where they do lie, before proceeding to the next decision. For this reason we shall, for convenience, call this the *Positive Check Model*. It should be emphasized that the term "inspection" does not refer only to the scrutiny of the signal, but implies a subdecision which includes elements of both identification of the signal and choice of the corresponding response.

(B) SIMULTANEOUS MODELS

These assume that the subject compares evidence from all the possible signal sources simultaneously, and decides in favour of the response which reaches a criterion value soonest, or for the response which is strongest after a critical time, or as soon as all comparisons have been completed. The process is essentially one of distinguishing the signal and response concerned from random variation in other possible signals and tendencies to response (e.g. Hick, 1952b; Christie and Luce, 1956; Rapoport, 1959; Laming, 1968). Two varieties of simultaneous model may be distinguished:

(i) Each source of signals and its corresponding response are assumed to be discrete, so that any confusion between signals or between responses is as likely to be with any one as with any other.

(ii) The several signals and responses are assumed to lie along a single continuum so that confusion is more likely between adjacent members than between those more remotely separated, and between members in certain positions as opposed to others on the continuum.

The simple serial-dichotomizing model A(i) appears to be untenable because it would not allow for a more frequent signal to be responded to faster than a less frequent signal in a two-choice task—one decision would be required in each case. Evidence relating to the other models is conflicting. Some experimental results are well fitted by the Positive Check model A(ii), but some others are not. We shall look first at some which are, and consider some which are not later in this chapter.

The Positive Check model is strikingly consistent with the results of a series of experiments in which subjects responded to lights in a horizontal row by pressing morse keys positioned under their eight fingers (Welford, 1971). Consider the eight-choice results shown by the heavy line in Fig. 3.3. Responses by the middle and ring fingers took about 90–100 msec longer than those by the index and little fingers. These results are inconsistent with the serial model A(i) and also with the simultaneous model B(i) according to both of which the reaction times by all fingers should have been the same, *unless* some motor factor was lowering performance by the middle and ring fingers and not by the others. This possibility seems to be excluded on two grounds. First, the differences in reaction time by the different fingers were reduced or absent in the four- and two-choice results also shown in Fig. 3.3. Second, when the lights corresponding to the little and ring and to the middle and index fingers were reversed, reactions by the little fingers, which were formerly the fastest, became the slowest, as shown in the upper line of Fig. 3.3.

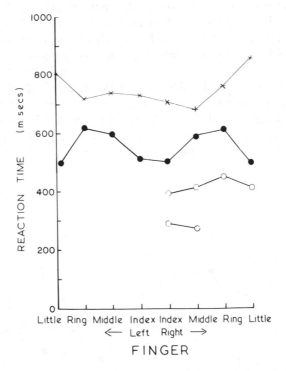

Fig. 3.3. Mean reaction times recorded in eight-, four-, and two-choice tasks (Welford, 1971). The relationships between the positions of the signal lights and response keys were direct except in the case shown in the top line. Here pairs of lights were reversed so that the one at the extreme left of the row was responded to by the left ring finger, the next by the left little finger, and so on.

The broad pattern of the results is accounted for well by a form of the parallel processing model proposed by Vickers (1979) and discussed by him in the previous chapter. Vickers suggests that the several signals in a task such as that of Fig. 3.3 have to be discriminated along a conceptual continuum of limited length as postulated in B(ii), so that the more signals there are, the more difficult the discrimination becomes. The subject is conceived as adjusting his criteria of identification so as approximately to

equalize the confidence of his judgements about signals in different positions. Discrimination is easy, and criteria therefore low, in positions at the
ends of the line (1 and 8) and also on either side of the centre line (4 and 5),
but discrimination is more difficult at intermediate positions, and criteria
therefore higher, making for longer reaction times. Concentration of attention on particular positions would have the effect of lowering criteria for
these positions and thus producing the dramatic reductions of reaction time
for these and adjacent positions shown in Fig. 3.4. At the same time, criteria
for more remote positions would be raised, although those for the end
positions, which would still benefit from their easy discriminability, might
be little changed.

Explanation in terms of differences in the discriminability of the light
positions corresponding to the various fingers is questionable because
Alegria and Bertelson (1970) found the ring and middle fingers were still
slower than the others when the signals were digits all shown in one
position. Such difficulty of discrimination as existed seemed to be between

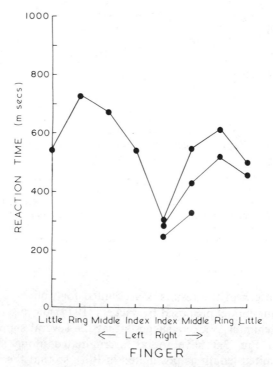

Fig. 3.4. Mean reaction times in eight-, four-, and two-choice tasks, showing the effects of
concentrating attention on the responses by the right index finger and its corresponding light
(Welford, 1971).

adjacent *keys* rather than signals: virtually all errors were due to pressing the key next to the one which was correct. This would not be inconsistent with Vickers' model, which is not confined to discrimination of signals but is applicable to all discriminating decisions. An alternative explanation of the errors might lie in the assumption that the build-up in the motor cortex which leads to the depression of a particular finger spreads to some extent to the cortical areas of other fingers. Such spread of effect, however, seems unlikely to have produced the differences between fingers shown in Fig. 3.3, as again it should have shown equally in the four-choice and eight-choice results. Further evidence against such an explanation is given by the results shown in Fig. 3.4. If the shortening of reaction time to the attended signal meant that the build-up for that finger was to some extent made in advance, we should expect a relatively high proportion of errors due to this response being given in place of adjacent ones, but no such bias was found. This same evidence tells somewhat against Vickers' model as the same bias would have been expected if the criterion for responding by the attended finger had been lowered.

The results shown in Figs 3.3 and 3.4 are satisfactorily accounted for by the Positive Check model A(ii) and the results obtained when concentrating on one of two alternatives in a two-choice task provide a means of testing it quantitatively. In a two-choice task, we may suppose that one inspection is needed to identify the signal and response on which attention is concentrated, and a second to identify the other signal and response. The difference between the average reaction times for the attended and unattended alternatives should therefore be one inspection time. Mean inspection times obtained in this way for different groups of subjects in this type of task have been about 80–100 msec (Welford, 1971, 1975). These figures are not very different from those obtained by Vickers *et al.* (1972) for easy discrimination, and it is tempting to regard the two measures as being of fundamentally the same functional unit. The assumption is questionable, however, because inspection times appear to differ substantially between one set of conditions and another.

A dichotomizing decision, such as that between the index and middle fingers in the two-choice task of Fig. 3.3, will require, as mentioned previously, an average of 1.5 inspection times since the correct signal and response will be reached on half the trials in one inspection, and on half in two. We can, therefore, think of a two-choice reaction time as being made up of two components: 1.5 inspection times and a "basic time", which includes the time required to observe that a signal has occurred, together with any time taken by purely sensory and motor processes and mechanical delays in the apparatus.

For the subjects who produced the results shown in Figs 3.3 and 3.4, mean inspection time was 92 msec and mean basic time was 142 msec. According to the Positive Check model a four-choice reaction time with equiprobable signals should require two decisions—say first between index plus middle as opposed to ring plus little, and second within the pair chosen. It should thus be 1.5 inspection times longer than a two-choice time—in this case it should be $142 + (3 \times 92) = 418$ msec. This compares well with the 415 $\pm$ 7 msec observed. Similarly the overall eight-choice time should be three inspection times longer than the two-choice time—that is $142 + (4.5 \times 92)$ $= 556$ msec, which is again close to the observed figure of 553 ± 8. The difference of reaction times for the middle and ring fingers from those of the index and little could perhaps be due to the subject, in his final decision in the eight-choice situation, always inspecting the "outer" positions corresponding to the index and little fingers before the "inner" corresponding to the middle and ring. If so, the index and little fingers should be reached in an average of four inspections and the middle and ring in five. The resulting predictions: $142 + (4 \times 92) = 510$ msec and $142 + (5 \times 92) = 602$ respectively, correspond well with the observed values of 502 ± 8 and 603 ± 12. Why there should be a bias in favour of the index and little fingers in the eight-choice situation and not in the four- or two-choice is not clear.

If the Positive Check model is correct, or approximately so, it follows that the effects of unbalance in the frequencies of different signals will follow not the "information" each transmits, but the number of inspections needed to distinguish them. In particular, for accurate performance of a two-choice task, the maximum mean difference between the reaction times to the more and less frequent signals will be one inspection time. Hyman (1953) noted that the reaction times to more and less frequent signals were closer together than a strict information analysis would predict, but he did not give examples from his two-choice tasks. In such of the literature as the author has been able to scrutinize, there seem to have been no cases reported in which mean differences in two-choice tasks with straightforward relationships between signal and response have appreciably exceeded the 92 msec postulated as the inspection time in the present experiments. In most cases they have been much less. The same appears to be true of other cases in which different classes of response in straightforward two-choice tasks have been separated, for example in studies of the repetition and alternation effects discussed in Chapter 4. Differences have been much greater, of course, with higher degrees of choice or with more complex relationships between signal and response.

In none of the cases has there been any way of estimating inspection time. A direct test was therefore made, using the same subjects as in the experiments of Figs 3.3 and 3.4 in a two-choice task with unbalanced signal frequencies. This confirmed that the difference of reaction time to the more and less frequent signals was well within the limits of one inspection time. One light appeared on 7/8 of occasions, the other on 1/8. Taking $1.5 \times 92 = 138$ msec as the time per bit, the mean reaction time to the more frequent signal at 0.19 bits should have been $142 + (0.19 \times 138) = 168$ msec, while that for the less frequent signal at 3 bits should have been $142 + (3 \times 138) = 556$ msec, a difference of 388. In fact, the mean time for the more frequent response was 242 ± 5 msec and for the less frequent 313 ± 13, giving a difference of only 71 msec. This is close to the difference of 69 msec expected if initial inspection had been biased to correspond with signal frequency—the difference between $142 + (0.875 \times 1 \times 92 + 0.125 \times 2 \times 92) = 246$ and $142 + (0.125 \times 1 \times 92 + 0.875 \times 2 \times 92) = 315$.

3. Strategies of choice

The last point serves to emphasize the fact that with the Positive Check model several different methods of search are possible and some are more efficient than others. For example, if inspection was biased so that the more frequent signal was *always* inspected first, the average number of inspections would be $7/8 \times 1 + 1/8 \times 2 = 1.125$ instead of 1.5. Interestingly, serial dichotomization is not always theoretically the most efficient strategy, and even within a dichotomizing system there is room for varying degrees of efficiency when the number of possibilities is not an exact power of 2. The results of various strategies are shown in Table 3.1 and will be briefly discussed in turn.

(a) Let us consider three ways of dichotomizing 3 equiprobable alternatives.

(i) The subject divides the 3 into $1 + 2$ and inspects each class first or second equally often, so that he reaches each, whether the 1 or the 2, in an average of 1.5 inspections. If the signal is within the class of 2, a further one or two inspections will be required to identify which of the two it is. One of the three signals and its corresponding reponse will thus be reached in an average of 1.5 inspections and the other two in 3. The overall average number of inspections is the sum, over all signals, of the mean number of inspections required for each, multiplied by the probability of its occurrence. In this case, the overall average will be $(0.33 \times 1.5) + (2 \times 0.33 \times 3) = 2.5$.

(ii) Some economy is achieved by biasing the initial inspection in proportion to probability, so that the class of 2 is inspected first twice as often as the class of 1. The average number of inspections then becomes $(0.67 \times 1) + (0.33 \times 2) + 1.5 = 2.83$ for the class of 2, and $(0.33 \times 1) + (0.67 \times 2) = 1.67$ for the class of 1, an average over the whole 3 of $(0.67 \times 2.83) + (0.33 \times 1.67) = 2.44$.

Table 3.1. Numbers of inspections required for different degrees of choice according to various strategies with the Positive Check model

Type of strategy	Degree of choice								
	2	3	4	5	6	7	8	9	10
(a) Dichtomizing									
(i) Strict	1.50	2.50	3.00	3.60	4.00	4.29	4.50	4.83	5.10
(ii) With frequency-matching bias		2.44		3.54	3.94	4.25		4.79	5.04
(iii) Class with greater probability always inspected first		2.33		3.40	3.83	4.14		4.67	4.90
(b) Serial inspection of individual items i.e. $(n + 1)/2$	1.50	2.00	2.50	3.00	3.50	4.00	4.50	5.00	5.50
(c) With initial division into 3 classes as nearly equal in size as possible, and initial inspection in proportion to class size			2.68	3.13	3.50	3.69	3.85	4.00	4.68
(d) As (a) or (c) above but with last group inspected seriatim									
(i) Last group always with 1 or 2 members			2.50	2.95	3.17				
(ii) Last group sometimes or always with 3 members				2.80	3.00	3.36	3.53	3.67	

(iii) Still greater economy is achieved if the class of 2 is always inspected first, so that the average number of inspections becomes $1 + 1.5 = 2.5$ for that class, and $1 + 1 = 2$ for the class of 1. The average for all three is then $(0.67 \times 2.5) + (0.33 \times 2) = 2.33$.

(b) If the total number of possibilities is 3, 4, 5, 6 or 7, dichotomizing is less efficient than simply inspecting the possibilities in turn until the one required is found. With this procedure the average number of inspections required is $(n + 1)/2$ where n is the number of possibilities.

(c) Further economies can often be obtained by dividing the possibilities at each stage into three or more classes instead of only two. For example, if 8 possibilities are divided initially into 4 classes of 2 which are inspected serially, identification will be achieved in an overall average of $2.5 + 1.5 = 4$

inspections instead of the 4.5 required with strict dichotomization. The optimum strategy of this kind for the degrees of choice shown in Table 3.1 appears to be an initial division into three classes as near equal in size as possible. For example, with six possibilities division is most efficiently made into 3×2 or with five possibilities $2 + 2 + 1$, followed by serial exploration of the members of the classes thus formed. With six possibilities it does not matter whether the initial division is into 3 or 2, i.e. 3×2 or 2×3, but in some cases it does; for instance with five possibilities an initial division into $2 + 2 + 1$ leads to an average total of 3.13 inspections, whereas an initial division into $3 + 2$ requires 3.28.

Variations from trial to trial in the number of inspections required is likely to be less with strategy (c) than with (b). For example with six choices, although the means are identical, the number of inspections to reach individual items will vary from 1 to 6 with strategy (b) but only from 2 to 5 with (c). The standard deviations are 1.61 and 0.96, respectively.

(d) When an array of possibilities has been divided into a number of classes and all except the last have been inspected without finding the signal, still further economy can be effected by neglecting to check the last class as a whole, but instead proceeding directly to inspect its members *seriatim*. Consider, for example, a six-choice task in which the initial division has been into three pairs of which two have been inspected without success. If the third pair was then inspected *seriatim* without prior check, one of its members would be reached in three inspections and the other in four, whereas if a prior check had been made they would have been reached in 4 and 5, respectively. The average number of inspections for all six possibilities would therefore be $[2(1 + 1.5) + 2(2 + 1.5) + 3 + 4]/6 = 3.17$, instead of $[2(1 + 1.5) + 2(2 + 1.5) + 2(3 + 1.5)]/6 = 3.5$. In this particular case economy would be even greater if the initial division was into two classes of three members, and the check omitted for the trio inspected second if the signal was not found in that inspected first. The average number of inspections would then be $[3(1 + 2) + 2 + 3 + 4]/6 = 3$.

A series of six-choice experiments produced results which were well accounted for in terms of these strategies and suggested that choice of strategy was affected by the layout of the display (Welford, 1975). The same apparatus was used as for the experiments of Figs 3.3 and 3.4 but omitting two of the lights and corresponding keys. Pre-tests using the two-choice concentration technique illustrated in Fig. 3.4 showed that the subjects had an average inspection time of 100 msec and basic time of 128 msec. The overall results for different arrangements of the display are shown in Table 3.2. The predicted mean number of inspections with strategy (c) of Table 3.1 is 2 for the initial division of the six possible signals and responses into three pairs, and a further 1.5 inspections to select the member of the pair

Table 3.2. Observed six-choice reaction times and predicted times calculated in terms of strategies shown in Table 3.1, assuming an average inspection time of 100 msec and a basic time of 128 msec. Data from Welford (1975)

Lights and keys ● Light used • Light not used	Observed reaction time and 95% confidence limits	Predicted reaction time	Strategy postulated
A · ● ● ● ● ● ● ·	478 ± 8	478	(c)
B · · ● ● ● ● ● ●	477 ± 7	478	(c)
C ● ● · ● ● · ● ●	443 ± 7	445	(c) + (d)(i)
D ● · ● ● ● ● · ●	443 ± 7	445	(c) + (d)(i)
E ● ● ● · · ● ● ●	521 ± 9	522	(a)(ii)

concerned—4.5 in all. The predicted mean reaction time is therefore 128 + (3.5 × 100) = 478 msec. In the two cases (A and B) where all six signals are in a single block, the observed times of 478 ± 8 and 477 ± 7 msec agree remarkably well with the prediction. Results in the case of C and D where the signals form three separate groups are in close accord with the predictions of strategy (d)(i) assuming an initial division into three pairs with the third pair scanned *seriatim* if the signal has not been found in the first or second pair. The predicted mean number of inspections in each case is 3.17 and the mean reaction time therefore 128 + (3.17 × 100) = 445 msec. The observed times of 443 ± 7 in each case again agree closely with prediction.

The relatively long reaction time for run E was surprising, since if the subjects divided the six possibilities into the two obvious groups of three and then dealt with these as trios, the expected mean time would have been 478 msec, the same as for runs A and B. If the trio reached second had been inspected *seriatim* in accordance with strategy (d), the time should have been 128 + (1 × 100) + (2 × 100) = 428 msec which is even shorter than the 445 msec predicted for runs C, D and E. Various possible reasons for the discrepancy were explored in subsidiary experiments. The most likely reason appeared to be that the layout of the display favoured an initial dichotomiz- ation, and that having started this way subjects continued to dichotomize even though this was not the most efficient strategy. According to strategy (a)(ii), a mean reaction time of 128 + (3.94 × 100) = 522 msec is predicted, which is close to the 521 ± 9 observed.

Three further points about these results may be briefly noted. First, in C and D the index fingers were on average faster than the others, and of the other remaining fingers, those of the right hand were on average faster than those of the left. In both cases the average times for the three pairs were in close agreement with the assumption that the subjects inspected the middle pair first on 5/6 occasions, the right-hand pair first on 1/6, and never inspected the left-hand pair first. Given that the same bias is maintained after the initial inspection, the subsequent inspections and mean reaction times would have been as in Table 3.3. Observed and predicted results are again in remarkably close agreement.

Second, as in the eight-choice task, reaction times by the middle and ring fingers tended to be some 100 msec slower than those by the index and little fingers unless they came in end positions as in *A* and *B*. A check was made to see if the differences of times for the different arrangements of the display could be accounted for in terms of the numbers of "slow" and "fast" fingers they contained, but results were not as well accounted for in this way as in terms of the strategies already proposed. As in the previous eight-choice task, changing the relationships between lights and keys indicated that the slower reactions were not associated with the middle and ring *fingers* but with the light positions that normally corresponded to them. There thus appears to be an anomaly between these results and those of Alegria and Bertelson (1970) who, as already noted, found that reaction times by middle and ring fingers were longer than those by others in circumstances in which the position of all signals was the same. There is perhaps some factor of *association between signal and response* which is important but not yet fully defined.

Third, it may be objected that the range of strategies possible, and the different predictions that follow from them, make the model proposed here so flexible that almost any results could be fitted by it. Such a criticism would seem, however, to be unjustified: almost without exception the results cluster closely around the predictions which the layouts of the display make plausible. Further, the author is all too well aware of the many possible ways of accounting for the data that were tried but found not to be satisfactory.

4. Errors of choice

So far in the present discussion the process of choice has been looked at mainly from the input end, and considered as the gradual elimination of possible alternative signals until the one which has occurred is identified and the response corresponding to it is chosen: first, broad classes are eliminated, then narrower ones until a final decision is made. It was, however, recognized in relation to eqn 3.6 that the process could also be regarded from the output end, seeing it as giving rise to build-up of activity in a small area of the motor cortex to an extent which causes, in the case we have been

Table 3.3. Numbers of inspections required with the Positive Check model to identify signals within three groups (or three single signals). The probabilities of groups A, B and C being inspected first are P_A, P_B and P_C respectively with $P_A + P_B + P_C = 1$ (Welford, 1973). The lower part of the table sets out the predicted mean reaction times for conditions C and D of Table 3.2, and the last two lines give the observed mean times

	Signal or group occurring		
	A (left)	B (centre)	C (right)
Number of inspections required to identify group			
1	P_A	P_B	P_C
2	$\dfrac{P_B \times P_A}{1-P_B} + \dfrac{P_C \times P_A}{1-P_C}$	$\dfrac{P_A \times P_B}{1-P_A} + \dfrac{P_C \times P_B}{1-P_C}$	$\dfrac{P_A \times P_C}{1-P_A} + \dfrac{P_B \times P_C}{1-P_B}$
3	$\dfrac{P_B \times P_C}{1-P_B} + \dfrac{P_C \times P_A}{1-P_C}$	$\dfrac{P_A \times P_C}{1-P_A} + \dfrac{P_C \times P_A}{1-P_C}$	$\dfrac{P_A \times P_B}{1-P_A} + \dfrac{P_B \times P_A}{1-P_B}$
1	0	0.83	0.17
2	0	0.17	0.83
3	1.0	0	0
Mean reaction time predicted	$128 + 3 \times 100$ $+ 0.5 \times 100 = 478$	$128 + 0.83 \times 100$ $+ 0.17 \times 200$ $+ 1.5 \times 100 = 395$	$128 + 0.17 \times 100$ $+ 0.83 \times 200$ $+ 1.5 \times 100 = 461$
Observed			
C	478 ± 12	394 ± 11	457 ± 13
D	475 ± 13	400 ± 10	454 ± 13

discussing, one finger to be moved while others remain stationary. We may suppose that excitation produced by the incoming signal is initially spread over all the alternatives, and that each successive stage of elimination concentrates it more and more on one of them, until it reaches the firing level C in eqn 3.6. This may be reasonable when considering actions by different fingers or limbs whose spatial mapping on the motor cortex is well recognized, but it is a far cry from processes of perceptual identification and the selection of non-manual responses such as nonsense syllables or names of letters or digits. The analogy is not, however, far fetched or unreasonable since perceptual identifications and verbal responses must be based on physical traces which have some kind of spatial location in the brain. Schouten and Bekker (1967) have suggested a somewhat similar approach to perceptual tasks in terms of "perceptual focusing".

There is likely to be some spread of the effect of the build-up in any area to adjacent areas and this, combined with random noise in the system, provides a plausible reason for the fact that virtually all the errors in the experiments we have been discussing were the result of pressing the key next to the one which was correct. We can further argue that the higher the criterion, the longer the buildup will take, but the fewer the errors that will be made. We can thus understand the tendency for accuracy to fall as speed rises.

Viewing the process of choice as one of a progressive build-up of activity to a critical level in the motor cortex provides an explanation of three further findings not easily accounted for otherwise. First, Seibel (1963) gave subjects a task in which all possible combinations of ten signal lights and response keys were used to yield 1032 choices. He found that reaction times were very little longer than those obtained in a similar task that used only five lights and keys with one hand to yield 31 choices. We may suppose that the build-up required to strike chords with several fingers at once virtually always distinguishes each finger from its neighbours, and that it does not differ appreciably whether all ten or only the five fingers of one hand are used.

Second, it seems reasonable to suppose that any spread of effect in the motor cortex would affect other areas in proportion to their distance from the focal point, so that errors would be related to the "neural distance" between correct and erroneous responses. There is some evidence from experiments by Blyth (1963, 1964) that this is so. He found that in a four-choice task in which responses were made by the two hands and two feet, the overwhelming majority of errors were due to the substitution of the wrong limb on the correct side. Occasional errors were made with the correct limb on the wrong side, but never with the wrong limb on the wrong side. Further studies by the same experimenter verified that this result did not depend on the layout of the signals but seemed clearly due to responses on the same side being more readily confused than those on opposite sides.

Third, since the build-up of activity would probably take an appreciable time to die away, it could be the basis of some of the tendency for repeated responses to be faster than others when the inter-response interval is short. The evidence on this point is discussed in Chapter 4.

Pew (1969), who reviewed the results of several studies, showed that the relation between reaction time and accuracy could be represented by the equation

$$\text{Mean reaction time} = a + b \log \frac{\text{proportion of correct responses}}{\text{proportion of errors}} \quad (3.8)$$

Pew points out that, where there are two alternatives, the log portion of eqn 3.8 is linearly related to the square of d' in the signal detection model. This is consistent with Hick's law, since $(d')^2$ is a linear function of information. Pew's formulation has, however, been challenged by Lappin and Disch (1972a,b) who reviewed various approaches to the problem and found that their own data were better explained by regarding reaction time as linearly related to d' instead of to its square. The difference between the linearity with d' and $(d')^2$ was, however, small, and their preference for d' seems to have been based largely on theoretical considerations. In either case, the speed-accuracy relationship depends on the magnitude of d' attained when the buildup reaches criterion. It is perhaps worth noting in this connection that in the results shown in Fig. 3.3, the average d' between each response and those adjacent to it, as calculated from the errors made, was practically constant at about 4 with all degrees of choice.

Equation 3.8 has been found to hold with several different methods of manipulating the relationship between speed and accuracy, such as restricting the time within which a response can be made or by providing explicit payoffs for fast and slow or for accurate and erroneous responses (Pew, 1969; Pachella and Fisher, 1972), for relationships spontaneously adopted by subjects (Lappin and Disch, 1972a) and for different intensities of signal (Lappin and Disch, 1972b) or of general illumination of the display (Pachella and Fisher, 1969). The last two cases serve to emphasize that, in principle, the process could be either a build-up of tendency to a particular *response* or the progressive focusing of attention on a particular signal as suggested by Schouten and Bekker (1967). Evidence surveyed here which was not available when Schouten and Bekker wrote, appears to make the former assumption preferable in at least many cases. Equation 3.6 would, however, apply equally to both, and each process may perhaps be regarded as the virtually inseparable counterpart of the other.

5. Factors affecting the extent to which reaction-time rises with number of alternatives

The slope constants K in eqns 3.1, 3.2 and 3.6 and b in eqn 3.5, for many studies of subjects in their twenties using conventional light signals and key-pressing or spoken responses, are remarkably constant at about 5–7 bits per sec (e.g. Merkel, 1885; Hick, 1952a; Hyman, 1953; Brown, 1960). Essentially the same rate was found by Pollack and Johnson (1963) as the maximum for monitoring a series of binary digits (0 or 1) briefly flashed one at a time on a screen. However, several other studies have shown rates much higher or lower than these. The rate appears to depend to a considerable extent upon the relationships between signals and responses or, as Fitts and Seeger (1953) termed it, *compatibility* between signal and response, and also upon the familiarity of these relationships. An example is contained in the results obtained by Brainard *et al.* (1962) who gave their subjects two-, four- and eight-choice tasks with all possible combinations of two types of signal and two types of response. The four combinations, ranging from least to most compatible and the results obtained are shown in Table 3.4. It can be seen that the rates vary from values similar to those found by Hick and Hyman in the less compatible conditions to very much higher values in the most compatible and familiar.

The two factors, compatibility and familiarity, will be considered in turn.

Table 3.4. Signal-response combinations used and results obtained by Brainard *et al.* (1962). Figures are in bits per second

Signal	Response	Incremental rates of information transmission between 2-, 4- and 8-choices
Numbers projected on screen	Pressing keys corresponding to the numbers, placed conveniently under the subject's fingers	5.5
Lights arranged in same pattern as keys	Speaking numbers corresponding to lights	4.9
Lights as above	Keys as above	9.0
Numbers as above	Repeating the numbers	90.9

(A) COMPATIBILITY

We may take, as an example, an experiment by Crossman (1956) who investigated the times taken to move from a central position to press particular keys in response to numbered signal lights. Two relationships between signal and response were studied. In one, the more compatible of the two, each signal light was located immediately above its corresponding key; in the other, they were scattered in random positions on a panel. The slope for the former was about 15 bits per sec and for the latter about 5.

Leonard (1959) attempted to produce complete compatibility by using as signals vibrations to the tips of the fingers which were to make the corresponding responses. He found an increase in reaction time from simple to two-choice conditions, but no further rise to four- or eight-choice. Some increase from simple to two-choice conditions is to be expected because, when only one response is required, it can be prepared to an extent that is not possible when two or more responses are called for. Leonard's results, however, can be questioned because he measured reactions from only one finger, which was used in all conditions, and also because he provided more practice with the higher degrees of choice so that effects of compatibility were not clearly distinct from those of practice. The importance of this latter point is emphasized by the fact that Broadbent and Gregory (1965), using apparatus similar to Leonard's and giving equal amounts of practice for two-choice and four-choice reactions, found that the latter were substantially slower than the former.

Smith (1978), in repeating Leonard's experiment, avoided these shortcomings. His results are shown in the first two lines of Table 3.5. On the first day there was a progressive increase of reaction time from two- to eight-choice, although it was small compared with those in, say, Fig. 3.3. On the second day, however, the increase was essentially nil, and the results confirm those of Leonard. The reason for the increase on the first day was that responses by the index fingers, which were used in the two-choice condition, were faster than those by the middle fingers which were added in the four-choice, and these were faster than those by the ring and little fingers added

Table 3.5. Mean reaction times (in msec) to vibratory stimuli delivered to the tips of fingers, with different degrees of compatibility between stimulus and response. Percentages of errors are given in brackets. Data from Smith (1978)

Relationship between stimulus and response	Runs			Bits per second for rise from 2-choice to 8-choice
	8-choice	4-choice	2-choice	
Direct — First day	256 (1.2)	249 (1.2)	236 (1.0)	100.0
Direct — Second day	216 (1.2)	203 (1.2)	212 (1.0)	500.0
Reflected	628 (13.3)	532 (9.7)	324 (6.9)	6.6
Shifted	858 (13.0)	698 (9.7)	385 (9.7)	4.2

in the eight-choice. The differences between fingers largely disappeared, however, on the second day. Smith raised the question of whether the lack of difference was due either to there truly being no increase with degree of choice in the time required to identify signals and relate them to highly compatible responses, or whether after some practice the times for all degrees of choice fell to a point at which they were determined by some minimum time. The latter view cannot be positively excluded on the evidence at present available, but the difference between different degrees of choice was in any case very small.

If there is a real difference it might reasonably be attributed to longer time taken for perceptual identification with increase in the number of possible signals. Work required to relate signals to their corresponding responses can be regarded as having been minimal in both Leonard's and Smith's experiments, so that the time taken to do this is presumably the main reason for increase of reaction time with degree of choice in other experiments. This view is supported when the top two lines of Table 3.5 are compared with the second and third lines, which set out results for two further conditions studied by Smith. In the "reflected" condition, the stimulus to any finger had to be responded to with the corresponding finger of the other hand, so that the mapping of signals to responses was by mirror-image reflection to positions on the opposite side of the body. In the "shifted" condition, the correct response had to be made by the other hand so that a stimulus to the left little finger was responded to by the right index finger, a stimulus to the left ring finger by the right middle finger, and so on. Both these conditions obviously involved a more complex relationship between signal and response than the direct condition, and in both, the increase in reaction time with degree of choice was in fact much greater. It is clear from the error percentages shown in Table 3.5 that the longer reaction times were not the result of greater accuracy.

1. Types of incompatibility

The requirement for relating signal to response in experiments which have studied compatibility—or perhaps more accurately *incompatibility*—can be divided into two main classes (Welford, 1968): *symbolic recodings or translations* as in Crossman's (1956) task, and *spatial transformations* as in Smith's (1977, 1978). Both types were incorporated in an experiment by Fitts and Deininger (1954) who compared the display and control shown in Fig. 3.5 with an arrangement in which the same control was used but the display was replaced by a window in which figures could be shown indicating clock positions—for example 12.00, 4.30, 9.00—corresponding to the different directions on the control panel. The average times taken to move from the centre of the control panel to the end of the appropriate

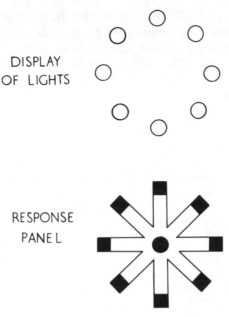

Fig. 3.5. Display and control panels used by Fitts and Deininger (1954). Each signal was one of the 8 lights. The subject responded by moving a stylus from the centre of the control panel to the end of one of the arms.

"spoke" and the errors made, are shown in the first two rows of Table 3.6, from which it is evident that the symbolic translation impaired both speed and accuracy: taking both into account, it about halved the rate of gain of information. The remaining four rows of Table 3.6 show the effects of increasing the complexity of the rule relating display to control by either mirror-image reversal so that if the display signalled 3.00 the subject moved to what would normally be the 9.00 position, or by complete randomization. It can be seen that the effect of these changes was greater for the normally compatible, spatial display than for the symbolic, so that when relationships were completely random the symbolic display yielded better performance. Why this was so is not clear. It seems, however, that adding one incompatibility to another may have several different effects. For example Kay (1954, 1955) whose results are discussed in Chapter 9, found that the effects of adding a symbolic translation to a spatial transposition were far greater than the sum of the effects of the two incompatibilities taken singly.

While the overall effects of incompatibility are clear, the precise reasons for them are still obscure. Several possible lines of explanation, not mutually exclusive, have, however, been suggested as worthy of consideration.

Table 3.6. Effects of symbolic translation between display and control. Results obtained by Fitts and Deininger (1954). Each figure is the mean time per response in sec or percentage of errors based on 128 readings from each of ten subjects

Correspondence between display and control positions		Type of display		
		Circular as in Fig. 3.5	Clock times shown in window	Difference
Straightforward	times	0.387	0.675	+0.288
	errors	1.9	5.0	+3.1
Mirror reversal	times	0.541	0.777	+0.236
	errors	4.4	7.2	+2.8
Random	times	1.111	0.885	−0.226
	errors	15.1	10.0	−5.1

(a) When signals on the right have to be responded with the left hand and vice versa, the signal may go to one hemisphere and the response come from the other. Appreciable increases of reaction time have been shown when such crossing over is required (e.g. Filbey and Gazzaniga, 1969; Jeeves and Dixon, 1970). However, this is an insufficient explanation, as shown by experiments in which responses were made with the hands crossed. In these experiments, a signal on the left has to be responded to by pressing a key on the right with the left hand, so that there is no crossover from one hemisphere to the other. Yet in these cases reaction times are longer than when a signal on the left is responded to on the right with the right hand which does require a crossover (Simon et al., 1970; Wallace, 1971; Brebner et al., 1972; Callan et al., 1974). It seems as if some lengthening of reaction time results when the spatial relationship is disturbed, either between positions of signal and response, or between positions of hand and response. Brebner (1973) has further shown that the effect of crossing hands is reduced by practice, implying that the main factor in this type of incompatibility is in disturbance of the *spatial* relationships between signals and responses.

(b) In some cases, such as Crossman's and Smith's already discussed, with the less compatible arrangement the subject has a double task of first identifying the signal and then identifying the response to be made to it. With the more compatible arrangement when the signal appears close to the point in which the response is made, or is delivered to the responding member, these two tasks are collapsed into one—when the signal has been identified, the response has been also. While this may be a valid partial explanation of some incompatibility effects, it cannot be complete because it does not account for the substantial difference of slope between the compatible conditions of Crossman's and Smith's experiments.

(c) An important—perhaps the most important—factor in compatibility seems to lie in the task of *recoding* or *translating* from perception to action. This is the essential process involved in the choice of response. It can be assumed to be at a minimum in experiments such as Leonard's (1959) and Smith's (1977) direct condition, but in less compatible conditions to involve more or less elaborate mediating processes such as the application of some *rule* for mapping signals onto responses. The mirror-image arrangement studied by Fitts and Deininger (1954) is a relatively simple example, while the random arrangement they used can be regarded as more elaborate and as giving rise to longer reaction times for that reason. The random case can, in fact, be thought of as one in which a different rule has to be used to relate each signal to its corresponding reponse, and the difficulty it produces as being due to more than one rule having to be used. A direct study of the effects of having two different rules has been made by Duncan (1977) who, with a four-choice task, used the four different arrangements shown in Fig. 3.6. He found that, not unexpectedly, reaction times were longer with the *P–O* arrangement than with the *P–C*. He also found that in the two "mixed" conditions *M*–1 and *M*–2, mean reaction times for both the compatible and incompatible signal-response pairs were longer than in the corresponding *P–C* or *P–O* conditions. Presumably the extra time was due to the subject having to precede his choice of response with a choice of rule by which to make it.

However, Smith (1978) using the vibrotactile task already described, found that when the correspondence between signal and response for one

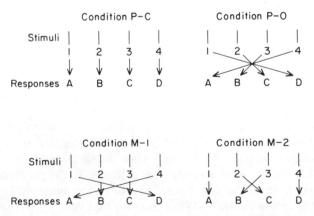

Fig. 3.6. Correspondences between signals and responses used by Duncan (1977).

hand was direct and for the other reversed, reaction times for both hands were intermediate between those obtained when the correspondence for both hands was either direct or reversed. The result is predicted by his model described in Chapter 5, but is clearly at variance with Duncan's. In a further experiment described in section 7(B) of Chapter 5, Smith obtained indications that the pattern changes from Duncan's to his own in the course of practice. In line with this, Duncan observed that performance improved with practice at his mixed tasks more than at either of his unmixed.

The effect of having a single rule has been shown to be capable of outweighing spatial correspondence effects. Hedge and Marsh (1975) used two signal lights, one on the left and one on the right, each of which could be either red or green; and two response buttons, one red and one green. They found that when the instruction was to press the button of the same colour as the signal, response was faster when the signal was on the same side as the button to be pressed. When, however, the instruction was to press the button of the opposite colour, response was faster when the light was on the opposite side: it seemed that in this case the task was easier if the same rule of "different" could be applied to both colour and location.

(d) Surprisingly, after more than twenty years' research there is no metric for compatibility that transcends particular experimental conditions. In a search for greater generality, three points seem worth bearing in mind. First, it has been shown that incompatibility can exaggerate the effects of other variables which affect reaction time such as a simultaneous distracting task or uncertainty about the time at which signals will arrive (Broadbent and Gregory, 1965), while very high degrees of compatibility may exaggerate the effects of unbalanced signal frequencies (Lamb and Kaufman, 1965; Kaufman and Levy, 1966). Second, effects of incompatibility are reduced when the signal is successfully predicted in advance, so allowing some of the work of translating from signal to response to be done before the signal arrives (Keele, 1969; Whitman and Geller, 1971, 1972; Craft and Hinrichs, 1975). Third, the results obtained by Smith and others who have used very high degrees of compatibility are obviously not fitted by the Positive Check model discussed earlier in this chapter with an inspection time of 90–100 msec. The question therefore arises of whether, if the model applies at all, the *number* of inspections is reduced by highly compatible conditions and perhaps increased by highly incompatible ones, or whether the number is unaffected but the *length* of each is changed. Present evidence is insufficient to decide this question, but two points may be noted: first Oldfield (1976) using a task somewhat similar to Smith's was able to account for his results in terms of the Positive Check model assuming an inspection time of about 30 msec: second, one may ask whether it was a mere coincidence that the mean reaction time for the incompatible conditions shown in Fig. 3.3

was 194 msec longer than that for the compatible condition, that is just over twice the inspection time of 92 msec?

(B) PRACTICE AND FAMILIARITY

Teichner and Krebs (1974) examined the effects of practice as shown in the published results of a large number of choice reaction time studies using visual signals and manual responses. They found a surprising uniformity, both of absolute times and of rates of reduction with practice, in different studies made under similar conditions. The practice effects were well represented by straight lines when reaction time was plotted against the logarithm of the number of trials. The regression equations for the two main groups of data they examined are given in Table 3.7, which shows that the rate at which reduction of reaction time occurred with practice increased both with degree of choice and with incompatibility between signals and responses. Broadly speaking, the reductions imply a decrease of K in eqns 3.1, 3.2 and 3.6 or of b in eqn 3.5, and represent an increase in the rate of information transfer.

Table 3.7. Regression equations obtained by Teichner and Krebs (1974) for effects of practice on choice reaction time. All times in sec. T = number of trials. All responses by key-pressing

Signals	Degree of choice	Equation
Lights (more compatible)	2	$0.335 - 0.018 \log_{10} T$
	4	$0.460 - 0.035 \log_{10} T$
	5	$0.620 - 0.042 \log_{10} T$
	8	$0.720 - 0.050 \log_{10} T$
Digits (less compatible)	2	$0.725 - 0.099 \log_{10} T$
	3	$1.050 - 0.156 \log_{10} T$
	4	$1.145 - 0.169 \log_{10} T$
	8	$1.540 - 0.217 \log_{10} T$

Plotting reaction times against the logarithm of number of trials has no particular basis in theory and, in some cases at least, a better fit is obtained by plotting the square-root of time against the square-root of the number of trials previous to the one concerned. An example of this type of plot is given in Fig. 3.7. The rationale for the plot is as follows. First, the discriminability of items to be recalled or recognized from other items in rote memory tasks, as measured in terms of d' in the signal detection model, has been found to rise linearly with the square-root of the number of trials (Welford, 1980).

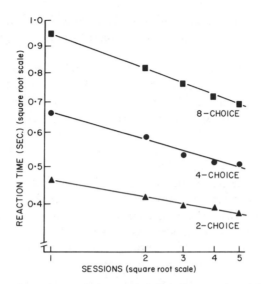

Fig. 3.7. Effects of practice on choice reaction-time. Data re-plotted from Hale (1968). The task was to press keys in response to numbers shown on an electronic tube. Two hundred responses were made in each session. Different groups performed with each degree of choice.

This would be expected from the statistical nature of signal detection theory, and from the rise of d' in detection tasks with the square-root of the time for which discriminanda are exposed (Green *et al.*, 1957). Second, it is plausible to suppose that in reaction time tasks, data are accumulated in any one trial linearly with the square-root of time until some criterion for responding with a given degree of accuracy is reached. Third, contributions to the data required can come either from accumulation in the trial concerned, or from what is brought from memory of previous trials.

It is evident from the results in Table 3.7 that with extensive practice the differences of reaction time with degree of choice would become very small. Indeed, as Teichner and Krebs suggest, they could become zero if the effect of practice was to bring the reactions for all degrees of choice down to what Piéron (1920) described as an irreducible minimum. If so, reaction time would be either the time taken to identify the signal and choose the response, or some basal time required for sensory and motor processes plus a minimal central time, whichever was greater. It seems reasonable to suppose that this irreducible minimum was attained by the subject studied by Mowbray and Rhoades (1959) who, after some 36 000 responses showed no difference of reaction time between three and six choices in a task using lights as signals and keys for responses. The alternative view is that extensive practice somehow increases the effective compatibility of the relationships between signals and responses, thus producing conditions which are similar to those studied by Leonard (1959) and Smith (1977, 1978).

Several further experiments have studied the effects of long practice by using transformations or material which have become highly familiar in the course of the subject's lifetime. Three approaches can be distinguished.

(a) Davis et al. (1961) measured the times taken to repeat digits, letters or nonsense syllables presented aurally, and found incremental rates of about 60–70 bits per sec between digits and letters and between nonsense syllables drawn from sets of 2, 4 and 8, indicating a very fast rate of information transfer between patterns of sound and the familiar patterns of muscular action required to produce the same sounds. Greenwald (1972) has argued that rapid performance in this type of task is not due to familiarity but to what he terms "ideomotor compatibility"—that is, the stimulus is similar to the feedback produced by the response. His view does not, however, account for the fact that even higher rates have been found for naming digits and letters shown *visually*: Morin et al. (1965) obtained an incremental rate of 130 bits per sec for letters drawn from sets of 2, 4 or 8. The rate was much higher than those obtained with the less familiar tasks of naming colours, geometric symbols or pictures of faces or animals—13, 10, 11 and 13 bits per sec respectively. Again, Brainard et al. (1962) found a rate of 90 bits per sec for naming digits as already shown in Table 3.4, and Mowbray (1960) obtained essentially equal mean reaction times for naming digits drawn from sets of 2, 4, 6, 8 and 10, although his result is questionable because he gave amounts of practice proportional to the degree of choice so that, for example, while subjects performing the two-choice task had 120 trials, those performing the ten-choice had 600. These rates are higher than that of 25 bits per sec found by Stone and Callaway (1964) between sets of two and four in a digit-naming task, but their responses were less familiar—"BUN", "BOO", "BEE" and "BOR" for 1, 2, 3 and 4, respectively. A relatively low rate of about 38 bits per sec has also been found for less familiar material by Pollack (1963a) whose subjects repeated words shown visually and drawn from vocabularies ranging from 2 to 1000.

(b) Oldfield and Wingfield (1965) related the reaction times for naming 36 pictures of objects to the frequencies with which the names occurred in the Thorndike-Lorge word list, and found that the increase of reaction time from names with a frequency of 1 per 10 000 to 1 per 3 000 000 represented about 13.5 bits per sec—a figure similar to that obtained by Morin and co-workers for naming pictures from different sizes of set.

(c) Several experiments have measured the rates for *reading* words or nonsense syllables continuously from lists drawn from different sizes of set. Conrad (1962) who compared rates of reading lists of 320 items drawn from sets of 4 or 32, found an incremental rate of 11 bits per sec for nonsense syllables and 300 bits per sec for the most frequent words in the Thorndike-Lorge list. However, Pierce and Karlin (1957) using sets of from 2 to 16 words drawn from the same source, found an incremental rate of only 60 bits per sec. The discrepancy may perhaps be due to the fact that it is difficult to assess the quality of reading in experiments of this kind, so that insofar as quality is an aspect of accuracy, the balance between speed and accuracy has not been fully controlled.

Experiments using each of these methods have shown that rates of information transfer with familiar material, already high compared with light-key or digit-key tasks, become even higher after some practice. For example with method (a) Pollack (1963a) found the rate for words rose from about 38 to about 77 bits per sec after practice of 40 mins per day, five days per week for four months. Again, Davis *et al*. (1961) found that after only 60 trials with nonsense syllables drawn from sets of 2, 4 or 8 the difference of reaction time with set size became virtually zero. The effect of practice in this latter case was probably to drive the times down to an irreducible minimum, because the times for syllables down from a set of 60, although reduced by practice, remained higher than those for the smaller sets. With method (b) Oldfield and Wingfield (1965) presented the pictures they used to some of their subjects on three occasions. The rates of information transmission they obtained were 14, 22 and 25 bits per sec for the first, second and third occasions respectively. With method (c) Conrad (1962) found that the incremental rate of 11 bits per sec for reading nonsense syllables rose to 17 when further lists were read the next day and to 18 when still further lists were read on a third day.

It seems clear that the main effects of practice are to shorten the time required either to identify signals or to map them onto responses, but how this is achieved is open to question. With light-key tasks, and perhaps some others, substantial improvement could arise with a move from less to more efficient strategies of the kinds listed in Table 3.1, and from optimizing the balance between speed and accuracy. However, some of the rates of information transfer with highly familiar material seem far too high to be accounted for in these ways. Some very high rates may be due to reaction time reaching an irreducible minimum, but again this is an insufficient explanation. The possibilities remain either that inspection times become greatly reduced or that the mapping of signals onto responses becomes, in some sense, "built into" the central mechanisms so that directly a signal appears the activation of the corresponding response occurs with little or no mediating activity. Both processes may occur.

Some evidence in favour of the first view comes from a re-calculation in terms of the Positive Check model, shown in Table 4.8 of data obtained by

Stone and Callaway (1964) whose subjects, as already mentioned, responded vocally to numbers 1, 2, 3 or 4 presented visually. Each number was presented with or without a light indicating whether or not a response was to be made. In conditions A, B, C and D the light appeared every time, while in conditions E, F, G and H it appeared only 40 per cent of the times. Assuming that the difference between conditions A and B should be 1.5 inspection times, we obtain an inspection time of 26 msec and a basic time of 303 msec. Applying these with the strategy of an initial inspection of signal 1 on 0.812 occasions in condition C and on 0.5 occasions in condition D, followed, if the signal is not 1, by a serial inspection of 2, 3 and 4 (not necessarily in that order), the times predicted are a very reasonable fit to those obtained. If it is assumed that in runs E, F, G and H there is an initial binary choice of whether to respond or not which, because response is called for on only 40 per cent of occasions, takes $(0.4 \times 1) + (0.6 \times 2) = 1.6$ inspection times, all these conditions should take 43 msec longer than their corresponding A, B, C and D condition. The predicted times in Table 3.8 agree fairly well with those observed.

Insofar as the second view—that signal-response connections become built in—is correct, the effects of selecting a small set of, say, three out of ten digits or 26 letters should make little or no difference to reaction time as compared with selecting from the whole set, because all the items would be equally ready whether they were in use or not. Some approach to this situation is perhaps indicated in results obtained by Fitts and Switzer (1962). They found that mean times to repeat digits projected on a screen rose progressively with the number of alternatives when familiar sub-sets were used such as 1, 2; 1, 2, 3, 4; or 1–8, but that results were less regular with unfamiliar sets such as 2, 7; 4, 7; or 4, 5, 6, 7. Similar results were obtained when the familiar sub-set A, B, C was compared with the unfamiliar E, B, P. The latter produced response times comparable with those when the whole alphabet was used, and suggests that when a subject has to deal with an *un*familiar sub-set drawn from a larger familiar set, he cannot rid his mind of the unwanted members of the larger set. In such cases, the failure of reaction time to rise with size of sub-set does not imply a breakdown of Hick's Law in any fundamental sense—it merely implies that the size of set from the subject's point of view is larger than it is from the experimenter's.

6. Attempts to separate stages in reaction time

Evidence will be presented in Chapter 6 that there are at least three stages which are distinct and successive in the central mechanisms leading from

Table 3.8. Reaction times observed and predicted by the Positive Check model. Calculated from results by Stone and Callaway (1964)

Condition	Probabilities of signals				Mean reaction time (msec)	Observed	Difference between observed and predicted as per cent of observed
	1	2	3	4	Predicted		
Respond to all signals							
A.	0.500	0.500	0.250	0.250	Used to calculate inspection time of 26 msec and basic time of 303 msec	343	
B.	0.250	0.250	0.250	0.250	303 + 0.812 × 26 + 0.188 × 54 = 334	382	+3.1
C.1	0.812				303 + 3 × 26* = 381	324	+1.3
C.2, 3, 4		0.062	0.062	0.062	303 + 0.5 × 26 + 0.5 × 52 = 342	376	−0.6
D.1	0.500				303 + 0.5 × 2.05 + 0.5 ×	344	
D.2, 3, 4		0.250	0.125	0.125	3.05 × 26† = 369	370	−0.3
Respond to only 40% of signals							
E.	0.500	0.500	0.250	0.250	As A plus 43 = 385	393	−2.0
F.	0.250	0.250	0.250	0.250	As B plus 43 = 424	415	+2.7
G.1	0.812				As C.1 plus 43 = 376	388	−3.1
G.2, 3, 4		0.062	0.062	0.062	As C.2, 3, 4 plus 43 = 423	418	+1.2
H.1	0.500				As D.1 plus 43 = 384	392	−2.0
H.2, 3, 4		0.250	0.125	0.125	As D.2, 3, 4 plus 43 = 411	409	+0.5

* If C.1 is inspected first, the average number of inspections for C.2, C.3 and C.4 would be 1 + 2 = 3. If C.1 is not inspected first, one inspection would be required to identify the signal as being one of the others and an average of 2 further inspections to decide which—again an average of 3.

† The average number of inspections required to distinguish between D.2, D.3 and D.4 was calculated using Table 3.3 and worked out at 2.05. A further inspection is required when D.1 is inspected first.

signal to response, in that one signal can be perceived while the response to a previous one is being chosen, and the response is being executed to the one previous to that. The first two of these stages are included within the reaction time as normally measured. Several attempts have been made to parcel out reaction time between these two stages and possibly others. They appear to fall into five broad groups.

(A) REACTION TO SOME ONLY OF THE SIGNALS PRESENTED

Donders in his pioneer work (1868) studied not only simple- and choice- (so-called a- and b-) reactions but a third arrangement which he termed the c-reaction, or as it has come to be called *selective response*. In this, two or more signals are presented, one at a time as in a b-reaction task, but response is made only to one. Donders found c-reaction times were intermediate between those for a- and b-reactions and argued that the difference between the b- and c-reaction times was the time required for choice of response, and the difference between the a- and c-reaction times was the time taken to identify the signal.

Results seemingly in line with Donders' have been reported by Taylor (1966) who used a two-choice task in which one of two coloured lights was presented after a warning signal followed by a foreperiod ranging from 0.8 to 1.5 sec. Taylor compared four conditions: (i) b-reactions in which responses were made to both lights, (ii) c-reactions in which responses were made to one light and the other was ignored, (iii) b-reactions in which only one light was used—one response was given this and the other response was given when the warning signal appeared but no light followed—and (iv) c-reactions with response to the one light and no response to no light. Using only responses to the "key" light, the difference between (ii) and (iv) provides a measure of the need to discriminate between signals and the difference between (iii) and (iv) a measure of the time taken for choice of response. The sum of these two differences should equal that between (i) and (iv). Taylor found that the first two differences were 25 and 22 msec, respectively, making a total of 47 compared with 44 msec observed for the third—a very substantial agreement.

However, several studies have shown that when the relationships between signal and response are highly compatible or familiar, the c-reaction may be equal to or longer than the b-reaction (see e.g. Smith, 1978). Mowbray (1960), in the study already mentioned in which subjects named digits shown visually, found no difference of b-reaction time between two and ten choices, but did find a difference of c-reaction time: when subjects had to respond to one digit and ignore others, c-reaction time was a little less than b-reaction time when only two signals were used, was about equal when four or six were used, and was longer when eight or ten were used. The result with two signals is consistent with Donders' position, but the other results imply that a complicating factor was operating. Mowbray suggested that this was the fact that as the total number of signals increases, the "key" signals to which a response has to be made become less and less frequent, so that reactions are likely to be slower because of temporal uncertainty effects. In confirmation he noted that c-reactions are affected by the *distribution* of intervals between key signals (Mowbray, 1964). Brebner and Gordon (1962, 1964) showed that the longer reaction times could not be due to *absolute* temporal uncertainty but to the *relative* infrequency of key signals.

Infrequency cannot, however, be the whole explanation because the signals concerned are no less frequent under c-conditions than under b-conditions. The solution of the problem seems to lie in recognizing, with Forrin and Morin (1966), that the c-reaction task is not merely to respond to the key signals but also to inhibit response to others. The task thus becomes a two-choice one between response and no-response. Moreover, if very familiar or compatible signal-response relationships have become "built-in", refraining from response will be less compatible than responding and will involve the application of a different rule for translating from signal to response. As has already been seen with Duncan's (1977) and Smith's (1978) experiments, such a conflict of rules affects all reactions, both incompatible and compatible. Support for this view comes from the results obtained by Forrin and Morin (1966) that in a digit-naming task c-reactions were slower than b-reactions, but that the slowing was less if the non-key signals were blank illuminated patches than if they were digits to be ignored. Both these conditions were, however, faster than one in which subjects had to respond by naming key digits and saying "NO" to non-key ones. This last finding confirms that omission of response in c-reaction tasks does, *other things being equal*, make c-reactions faster than b-reactions.

If the relationships between signal and response under b-conditions are incompatible, the c-reaction will be faster because the translation from signal to response for the key signals can be prepared in advance to a greater extent than is possible in the b-condition. Confirmation of this point has been given by Broadbent and Gregory (1962) who found that although c-reactions were slightly slower than b-reactions under highly compatible conditions, they were faster under incompatible conditions.

The evidence suggests that Donders' approach was correct in that, except under very highly compatible or familiar conditions, the c-reaction involves less choice of response than the b-reaction, but was wrong in assuming that *all* choice of response was eliminated. The difference between b- and c-reactions will therefore underestimate the time taken by choice, and the difference between c- and a-reactions will overestimate the time taken to identify signals.

(B) FEWER CATEGORIES OF RESPONSE THAN OF SIGNAL

Several experiments investigating the relative effects on reaction time of uncertainty regarding signal and response have used tasks in which one response has had to be given to any of two or more signals. The earliest is that of Crossman (1953) who found that the time taken to sort playing cards into two piles, one of Red Pictures plus Black Plain and the other of Black Pictures plus Red Plain, was similar to that for sorting into four suits and substantially greater than for sorting into two colours. This result was obtained from only one subject, but he had been well practised. It seems to favour the view that both the number of signal categories and response categories, or the number of *signal-response connections*, determines sorting time.

On the other hand, Morin *et al.* (1961), using a conventional choice-reaction task obtained indications that only the number of response categories was important, at least for well-practised subjects. They compared the five conditions set out in Fig. 3.8. Of these, the first three are straightforward simple, two- and four-choice arrangements. Condition IV can also be regarded as a straightforward two-choice between circles and squares. The times for these four conditions rose with degree of choice as expected, although the increase from simple to two-choice was somewhat larger than usual. Times for both two-choice conditions II and IV were closely similar. The crucial question concerned condition V, which was analogous to Crossman's task. The times for thic condition were intermediate between those for the two- and four-choice tasks early in practice, but became virtually identical with those for two-choice after about 180 trials.

In order to pursue the apparent discrepancy of fact between the results of Crossman and of Morin and co-workers, Cameron (1964) used the latter's designs in a card-sorting task, reproducing conditions II, III, IV and V of Fig. 3.8. He found that the times for condition·V were a little *longer* than for

Signals:	●	■	●●	■■
Conditions:				
I	1			
II	1	2		
III	1	2	3	4
IV	1	2	1	2
V	1	2	2	1

Fig. 3.8. Conditions used in a choice-reaction experiment by Morin *et al.* (1961). The numbers 1, 2, 3 and 4 refer to the responses made to the signals under the various conditions.

the four-choice condition III and much longer than for the two-choice conditions II and IV. Essentially similar results were reported by Fitts and Biederman (1965) who repeated conditions II–V of Fig. 3.8 in a task similar to that used by Morin and co-workers. A possible explanation of the discrepancy between the results of the original and subsequent investigators lies in the fact that the subjects employed by Morin and co-workers were strikingly inaccurate, least so in the four-choice condition and most in condition V. The subjects in the other experiments made relatively few errors and their findings seem therefore to be the more worthy of acceptance.

The technique has been combined with that of the *c*-reaction by Nickerson and Feehrer (1964) who presented subjects with single letters and required them to respond to key letters and to make no response to others. In each run there were twice as many non-key as key letters, while in different runs there were 1, 2 or 4 key letters. Reaction time rose substantially, and approximately linearly, with the logarithm of the number of key letters, showing an incremental rate of about 16 bits per sec. The familiarity of the material used would mean that a uniform response to several signals would be less compatible than the different built-in responses to each, and would in a sense represent the application of a different rule of translation to each. It is therefore understandable that the incremental rate was relatively low compared with that found for letter naming by Davis *et al.* (1961).

The ultimate limit of the technique is exemplified in an experiment by Teichner and Krebs (1974) who exposed digits one at a time and required subjects to press the same microswitch to all of them. In different runs the digits were either all the same or any of three or of seven. Again reaction time rose approximately linearly with the logarithm of the number of digits. The incremental rate in this case was much higher—about 140 bits per sec which was comparable with that for choice tasks using highly familiar material under compatible conditions. The surprising fact is that there was any increment at all. However, the giving of a uniform response to different digits would still be less compatible than a built-in different response to each *unless* the subjects could merely regard all the digits as a simple stimulus ignoring their differences. This they appeared not to do: the result, as Teichner and Krebs say, "suggests that people are compulsive stimulus encoders even when coding is not required".

The results surveyed so far imply that the technique is not a good one for separating stages of identification and choice. It is impossible to distinguish between them because choice reaction time appears not to be so much a function of the number either of signals or of responses but of *signal-response connections*, so that in Crossman's task and condition V of Fig. 3.8 four rather than two connections were involved. To be precise it should be the probability of such connections rather than their number which influences reaction time, as is indicated in results obtained by La Berge and Tweedy (1964). Their subjects responded with one hand to a green signal and with the other to either a red or a blue. Reaction times to red and blue were influenced by altering their relative frequencies even though their combined frequencies, and thus the frequency of the response made to them, remained the same.

A somewhat different technique and pattern of results is presented in an experiment by Rabbitt (1959) whose subjects sorted packs of cards on which letters or digits had been stencilled into 2, 4, 6 or 8 piles. With some packs only one letter or digit had to be sorted onto each pile, with others 2, 3, 4 or 8. He found that the times taken rose sharply as the number of symbols per pile increased from one to two, but relatively little thereafter. Rabbitt repeated the experiment using a more conventional reaction-time apparatus with which subjects pressed keys in response to digits or letters projected on a screen, and found the same pattern of results, although only after fairly long practice. Very similar results were obtained by Pollack (1963b) who timed subjects classifying lists of words into superordinate classes and varied in different lists the number of words belonging to each class. The times rose substantially with the number of superordinate classes. In most cases they also rose substantially with the number per class from one to two but relatively little thereafter.

The increase of time from one to two symbols per pile in Rabbitt's experiment was the same for all numbers of piles which, as will be seen later, is an indication of a separate stage of processing concerned with the transition from single symbol categories to those of more than one symbol. No further rise occurred until the total number of symbols in use exceeded 16. Presumably up to 16 symbols could be identified in parallel with the time taken by other components of the sorting time. Just where the overlap occurred is impossible to say from Rabbitt's results. It seems likely, however, that the lack of increase of time beyond two symbols per pile in Rabbitt's card sorting task was in some way due to the familiarity of the symbols used since in his more conventional reaction time task the similar result required a substantial amount of practice to achieve. Further indications come from an experiment by Smith (1967) who presented subjects with words in a tachistoscope and required them to signify, by pressing one of two buttons, whether or not they had been previously designated as key words or belonged to previously designated classes of key words. In different runs one, two or four key words or classes were used. He found that reaction time rose linearly with the logarithm of the numbers of unfamiliar key words at about 13 bits per sec and of unfamiliar key classes at about 10 bits per sec. With familiar key words or classes the rise from one to two was about the same as for unfamiliar, but the rise from two to four was much less—the incremental rates were about 40 and 34 bits per sec respectively.

The results outlined in the last two paragraphs confirm that times to respond rise with number of signals independently of number of responses, but they are complicated as measures because the amount of increase is affected by familiarity. They do, however, raise a side issue of considerable interest. The much greater increase of time from one to two signals per response compared with increase beyond two, suggests that the increase from simple to the two-choice reaction times found by Leonard (1959) and Smith (1977, 1978) may not have been due wholly or even mainly to the opportunity to prepare *responses* more completely in the simple than in the choice task, but has to do with a transition from one to two *signals*.

(C) DIRECT ATTEMPTS TO SEPARATE IDENTIFICATION FROM CHOICE

Several experiments have attempted to parcel out reaction time between identification and choice by requiring a response in two stages, the first of which is presumed to indicate the end of the identification process, and the second the time taken by choice. An example is that of Hilgendorf (1966) using a task in which the signals were illuminated digits or other symbols shown on a small screen and the responses were made by pressing type-writer keys. Each trial started with the subject pressing an additional "home" key with the palm of the hand. He was instructed that as soon as the signal appeared he was to identify it and then press the appropriate key or keys on the typewriter. As soon as he raised his hand from the home key the light illuminating the signal went out, so there was no chance of continuing to observe the signal once the responding movement had begun. Hilgendorf found that the total time to raise the hand from the home key, press the necessary typewriter key or keys and return to the home key was well fitted by eqn 3.1 with a slope of about 5.5 bits per sec—a figure close to Hick's. The time between the appearance of the signal and raising the hand from the home key was also well fitted by eqn 3.1 but with a slope of about 27 bits per sec.

In this and similar cases it is assumed that choice of response overlaps with movement time from the home key to those which have to be pressed to make the responses. How far it does so, however, is open to question. When all the response keys lie in roughly the same direction from the starting point, it is reasonable to suppose that modifications can take place to the movement as the process of choice proceeds— as was indicated to be the case with Crossman's (1953) card sorting task; the results of which are shown in Fig. 3.2. When, however, the movements have to be in very different directions from the starting point—say to either side of it in a two-choice task or, with higher degrees of choice, in a semicircle round it—the response is likely to have been at least partly chosen by the time the subject leaves the home key. Even if no choice of response to the signal is made before leaving the home key, some element of decision to respond and of initiation of action to leave the home key will be included with the time required to identify the signal. Perhaps, this latter element can be eliminated by assessing identification time from the incremental rate of increase with number of signals, as was done by Hilgendorf, but doing so does nothing to eliminate the possibility that the response is partly chosen before the home key is released. The technique therefore appears likely to overestimate the time taken to identify the signal and to underestimate the time required for choice of response.

(D) INCREASE OF REACTION TIME WITH NUMBER OF SIGNALS WHEN THERE ARE HIGHLY COMPATIBLE OR FAMILIAR RELATIONSHIPS BETWEEN SIGNALS AND RESPONSES

Several experiments discussed earlier in this chapter have shown that when relationships between signals and responses are highly compatible or very familiar, the increase of reaction time with degree of choice is very small. It has been suggested that this may be due to a "building-in" of the connections reducing the task of relating signals to responses to an extent that it does not differ with degree of choice. It is intuitively obvious, however, that even in these cases the subject must still identify each signal as it comes, and that the time required to do so is likely, in many cases at least, to rise with the number of possible signals because the greater the number of signals the more detail will have to be observed to distinguish between them. If so, this time is presumably represented by the small but appreciable increase of reaction time with number of signals that commonly remains in these tasks.

As has been seen, the incremental rate of information transfer is usually high, ranging from about 60 to 100 or more bits per sec (e.g. Davis *et al.*, 1961; Brainard *et al.*, 1962; Smith, 1977, 1978)—much higher than 5–10 bits per sec in most light-key or digit-key tasks. It should be added that similar high rates, of about 65 bits per sec were found by Brebner and Gordon (1964) in *c*-reaction tasks for increase in the number of *non-key* signals from two to four. The authors did not claim significance for this increase, but it is clear from their published results that it was significant since all their four subjects showed it in each of two tasks. Similarly Rabbitt (1964) whose subjects sorted packs of cards on which there was one relevant letter or digit and varying numbers of irrelevant, found that the increase of sorting time as the number of irrelevant symbols rose from one to seven or eight was 30–56 bits per sec for sorting into two piles, although for sorting into eight piles it was much less—10–11 bits per sec.

It is perhaps fair to argue that there is a biological advantage in having the perceptual mechanism work substantially faster than the mechanism concerned with choice of response since it is much more at the mercy of external events which must be perceived as they occur. To do this, a high peak capacity is needed even if on most occasions it is not fully used. Action, although it may have to keep approximately in step with events, usually permits some flexibility of timing and can thus be adequate with a lower maximum rate of information handling. The main doubts which attach to the present technique are, first, that some increase of time with number of signals may still be due to choice of response, so that time for identification might be overestimated; and second, that in some cases reaction time may be down to an irreducible minimum. This would reduce the increase of reaction time for different numbers of signals and mean that the time for identification would be underestimated.

(E) ADDITIVITY AND INTERACTION IN FACTORIAL EXPERIMENTS

Perhaps the most stimulating attempt to identify and separate stages in the process of responding to signals is that described by Sternberg (1969). It is well illustrated by one of his experiments. Highly practised subjects were required to give verbal responses to digits. These could be shown either clearly or degraded by the superposition of a chequerboard pattern. In any run there could be either two digits (1 and 2) or eight (1–8). The response could be either compatible—repeating the digit shown; or incompatible—giving the digit shown plus 1, that is if 1 appeared saying 2, if 2 appeared saying 3, and so on. The results are shown in Fig. 3.9. The lines joining the points for the intact and degraded signals between the two degrees of compatibility are parallel for each number of alternatives taken separately. This means that the effects of signal quality and of incompatibility are additive. Sternberg argues that if this is so, they must result from distinct non-overlapping stages, one concerned with the encoding of stimuli and the other with translation from signal to response. However, both factors interact with number of alternatives, as shown in Fig. 3.10. The interaction of degradation is weak while that of compatibility is strong. Sternberg points out that these interactions mean that number of alternatives affects both stages: stimulus encoding is affected slightly, translation substantially. The results are clearly in line with the broad conceptual model implied in this chapter: stimulus encoding—the perceptual stage—is separate from the relating of signal to response, and it is the latter which is more affected by

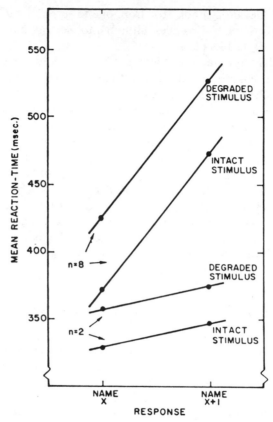

Fig. 3.9. Mean *RT*s for the eight conditions in an experiment by Sternberg (1969). On the abscissa are indicated the two levels of compatibility; parameters are number of alternatives (*n*) and stimulus quality. For each value of *n* is also shown the best-fitting pair of parallel lines, which represent perfect additivity of the effects on mean reaction time of stimulus quality and compatibility.

number of alternatives, as would be expected if it occupied a larger share of the total choice-reaction time.

Sternberg goes on to emphasize that, in many cases, more than these two stages are involved, but that their separate entities can in all cases be identified by examining the interactions and absences of interaction between factors in a factorially designed experiment. He also stresses that while the times taken in the various stages may be independent, the model does not require this—times for two or more stages might be correlated because of some factor affecting them all. Applying his method to other results, he shows that in a classification experiment of his own which resembled Smith's (1967) already mentioned, practice did not affect the process of

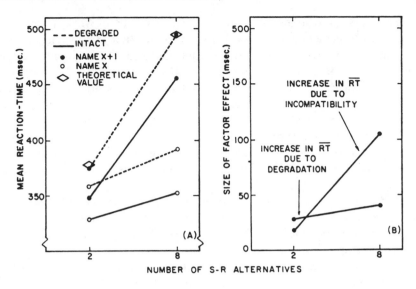

Fig. 3.10. Interactions between number of alternatives (*n*) and the other factors in Sternberg's experiment. A: Mean reaction times to stimuli "1" and "8" as a function of *n* under four conditions. Theoretical values of the topmost points in each set of four are the values expected from the other three points, combined with the assumption that effects of compatibility and stimulus quality are additive for each value of *n*. B: Effects of stimulus quality (averaged over compatibility levels) and of compatibility (averaged over quality levels) as a function of *n*; derived from values in panel A. Lines would be horizontal if these factors did not interact with *n*.

serial comparison of a signal (digit) to ascertain whether or not it belonged to the key set, but did affect other stages. The same conclusions can be drawn from Smith's own results, which show that practice affected reaction times equally for all sizes of key-signal set. Sternberg also notes results by Raab *et al.* (1961) who found the effects of foreperiod length and stimulus luminance to be additive, implying that they affected different stages. Presumably since luminance must affect the perceptual stage, foreperiod has its effect upon the organization of the response. We may add the point already noted that in Rabbitt's (1959) card-sorting task, the effects of numbers of piles and of placing two different items as opposed to one on each were additive, indicating that these factors affected different stages. Also in Teichner and Krebs' (1974) experiment in which the same response was given to all of varying numbers of digits, presenting the digits in mirror image had an effect which was additive with size of set, implying that incompatibility and size of set affected different stages. Sternberg's original result has since been confirmed in an experiment by Blackman (1975) who manipulated relative frequencies of signals rather than number. He also surveys other experiments in this field.

Sanders (1977), who also provides a valuable survey of work in this field together with further results of his own, concludes that the evidence points to a series of the three central stages mentioned at the beginning of this chapter which he labels (perceptual) *encoding*, *choice* (of response) and *motor adjustment*. He notes, however, that these stages do not sufficiently account for certain effects of intensity of signals and warning stimuli. He therefore suggests that a further factor, which he identifies as general orientation or *arousal*, can affect the operation of all stages. This view is in line with what is known on other grounds of the broad activating effects of arousal (see Welford, 1976). Sternberg's approach is further discussed in Chapter 5.

Taylor (1976) has emphasized that Sternberg's model assumes a series of processes each of which cannot begin until the previous one has finished, and that his method would fail if these processes overlapped as, for example, if choice of response could proceed in parallel with identification of signal. Stanovich and Pachella (1977) have produced evidence that such overlap is in some cases the most parsimonious explanation of results. Taylor also notes that Sternberg's method would fail if longer time spent over one process saved time over another in the chain, or if two simultaneous processes both drew upon a common limited "pool" of capacity so that the time taken depended on the sum of the demands of both. Some of the further possibilities he suggests seem less likely to occur, but his arguments serve to emphasize that the sorting out of factors influencing reaction time, and the ways in which they do so, is still far from complete. A lead to further clarification is perhaps given by Townsend (1976) who has shown that mathematically every parallel model is equivalent to a serial model, although the converse is not true. In the last analysis, choices between models cannot be made on mathematical grounds alone. In this connection, it should be mentioned that evidence for the separation of stages like those postulated by Sanders is forthcoming from the quite different approach discussed in Chapter 6.

A question arises of how Sternberg's and other concepts of stages relate to the Positive Check model. Broadly speaking, there seem to be two possibilities. First, that in the experiments to which the Positive Check model has been applied, the time required for identification of the signal has been so short that it can be neglected, so that the model deals essentially with choice of response and that alone. Second, identification of signal and choice of response may both involve a similar pattern of sub-decisions so that inspection times contain appreciable elements of both. In this case the further question arises of whether all the sub-decisions involved in identification take place before any of those concerned with choice, or whether the process is an iterative one (cf. Smith's model described in Chapter 5) in which there is a succession of inspection times, each containing a stage of identification followed by one of choice. It does not seem possible at present to choose clearly between these alternative possibilities.

7. Reaction time in relation to duration or complexity of response

The counterpart of the studies attempting to distinguish identification and choice are those examining relationships between reaction time and response time—that is between identification and choice on the one hand, and on the other the further central stage which controls the execution of phased and coordinated action. Experiments fall into two groups according to whether the responses are manual or verbal.

(A) REACTION TIME AND MANUAL RESPONSES

Because, as will be discussed in Chapter 6, it takes an appreciable time to modify action once it has been initiated, any action must be ballistic in the sense that it is to some extent programmed before it is begun. The programme must be of long enough duration to span the minimum time required to modify an action. For visually guided movements this has been estimated at about 0.4 sec (Vince, 1948) although limited modifications as the result of kinaesthetic feedback can be made more rapidly than this. The actions of expert pianists and other skilled performers make it clear that the programmes are often much longer than this minimum.

Henry and Rogers (1960) argued that the time required to lay down a programme should be longer for more complex than for simple movements, and that if the programme is laid down before the start of the action, the reaction time preceding complex movements should be lengthened. They found that, as they expected, the time taken to raise the hand from a key was about 20 per cent longer when the task was to raise the hand and grasp a tennis ball hanging on a string, than when the grasping movement was not required. The time was about 7 per cent longer again when a still more elaborate movement was involved.

Some, but by no means all, subsequent studies have confirmed Henry and Rogers' results. The reason appears to have been that, while in some cases programming must be carried out during the reaction time, in others it can be completed before the reaction time begins, and in still others it can be continued during the course of the responding movement. Thus Klapp et al. (1974) whose subjects responded to lights which signalled that either a "dot" or a "dash" should be tapped on a morse key, found that reaction time before a dash was some 9 per cent longer than before a dot. They argued that depressing the key and holding it down before releasing it in order to produce a dash required a more complex programme than the simple down and up movement needed for a dot. The same difference was found between simple reaction tasks in which only dots or dashes were required, but in these it disappeared with practice while in the choice reaction task it did not. Presumably with the simple task, subjects learnt to shorten their reaction times by programming their actions in advance of the signals.

Klapp and Wyatt (1976) in a four-choice task in which different lights signalled responses of either "dot-dot", "dash-dash", "dot-dash" or "dash-dot" found that reaction times were shorter when responses began with a dot than with a dash, and also found that they were shorter when both items in the response were the same than when they were different. The differences associated with the second item disappeared, however, with practice. At the same time, the inter-response interval was longer when dashes were part of the response. This slowing could be due to the frequently demonstrated effect that one slow item can reduce the speed of others in a sequence (e.g. Wehrkamp and Smith, 1952; Simon and Simon, 1959). It was, however, interpreted by Klapp and Wyatt as suggesting that while the response "dot-dot" may have been programmed as a whole, other responses might not have been fully programmed before they began.

As regards other possible complexities of response, Glencross (1976) found no significant differences of reaction time before unaimed movements requiring different amounts of force, and Lagasse and Hayes (1973) similarly found no differences for unaimed movements of different extents. Both experiments, however, required simple and not choice reactions so that actions could have been programmed in advance. With a choice task Glencross (1973) found increases of reaction time of about 4 and 11 per cent before unaimed movements of 6 and 18 inches respectively by the preferred hand. The corresponding percentages for the non-preferred hand were 0 and 5.

With movements aimed at a target, results are conflicting. In a task in which subjects had continually to tap with a stylus between two targets, using in different runs all combinations of 2 and 1 inch target diameters 1 and 2 ft apart, the time spent on the targets, which could be construed as a kind of reaction time, rose by only about 3 per cent with doubling of distance, but by about 24 per cent with halving of target diameter (see Welford, 1958, p. 103). The small effects of distance were confirmed by Fitts and Peterson (1964) who found a rise in reaction time of only 2 per cent with doubling of distance between 3 and 12 ins and by Glencross (1972) who found less than 1 per cent between distances of 6 and 18 ins. As regards target size, Glencross (1976) found increases of reaction time of between about 1 and 6 per cent with reduction of target size from 2 to 1 or 0.5 ins over distances of 6 and 18 ins, but Fitts and Peterson (1964) found none for reductions of target size from 1 to 0.125 ins, and Ells (1973) found none between targets 7.6 and 1.3 cms wide at 47 cms from the starting point.

Some of the confusion is perhaps resolved in an experiment by Klapp (1975) which compared movements in tasks in which they had to be made either right or left from a starting point over varying distances and to targets of various diameters. The movement times ranged from about 0.13 sec for the largest targets at the shortest distance to about 0.83 sec for the smallest targets at the longest distances. The reaction times preceding them are shown in Table 3.9. It can be seen that reaction time shortens substantially with target size at the shorter distances, but does so hardly at all at the longest. Klapp suggests that the short movements are made ballistically so that the amount of programming done during the reaction time increases as the targets become smaller, whereas longer movements are modified during their course by feedback control so that programming is at least partly

Table 3.9. Reaction time (msec) in relation to length of movement and diameter of target. Data from Klapp (1975)

	Length of movement (mm)			
	2	11	70	336
Diameter of target (mm)				
2 and 4	374	347	322	327
8 and 16	327	336	318	329
32 and 64	304	229	307	323
Difference $(2 + 4) - (32 + 64)$	70	48	15	4

carried out during their course. He confirmed this view by showing that the accuracy of the longer movements was much more affected than that of the shorter by excluding sight of the target once movement had begun.

Two further types of variation in movement deserve to be mentioned briefly. First, Loockerman and Berger (1972) in a four-choice task found the reaction times preceding movements either by the hand or by the whole body to the right or left were slightly shorter than those preceding movement backward, and those again slightly shorter than for movements forward. Second, a few studies have compared reaction times preceding simple and compound movements. For example, Singleton (see Welford, 1958, p. 99) found that reaction time to a light signalling a movement of 18 ins from left to right was significantly shorter by about 5 per cent than when the movement had to be made from left to right and back again. On

the other hand Glencross (1972, 1973) found no consistent differences
between reaction times preceding single and double movements of 6 or
18 ins. He did, however, find a substantial increase of reaction time from
when the response was merely lifting the finger from a key to when it was
the making of an 18 ins movement during the course of which two or three
taps had to be made. The increase was 14 per cent with two taps and 20 per
cent with three.

(B) REACTION TIME AND VERBAL RESPONSES

Several experiments have shown that the reaction time to repeat words or
numbers shown visually rises with the number of syllables to be pro-
nounced, and have argued that the greater the number of syllables the more
programming of the response is required. Essentially, two conditions have
been used, an experimental in which the word or number is given and
response is required as fast as possible, and a control condition in which
there is gap of a few seconds after giving the word or number, during which
programming can occur in readiness for a signal to which the actual
response is to be made. Reaction time in the control condition has been
found not to vary with the number of syllables in the response. For the
experimental condition the results of several studies summarized in Table
3.10 show appreciable rises of reaction time with number of syllables in the
response up to 3, but small and inconsistent rises from 3 to 4. The latter
result has been shown, however, only for two-digit numbers and all the four-
syllable numbers used have inevitably contained 7 which when spoken
rapidly is often contracted from the two-syllable "sev-en" to the monosyl-
lable "semn". Alternatively part of the programming of four-syllable numbers may have taken place during the response. Henderson et al. (1973) also
argued that the actual two-syllable numbers used by Eriksen et al. (1970) on
which the number studies were based, were easier to identify than the
others. Using an alternative set in which identifiability was better controlled
they found, as shown in Table 3.10, that differences were relatively small
and were further reduced after practice.

The problem with the experiments of Table 3.10 has been that, in the
experimental condition, programming has been confounded with identification, and in the control condition the task has been one of simple reaction
in which pre-programming has been possible. Sternberg et al. (1978)
avoided these problems by allowing a gap between the presentation of the
material and the signal to respond but, by sometimes omitting the latter,
introduced an element of choice between responding and not responding.
Using in different trials sequences of 1–5 different digits presented visually,

Table 3.10. Reaction times (in msec) in relation to length of verbal responses when the response is not known in advance

Experimenter and type reaction	Number of syllables in response				Differences (per cent shown in brackets)				
	1	2	3	4	2–1	3–1	3–2	4–2	4–3
Words									
Eriksen et al. (1970)									
Naive subjects	455		474			19 (4.2)			
Practised subjects	474		501			27 (5.7)			
Klapp et al. (1973)	518	533			15 (2.8)				
Numbers (set originated by Eriksen et al.)					–				
Eriksen et al. (1970)		406	423	428			17 (4.2)	22 (5.4)	5 (1.2)
Klapp (1971)		503	522	536			19 (3.8)	33 (6.6)	14 (2.3)
Henderson et al. (1973)		518	536	534			18 (3.5)	16 (3.1)	–2 (–0.4)
Numbers (other sets)									
Henderson et al. (1973)*									
1st session	473		485					12 (2.5)	
4th session	454		456					2 (0.4)	
Klapp (1974)†		421	428						7 (1.6)

* The figures given are for a set of decades (two syllables) and of seventies (four syllables). Results using a set of teens for two syllables are not given as these involve the incompability of pronouncing the second digit first. They did in fact take longer than decades.
† Comparison of three-syllable, two-digit numbers ending in 6 or 4, with four-syllable, two-digit numbers ending in 7.

and a gap of 4 sec, they found that reaction time rose by 12.6 msec per item. When the material was divided into two sub-lists, the first to be recited quickly and the second slowly, there was a rise of about 11 msec per item for the fast list, while the length of the slow had no effect. Presumably programming within the reaction time was necessary for the former, while for the latter it could be carried out during recitation. Substituting days of the week for digits they found a rise which did not differ significantly from that for digits, thus indicating that the number of syllables as such was not important. Instead they found that the important variable was neither syllables nor words but the number of primary stresses—a result in line with those of Table 3.10 since almost all two-syllable numbers have only one primary stress and almost all three or four-syllable numbers, two. The authors also showed that randomness of the material was unimportant in that results with an ordered sequence of digits such as 3, 4, 5, 6 were similar to those with a random sequence, and saying the same day of the week several times produced approximately the same result as the same number of different days. Finally, they found that reaction time ceased to increase with sequences longer than 6–7, presumably because either the response took long enough for programming to overlap with it, or because there is a maximum length of programme of about 6–7 items under conditions of this kind.

References

Alegria, J. and Bertelson, P. (1970). Time uncertainty, number of alternatives and particular signal-response pair as determinants of choice reaction time. *Acta Psychologica* **33**, 36–44.

Blackman, A. R. (1975). Test of the additive-factor method of choice reaction time analysis. *Perceptual and Motor Skills* **41**, 607–613.

Blyth, K. W. (1963). Ipsilateral confusion in 2-choice and 4-choice responses with the hands and feet. *Nature* **199**, 1312.

Blyth, K. W. (1964). Errors in a further four-choice reaction task with the hands and feet. *Nature* **201**, 641–642.

Brainard, R. W., Irby, T. S., Fitts, P. M. and Alluisi, E. A. (1962). Some variables influencing the rate of gain of information. *Journal of Experimental Psychology* **63**, 105–110.

Brebner, J. (1973). S–R compatibility and changes in RT with practice. *Acta Psychologica* **37**, 93–106.

Brebner, J. and Gordon, I. (1962). Ensemble size and selective response times with a constant signal rate. *Quarterly Journal of Experimental Psychology* **14**, 113–116.

Brebner, J. and Gordon, I. (1964). The influence of signal probability and the number of non-signal categories on selective response times. *Quarterly Journal of Experimental Psychology* **16**, 56–60.

Brebner, J., Shephard, Maxine and Cairney, P. (1972). Spatial relationships and S–R compatibility. *Acta Psychologica* **36**, 1–15.

Broadbent, D. E. and Gregory, Margaret (1962). Donders' *B*- and *C*-reactions and S–R compatibility. *Journal of Experimental Psychology* **63**, 575–578.

Broadbent, D. E. and Gregory, Margaret (1965). On the interaction of S–R compatibility with other variables affecting reaction time. *British Journal of Psychology* **56**, 61–67.

Brown, I. D. (1960). Many messages from few sources. *Ergonomics* **3**, 159–168.

Callan, J., Klisz, Diane and Parsons, O. A. (1974). Strength of auditory stimulus-response compatibility as a function of task complexity. *Journal of Experimental Psychology* **102**, 1039–1045.

Cameron, C. G. (1964). Unpublished B.A. Thesis. University of Adelaide.

Christie, L. S. and Luce, R. D. (1956). Decision structure and time relations in simple choice behaviour. *Bulletin of Mathematical Biophysics* **18**, 89–111.

Conrad, R. (1962). Practice, familiarity and reading rate for words and nonsense syllables. *Quarterly Journal of Experimental Psychology* **14**, 71–76.

Craft, J. L. and Hinrichs, J. V. (1975). Effects of stimulus-response correspondence and verbal expectancy on choice reaction time. *Perceptual and Motor Skills* **41**, 323–326.

Crossman, E. R. F. W. (1953). Entropy and choice time: the effect of frequency unbalance on choice-response. *Quarterly Journal of Experimental Psychology* **5**, 41–51.

Crossman, E. R. F. W. (1956). The information capacity of the human operator in symbolic and non-symbolic control processes. *In* "Information Theory and the Human Operator". Ministry of Supply Publication WR/DZ/56.

Davis, R., Moray, N. and Treisman, Anne (1961). Imitative responses and the rate of gain of information. *Quarterly Journal of Experimental Psychology* **13**, 78–89.

Donders, F. C. (1868). Over de snelheid van psychische processen. *Onderzoekingen gedaan in het Physiologisch Laboratorium der Utrechtsche Hoogeschool*, 1868–1869, *Tweede reeks*, II, 92–120. Translated by W. G. Koster, 1969, On the speed of mental processes. *Acta Psychologica* **30**, 412–431.

Duncan, J. (1977). Response selection rules in spatial choice reaction tasks. *In* "Attention and Performance VI" (S. Dornic, ed.), pp. 49–61. Lawrence Erlbaum, Hillsdale, N.J.

Ells, J. A. (1973). Analysis of temporal and attentional aspects of movement. *Journal of Experimental Psychology* **99**, 10–21.

Eriksen, C. W., Pollack, M. D. and Montague, W. E. (1970). Implicit speech: mechanism in perceptual encoding? *Journal of Experimental Psychology* **84**, 502–507.

Filbey, R. A. and Gazzaniga, M. S. (1969). Splitting the normal brain with reaction time. *Psychonomic Science* **17**, 335–336.

Fitts, P. M. (1966). Cognitive aspects of information processing: III. Set for speed versus accuracy. *Journal of Experimental Psychology* **71**, 849–857.

Fitts, P. M. and Biederman, I. (1965). S–R compatibility and information reduction. *Journal of Experimental Psychology* **69**, 408–412.

Fitts, P. M. and Deininger, R. L. (1954). S–R compatibility: correspondence among paired elements within stimulus and response codes. *Journal of Experimental Psychology* **48**, 483–492.

Fitts, P. M. and Peterson, J. R. (1964). Information capacity of discrete motor responses. *Journal of Experimental Psychology* **67**, 103–112.

Fitts, P. M. and Seeger, C. M. (1953). S-R compatibility: spatial characteristics of stimulus and response codes. *Journal of Experimental Psychology* **46**, 199–210.

Fitts, P. M. and Switzer, G. (1962). Cognitive aspects of information processing: I. The familiarity of S-R sets and subsets. *Journal of Experimental Psychology* **63**, 321–329.

Forrin, B. and Morin, R. E. (1966). Effect of contextual associations upon selective reaction time in a numeral-naming task. *Journal of Experimental Psychology* **71**, 40–46.

Glencross, D. J. (1972). Latency and response complexity. *Journal of Motor Behavior* **4**, 251–256.

Glencross, D. J. (1973). Response complexity and the latency of different movement patterns. *Journal of Motor Behavior* **5**, 95–104.

Glencross, D. J. (1976). The latency of aiming movements. *Journal of Motor Behavior* **8**, 27–34.

Green, D. M., Birdsall, T. G. and Tanner, W. P. (1957). Signal detection as a function of signal intensity and duration. *Journal of the Acoustical Society of America* **29**, 523–531.

Greenwald, A. G. (1972). On doing two things at once: time sharing as a function of ideomotor compatibility. *Journal of Experimental Psychology* **94**, 52–57.

Hale, D. (1968). The relation of correct and error responses in a serial choice reaction task. *Psychonomic Science* **13**, 299–300.

Hedge, A. and Marsh, N. W. A. (1975). The effect of irrelevant spatial correspondences on two-choice response-time. *Acta Psychologica* **39**, 427–439.

Henderson, L., Coltheart, M. and Woodhouse, D. (1973). Failure to find a syllabic-effect in number-naming. *Memory and Cognition* **1**, 304–306.

Henry, F. M. and Rogers, D. E. (1960). Increased response latency for complicated movements and a "memory drum" theory of neuromotor reaction. *Research Quarterly* **31**, 448–458.

Hick, W. E. (1952a). On the rate of gain of information. *Quarterly Journal of Experimental Psychology* **4**, 11–26.

Hick, W. E. (1952b). Why the human operator? *Transactions of the Society of Instrument Technology* **4**, 67–77.

Hilgendorf, Linden (1966). Information input and response time. *Ergonomics* **9**, 31–37.

Howell, W. C. and Kreidler, D. L. (1963). Information processing under contradictory instructional sets. *Journal of Experimental Psychology* **65**, 39–46.

Hyman, R. (1953). Stimulus information as a determinant of reaction time. *Journal of Experimental Psychology* **45**, 188–196.

Jeeves, M. A. and Dixon, N. F. (1970). Hemisphere differences in response rates to visual stimuli. *Psychonomic Science* **20**, 249–251.

Kaufman, H. and Levy, R. M. (1966). A further test of Hick's law with unequally likely alternatives. *Perceptual and Motor Skills* **22**, 967–970.

Kay, H. (1954). The effects of position in a display upon problem solving. *Quarterly Journal of Experimental Psychology* **6**, 155–169.

Kay, H. (1955). Some experiments on adult learning. In "Old Age in the Modern World". Report of the Third Congress of the International Association of Gerontology, London, 1954, pp. 259–267. Livingstone, Edinburgh.

Keele, S. W. (1969). Repetition effect: a memory-dependent process. *Journal of Experimental Psychology* **80**, 243–248.

Klapp, S. T. (1971). Implicit speech inferred from response latencies in same-different decisions. *Journal of Experimental Psychology* **91**, 262–267.

Klapp, S. T. (1974). Syllable-dependent pronunciation latencies in number naming: a replication. *Journal of Experimental Psychology* **102**, 1138–1140.

Klapp, S. T. (1975). Feedback versus motor programming in the control of aimed movements. *Journal of Experimental Psychology, Human Perception and Performance* **104**, 147–153.

Klapp, S. T. and Wyatt, E. P. (1976). Motor programming within a sequence of responses. *Journal of Motor Behavior* **8**, 19–26.

Klapp, S. T., Wallace, G. A. and Berrian, R. W. (1973). Implicit speech in reading, reconsidered. *Journal of Experimental Psychology* **100**, 368–374.

Klapp, S. T., Wyatt, E. P. and MacLingo, W. (1974). Response programming in simple and choice reactions. *Journal of Motor Behavior* **4**, 263–271.

La Berge, D. and Tweedy, J. R. (1964). Presentation probability and choice time. *Journal of Experimental Psychology* **68**, 477–481.

Lagasse, P. P. and Hayes, K. C. (1973). Premotor and motor reaction time as a function of movement extent. *Journal of Motor Behavior* **5**, 25–32.

Lamb, J. and Kaufman, H. (1965). Information transmission with unequally likely alternatives. *Perceptual and Motor Skills* **21**, 255–259.

Laming, D. R. J. (1968). "Information Theory of Choice-reaction Times". Academic Press, London.

Lappin, J. S. and Disch, K. (1972a). The latency operating characteristic: I. Effects of stimulus probability on choice reaction time. *Journal of Experimental Psychology* **92**, 419–427.

Lappin, J. S. and Disch, K. (1972b). The latency operating characteristic: II. Effects of visual stimulus intensity on choice reaction time. *Journal of Experimental Psychology* **93**, 367–372.

Leonard, J. A. (1959). Tactual choice reactions: I. *Quarterly Journal of Experimental Psychology* **11**, 76–83.

Loockerman, W. D. and Berger, R. A. (1972). Specificity and generality between various directions for reaction and movement times under choice stimulus conditions. *Journal of Motor Behavior* **1**, 31–35.

Merkel, J. (1885). Die zeitlichen Verhältnisse der Willensthätigkeit. *Philosophische Studien* **2**, 73–127.

Morin, R. E., Forrin, B. and Archer, W. (1961). Information processing behavior: the role of irrelevant stimulus information. *Journal of Experimental Psychology* **61**, 89–96.

Morin, R. E., Konick, A., Troxell, Nola and McPherson, Sandra. (1965). Information and reaction time for "naming" responses. *Journal of Experimental Psychology* **70**, 309–314.

Mowbray, G. H. (1960). Choice reaction times for skilled responses. *Quarterly Journal of Experimental Psychology* **12**, 193–202.

Mowbray, G. H. (1964). Subjective expectancy and choice reaction times. *Quarterly Journal of Experimental Psychology* **16**, 216–223.

Mowbray, G. H. and Rhoades, M. V. (1959). On the reduction of choice reaction times with practice. *Quarterly Journal of Experimental Psychology* **11**, 16–23.

Nickerson, R. S. and Feehrer, C. E. (1964). Stimulus categorization and response time. *Perceptual and Motor Skills* **18**, 785–793.

Oldfield, R. C. and Wingfield, A. (1965). Response latencies in naming objects. *Quarterly Journal of Experimental Psychology* **17**, 273–281.

Oldfield, S. R. (1976). Hemisphere and attentional effects on the transmission of somatosensory information. Unpublished Thesis: Australian National University, Canberra.

Onishi, N. (1966). Changes of the jumping reaction time in relation to age. *Journal of Science of Labour* **42**, 5–16.

Pachella, R. G. and Fisher, D. (1969). Effect of stimulus degradation and similarity on the trade-off between speed and accuracy in absolute judgements. *Journal of Experimental Psychology* **81**, 7–9.

Pachella, R. G. and Fisher, D. (1972). Hick's Law and the speed-accuracy trade-off in absolute judgement. *Journal of Experimental Psychology* **92**, 378–384.

Pew, R. W. (1969). The speed-accuracy operating characteristic. *Acta Psychologica* **30**, 16–26.

Pierce, J. R. and Karlin, J. E. (1957). Reading rates and the information rate of a human channel. *Bell System Technical Journal* **36**, 497–516.

Piéron, H. (1920). Nouvelles recherches sur l'analyse du temps de latence sensorielle et sur la loi qui relie ce temps à l'intensité de l'excitation. *Année Psycholigique* **22**, 58–142.

Pollack, I. (1963a). Verbal reaction times to briefly presented words. *Perceptual and Motor Skills* **17**, 137–138.

Pollack, I. (1963b). Speed of classification of words into superordinate categories. *Journal of Verbal Learning and Verbal Behavior* **2**, 159–165.

Pollack, I. and Johnson, L. (1963). Monitoring of sequential binary patterns. *Perceptual and Motor Skills* **16**, 911–913.

Raab, D., Fehrer, Elizabeth and Hershenson, M. (1961). Visual reaction time and the Broca-Sulzer phenomenon. *Journal of Experimental Psychology* **61**, 193–199.

Rabbitt, P. M. A. (1959). Effects of independent variations in stimulus and response probability. *Nature* **183**, 1212.

Rabbitt, P. M. A. (1964). Ignoring irrelevant information. *British Journal of Psychology* **55**, 403–414.

Rapoport, A. (1959). A study of disjunctive reaction times. *Behavioural Science*, **4**, 299–315.

Sanders, A. F. (1977). Structural and functional aspects of the reaction process. *In* "Attention and Performance VI" (S. Dornic, ed.), pp. 3–25. Erlbaum, Hillsdale, N.J.

Schouten, J. F. and Bekker, J. A. M. (1967). Reaction time and accuracy. *Acta Psychologia* **27**, 143–153.

Seibel, R. (1963). Discrimination reaction time for a 1023-alternative task. *Journal of Experimental Psychology* **66**, 215–226.

Shannon, C. E. and Weaver, W. (1949). "The Mathematical Theory of Communication". University of Illinois Press, Urbana, Illinois.

Simon, J. R. and Simon Betty, P. (1959). Duration of movements in a dial setting task as a function of the precision of manipulation. *Journal of Applied Psychology* **43**, 389–394.

Simon, J. R., Hinrichs, J. V. and Craft, J. L. (1970). Auditory S–R compatibility: reaction time as a function of ear-hand correspondence and ear-response-location correspondence. *Journal of Experimental Psychology* **86**, 97–102.

Smith, E. E. (1967). Effects of familiarity on stimulus recognition and categorization. *Journal of Experimental Psychology* **74**, 324–332.

Smith, G. A. (1977). Studies in compatibility and a new model of choice reaction time. *In* "Attention and Performance VI" (S. Dornic, ed.), pp. 27–48. Erlbaum, Hillsdale, New Jersey.

Smith, G. A. (1978). Studies of compatibility and investigations of a model of reaction time. Unpublished Ph.D. thesis. University of Adelaide.

Stanovich, K. E. and Pachella, R. G. (1977). Encoding, stimulus-response compatibility, and stages of processing. *Journal of Experimental Psychology: Human Perception and Performance* **3**, 411–421.

Sternberg, S. (1969). The discovery of processing stages: extension of Donders' method. *Acta Psychologica* **30**, 276–315.

Sternberg, S., Monsell, S., Knoll, R. L. and Wright, C. E. (1978). The latency and duration of rapid movement sequences: comparisons of speech and typewriting. *In* "Information Processing in Motor Control and Learning" (G. E. Stelmach, ed.), pp. 117–152. Academic Press, New York.

Stone, G. C. and Callaway, E. (1964). Effects of stimulus probability on reaction time in a number-naming task. *Quarterly Journal of Experimental Psychology* **16**, 47–55.

Taylor, D. A. (1976). Stage analysis of reaction time. *Psychological Bulletin* **83**, 161–191.

Taylor, D. H. (1966). Latency components in two-choice responding. *Journal of Experimental Psychology* **72**, 481–487.

Teichner, W. H. and Krebs, Marjorie, J. (1974). Laws of visual choice reaction time. *Psychological Review* **81**, 75–98.

Townsend, J. T. (1976). Serial and within-stage independent parallel model equivalence on minimum completion time. *Journal of Mathematical Psychology* **14**, 219–238.

Vickers, D. (1979). "Decision Processes in Visual Perception". Academic Press, London.

Vickers, D., Nettelbeck, T. and Willson, R. J. (1972). Perceptual indices of performance: the measurement of "inspection time" and "noise" in the visual system. *Perception* **1**, 263–295.

Vince, Margaret A. (1948). Corrective movements in a pursuit task. *Quarterly Journal of Experimental Psychology* **1**, 85–103.

Wallace, R. J. (1971). *S–R* compatibility and the idea of a response code. *Journal of Experimental Psychology* **88**, 354–360.

Wehrkamp, R. and Smith, K. U. (1952). Dimensional analysis of motion: 2. Travel-distance effects. *Journal of Applied Psychology* **36**, 201–206.

Welford, A. T. (1958). "Ageing and Human Skill". Oxford University Press for the Nuffield Foundation. (Reprinted 1973 by Greenwood Press, Westport, Connecticut.)

Welford, A. T. (1960). The measurement of sensory-motor performance: survey and reappraisal of twelve years' progress. *Ergonomics* **3**, 189–230.

Welford, A. T. (1968). "Fundamentals of Skill". Methuen, London.

Welford, A. T. (1971). What is the basis of choice reaction-time. *Ergonomics* **14**, 679–693.

Welford, A. T. (1973). Attention, strategy and reaction time: a tentative metric. *In* "Attention and Performance IV" (S. Kornblum, ed.), pp. 37–53. Academic Press, New York.

Welford, A. T. (1975). Display layout, strategy and reaction time: tests of a model. *In* "Attention and Performance V" (P. M. A. Rabbitt and S. Dornic, eds), pp. 470–484. Academic Press, London.

Welford, A. T. (1976). "Skilled Performance: Perceptual and Motor Skills". Scott Foresman, Glenview, Illinois.

Welford, A. T. (1980). Memory and age: a perspective view. *In* "New Directions in Memory and Aging: Proceedings of the George Talland Memorial Conference"

(L. W. Poon, J. L. Fozard, L. S. Cermak, D. Arenberg and L. W. Thompson, eds). Erlbaum, Hillsdale, New Jersey.

Whitman, C. P. and Geller, E. S. (1971). Prediction outcome, S-R compatibility, and choice reaction time. *Journal of Experimental Psychology* **91**, 299–304.

Whitman, C. P. and Geller, E. S. (1972). Stimulus anticipation in choice reaction time with variable S-R mapping. *Journal of Experimental Psychology* **93**, 433–434.

Chapter 4

Sequential Effects in Choice Reaction Time

NEIL KIRBY

Introduction and definitions

In the application of information theory measures to choice reaction time (*RT*) studies, Hyman (1953) listed three ways in which the average amount of information accompanying the presentation of a single stimulus could be independently varied. These were by varying (a) the number of equiprobable alternatives from which it could be chosen, (b) the proportion of times it could occur relative to the other possible alternatives, and (c) the probability of its occurrence as a function of the immediately preceding stimulus presentation.

While Hyman's main interest was in the effects of varying uncertainty on the overall mean *RT*, he noted that

> whenever a stimulus was immediately followed by itself in series, *S* seemed to respond unusually fast to it

and that

> an examination of the data showed that this phenomenon was quite marked for the situation with four or more alternatives and steadily declined until it disappeared or became slightly negative for the case with just two alternatives.

The tendency to respond faster to a stimulus which is the same as the one preceding it has been termed a "recency" or *"repetition effect"*. The opposite tendency, to respond faster to a stimulus which is different from the one preceding it has been termed a "negative recency" or *"alternation effect"*. In this chapter a *repetition RT* will be defined as the *RT* for a stimulus-response pair which is the *same* as the immediately preceding stimulus-response pair and an *alternation RT* will be defined as the *RT* for a stimulus-response pair which is *different* to the immediately preceding stimulus-response pair. A *repetition effect* will refer to a situation in which the repetition *RT* is faster

129

than the alternation *RT* and an *alternation effect* will refer to a situation in which the alternation *RT* is faster than the repetition *RT*. Since these repetition and alternation effects refer to the effects of the immediately preceding stimulus and response they may therefore be described as "first order" sequential effects. The effects of stimuli and responses more than one back in the sequence have been termed *"higher order" repetition or alternation effects*. These effects will be specifically referred to as such. The terms, "repetition effect" and "alternation effect" will refer to first order effects only.

Following Hyman's original observation, a considerable number of experiments have reported changes in both first order and higher order sequential effects with changes in certain parameters associated with the reaction time procedure. Unfortunately, the results have not always been consistent and this has made it difficult to evaluate explanations for sequential effects which have been based upon them. Before considering such explanations, therefore, an attempt will be made to establish certain facts and generalizations concerning sequential effects.

The effects of four main parameters have been examined:

1. the number of stimulus-response alternatives,
2. the time interval between the last response and the following stimulus,
3. the compatibility of the stimulus-response arrangements, and
4. the probability of repetitions and alternations.

The evidence concerning these parameters will be considered first in terms of first order sequential effects since most experiments have only reported these effects.

A following section will consider explanations of sequential effects in the light of more detailed analyses of sequential data; in particular, higher order effects and more complex analyses of eight-choice data. Finally, some consideration will be given to attempts which have been made to determine the location of sequential effects within the information processing system.

1. Facts and generalizations

(A) SEQUENTIAL EFFECTS AND THE NUMBER OF STIMULUS-RESPONSE (S–R) ALTERNATIVES

All the evidence to be discussed in this section will be taken from conditions in experiments with compatible *S–R* arrangements and where all stimuli were equiprobable and balanced sequentially. This means that the probabilities of repetitions and alternations in a two-choice task were both 0.5; in a four-choice task 0.25 and 0.75; and in an eight-choice task 0.125 and 0.875, respectively. The reason for this will be made clear in two later sections which will examine the effects of incompatible $S-R$ arrangements, and of varying the probabilities of repetitions and alternations.

Hyman's finding of the repetition effect for RT tasks with greater than two choices has been confirmed for eight-choice tasks by Hale (1969), Kornblum (1968), Rabbitt (1965, 1968), Hoyle and Gholson (1968), Kirby (1975, 1976a), for a five-choice task by Leonard, Newman and Carpenter (1966), and for four-choice tasks by Kornblum (1967), and Hoyle and Gohlson (1968), Smith (1968), Hale (1969), Kornblum (1969), Schvaneveldt and Chase (1969) and Remington (1971).

There are suggestions from several experiments reported in the literature that the repetition effect tends to be greater with more alternatives (Hyman, 1953; Hoyle and Gohlson, 1968; Hale, 1969; Remington, 1969, 1971). This increase in the repetition effect appears to be due to the fact that while both repetition and non-repetition RTs increase with increasing number of $S-R$ alternatives, non-repetition RTs increase more than do repetition RTs (Kornblum, 1969; Hoyle and Gohlson, 1968; Remington, 1969, 1971).

In these experiments the RTs to the various stimuli have usually been collapsed to give one average repetition RT and one average alternation RT. Alternatively, only responses common to all conditions have been used. However, Kirby (1975) analyzed the repetition effects in an eight-choice task for all stimulus-response pairs separately. A display of eight circular lights was used, arranged in a horizontal row and divided into two groups of four by a thin white line. The subject responded with the index, middle, ring and little fingers of both hands in a compatible arrangement. Repetition effects were much larger for middle and ring fingers than for index and little finger responses.Thus an increase in repetition effect with increasing $S-R$ alternatives may depend upon whether overall or individual $S-R$ sequential effects are considered.

Error analyses have shown that repetition effects tend to be associated with proportionally less errors on repetition trials for two, four and eight choice tasks (Bertelson, 1965; Hale, 1969; Remington, 1973).

While repetition effects have generally been found for RT tasks involving more than two choices, alternation effects as well as repetition effects have been found in two-choice tasks. One important parameter determining which of these two effects is obtained seems to be the interval between the end of the last response and the onset of the next stimulus.

(B) SEQUENTIAL EFFECTS AND THE RESPONSE-STIMULUS INTERVAL (*RSI*)

Again, all evidence to be considered in this section will be taken from compatible $S-R$ conditions with equiprobable and sequentially balanced stimuli.

1. *Two-choice tasks*
Generally, with increasing *RSI*, repetition effects have been found either to decrease (e.g. Bertelson, 1961; Bertelson and Renkin, 1966), or to change to an alternation effect (e.g. Hale, 1967; Entus and Bindra, 1970; Kirby, 1976b). Kirby (1972) failed to find a significant change in alternation effects with change in the *RSI*.

The point at which this change from a repetition to an alternation effect takes place appears to be approximately half a second. Thus, repetition effects have been found for *RSIs* of less than approximately half a second by Bertelson (1961, 1963), Bertelson and Renkin (1966), Hale (1967), Kornblum (1967), Hale (1969), Eichelman (1970), Kirby (1976b) and alternation effects with intervals greater than half a second by Williams (1966), Hale (1967), Moss, Engel and Faberman (1967), Kirby (1972, 1976b). At intervals of, or close to, half a second, repetition, alternation and non-significant sequential effects have been reported (e.g. Bertelson, 1961; Hale, 1967; Schvaneveldt and Chase, 1969; Eichelman, 1970; Kirby, 1976b).

There are, however, a number of anomalous results, some of which might be explained by the influence of other variables. For example, the failure of Schvaneveldt and Chase (1969) to find a significant repetition effect at a 100 msec interval could be due to their use of only 300 trials. Generally, experiments reporting repetition effects have used much larger numbers of trials: for instance, Kirby (1976b) found a significant repetition effect with a 50 msec interval only after 300 trials.

Bertelson and Renkin (1966), Entus and Bindra (1970), Remington (1969) and Hannes (1968) reported repetition effects with *RSIs* of one second or more. The former two experiments used numerals and circular patches of light respectively as stimuli. Each stimulus was arbitrarily assigned to a response. This constituted a more complicated *S–R* relationship than the usual position mapping in which the left key is pressed in response to the left light and the right key in response to the right light. Since (as will be more fully discussed in a later section) repetition effects are more likely to occur or to increase in size with an increase in *S–R* incompatibility, this could account for these results. There appear to be no obvious explanations for the results of the latter two experiments.

While the evidence is generally consistent with regard to the ranges of *RSIs* at which repetition and alternation *effects* occur, Kornblum (1973) has pointed out that there is little consistency with respect to changes in repetition and alternation *RTs* with changes in the *RSI*. He considered a number of studies which indicated that changes in sequential effects can be due to changes in repetition or alternation *RTs*, or both. Furthermore, these changes can be either in the same direction or in opposite directions. The variety of changes reported suggests that other factors apart from those responsible for sequential effects may be operating, but it seems unlikely that changes in sequential effects can be explained in terms of processes to do with either the repetition or the alternation response alone.

In summary, generally in two-choice compatible tasks with repetitions and alternations equiprobable, repetition effects appear to occur with *RSI*s of less than approximately half a second and alternation effects with *RSI*s of greater than half a second. It would appear that changes in sequential effects with *RSI* can be due to changes in processes associated with either the repetition *RT* or the alternation *RT* or both.

2. *Greater than two-choice tasks*

While no alternation effects have been reported for *RT* tasks with greater than two choices, several experiments have failed to find any significant changes in overall sequential effects with increasing *RSI* (e.g. Keele, 1969; Schvaneveldt and Chase, 1969; Kirby, 1975).

However, using an eight-choice task, Kirby (1975) did find a slight decrease with increasing interval for middle and ring finger responses but not for index and little finger reponses.

A decrease in the overall repetition effect with increasing *RSI* was found by Smith (1968) who used a very complicated *S–R* relationship, and by Umilta, Simon and Hyman (1976) who used pairs of letters as stimuli.

Hence it would appear that with two-choice and to a lesser extent with greater than two-choice tasks, the evidence generally suggests a decrease in the repetition effect with increasing *RSI*. However, it appears that the number of trials given, the difficulty of the task and the particular stimulus-response pairs considered may be important factors qualifying this conclusion. Variations in the difficulty of the task and the resulting sequential effects will be dealt with in the following section.

(c) STIMULUS-RESPONSE COMPATIBILITY

One way in which the difficulty of choice *RT* tasks has often been increased, is by impairing the compatibility between stimulus and response. This has been done by altering the relationship between either lights and keys, or numbers and keys. For example, the compatible relationship of left key pressed to left light and right key to right light, has been made incompatible by having the subject respond with the left key to the right light and *vice versa*. A compatible numbers-keys code usually involves the first key on the left being pressed in response to number 1, the second to 2, and so on. An incompatible code involves altering this relationship.

Increasing incompatibility has been found to increase the size of the repetition effect for two-choice tasks (Bertelson, 1963), four-choice

(Bertelson, 1963; Schvanevelde and Chase, 1969) and eight-choice (Kirby, 1976a). Generally, the increase in repetition effect has been either completely or largely due to an increase in the RT to new signals. In the above experiments, only Schvaneveldt and Chase found a decrease in repetition RT as well as an increase in alternation RT.

While alternation effects might be expected to decrease and even change to repetition effects with increasing incompatibility, this has not always been found to be so. For example, both Shaffer (1965) and Kirby (1974) found that alternation effects obtained from compatible $S–R$ conditions did not change with increasing incompatibility, even though the overall mean RT did increase significantly. In both these experiments, incompatibility was obtained by having the left key pressed in response to right light and *vice versa*. When the spatial relationship was made variable, that is sometimes left key to right light, sometimes left key to left light etc., Shaffer did find a repetition effect along with an increase in overall mean RT. Similarly, Williams (1966) found that an alternation effect in a compatible condition changed to a repetition effect when the $S–R$ relationship was made much more difficult.

The evidence, therefore, indicates that increasing incompatibility will tend to increase an already existing repetition effect; it may not change an alternation effect unless the increase in incompatibility is large.

Another type of $S–R$ incompatibility is that of mapping two or more stimuli onto one response. However, it seems more appropriate to deal with these experiments in a later section concerned with the role of the repetition of the stimulus and of the response in determining the overall repetition effect.

(D) PROBABILITY OF REPETITIONS AND ALTERNATIONS

When the number of $S–R$ alternatives in two-choice tasks is equiprobable, a bias in the proportions of repetitions and alternations tends to lower the RT to the particular stimulus sequence which is favoured (Bertelson, 1961; Moss, Engel and Faberman, 1967). The size of the resulting repetition or alternation effects will depend on the type and size of sequential effect obtained in the equiprobable condition. Thus, using an RSI of 0.05 sec, Bertelson found a repetition effect when the sequential probabilities were equal. This changed to a larger repetition effect when the probability of repetitions was made 0.75 and to a small alternation effect when the probability of alternations was 0.75. Using a 12 sec RSI, Moss and co-workers found an alternation effect in their equiprobable condition. This changed to a larger alternation effect when the probability of alternations was made 0.75 and to a small repetition effect when the probabillity of repetitions was 0.75.

With tasks of greater than two choices, random sequences will result in greater numbers of alternations from one stimulus to another than re-petitions of the same stimulus. It has already been pointed out that repetition effects are, nevertheless, consistently reported with such tasks.

Keele and Boies (1973) found with a four-choice task that the repetition effect increased when the probability of repetitions was increased from 0.25 in a random sequence to 0.61. When a particular sequence of alternations was given a probability of 0.61, *RTs* to these stimuli were faster than to repetitions and other alternations both of which had low probabilities of occurrence. However, the resulting "alternation" effect was less than the repetition effect found with the equivalent high probability repetition condition.

Thus, while an alternation effect can be produced in greater than two-choice tasks by biasing the sequence towards particular sequences of alternations, as for two-choice tasks, the size of the repetition or alternation effect obtained from biased sequences would seem to depend upon the size of the sequential effect in the random sequence condition.

Altering the probabilities of individual stimuli has also been found to change the resulting sequential effects. Leonard, Newman and Carpenter (1966) studied the effects of stimulus frequency imbalance on sequential effects in a five-choice task in which one stimulus occurred more often than the others. The data were divided into three categories in which the proportion of that particular stimulus was either high, approximately equal or low. Sequential analysis of runs of the more probable stimulus showed a strong repetition effect and the analysis of response times for each stimulus showed that while those for the more probable stimulus were shortest, they varied with the amount of local bias, being shortest with the high local bias and longest with the low bias.

Remington (1970) in a methodological consideration relevant to the above experiment discusses data from a previous experiment (Remington, 1969) in which two two-choice conditions were compared, one in which the two stimuli were equiprobable and the other in which one of the stimuli occurred 70 per cent of the time. Repetition and alternation probabilities were nearly equal for both conditions. The first order repetition effect appeared to be larger for the 70 per cent condition, but this was found to be due to averaging over the two components that made up the condition; while both 70 and 30 per cent components contributed equally to the overall alternation *RT*, the 70 per cent component, with a greater number of repeti-tions and faster *RTs*, largely determined the overall mean *RT* for the initial repetitions. Thus, Newman and Carpenter's "strong" repetition effect may have resulted from averaging over components.

Remington (1971) used a task with four lights, numbered 1, 2, 3 and 4, and four keys in a compatible arrangement. In one condition all stimuli were equiprobable. In the other, stimulus light "1" occurred 40 per cent of the time and the others each 20 per cent of the time. The repetition effect for stimulus "1" in the equiprobable condition was found to vary depending on whether it was preceded by stimulus 2, 3 or 4. Higher order sequential effects were also found of stimuli two before the stimulus to which the subject was responding. In the 40:20:20:20 condition, the RT to stimulus "1" (40 per cent) was found to be faster than those to the other stimuli, as expected. A larger repetition effect was also observed for stimulus 1 when compared with the equiprobable condition even when no averaging of data took place.

In conclusion, the evidence reviewed suggests that, given the size of the sequential effect (whether repetition or alternation) with a random stimulus sequence, altering the probability of repetitions and alternations will change the sequential effect in the direction of the one with the greater probability. The repetition effect may also vary with the relative probabilities of occurrence of each stimulus but, as Remington (1970) has pointed out, care must be taken that this is not due to averaging over RTs to different stimuli.

(E) SUMMARY

From the foregoing review of the empirical findings in the literature, it would appear that generally:

(i) Repetition effects occur for greater than two-choice tasks and their overall magnitude increases with the number of $S–R$ alternatives although this may depend upon which $S–R$ alternatives are considered. The main increase in RT with number of alternatives is in response to alternations.

(ii) Repetition effects generally occur in compatible equiprobable two-choice tasks with RSIs of less than approximately 0.5 sec, while alternation effects occur with RSIs of greater than 0.5 sec. Repetition effects tend to decrease and to change to alternation effects with increasing RSI. Alternation effects do not appear to change very much with increasing RSI. Both repetition and alternation RTs may be involved in changes in sequential effects with changes in RSI.

(iii) The repetition effect increases with decreasing compatibility of the task, the main increase in RT being on responses to alternations. The alternation effect need not increase with significant increases in incompatibility unless the increase is large.

(iv) The size of the repetition or alternation effect is directly related to the probability of repetitions or alternations in the sequence, given the size of the sequential effect, whether repetition or alternation, for the same situation with a random stimulus sequence.

2. Explanations of sequential effects

(A) BASIC TYPES OF EXPLANATION

There have been two basically different types of explanation for sequential effects. The first has been based on the analysis of the human operator into subsystems (e.g. Welford, 1960). This explanation assumes that a sequential effect is due to some *automatic facilitation* in one or more of these subsystems. The term "automatic facilitation" can refer to either:

(a) some residual activity in a more peripheral stimulus or response subprocess which facilitates its repetition, or
(b) to a saving in processing time in the more central coding subprocesses such that some or all of such a subprocess can be bypassed on a subsequent trial if its outcome is already known from the previous trial.

The second type of explanation has been in terms of various *"strategies"* adopted by the subject. These strategies can themselves be divided into two types; those that assume that the subject carries out his strategy *prior* to the arrival of the stimulus, for example, preparing for a particular stimulus-response pair on the basis of some expectation; and those that assume that the subject carries out his strategy *after* the arrival of the stimulus, for example, identifying the correct stimulus by inspecting the stimulus array in a particular order.

While both types of explanation assume some kind of saving in processing time, the "automatic facilitation" hypothesis implies that this saving is not under the subject's control whereas the "strategy" hypothesis generally implies that the subject could do otherwise if he wished. These hypotheses are *not*, of course, mutually exclusive and some explanations for sequential effects have incorporated both.

None of the explanations can in fact individually account for all of the findings concerning first-order sequential effects. For example, both types of automatic facilitation can account for the existence of repetition effects and, if it is assumed that the facilitation reduces with time, both can also account for the decrease in repetition effects with increasing *RSI*. However, neither type of facilitation can explain the change to an alternation effect in two-choice tasks.

Both types of facilitation can also account for increases in the size of the repetition effect with an increase in the probability of repetitions but again neither can account for a change to an alternation effect as the probability of alternations increases.

The increase in the repetition effect with increasing numbers of S–R alternatives and with increasing incompatibility cannot be accounted for in terms of a "peripheral" facilitation but could be accounted for by assuming that repetitions bypass extra central coding which is required for all non-repetition responses under these conditions.

Both types of strategy could also account for the existence of either repetition or alternation effects. However, neither could explain the change from a repetition effect to alternation effect with increasing RSI in two-choice tasks unless some further explanation is given as to why the subject changes his strategy from either preparing or checking for repetitions to preparing or checking for alternations.

Both types of strategy can account for the reported changes in sequential effects with changes in the probabilities of repetitions and alternations since it would be reasonable to assume that the subject could and would adjust his strategy to match sequential probabilities.

Increases in repetition effects with increasing number of S–R alternatives and with increasing incompatibility can also be accounted for by assuming that both strategies would bypass extra central coding required for all non-repetition responses under these conditions.

Thus, while it is clear that the above explanations can each account satisfactorily for at least some of these findings, it is difficult to determine their relative merits by considering first-order sequential effects alone. More decisive evidence concerning the adequacy of these explanations can, however, be obtained from more detailed analyses of sequential data.

The following section will therefore consider the above basic types of explanation in terms of the results of these more detailed sequential analyses. Results for two and greater than two-choice tasks will be examined separately.

(B) TWO-CHOICE TASKS

The most complete higher-order analyses for two-choice tasks have been carried out by Remington (1969) and Kirby (1972, 1976b). To illustrate these effects, Fig. 4.1 shows higher-order analyses for first-order repetition and alternation effects. The results are taken from Kirby (1976b); the RSIs were 50, 500 and 2000 msec and the task was a compatible two-choice. Results are shown for the first and last three runs. There were 100 trials for each run. In Fig. 4.1, A represents the first order or overall mean RT, AA and BA represent the two second-order RTs, the former representing the

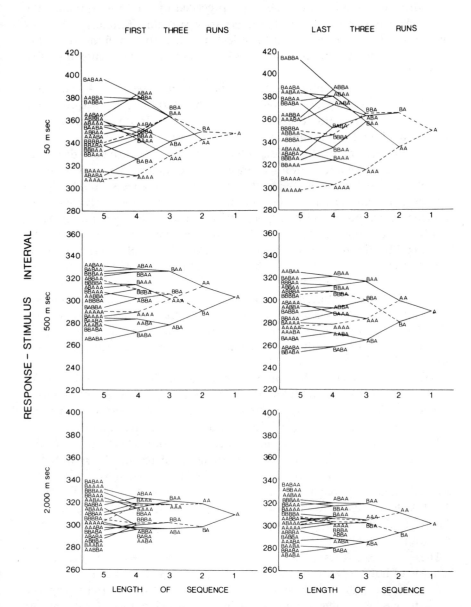

Fig. 4.1. Tree diagram analysis with *RT* in milliseconds for each response-stimulus interval and for the first three and last three runs.

case when the stimulus responded to is preceded by the same stimulus, the latter when it is preceded by the alternative stimulus. Similarly, the four third-order RTs, the eight fourth-order, and the sixteen fifth-order RTs represent all the possible combinations of the two stimulus events up to five in length.

The first-order *sequential effects*, that is differences between AA and BA, are similar to those generally reported in the literature; a repetition effect changes to an alternation effect as the RSI increases. In this experiment the change was found to be more marked for the last three runs.

It can be seen for the first-order alternation effects that the RT decreases as the length of the alternation sequence increases in length, that is from BA to ABA to BABA to ABABA. These alternation effects could not be explained by an automatic facilitation since this could only apply to repeated events but could be explained by a strategy of preparation based on expectancy which increases as the sequence length increases. Similarly, they could be explained by a strategy of checking for an alternation after the arrival of the stimulus, if it is further assumed that the tendency to do this increases with the length of the sequence.

Both of these explanations would predict that the RT to a discontinuation of an alternation sequence would increase if the prediction or check is incorrect. Thus, as preparation or the tendency to check for an alternation increases, so the RT to a discontinuation of the alternation sequence should increase.

If we now consider the discontinuation of alternation sequences, that is AA to BAA and ABAA to BABAA, RT does tend to increase as the sequence increases in length. Thus, the higher-order alternation effects are consistent with an explanation in terms of either of the above strategies.

It can be seen that for the first-order alternation effects the RT also decreases as the length of the repetition sequence increases in length, that is from AA to AAA to AAAA to AAAAA. Similarly, if we now consider the discontinuations of repetition sequences, that is BA to BBA to BBBA to BBBBA the RT tends to increase as the sequence increases in length. Again this result is more consistent with an explanation in terms of preparing or checking for repetitions.

These results suggest that the subject is sensitive to the occurrence of patterns of both repetitions and alternations in a random sequence.

A strategy explanation would have to assume that the subject is capable of changing his strategy from preparing or checking for alternations to preparing or checking for repetitions. Such a change would tend to occur when a run of alternations is discontinued and succeeded by a run of repetitions. Similarly, the repetition strategy would again change to an alternation strategy after the repetition sequence is succeded by another alternation sequence.

The existence of first-order alternation effects would, however, require some additional explanation. The fact that the subject's strategy seems to favour alternations overall can perhaps be related to a tendency to expect more alternations in a random sequence in a way analogous to the Gambler's fallacy phenomenon (Jarvik, 1951). Further evidence in support of the role of subjective expectancy in two-choice *RT* tasks will be considered in a following section.

If, on particular trials of an equiprobable two-choice task, the subject is assumed to expect one stimulus alternative more than the other, it is perhaps more likely that this kind of expectancy would lead to a strategy of preparation for the particular stimulus, whether a repetition or alternation, before its arrival. It is perhaps less likely that such expectancy would be associated with a checking strategy which could only be carried out after the arrival of the expected stimulus.

Let us now consider the higher-order effects associated with the first-order repetition effects. It can be seen that the *RT* decreases as the repetition sequence increases in length, that is from AA to AAA to AAAA to AAAAA. This effect is consistent with either an automatic facilitation which increases as the sequence length increases or with a strategy hypothesis. However, increased facilitation would not be expected to have any effect on the *RT* to a discontinuation of a repetition sequence whereas the strategy hypothesis would predict increased *RT* as the repetition sequence prior to the discontinuation increases. It can be seen that as the repetition sequence increases in length prior to its discontinuation, that is BA to BBA to BBBA to BBBBA, the *RT* does not change very much. These higher-order repetition effects are therefore more consistent with an automatic facilitation explanation.

Within the first-order repetition effects there are also higher-order alternation effects and these are consistent with a strategy hypothesis, that is *RT* decreases as the alternation sequence increases in length and increases as the sequence prior to its discontinuation increases in length.

Overall, these results suggest that an adequate explanation of sequential effects in compatible two-choice tasks must involve both subjective expectancy and some kind of automatic facilitation. An explanation in terms of subjective expectancy alone (e.g. Laming, 1969) would have to explain not only why the subject's overall expectancy changes from repetitions to alternations as the *RSI* increases but also why the higher-order expectancy effects for repetitions differ at different *RSI*s while those for alternations do not. Instead, it appears that while expectancy operates at all *RSI*s (with the subject having an overall bias towards alternations), at short *RSI*s, the main determination of the repetition effect is some kind of automatic facilitation. The fact that this facilitation occurs only at short *RSI*s can be explained by assuming that it dissipates with time. The shorter overall *RT* at the longer *RSI*s would be partly due to greater time for preparation at these intervals.

Kirby (1976b) has reported two attempts to test the hypothesis that sequential effects in two-choice *RT* tasks are due to expectancy and preparation plus some automatic facilitation.

In one experiment the probabilities of sequences were changed without informing the subject. The sequential effects from three sequences were compared. In the first two-thirds of the sequences, the probabilities of repetitions and alternations were either 70:30, 50:50 or 30:70. In the last one third of each sequence the probabilities were 50:50. The sequences were each presented without a break and the subject was informed of the initial sequential probabilities but not that they would change. First-order repetition effects were found when the probability of repetitions was 70 per cent and first-order alternation effects when the probability of alternations was 70 per cent. But more importantly, these sequential effects were found to continue significantly into the last one-third of the sequence where the probabilities of repetitions and alternations were equal. If sequential effects were solely determined by the stimulus sequence (as would be the case for an automatic facilitation or a checking strategy not based on expectancy), there should have been no difference in the sequential effects between the three sequences for the last one third of the trials. Thus, subjects appeared to carry over their subjective expectancy and preparation into the last one-third of each run.

Two *RSI*s were used in the experiment, 1 msec and 2000 msec. If some automatic facilitation was operating at the short *RSI* which tended to produce repetition effects, then the structure of the stimulus sequence should be more important at these intervals. There was some evidence for this in so far as there appeared to be larger changes from the first two-thirds to the last third of the sequence for the 1 msec *RSI* than for the 2000 msec *RSI*.

An explanation of two-choice sequential effects in terms of subjective expectancy and preparation implies that sequential effects are largely under the control of the subject. In a second experiment it was found that subjects could produce first-order repetition or alternation effects upon demand with a 2000 msec *RSI*. First-order repetition effects could be produced with a 50 msec *RSI* but not all subjects could produce a first-order alternation effect at the same interval. This is as would be expected if there was some automatic facilitation at short *RSI*s which favours repetitions and might interfere with a subject's attempt to produce an alternation effect. That this facilitation could be over-ridden with practice was suggested by the fact that a group of subjects who had had considerable experience with *RT* tasks were found to be able to produce both sequential effects with a 1 msec *RSI*. Comparisons of *RT*s and error rates showed that these effects were not achieved at the cost of speed or accuracy.

(C) FURTHER SUPPORT FOR AN EXPECTANCY HYPOTHESIS IN TWO-CHOICE *RT*
TIME TASKS: GUESSING TASKS

Schvaneveldt and Chase (1969) found further evidence in favour of an expectancy hypothesis for two-choice tasks by comparing the sequential effects in an *RT* task with those in a guessing task not involving *RT*. With a highly compatible code, the higher-order sequential effects for a two-choice *RT* task resembled the pattern of responses in a guessing experiment.

Evidence which appears to support an explanation in terms of expectancy plus some other factor comes from *RT* tasks which have required the subject to predict which stimulus will occur prior to its occurrence.

If sequential effects were entirely due to subjective expectancy, then they should only be reflected in the difference between the *RT*s for responses following correct guesses and those following incorrect guesses. There should therefore be no sequential effects within these separate "correct" and "incorrect" *RT*s. That is, there should be no difference between *RT*s for "correct guess" responses which involve the same stimulus-response pair as on the previous trial and those which involve a different stimulus-response pair. Similarly, there should be no difference between the *RT*s for incorrect guess responses which involve the same stimulus-response pair as on the previous trial and those which involve a different stimulus-response pair. If, on the other hand, sequential effects were independent of subjective expectancy, these effects should still be evident within the separate *RT*s for "correct" and "incorrect" guesses.

Williams (1966) found that alternation effects were generally still evident in the *RT*s for correct and incorrect predictions, while Hale (1969) found only a slight effect for incorrect predictions. Geller and Pitz (1970) reported slight first-order repetition effects for predicted and non-predicted stimuli but with more marked higher order effects.

These results would seem to imply that sequential effects are not wholly due to subjective expectancy. But the relevance of these results to sequential effects in choice *RT* rests on the assumption that guessing provides a measure of the total expectancy in the situation. That this may not be so is indicated by the results of Geller and Pitz (1970) and Geller, Whitman, Wrenn and Shipley (1971). They found that in a two-choice task, prediction outcome, stimulus probability and stimulus run length independently influenced *RT*. This was taken as support for an expectancy hypothesis insofar as changes in these independent variables, which might be assumed to reflect an increase in expectancy, were accompanied by a decrease in *RT*. An implication of this is that overt prediction alone may not reflect the total expectancy occurring in this situation.

That a single overt prediction may not provide a measure of the subject's total expectancy has been shown by Hacker and Hinrichs (1974). Subjects were required to predict the stimuli that they felt would be first and second most likely to occur. Correct first prediction responses were faster than correct second prediction responses which were in turn faster than responses to unpredicted stimuli.

In experiments using an extension of the guessing task, Whitman and Geller (1971a,b) analyzed the effects of past predictions on RTs to present predictions in two-choice tasks. With incompatible $S–R$ relationships, an expectancy hypothesis was not supported. Instead, preceding correct predictions facilitated, and preceding incorrect predictions inhibited, the RTs to both correct and incorrect predictions. With a compatible $S–R$ relationship, the results did support an expectancy hypothesis: a preceding correct prediction tended to decrease RT to a subsequent correctly predicted stimulus and to increase RT to a subsequent incorrectly predicted stimulus while a preceding incorrect prediction reduced both these effects. However, with the compatible $S–R$ relationship there were no higher-order effects of previous predictions; maximum facilitation and inhibition occurred after two consecutive predictions. Nevertheless in a subsequent study Whitman and Geller (1972) did find reliable third-order prediction effects which appear to be similar to the higher-order sequential effects found in two-choice RT tasks.

The relevance of these results for expectancy in RT tasks not requiring overt prediction rests on the assumption that the subject's degree of anticipation does not differ from one situation to the other. But if the subject is required to predict the next stimulus overtly, he might well commit himself to anticipation of that stimulus in a more marked way than he would when overt prediction is not required. If this were so, it would explain why expectancy might produce more marked higher order effects in RT tasks than in guessing tasks.

Geller (1975) found that RTs to stimuli not requiring verbal prediction were slower when some stimuli in the sequence did require prediction than when none did so. This result questions the assumption that verbal prediction does not change the way in which the subject carries out the task. In fact De Klerk and Eerland (1973) have suggested that different results may be obtained in guessing tasks depending upon the type of response the subject uses to indicate his prediction.

The assumption has also been questioned by Hinrichs and Craft (1971a) who examined the effect of probability of stimulus occurrence on RT. They found ambiguous results in a comparison between the same condition requiring and not requiring prediction and pointed out that

the validity of interpreting the probability effect in experiments where verbal predictions are not required on the basis of results where predictions are made, must remain an open question.

Thus, while the evidence from "guessing" tasks suggests that expectancy may contribute to the determination of sequential effects in RT tasks, it does not indicate whether or not something other than expectancy must also be involved.

(D) THE ROLE OF SHORT-TERM MEMORY IN TWO-CHOICE TASKS

The higher-order effects found by Kirby (1976b) have ruled out two explanations which have assumed that sequential effects are primarily due to short-term memory processes. Both explanations assume a strategy which the subject carries out after the arrival of the stimulus.

For example, Bertelson (1963) hypothesized that the subject uses a memory trace of the preceding stimulus in order to check whether the new stimulus is identical to the immediately preceding stimulus. If it is not, in the two-choice case the subject then checks to see if it is the other stimulus. For more than two stimuli, the identification of the correct non-repetition would require more than these two steps and, similarly, more incompatible $S-R$ relationships would involve more classification steps than compatible ones. Thus the model can explain an increase in repetition effects with increase in the number of $S-R$ alternatives and with an increase in incompatibility. To explain the decrease in the repetition effect with increased RSI, it was assumed that the memory trace of the preceding stimulus decays with time so that the "repeat" question can no longer be asked reliably.

Hale (1967) suggested that the model could explain the progressive decrease in RT as the number of repetitions increased, if it is assumed that the repeat question is not always asked first, but tends to be, after being reinforced repeatedly by a series of repetitions. But this would imply, contrary to the results of higher-order sequential analyses, a corresponding increase in RT for discontinuations of repetition sequences as the repetition sequence prior to its discontinuation increased. More importantly, the model cannot explain the existence of significant alternation effects.

A more sophisticated short-term memory hypothesis is considered by Smith, Chase and Smith (1973). Memory is searched sequentially and the order in which alternatives are compared is determined probabilistically by their recency of occurrence. Thus the repetition effect is due to the last stimulus often being among the first to be searched. It explains the possibility of alternation effects insofar as a stimulus might not have occurred on the last trial but may have occurred frequently in preceding trials and hence be higher in the search order.

However, while the theory does explain the progressive decrease in RT as the length of a repetition sequence increases in length, it does not explain the lack of change in *RT* at short *RSI*s as the repetition sequence increases in length prior to its discontinuation. Nor does it explain the progressive decrease in *RT* as the alternation sequence increases in length, as a number of alternations should tend to equalize the position of each stimulus in the search order and hence equalize their *RT*s. Nor does it explain the progressive increase in *RT* as the alternation sequence increases prior to its discontinuation, nor why this can be so much longer than the *RT* for the equivalent alternation sequence. The discontinuation itself constitutes a first-order repetition effect. This should increase the likelihood of that particular stimulus being searched and hence lower its *RT* when compared with the same stimulus preceded by an alternation sequence.

The evidence for two-choice tasks, therefore, seems to be against explanations of sequential effects in which the subject is assumed to use short-term memory for some strategy which operates after the occurrence of the stimulus. However, it is clear that expectancy and preparation must be based to some extent on memory of the preceding stimulus sequence. But, in this case, the subject must use his knowledge of the preceding sequence in order to determine his degree of preparation *prior* to the occurrence of the stimulus. This being so, it follows that there must be some optimum *RSI* which would be long enough for maximum preparation to take place and short enough to ensure the most accurate memory of the preceding sequence. If the *RSI* is too short, the subject will have insufficient time to prepare for the next stimulus. If the *RSI* is too long, the memory traces of stimuli more than one or two back may have faded to a point where they cannot be used reliably. If this were so, it would be expected that higher-order effects should eventually diminish with increasing *RSI*. Schvaneveldt and Chase (1969) provide some evidence for such a decrease and a similar trend is apparent in the data of Kirby (1976b).

As the *RSI* decreases, less and less time would be available for preparation. The evidence of higher-order effects suggests that, at short *RSI*s, the repetition effect is due to some automatic facilitation. An explanation in terms of residual activity in one or more of the peripheral subprocesses linking the stimulus to the response would not involve short-term memory. However, the bypassing of central coding operations might well depend upon the subject remembering the outcome of the previous stimulus-response translation when the stimulus is repeated.

It is perhaps unlikely that the primary function of a memory trace of the last stimulus and response would be to facilitate repetitions. A more important function of such a memory trace might be to monitor the accuracy of responses. This would presumably involve retrieval of some memory trace of the *S–R* code as well as the stimulus responded to and the response made. Thus the subject may have already retrieved the essential components of the previous trial from memory for checking purposes prior to the onset of the next signal. Depending upon the length of the *RSI*, this could not only limit the amount of time available for preparation for the next stimulus but facilitate processing of the next stimulus if it is a repetition of the previous stimulus. As the number of repetitions increased so more *S–R* processing time could be saved. This is provided that the next signal arrives after monitoring is complete and before the memory traces have faded or been overwritten by memory processes concerned with the anticipation of the next stimulus. If the next stimulus arrived before monitoring is complete, both repetition and alternation responses might be delayed. Welford (1975) provides some evidence concerning this possibility and also discusses the possible contribution of monitoring to the explanation of changes in sequential effects with age. Such a delay would partly account for the longer overall *RT* at the shortest *RSI* reported previously in the data of Kirby (1976b). Since there is also evidence that extensive practice can reduce the time the subject needs to spend attending to feedback (Welford, 1968, p. 112), practice would allow the subject to spend more time in preparation. Thus, if some minimum preparation had not occurred when the next stimulus arrived, the automatic facilitation would predominate in determining the sequential effects. But this effect might be overriden to the extent that the subject could decrease the time needed for monitoring and increase his preparation by practice and effort. This would account for the finding by Kirby (1976b) that first-order alternation effects can be produced at very short *RSI*s by subjects with considerable experience in such tasks.

The increase in the repetition effect with increasing incompatibility is most easily accounted for in terms of an increased bypasing of some of the central coding processes. Alternation *RT*s would increase more then repetition *RT*s because the more complicated *S–R* code would have to be fully used on alternation trials.

Since the probability of error tends to increase with increasing incompatibility, it is likely that monitoring will also become more important and take more time. In such cases, monitoring an alternation will require checking of the *S–R* code. However, a repetition may reduce the necessity of checking the code so that monitoring of repetitions could take less time than alternations. If this was true it would help to explain the finding with a short *RSI* that an incompatible *S–R* arrangement increases not only a first-order repetition effects but also the spread of higher-order effects around the mean *RT*s for AA and BA (Kirby, 1974). The increased spread of higher order *RT*s around AA would be due in part to the increased saving in processing time which is usually assumed to accompany repetitions in incompatible *S–R* arrangements. The increased spread of higher-order *RT*s around

BA could be due to accumulated monitoring time associated with alternations.

In the same experiment (Kirby, 1974) it was found with a longer *RSI* that
although an incompatible *S–R* arrangement produced a significant increase
in overall mean *RT*, there was no change in a first-order alternation effect or
in any of the higher-order effects. In terms of the above explanations, this
could be due to an *RSI* which was long enough to allow monitoring to be
completed. It should be pointed out that although it would appear from the
above experiment that higher-order effects tend to increase or decrease with
the size of the first-order sequential effect, this need not be so. For example,
Kirby (1976b) found that when subjects were instructed to try to produce
either repetition or alternation effects by preparing for the appropriate next
event, whether repetition or alternation, first-order sequential effects were
increased substantially from a "no preparation" condition but with either
little change or indeed some reduction in the associated higher-order effects.

In summary, there are two ways in which short-term memory seems likely
to influence sequential effects in two-choice tasks. First, expectancy and
preparation must be based on memory traces of the preceding stimulus
sequence structure. Second, a short-term memory trace of a preceding trial
may enable some of the more central coding processes to be bypassed on a
subsequent repetition of that trial.

Thus, the evidence is against an explanation of sequential effects in two-
choice tasks in terms of some kind of strategy which operates after the
arrival of the stimulus. Instead, these effects seem to be largely determined
by a strategy of expectancy and preparation which occurs prior to the
arrival of the stimulus. The evidence also suggests that repetition effects at
short *RSI*s are partly determined by some kind of automatic facilitation. It
is likely, given the increase in repetition effects with more incompatible *S–R*
relationships, that some of the facilitation is due to the bypassing of some of
the more central coding processes. It is also possible that part of this
facilitation is due to some residual activity in the more peripheral stimulus
or response processes or both.

(E) GREATER THAN TWO-CHOICE TASKS

Higher-order sequential effects have also been reported for four-choice tasks
by Schvaneveldt and Chase (1969), Remington (1971) and Peeke and Stone
(1972). All three experiments found a decrease in *RT* with increase in the
lengths of the repetition sequence. Discontinuations of repetition sequences
and alternation effects are more difficult to evaluate since an alternation
may be any of three other stimuli. However, there is some suggestion from
Remington's data that *RT* increased as the repetition sequence increased

prior to its discontinuation. Complete analyses of higher-order effects have not been investigated with eight-choice tasks, due partly, no doubt, to the difficulty of constructing sequences balanced more than one back, and also because of the large numbers of possible sequential combinations. In fact, not only have such experiments restricted their analyses to first-order sequential effects but generally RTs have been combined to form one overall repetition RT and one overall alternation RT. This procedure obviously conceals a good deal of potential information.

A more detailed analysis of first order sequential effects in an eight-choice task has been provided by Kirby (1975) using the same apparatus as Welford which is described in Chapter 3. The stimulus display consisted of eight lights in a row divided into two groups of four by a thin line. Lights were assigned to keys pressed by the four fingers of each hand in a compatible arrangement. Two RSIs were used; 1 msec and 2000 msec. The results are shown in Fig. 4.2. RTs differed for the different stimuli, being shortest to lights at each end of the display and adjacent to the midline. These "outer" lights were associated with the little and index fingers (outer fingers); longer RTs were associated with the "inner" lights responded to by the middle and ring fingers (inner fingers). This effect was previously demonstrated by Welford (1971).

All possible combinations of each stimulus followed by each other stimulus were examined. On the basis of this examination, the data were collapsed to form three types of sequential response; repetitions (REP), responses following a response by the Same Hand but Not a Repetition ($SHNR$) and responses following a response by the Other Hand (OH). It can be seen from Fig. 4.2 that generally REP responses tended to be faster than $SHNR$ which in turn were faster than OH. However, a comparison of these responses for each stimulus position showed large repetition effects for "inner" stimuli with only slight effects for "outer" stimuli.

In addition, with an RSI of 1 msec it was found that RTs for the response adjacent to the last response were as fast as repetition responses. With a 2000 msec RSI they were significantly slower.

It is clear from these results that there is more to be explained in sequential effects than the mere fact that repetitions are often faster than alternations. The fact that the size of repetition effects differed markedly among stimulus response pairs argues against an explanation of repetition effects in greater than two-choice tasks wholly in terms of an automatic facilitation involving some residual peripheral activity since this kind of facilitation would be expected to affect all stimulus response pairs equally. Further evidence against such an explanation comes from the existence of proximity effects, that is, the fact that responses to stimuli adjacent to the last stimulus can, under some circumstances, be almost as fast as repetitions.

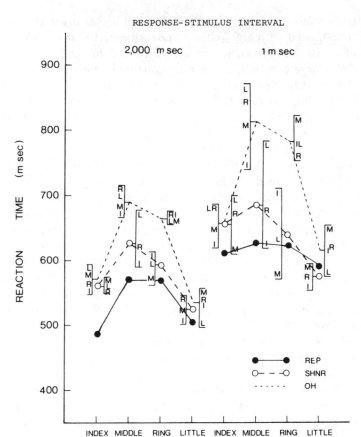

Fig. 4.2. Mean *RT*s in milliseconds for the response-stimulus intervals for the index, middle, ring and little finger responses when each; (1) is a repetition of the last response (REP), (2) follows a response by a finger of the same hand but is not a repetition (SHNR) and, (3) follows a response by a finger of the other hand (OH). Also shown are the *RT*s which constitute each of these mean *RT*s. These are indicated by letters each of which represents the preceding response whether little (L), ring (R), middle (M) or index (I) of the same hand or of the other hand.

An explanation in terms of this kind of facilitation alone would predict that repetitions should be significantly faster than all other responses. Thus although this kind of facilitation might still play some small part in determining sequential effects, this evidence appears to imply that an explanation must be made largely in terms of a facilitation involving the bypassing of central coding processes or in terms of some form of strategy. That the strategy is unlikely to be one in terms of guessing and preparation for repetitions is suggested by the fact that when more than two choices are involved, the probability of a repetition in a random sequence will be much less than that of an alternation. Hence, such a strategy would not appear to be very efficient.

Evidence against a strategy in terms of expectancy for repetitions is provided by Rabinowitz (1970) who reported that subjects tended not to repeat responses in guessing tasks with more than two choices. Similarly Keele (1969), using a six-choice task, and Schvaneveldt and Chase (1969), using a four-choice task, found a tendency for subjects not to guess repetitions.

Since the probability of any particular alternation in greater than two-choice tasks with balanced sequences will be as low as that of a repetition, any expectancy that does occur is more likely to take the form of a general expectation that the next stimulus will occur in a part of the display where one has not recently occurred. As the probability of occurrence of each stimulus decreases with increasing number of S–R alternatives, so the extent to which specific expectation determines sequential effects might be expected to decrease.

Given that a strategy in terms of expectancy and preparation is unlikely as an explanation for repetition effects, the alternative is one in which the subject processes the information in a particular order *after* the arrival of the stimulus.

One possible strategy of this type would be for the subject to check for a match with the preceding stimulus. If the stimulus is a repetition then some central translation time would be saved (e.g. Schvaneveldt and Chase, 1969). Again, this does not appear to be a very efficient strategy given the relatively low probability of occurrence of a repetition. Such a strategy becomes more plausible if it is assumed that checking for a repetition would enable the subject to take advantage of some residual activity in peripheral subprocesses which faded with time (Rabbitt, 1968). Unless a repetition was checked for first, the extra time taken checking other stimuli might allow whatever facilitation was initially available to dissipate. However, this explanation would also predict that repetitions should always be faster than all other responses and could not therefore account for proximity effects.

An alternative strategy, but one which still assumes that processing occurs after the arrival of the stimulus, has been proposed by Kirby (1975). It was assumed that the ends of the display, the midline and the position of the last stimulus act as reference points and that the subject first detects the presence of a stimulus and then attempts to locate it in the display by seeking its nearest reference point.

Thus, stimuli corresponding to index and little fingers would be located relatively quickly as being next to either the ends of the display or to the midline. This could be done regardless of the position of the previous stimulus. Stimuli corresponding to middle and ring fingers would have to be located as next to stimuli corresponding to index and little fingers unless they are repetitions of the previous stimulus and hence reference points themselves.

The proximity effect could be due to the subject using the repetition of the last stimulus as a guide to the position of the adjacent stimulus. If the position of the last stimulus is dependent upon a memory trace which fades with time, it might not be available as a reference point after 2000 msec. At the 1 msec RSI, "inner" $SHNR$ responses would contain proximity effects and this would make them faster than their equivalent OH responses. As the RSI increases and the last stimulus becomes less effective as a reference point, "inner" REP and $SHNR$ responses should increase relative to their OH equivalents and to all "outer" responses. The effectiveness of the memory trace of the last stimulus might also be reduced by any general expectation for alternations that directs attention away from the position of the last stimulus to other parts of the display. This kind of expectation would be based on memory of the previous sequence and might be expected to increase to some extent with the RSI just as for the more specific expectation in two-choice tasks.

The results reported by Kirby (1975) were generally in agreement with the above explanation which implies that basically the repetition effect in an eight-choice situation is due to a saving in identification of the stimulus. However, because of the identical relationship between the position of a stimulus and the position of its response within their respective displays, it is possible that faster identification of a stimulus also allows for faster identification of its response. Thus reference points in a compatible task may provide not only a simpler means of identifying some stimuli but also simpler $S-R$ codes for identifying their corresponding responses. Because of the relatively small sequential effects for outer stimuli and because of proximity effects, it is evident that position effects and sequential effects must both be due either to stimulus or to stimulus plus central translation effects.

That the explanation is more likely to be in terms of stimulus plus central translation effects is suggested by the results in an experiment using the same sequential analyses on similar eight-choice tasks but comparing compatible and incompatible $S-R$ arrangements (Kirby, 1976a). The incompatible arrangement was similar to that used by Welford (1971); that is, "outer" stimuli were mapped onto their adjacent "inner" responses and *vice versa*. If faster stimulus identification alone was responsible for the sequential effects and position effects in compatible tasks, the incompatible $S-R$ arrangement should add a constant to all RTs so that the same stimulus position and sequential effects should be evident. If, however, these effects are also due to savings in central translation time, repetitions and non-repetitions should be affected differently by the incompatible *S–R* code. Repetitions would still be able to bypass the code to some extent since the identification of a stimulus as the same as the last would enable the subject simply to re-select the same response as the last one. However, the position of a stimulus in the display as next to a reference point such as the last stimulus, would not necessarily mean that the correct response was adjacent to the same reference point in the response display. If this explanation is correct, the incompatible arrangement should eliminate proximity effects, reduce the overall difference between inner and outer *RT*s and lead to a significant advantage of outer repetition responses over other responses.

The results of the experiment were consistent with these latter predictions. That is, they supported an explanation of sequential effects and position effects in terms of savings in both stimulus identification and central coding processes.

This explanation is relevant to the results of an experiment by Rabbitt (1965) who used a ten-choice task with a sequence in which no stimulus ever followed itself. Responses following responses with the same hand were found to be faster than those following responses with the other hand. While Rabbitt argued that merely selection of the limb with which a response was made was sufficient to produce a sequential effect, these results could be equally well explained in terms of the use of reference points. The *RSI* of 20 msec used by Rabbitt would have enabled the subject to use the position of the last stimulus to locate the position of adjacent stimuli and their corresponding responses quickly. This would tend to lower the overall *RT* for responses following responses with the same hand when compared with those following the other hand.

The stimuli used in the above experiments were lights placed in a horizontal row. The question arises as to whether similar results would be expected when the stimuli were numbers presented in the same position. Some evidence that this may be so is reported in the work of Smith, Chase and Smith (1973). The numbers 1, 2, 3 and 4 were used as stimuli in an information-reduction paradigm. They found that *RT*s to 1 and 4 were faster than those to 2 and 3 for non-repetitions but that the difference was greatly reduced for stimulus repetitions. There was no difference for stimulus repetitions when a 100 msec *RSI* was used and only slight differences with *RSI*s of 500 and 1000 msecs. The same kind of effects were also revealed in the error rates.

These results were very similar to those of Kirby (1975, 1976a) and support a suggestion made by Welford (1971) that

> when symbols such as digits have to be related to a spatial response, there is some mediating process which translates from the symbolic to a spatial code, and it is in this transformed display that difficulties of discrimination occur.

The results of these experiments therefore support an explanation of the sequential effects in eight-choice tasks in terms of a strategy in which the subject uses certain reference points including a memory trace of the position of the last stimulus, in order to identify stimuli and their corresponding responses. In a compatible S–R task, faster identification of the stimulus also allows for a simpler S–R code which can facilitate identification of the correct response. In an incompatible task only repetitions can benefit from a simpler S–R code.

Thus, as for two-choice tasks, the evidence suggests that sequential effects are due to a combination of strategy and facilitation effects. The facilitation in both cases is perhaps most likely to be due to the use of simpler S–R codes. While the strategy in two-choice tasks tends to be one of expectancy and preparation prior to the arrival of the stimulus, the strategy in eight-choice tasks appears to be one of using certain reference points to locate the position of the stimulus in the display after its arrival.

If the use of reference points is to be termed a strategy, it should be under the control of the subject. To test this explanation in terms of a strategy plus a facilitation, Kirby (1974) asked subjects to prepare for either (1) a repetition of the last stimulus, (2) stimuli associated with the same hand (SH) as that involved in the last response, or (3) stimuli associated with the other hand (OH) as that involved in the last response. Two RSIs were used; 2000 msec and 1 msec. It was found for both RSIs and all stimulus positions that repetitions could be made significantly faster than all other responses, and SH responses could be made significantly faster than all OH responses. However, OH responses could be made significantly faster than all other responses, including repetitions, only in the 2000 msec condition. These results are similar to those found by Kirby (1976b) using a two-choice task and again suggest that sequential effects are partly but not wholly under the control of the subject. No attempt was made to see whether experienced subjects could, with practice and effort, make OH responses faster than other responses in the eight-choice task.

In the 2000 msec condition of the above experiment it was found that repetition responses were still slightly faster than non-repetition responses made with the same hand even though subjects had successfully directed their attention and preparation to OH responses. This suggests that the memory trace of the last stimulus still retains some of its effectiveness as a reference point even when attention has been directed away from it.

While the sequential analyses in these experiments were more detailed than is usual in eight-choice tasks, higher order effects were not examined. Nevertheless such effects have been reported for four-choice and eight-choice tasks (Remington, 1971; Hale, 1969; Peeke and Stone, 1972). The presence of these effects in two-choice tasks suggested both the operation of subjective expectancy and some automatic facilitation. In greater than two-choice tasks the examination of higher-order effects has been insufficiently detailed to draw any firm conclusions concerning the possible contributions of expectancy and preparation. It would seem reasonable to assume that they would also make at least some contribution, although not the major one, to sequential effects in these tasks.

Thus, generally the evidence suggests that the subject can and does use different strategies depending upon the type of task and the instructions being given. Basically, he is assumed to take a much more active role in the two-choice situation, preparing for particular stimuli prior to their occurrence. In the eight-choice situation, he is assumed to be more passive, most of the specific identification of the stimulus and preparation of the response occurring after the arrival of the stimulus.

Of course, the above conclusions apply only to situations using balanced stimulus sequences. Expectancy and preparation would occur to a much greater extent in tasks where there was an obvious bias towards a particular stimulus or stimuli or when the sequential probabilities were biased. This kind of expectancy would, of course, be reflected in faster RTs to the most probable events but it has also been found to be reflected in the proportions of different types of errors made in repetition and alternation trials (Kornblum, 1969). Preparation for alternation would direct attention away from the last stimulus and response and would also require retrieval of information concerning the previous stimulus sequence. These operations would be expected to override the memory trace of the last stimulus and hence reduce its effectiveness both as a reference point and as a means of bypassing central coding processes. Keele and Boies (1973) used a four-choice task and reported that

> when some event other than a repetition has a high probability, the RT to repetitions is little different than other low-probability events.

In fact their data do indicate some small but consistent advantage of repetitions over other low-probability events even under these conditions. Using a ten-choice task, Summers (1977) found a significant advantage of repetitions over other low probability events. Thus, it would appear that repetitions are likely to retain some advantage even when other sequences of events have high probabilities.

The effectiveness of the repetition as a reference point appears to be only slightly affected by additional processing associated with a simultaneous second task. Hale (1969) and Keele and Boies (1973) added a memory task to the RT task and found a greater increase in overall RT for alternations than for repetitions. This result suggests that the memory task interfered not with the memory trace of the last stimulus but with the processing of the stimulus being responded to. The greater effect on alternations is consistent with the assumption that the last stimulus as reference point allows a simpler S–R code and hence less processing for a repetition than for an alternation.

(F) THE LOCATION OF SEQUENTIAL EFFECTS: THE INFORMATION REDUCTION PARADIGM

Most explanations of sequential effects have assumed that these effects occur in one or more of the subprocesses of the information-processing system. A common aim of many investigations has been to determine the exact location of these effects. In information-processing terms, the basic question has been, is the automatic facilitation or strategy primarily concerned with stimulus processing or response processing or with central processing mediating between the stimulus and the response?

Unfortunately, this question has not been as easy to answer as it might seem. This is because the information-processing model has not always been partitioned into only the above three subprocesses.

The assumed number and nature of the subprocesses has varied depending upon (a) the particular theoretical question being investigated; (b) the particular RT paradigm being used; and (c) the results obtained. While distinctions between numerous subprocesses can easily be made at a conceptual or explanatory level, as Sanders (1970) points out,

> proper use of these hypothetical mechanisms is only guaranteed when they can be made operational in the sense that reaction tasks can be defined in which all mechanisms except one are involved.

One problem has been that RT paradigms have differed in the number of subprocesses into which they allow the RT to be divided. Thus, some paradigms force the experimenter to confine his explanation to a particular number of subprocesses; for example, only those of stimulus and response.

A further problem is that it is possible on a conceptual level to group various minor subprocesses into major ones. Unfortunately it is not always obvious to which group of major subprocesses a particular minor one should belong. For example, a repetition effect due to

> regenerating a decaying trace or organization or neural elements that correspond to the "elements" making up the physical event (Eichelman, 1970)

is obviously a peripheral stimulus process. Similarly, a repetition effect due not to

> the properties of decision processing, but the properties of a response system which has not come fully to rest between trials (Williams, 1966)

is obviously a peripheral response effect. Both these effects would be categorized as automatic facilitations since neither is likely to be under the control of the subject. Similarly, it is obvious that an increased repetition effect due to an increase in S–R incompatibility must involve central processes to some extent. But it is not so clear as to whether strategies involving stimulus selection or response organization should be classified as stimulus and response processes, respectively, or as central translation processes.

The most commonly used paradigm for determining the exact location of sequential effects within the information processing system is the information-reduction paradigm developed by Bertelson (1965). It was designed to separate the contribution of stimulus from response factors.

Equiprobable signals were mapped into two responses, two signals to each response. Such a task allows three categories of *RT*: the relationship of a stimulus and its response to the preceding stimulus and response can be one of "identity" (same signal, same response), of "equivalence" (different signal but same response), or of "difference" (different signal, different response). If only repetition of the signal is important then "identical" *RT*s should be faster than "equivalent" and there should be no difference between "equivalent" and "different" *RT*s. If, however, only repetition of the response is important, then "equivalent" *RT*s should equal "identical" and both should be faster than "different". An intermediate value for the "equivalent" *RT*s between those for "identical" and "different" would implicate repetition of both the signal and the response.

Thus, the paradigm allows a distinction only between stimulus and response subprocesses. It allows no distinction to be made between the more peripheral stimulus processes and more central encoding processes. Similarly, no distinction is made between more peripheral and more central response processes. Nor does the paradigm allow a distinction between central translation processes on the one hand and stimulus input and response output processes on the other.

The paradigm simply assumes that the extent of a stimulus repetition effect can be measured by subtracting the "identical" *RT* from the "equivalent", and that the extent of a response repetition effect can be measured by subtracting the "equivalent" *RT* from the "different". These two effects when added together give the total repetition effect. Bertelson found in his experiment that while "identical" *RT*s were slightly less than "equivalent", implying some effect due to repetition of the signal, the main difference in *RT* was between "different" and "equivalent", implying that the main effect was due to repetition of the response.

However, further studies have shown that the situation is more complex than this. For example, the relative position of "equivalent" *RT*s appears to depend upon such factors as the *number of trials* given. Rabbitt (1968) found a stimulus effect in the first 300 of 600 trials; "identical" *RT*s were faster than either "equivalent" or "different" *RT*s with little difference between the latter two. In the last 300 of 1500 trials, "equivalent" *RT*s were faster than "different" *RT*s, although not quite as fast as "identical". These results implied an initially strong stimulus effect which changed in the course of trials to a strong response effect.

The relative position of "equivalent" *RT*s also appears to depend upon the *response-stimulus* interval. Eichelman (1970) used *RSI*s of 200 and 700 msecs. At both *RSI*s "identical" *RT*s were faster than "equivalent" which were in turn faster than "different". However, while "identical" and "different" *RT*s decreased slightly with increasing *RSI*, "equivalent" *RT*s decreased much more. This implied that there was a decrease in stimulus effect and a corresponding increase in response effect with increasing *RSI*.

While these results implied that sequential effects could not be explained in terms of the facilitation of either stimulus or response processes alone, they were still consistent with the assumption that the contribution of stimulus and response effects could be measured by the difference between the appropriate *RT*s. This is because "equivalent" *RT*s were always found to lie between "identical" and "different" *RT*s. However, this assumption has been challenged by studies which have used *complex S–R relationships*. For example, Smith (1968) used a number-colour code; left key to be pressed for either a red "1" or a green "2", and right key to be pressed for either a green "1" or a red "2". Peeke and Stone (1972) used different colours and also different geometric forms as stimuli. In both these experiments "identical" responses were again found to be faster than "different" responses but "equivalent" responses were in fact found to be slower than "different" responses.

Further evidence against the assumptions underlying the information-reduction paradigm is provided by Ells and Gotts (1977). In their experiment numbers could appear on different displays. The subject had to move a toggle switch in the direction of the display if the number presented was one of a predetermined target set. This allowed separate estimates of "stimulus only" repetitions and "response only" repetitions. The sum of these two estimates was found to be substantially different from the savings due to the repetition of both the stimulus and the response.

Although some explanations for the results obtained with the information-reduction paradigm have included stimulus facilitation (e.g. Eichelman, 1970) or response facilitation (e.g. Rabbitt, 1968), the complexity of the results has strongly suggested that more complex central processes must also be involved. Thus, Eichelman additionally assumed the operation of a strategy which involved preparing to execute a response, while Rabbitt additionally assumed a stimulus classification strategy. Changes in the relative position of "equivalent" RTs were largely explained in terms of changes in strategy.

Unfortunately, these strategies may apply only to the information-reduction situation. The fact that "equivalent" RTs can be longer than "different" RTs strongly suggests that some factor or factors must be operating apart from those responsible for sequential effects in a one-to-one choice RT situation.

A number of such factors have been suggested. For example, Bertelson and Tisseyre (1966) point out that perceptual similarity may cause stimulus generalization so that

> the analysis of the stimuli could presumably be reduced to the time necessary for the detection of the common elements, and results suggestive of a response effect might be produced.

Thus, equal repetition and equivalent RTs could still be compatible with a stimulus based repetition effect. This criticism has been applied by Smith (1968) to the results of Bertelson (1965). Bertelson used the numerals "2" and "4" as stimuli for the left-hand response and "5" and "7" for the right. Thus it is possible that subjects would code the stimuli as "even number respond with left hand, odd number respond with right" and so produce an apparent response effect.

Other factors could also account for an apparent stimulus effect. Thus, Sanders (1970) has suggested that

> more dissimilar signals are likely to produce mutual associative inhibition or a negative transfer effect.

For example, if two signals are mapped onto a response with unequal probability, the signal with high probability will have its connection reinforced in the majority of responses, and the signal with low probability will suffer most from inhibition. Results in the direction of a perceptual bias would then be produced, e.g. Bertelson and Tisseyre (1966). Hence, rather than measuring differences in speed of identification or response, the paradigm may measure the degree of $S–R$ interference.

Similarly, Smith (1968) suggested that "equivalent" RTs might be slower than "different" RTs because of a slight reluctance on the part of the subject to make the same response to a new stimulus that he had just made to a different stimulus. Thus equal equivalent and different RTs could still be compatible with a response-based repetition effect.

One factor which may be of importance in both the one-to-one and the information-reduction situations is monitoring or checking of accuracy. Thus, Peeke and Stone (1972) suggested that because of possible confusion with "different" responses, there was an increased need to check the accuracy of "equivalent" responses prior to execution. This would also explain why "equivalent" *RT*s could be longer than "different", particularly with complex *S–R* codes. Their suggestion is supported by the results of a similar experiment by Smith *et al.* (1973). They found that "equivalent" *RT*s were slightly faster than "different", but that error rates were also much higher. This suggests that the difference between these two *RT*s could have been due to a speed-accuracy trade off.

In addition to explaining why "equivalent" *RT*s can sometimes be longer than "different", there are a number of other facts concerning "equivalent" *RT*s which a "monitoring" hypothesis might explain. First, the relatively larger decrease in "equivalent" *RT*s with practice (Rabbitt, 1968) could be due to less need to check these *RT*s as the *S–R* relationships becomes more firmly established.

Second, if it is assumed that "equivalent" responses are checked both before as well as after execution of the response, a shorter *RSI* would give less time for checking accuracy after the response. In order to maintain accuracy, more time would need to be spent checking accuracy before the response. This would explain the relatively larger increase in "equivalent" *RT*s as the *RSI* decreases (Eichelman, 1970).

Third, a "monitoring" hypothesis might help to explain some of the higher-order sequential effects reported by both Peeke and Stone (1972) and Smith *et al.* (1973). These second-order effects were also defined in terms of the stimulus being responded to. Both studies found that "different" responses were not affected by the preceding sequential combination, whether "repetition", "equivalent" or "different". First-order "equivalent" responses were reduced by a preceding "identical" response, but there was little difference between them when preceded by "equivalent" or "different" responses. This difference is unlikely to be due to a second-order response repetition effect since this should also apply when an "equivalent" response is preceded by an "equivalent" response. But when "equivalent" responses are preceded by "identical" responses, the same two stimuli involved in the first-order sequential effect are also involved in the second-order effects. Since both these stimuli share a common response, any possible confusion concerning the correctness of the response would have already been resolved by checking on the previous trial. This particular higher-order "equivalent" *RT* would be faster than the two other higher-order "equivalent" *RT*s since this possible confusion could not have been resolved for them and extra time would still be needed to check their accuracy. Unfortunately, the worth of this explanation cannot be evaluated with respect to identical *RT*s since there was a difference between the experiments in the second-order sequential effects for these responses.

It is clear that given the operation of one or more of the above factors, the results obtained with the information-reduction paradigm can be made consistent with either a stimulus or a response based repetition effect in the one-to-one situation. While the complexity of the results has led to some interesting hypotheses concerning the possible processes involved in this kind of *RT* task, the paradigm must be considered to have failed in its original purpose, which was to determine the location of repetition effects in the one-to-one situation.

The information-reduction paradigm has also been used in conjunction with guessing tasks in order to determine whether expectancy is primarily a stimulus or a response effect. In an experiment by Hinrichs and Kranz (1970), subjects had to predict which of three stimuli would occur when two stimuli were mapped onto one response and the remaining stimulus onto a second response. The results indicated that subjects' expectancy is primarily a set to perceive a particular stimulus rather than to execute a particular response. These results are consistent with those of Hawkins, Thomas and Drury (1970), Orenstein (1970), Hinrichs and Craft (1971b) and Hacker and Hinrichs (1974), who used similar *S–R* paradigms and concluded that generally perceptual bias occurs.

Whitman and Geller (1972) pointed out that the information-reduction paradigm does not allow correct prediction of the stimulus without antici-pation of the correct response. Using a two-stimulus-two-response task, they required subjects to predict both the stimulus and the rule relating the stimuli to their responses. Both the stimulus and the rule could change from trial to trial. This procedure allowed a situation in which the subject could incorrectly predict both the stimulus and the rule yet correctly anticipate the response. The fact that *RT* was longest under this condition was taken as further support for perceptual rather than response bias in guessing tasks. However, a different interpretation of this result seems possible. The natural tendency of the subject might well be to inhibit the response he has prepared as soon as he realizes that he has predicted the wrong stimulus. The response would then have to be reactivated after application of the correct rule had shown that the response anticipated was indeed the correct one. Thus, the *RT* for this particular combination of stimulus and rule prediction could take longer than all others yet still be compatible with response preparation.

Higher-order sequential analyses in two-choice tasks not requiring predic-tion have, as noted previously, suggested that expectancy plays a large part in determining sequential effects. Whether this expectancy is also primarily a set to perceive a stimulus rather than a response depends upon the extent to which the results of information-reduction and guessing tasks can be generalized to the one-to-one choice *RT* situation. The evidence reviewed suggests that it is doubtful whether such a generalization can be made.

Rabbitt and Vyas (1973) have attempted to provide a preliminary taxonomy of repetition effects. It includes six stages: perceptual identification, signal coding, signal-reponse mapping, response "retrieval" or "selection", response programming and response execution. For each subprocess except the last, they cite experiments whose results suggest the presence of repetition effects in that particular process. But much of the evidence which they consider is taken from experiments using the information-reduction paradigm, and we have already seen how results which appear to indicate evidence in favour of one subprocess can be equally well explained in terms of another. For example, in support of the perceptual identification and signal-coding stages, Rabbitt and Vyas cite Rabbitt's (1968) experiment mentioned earlier. But these results are compatible with a response based repetition effect, given some additional factor such as an increased need to check the accuracy of "equivalent" RTs.

Since the relative extent of stimulus and response effects change with practice and condition, they argue that it is unlikely that each of the possible processes contributing to sequential effects is independent of the others. They say:

> There is no "prima facie" reason to suppose that (a) these processes are all functionally successive in time, without delays, or (b) the complexity and duration of any one of these processes does not affect the duration of others.

An important implication of such interactive effects is that it may be wrong to make the usual assumption that a change in the task, such as in the display of information, the $S-R$ compatibility or the response requirements, primarily affects only the corresponding perceptual, central or response processes within the subject. For example, the effect of altering the compatibility between the stimulus and the response might also be to alter the extent to which the subject anticipates a particular stimulus or prepares a particular response. Similarly, a change in the response requirements of a task might also lead to changes in the way in which the subject decides to encode the stimulus.

While the evidence reviewed so far has failed to demonstrate the contribution to sequential effects of any of these subprocesses individually, Rabbitt and Vyas (1973) provide evidence that repetition effects can occur in the central processing stages without at the same time occurring in the peripheral perceptual identification and response execution stages. They used two different classes of signals (numbers and neon bulbs), and found that transitions within classes were faster than transitions between classes. Errors were also found to be largely due to within class confusion, that is "number" responses to the wrong number or "neon" responses to the wrong neons rather than between classes. In a second experiment the same result was obtained when the $S-R$ mapping for some stimuli was different from that for other stimuli. These results indicate that the repetition of central processes alone is sufficient to produce a facilitative repetitive effect. In a third experiment, subjects were found to respond faster when successive different nouns had to be generated from the same super-ordinate class than when successive nouns were generated from different classes. This experiment has the unique feature of having "identical" and "different" transitions between stimuli, but without repetition of any response. Thus the repetition effect in this experiment was independent of any response effect.

Marcel and Forrin (1974) have extended the above findings by demonstrating that the amounts of facilitation within a category of numbers depends upon the ordinal distance between the number being responded to and the preceding one in the sequence. The authors suggested that the repetition effect may therefore be

> a special case of a more general phenomenon: a gradient of facilitation based on the degree of association between the current stimulus and earlier events, resulting from a spread of excitation over locations in memory.

A category facilitation effect was still found even when subjects were given false information about the category of the next signal. This result suggests that this facilitation is automatic and not under the control of the subject.

Using a similar kind of paradigm Higgins and Gettys (1977) used a four stimulus, four response task where some of the stimuli shared common attributes. They found evidence for a partial repetition effect; that is, RT was faciliated if the stimulus responsed to shared some common attribute with the immediately previous stimulus. Facilitation increased with the number of common attributes. This result does seem to be evidence for a stimulus based repetition effect although it does not indicate whether the location of the effect is at the more peripheral or at the more central processing stage.

A study by Brewer (1978) has suggested that, at least in eight-choice tasks, relatively little of the overall repetition effect is due to peripheral stimulus or response processes. He found that the use of vibrotactile keys not only substantially reduced the overall mean RT when compared with a lights and keys condition, but also reduced a substantial repetition effect to a small one. If vibrotactile keys largely eliminate the time required for stimulus encoding, $S-R$ translation and response selection, presumably the substantial repetition effect found with lights and keys reflected these processes. The small remaining repetition effect in the vibrotactile condition would then indicate that repetition savings in peripheral stimulus input and response output processes are relatively small.

While Rabbitt and Vyas (1973) may well be correct in their view that repetition effects can occur in any or all of the subprocesses which they specify, the only firm conclusion that the evidence reviewed allows is that repetition effects are predominantly caused by central processes involved in choice rather than peripheral stimulus identification and response execution processes.

If sequential effects do largely reflect central processes involved in choice, the presence or absence of such effects in a RT task might then be used as an indicator of whether or not choice is involved. For example, Kirby, Nettelbeck and Tiggemann (1977) compared retarded and non-retarded subjects in a two-choice RT task in which subjects were required to move a particular finger from a home key to one of two keys each of which was associated with one of two lights. While time to lift the finger from the home key (decision time) was found to be longer than movement time for non-retarded subjects, the opposite was the case for retarded subjects. Although it could have been argued that the latter result was due to the retarded subjects making part of their choice duing movement, the fact that sequential effects were found in the "decision" times and not in the movement times for both groups of subjects, suggests that this was not so. It was therefore possible to conclude that the proportionately longer movement times for the retarded subjects were due to genuine difficulties in movement rather than in choice.

3. Overview

The investigation of sequential effects in choice RT began with the observation that in a choice RT task, a response that was the same as the preceding response was faster than a response that was different. Since that first investigation it has become clear that sequential effects are far more complex than was initially anticipated. Higher-order effects were discovered and these and first-order effects were found to be influenced by a large number of other factors such as the number of $S–R$ alternatives, the RSI, $S–R$ compatability, the probabilities of repetitions and alternations and the position of stimuli in the display. As new relationships between sequential effects and these factors were established, so the explanations for these effects became more complex.

The two basic types of explanation for sequential effects have been in terms of either an automatic facilitation or some kind of cognitive strategy. The evidence reviewed suggests that both explanations are correct. Moreover, it appears that the subject is not limited to one strategy. Instead, he is flexible and can change strategies depending upon the type of task or the instructions given, and these factors will thus determine the extent to which sequential effects depend upon facilitation or strategy.

The evidence suggests that an automatic facilitation due to some residual activity in the more peripheral stimulus or response subprocesses contributes relatively little to repetition effects. Sequential effects appear to be largely determined by the more central coding processes such as identification of the stimulus, the use of the S–R code and selection of the response. Attempts to determine the relative contribution of these different subprocesses have generally failed. Instead the results suggest that these and other subprocesses interact in complex ways.

One particular central process that does seem to play an important role in determining sequential effects is short-term memory. The subject in a choice RT task is required to respond both quickly and accurately. In order to maintain accuracy each trial must be monitored after its completion and this monitoring must be based on some memory of the stimulus, the S–R code used and the response made. These memory traces would presumably dissipate with time. While they remain available, they appear to be used in a number of ways which are reflected in sequential effects.

First, memory of the immediately previous stimulus-response pair enables the subject to select the correct response for a repetition of the previous stimulus by a simpler S–R code than that generally required for non-repetitions. The extent of the savings in coding time will depend upon both the complexity of the code required for non-repetition responses and the number of alternatives from which a correct response must be chosen. It is assumed that this saving in central processing time is automatic and not the result of some deliberate strategy on the part of the subject. Clearly, an efficient information processing system would be one which tends to simplify decision making processes wherever possible.

The memory traces of previous stimulus-response pairs also accumulate so as to provide the subject with a running memory of the preceding pattern of stimuli. On the basis of such a pattern the subject may anticipate and prepare for the next stimulus and its associated response. This is clearly an efficient strategy to adopt when the stimulus sequence is biased either sequentially or towards certain stimuli. But it appears that a subject may also anticipate and prepare for stimuli in a random sequence even though he may know that there is no objective way of predicting the next event. This kind of expectancy appears to influence sequential effects most in two-choice RT tasks when the RSI is relatively long. This is presumably because the sequential pattern of repetitions and alternations is most obvious in a two-choice sequence and because a certain amount of time is required in order to predict and prepare. Of course, if the RSI is too long, the relevant memory traces may dissipate or be overriden so that prediction is made more difficult. The subject is sensitive to patterns of both repetitions and alternations in these sequences but appears to expect slightly more alternations overall than repetitions. This strategy is clearly under the subject's control since, given a sufficiently long *RSI*, he can produce repetition or alternation effects to the same extent, at will. As the *RSI* shortens less time is available for preparation and an automatic facilitation is more likely to determine the overall sequential effect. Sequential effects at short *RSIs* are therefore less under the control of the subject although there is some evidence that the automatic facilitation can be overriden with practice and effort.

Where more than two stimulus response pairs are involved, expectancy will also operate when the sequence is biased sequentially or towards a certain stimulus or stimuli. However, when the sequence is random, expectancy is likely to decrease as the increasing number of possible alternative stimuli makes prediction more difficult. The subject is therefore more likely to carry out a strategy of responding after the arrival of the stimulus rather than before it. The evidence suggests that the strategy usually adopted in these tasks uses what may be termed "reference points" in the display. The position of the stimulus in relation to these points will determine the size of the sequential effect associated with it, even when the display is not spatial. If the stimulus is next to a reference point, for example, a midline or end of the display, it is reacted to relatively quickly. The memory trace of the last stimulus also appears to act as a reference point which facilitates reactions to repetitions of itself or to stimuli immediately adjacent to it. The latter "proximity" effect appears to be more dependent than the repetition effect upon the memory trace as it diminishes more rapidly as the *RSI* increases. Both the proximity effect and the influence of the position of the stimulus in the display upon repetition effects appear to be due not only to faster stimulus identification but also to an automatic facilitation based on bypassing some of the central translation required for the selection of other responses. However, whereas the central processing facilitation is likely to increase for repetitions as the *S–R* code becomes more complex, proximity effects and the effects of non-repetition reference points may decrease. This is because the simpler *S–R* code which they allow depends upon the spatial relationships between the stimulus and its reference point being the same as that for the response and its corresponding reference point.

As for two-choice tasks, the repetition effect in tasks with more than two-choices appears to be due to a combination of automatic facilitation and strategy effects.

Changes in sequential effects with practice suggest that the subject is capable of modifying his strategy as the tasks proceeds. Thus, Fletcher and Rabbitt (1978) found evidence which suggested that with increasing practice, subjects tended to respond less in terms of the stimulus display itself and more in terms of change or constancy between successive displays.

Changes in strategy may be carried out on the basis of either short-term or long-term sampling of the stimulus input. They may also result from more efficient coding of the stimulus input and better learning and more efficient use of the *S–R* code. Part of these changes may also be due to less need to monitor the accuracy of responses.

Another important implication of an explanation in terms of strategies is that the subject's performance will be determined not only by the nature of the task itself and the information the subject is given about it, but also by his own evaluation of it. For example, Rabbitt, Clancy and Vyas (1977) point out that there may be more than one *S–R* mapping rule that can be used in a *RT* task and subjects may differ in which rule they adopt. The subject must attempt to fulfil the demands of the task as efficiently as possible. Where these demands conflict to some extent, as when instructed to be fast but accurate, his strategy may be determined by (a) which demand is most emphasized in the instructions, (b) which demand *he* sees as being most important, or (c) which of the demands he is most able to fulfil at the time.

In his everyday activities, the subject is not given precise instructions as to what he must do with the information with which he is confronted. Circumstances may call upon him to make a number of quite unexpected decisions. He is, therefore, likely to store a large amount of information about the stimulus input. In laboratory tasks, he is called upon to use only a certain amount of it. But the experimental evidence (for example, Rabbitt and Vyas, 1974; Felfoldy, 1974) indicates that much more is stored than would be required to perform the task efficiently. In fact some of the information stored may conflict with the demands of the task so that the subject performs less efficiently than he might otherwise do. Clearly, this is because, given the varying demands of his everyday activities, he must ordinarily store information that *might* be useful as well as that which he knows will be useful. In order to carry this information in an efficient way, it must be coded in some form. Thus not only is it likely that information irrelevant to the task in hand is stored but that additional decisions are also made about coding that information in a particular way.

Thus, as Rabbitt and Vyas (1973, 1974) argue, there appears to be a number of component processes intervening between the onset of a signal and the subjects' reponse to it and these processes may interact with others in complex ways which either facilitate or inhibit the efficient carrying out of the task.

The complexity of the results obtained in the study of sequential effects would appear to have a number of implications for the use of *RT* in the study of human behaviour.

First, *RT* can no longer be considered as a measure of basic information processing which is independent of the subject's general expectations. The instructions to the subject may therefore be of considerable importance in explaining results and since different subjects may use different strategies even with identical instructions, their comments on how they perceived the task may also be very important.

Second, much more consideration needs to be given to the design of RT paradigms which attempt to examine particular parts of the information processing system. Care must be taken to ensure that such paradigms do not confound the effects of a particular component process with the effects of additional processes specific to the paradigm.

Third, models based upon simple additive assumptions are likely to be of only limited explanatory value since the evidence suggests that subprocesses may combine in quite different ways after considerable practice or when the experimental situation changes. Since the effects of practice on RT measures can be quite revealing in this regard, more emphasis should therefore be given to examining changes in RT with practice.

Fourth, since sequential effects seem to reflect central choice processing, the presence or absence of such effects may provide a useful indicator of the presence or absence of choice processing in particular RT tasks.

Finally, since sequential effects are likely to occur to some extent in almost all RT tasks involving choice, it is clear that explanations can no longer be confined to a hypothetical average trial. An adequate explanation will also have to include some consideration of both the subject's experience and behaviour on previous trials and his expectations concerning future trials.

It should perhaps be pointed out that Neisser (1976) has reached similar conclusions in a more general discussion of the use of the information processing model in the study of cognition.

References

Bertelson, P. (1961). Sequential redundancy and speed in a serial two-choice responding task. *Quarterly Journal of Psychology* **13**, 90–102.

Bertelson, P. (1963). S–R relationships and reaction times to a new versus repeated signals in a serial task. *Journal of Experimental Psychology* **65**, 478–484.

Bertelson, P. (1965). Serial choice reaction-time as a function of Response versus Signal-and-Response Repetition. *Nature* **206**, 217–218.

Bertelson, P. and Renkin, A. (1966). Reaction times to new versus repeated signals in a serial task as a function of response-signal time interval. *Acta Psychologica* **25** (2), 132–136.

Bertelson, P. and Tisseyre, F. (1966). Choice reaction time as a function of stimulus versus response relative frequency of occurrence. *Nature* **212** (5066), 1069–1070.

Brewer, N. (1978). Motor components in the choice reaction time of mildly retarded adults. *American Journal of Mental Deficiency* **82** (6), 565–572.

De Klerk, L. F. W. and Eerland, E. (1973). The relation between prediction outcome and choice reaction speed: comments on the study of Geller *et al.* (1973). *Acta Psychologica* **37**, 301–306.

Eichelman, W. H. (1970). Stimulus and response repetition effects for naming letters at two response-stimulus intervals. *Perception and Psychophysics* **7** (2), 94–96.

Ells, J. G. and Gotts, G. H. (1977). Serial reaction time as a function of the nature of repeated events. *Journal of Experimental Psychology, Human Perception and Performance* **3**, 234–262.

Entus, A. and Bindra, D. (1970). Common features of the "repetition" and "same-different" effects in reaction time experiments. *Perception and Psychophysics* **7**, 143–148.

Felfoldy, G. L. (1974). Repetition effects in choice reaction time to multidimensional stimuli. *Perception and Psychophysics* **15** (3), 453–459.

Fletcher, B. L. C. and Rabbitt, P. M. A. (1978). The changing pattern of perceptual analytic strategies and response selection with practice in a two-choice reaction time task. *Quarterly Journal of Experimental Psychology* **30**, 417–427.

Geller, E. S. (1975). Prediction outcome and choice reaction time: inhibition versus facilitation effects. *Acta Psychologica* **39**, 69–82.

Geller, E. S. and Pitz, G. F. (1970). Effects of prediction, probability and run length on choice reaction speed. *Journal of Experimental Psychology* **84** (2), 361–367.

Geller, E. S., Whitman, C. P., Wrenn, R. F. and Shipley, W. G. (1971). Expectancy and discrete reaction time in a probability reversal design. *Journal of Experimental Psychology* **90** (1) 113–119.

Hacker, M. J. and Hinrichs, J. V. (1974). Multiple predictions in choice reaction time: a serial memory scanning interpretation. *Journal of Experimental Psychology* **103** (5), 999–1005.

Hale, D. J. (1967). Sequential effects in a two choice serial reaction task. *Quarterly Journal of Experimental Psychology* **19**, 133–141.

Hale, D. J. (1969). Repetition and probability effects in a serial choice reaction task. *Acta Psychologica* **29** (2), 163–171.

Hannes, M. (1968). The effect of stimulus repetitions and alternations on one-finger and two-finger responding in two-choice reaction time. *Journal of Psychology* **69** (2), 161–164.

Hawkins, H. L., Thomas, G. B. and Drury, K. B. (1970). Perceptual versus response bias in discrete choice reaction time. *Journal of Experimental Psychology* **84** (3), 514–517.

Higgins, D. L. and Gettys, C. F. (1977). A partial repetition effect in choice reaction time for multi-dimensional stimuli. *Perception and Psychophysics* **21** (4), 298–306.

Hinrichs, J. V. and Craft, J. L. (1971a). Verbal expectancy and probability in two-choice reaction time. *Journal of Experimental Psychology* **88** (3), 367–371.

Hinrichs, J. V. and Craft, J. L. (1971b). Stimulus and response factors in discrete choice reaction time. *Journal of Experimental Psychology* **91** (2), 305–309.

Hinrichs, J. V. and Kranz, Patricia, L. (1970). Expectancy in choice reaction time: Anticipation of stimulus or response? *Journal of Experimental Psychology* **85** (3), 330–334.

Hoyle, R. H. and Gholson, B. (1968). Choice reaction times with equally and unequally probable alternatives. *Journal of Experimental Psychology* **78** (1), 95–98.

Hyman, R. (1953). Stimulus information as a determinant of reaction time. *Journal of Experimental Psychology* **45**, 188–196.

Jarvik, M. E. (1951). Probability learning and a negative recency effect in the serial anticipation of alternative symbols. *Journal of Experimental Psychology* **41**, 291–297.

Keele, S. W. (1969). Repetition effect: a memory-dependent process. *Journal of Experimental Psychology* **80** (1), 243–248.

Keele, S. W. and Boies, S. J. (1973). Processing demands of sequential information. *Memory and Cognition* **1**, 85–90.

Kirby, N. H. (1972). Sequential effects in serial reaction time. *Journal of Experimental Psychology* **96** (1), 32–36.

Kirby, N. H. (1974). Sequential effects in serial reaction time. Unpublished doctoral thesis, University of Adelaide.

Kirby, N. H. (1975). Sequential effects in an eight choice serial reaction time task. *Acta Psychologica* **39**, 205–216.

Kirby, N. H. (1976a). Sequential effects in an eight-choice serial reaction time task using compatible and incompatible stimulus-response arrangements. *Acta Psychologica* **40**, 207–216.

Kirby, N. H. (1976b). Sequential effects in two-choice reaction time: automatic facilitation or subjective expectancy? *Journal of Experimental Psychology: Human Perception and Performance* **2** (4), 567–577.

Kirby, N. H., Nettelbeck, T. and Tiggemann, M. (1977). Reaction time in retarded and nonretarded young adults: sequential effects and response organization. *American Journal of Mental Deficiency* **81** (5)5, 492–498.

Kornblum, S. (1967). Choice reaction time for repetitions and nonrepetitions: a re-examination of the information hypothesis. *Acta Psychologica* **27**, 178–187.

Kornblum, S. (1968). Serial-choice reaction time: Inadequacies of the information hypothesis. *Science* **159** (3813), 432–434.

Kornblum, S. (1969). Sequential determinants of information processing in serial and discrete choice reaction time. *Psychological Review* **76** (2), 113–131.

Kornblum, S. (1973). Sequential effects in choice reaction time. A tutorial review. *In* "Attention and Performance IV" (S. Kornblum, ed.), pp. 259–288. Academic Press, New York.

Laming, D. R. (1969). Subjective probability in choice reaction experiments. *Journal of Mathematical Psychology* **6** (1), 81–120.

Leonard, J. S., Newman, R. C. and Carpenter, A. (1966). On the handling of heavy bias in self paced tasks. *Quarterly Journal of Experimental Psychology* **18**, 130–141.

Marcel, T. and Forrin, B. (1974). Naming latency and the repetition of stimulus categories. *Journal of Experimental Psychology* **103** (3), 450–460.

Moss, S. M., Engel, S. and Faberman, D. (1967). Alternation and repetition reaction times under three schedules of event sequencing. *Psychonomic Science* **9** (10), 557–558.

Neisser, U. (1976). "Cognition and Reality". W. H. Freeman, San Francisco.

Orenstein, H. B. (1970). Reaction time as a function of perceptual bias, response bias and stimulus discriminability. *Journal of Experimental Psychology* **86** (1), 38–42.

Peeke, S. C. and Stone, G. C. (1972). Sequential effects in two- and four-choice tasks. *Journal of Experimental Psychology* **92** (1), 111–116.

Rabbitt, P. M. A. (1965). Response facilitation on repetition of a limb movement. *British Journal of Psychology* **56**, 303–304.

Rabbitt, P. M. A. (1968). Repetition effects and signal classification strategies in serial choice-response tasks. *Quarterly Journal of Experimental Psychology* **20**, 232–239.

Rabbitt, P. M. A. and Vyas, S. (1973). What is repeated in the "repetition effect"? *In* "Attention and Performance IV" (S. Kornblum), ed.). Academic Press, New York.

Rabbitt, P. M. A.and Vyas, S. M. (1974). Interference between binary classification judgements and some repetition effects in a serial choice reaction time task. *Journal of Experimental Psychology* **103** (6), 1181–1190.

Rabbitt, P. M. A., Clancy, M. and Vyas, S. M. (1977). After-effects of responding and of withholding responses in C.R.T. tasks. *Quarterly Journal of Experimental Psychology* **29**, 425–436.

Rabinowitz, M. F. (1970). Characteristic sequential dependencies in multiple-choice situations. *Psychological Bulletin* **74** (2), 141–148.

Remington, R. J. (1969). Analysis of sequential effects in choice reaction times. *Journal of Experimental Psychology* **82**, 250–257.

Remington, R. J. (1970). The repetition effect: A methodological consideration. *Psychonomic Science* **20**, 221–222.

Remington, R. J. (1971). Analysis of sequential effects for a four-choice reaction time experiment. *Journal of Psychology* **77** (1), 17–27.

Remingtion, R. J. (1973). Sequential effects analysis of choice reaction error data. *Perceptual and Motor Skills* **36**, 1211–1216.

Sanders, A. F. (1970). Some variables affecting the relation between relative stimulus frequency and choice reaction time. *Acta Psychologica* **33**, 45–55.

Schvaneveldt, R. W. and Chase, W. G. (1969). Sequential effects in choice reaction time. *Journal of Experimental Psychology* **80** (1), 1–8.

Shaffer, L. H. (1965). Choice reaction with variable *S–R* mapping. *Journal of Experimental Psychology* **70**, 284–288.

Smith, M. C. (1968). The repetition effect and short term memory. *Journal of Experimental Psychology* **77**, 435–439.

Smith, E. E., Chase, W. G. and Smith, P. G. (1973). Stimulus and response repetition effects in retrieval from short-term memory: trace decay and memory search. *Journal of Experimental Psychology* **98** (2), 413–422.

Summers, J. J. (1977). Adjustments to redundancy in reaction time: A comparison of three learning methods. *Acta Psychologica* **41**, 205–223.

Umilta, C., Simion, F. and Hyman, R. (1976). The repetition effect for verbal and non-verbal stimuli in the two visual fields. *Italian Journal of Psychology* **3** (2), 305–316.

Welford, A. T. (1960). The measurement of sensory-motor performance: survey and reappraisal of twelve years' progress. *Ergonomics* **61** (3–4), pp. 189–230.

Welford, A. T. (1968). "Fundamental of Skill". Methuen, London.

Welford, A. T. (1971). What is the basis of choice reaction-time? *Ergonomics* **14** (6), 679–693.

Welford, A. T. (1975). Serial reaction times, continuity of task, single-channel effects and age. "Attention and Performance VI", pp. 79–97. Academic Press, New York.

Whitman, C. P. and Geller, E. S. (1971a). Runs of correct and incorrect predictions as determinants of choice reaction time. *Psychonomic Science* **23**, 421–423.

Whitman, C. P. and Geller, E. S. (1971b). Prediction outcome, *S–R* compatibility and choice reaction time. *Journal of Experimental Psychology* **91** (2), 299–304.

Whitman, C. P. and Geller, E. S. (1972). Stimulus anticipation in choice reaction time with variable *S–R* mapping. *Journal of Experimental Psychology* **93** (2), 433–434.

Williams, J. A. (1966). Sequential effects in disjunctive reaction time: Implications for decision models. *Journal of Experimental Psychology* **71**, 665–672.

Chapter 5

Models of Choice Reaction Time

G. A. SMITH

1. Introduction

Before reviewing relevant models of choice reaction processing, it is useful to consider the general problem of modelling. By modelling is meant a set of specifications more or less closely tied to some theory, which describes the measured variable, RT in this case, under specified conditions. Any accompanying theory must be explanatory and a valid representation or analogue of the behaviour being modelled. A complete model will match experimental data in every testable respect, but this is seldom attempted. Ultimately it may be possible to develop a model which emulates the full complexities of choice reaction behaviour, but certainly no current model does this. The path to a complete model must be via successive approximations, for which one must decide which aspects are of primary interest, and concentrate on them. In this way we try to add to our understanding by simplifying the model to an acceptable level. As Edwards (1965) pessimistically noted concerning a model which he developed

> No model that makes many specific and easily checkable predictions has any possibility of being consistent with substantial amounts of data: only vague models or models with plenty of fittable parameters survive such confrontations.

Models must therefore be developed for a set purpose and a limited domain of interest selected after assessing the costs and payoffs of comprehensive accuracy versus comprehensible but restricted application. This means that direct comparisons of models must be approached with caution as each tackles a slightly different area of RT knowledge. The usual method involves classifying models on a few broad dimensions and is arguably the fairest. For example, Audley and Pike (1965) separated three groups of models which they classified as statistical uncertainty models, Markov chain

173

models, and stimulus sampling to criterion models, choosing the latter as the best approach for modelling *RT*, while Welford (1976) used the dichotomy, serial versus simultaneous processing.

All choice *RT* models follow broadly similar lines: the subject starts a trial without knowledge of the particular stimulus (although possibly with expectations) and either repeatedly takes evidence about the stimulus or its preprocessed internal representation, or analyzes deeper the evidence gained to date, until one possibility is adequately supported, on the basis of the current sample or accumulated evidence from discrete or continuous samples. Models can be differentiated along two separate aspects: how the fate of each alternative changes during a trial and the time course of these changes. Each model favours a different "criterion dimension", by which is meant broadly the transformation of the stimulus input on which the alternatives are assessed. For example, in one model this involves a complete matching of the received stimulus with internal representations of the alternatives, while another assesses the probability that the received input comes from each possibility. Models also vary as to the "criterion state" used, i.e. the grounds for deciding that one alternative is the best choice on the current trial. This will be explained in context for each model. This is not to say that such representation would be viewed by each model's originator as in the spirit of his model, but is superimposed by this reviewer to facilitate direct comparisons of the models.

Two broad classes of models can be distinguished on the basis of the style of criterion state they employ. Some models completely reject alternatives during the trial before the final choice is made, and others keep assessing each possibility relative to the rest until one is sufficiently justified to be accepted. These can be called *complete criterion* models and *relative criterion* models. In the first of these, the processing of the alternatives is complete in that they are all assessed to the level of rejection apart from the one which is chosen. The decision in these models is simple, merely choosing the only non-rejected option. In relative criterion models on the other hand, none of the alternatives is discarded prior to the decision point. In general, these models assess the evidence in favour of each alternative until one is deemed adequate in its own right or superior to the rest. The two types will become clearer with the presentation of actual examples as below.

The major areas of interest here are the relationship between mean *RT* and p, the probabilities of the alternatives, i, $i = 1, 2, \ldots, N$, given by

$$RT = A + B \cdot \sum_{i=1}^{N} (-p_i \log p_i) \tag{5.0}$$

which reduces to a log increase in *RT* with N for equiprobable stimuli:

$$RT = A + B \cdot \log(N + D) \qquad 0 \leqslant D \leqslant 1 \tag{5.1}$$

and the range of values of B (or its reciprocal, C, which is a measure of the task's stimulus-response compatibility) obtained from various tasks. Models which do not cover these points will not be detailed here, although the recent model of Grice, Nullmeyer and Spiker (1977) deserves a mention as a good attempt to describe the distribution of RT rather than just its mean—without, however, considering its increase with N. Other models are put forward only in terms of $N = 2$, without specifying how they apply for larger N. These also will not be considered.

2. Complete criterion models

(A) SUCCESSIVE GROUP ELIMINATION MODELS

Hick (1952a) designed one of the simplest models of the choice process. He suggested that the subject makes a chain of subdecisions or steps each of equal duration, which Welford (1971) called an "inspection time". One subdecision locates the stimulus as being in half of the remaining possibilities, and rejects the others. This process is repeated until only one alternative is left whereupon the corresponding response is selected and made. Under this successive dichotomization, the number of steps equals $\log_2 N$, at least where N is a power of 2. For example if the subject has eight alternatives, at the start of the trial any one of the eight may be correct. During the first inspection time, four of these are rejected and the other four are left. Two of these are discarded in the second inspection time. The third and final step chooses between the remaining two, rejecting one and leaving the selected alternatives. The criterion dimension is matching between the stimulus and internal representations, or templates, of the possible stimuli, and each possibility is processed, i.e. to rejection or acceptance completely.

Since Hick found that $\log(N + 1)$ gave a better fit than $\log(N)$, he suggested that the effective number of alternatives was one more than the number of stimuli. He felt that this additional one represented the fact that subjects had to decide not only which of N stimuli had occurred but whether any stimulus had occurred, and hence had to decide between the N stimulus states and one non-stimulus state. If N is not a power of 2, the processor is faced with an odd number of possibilities in at least one stage. When this happens an unequal division is made, and one of the subgroups is rejected. The model suggests that there should be evidence of a periodicity in the RTs corresponding to the inspection time. Such lumpiness was not apparent in the RT distributions Hick examined. More recently, Stone (1976) reviewed the evidence for periodicity in RT distributions, and concluded that it has not been found. Nor can the model predict observed differences in RTs to stimuli of unequal probabilities, with the more probable stimuli being reacted to faster. To overcome this, Welford (1960) extended the model so that cognitive strategies can be adopted which influence RT. Like Hick, he envisaged a series of steps, each searching for the stimulus in half the remaining alternatives, but he proposed that the subject must test a matching half set before proceeding to the next step. Thus for $N = 4$, the subject compares the given stimulus with two of the alternatives. If the stimulus is in that half set, he proceeds immediately with the next dichotomization; if not, he checks the other two and gets a match there before moving to the next step. Each halving subdivision takes either one or two inspection times. If the stimuli are equiprobable and random, each step will take 1.5 inspections on average. However, if one stimulus or group of stimuli are more frequent, the subject can check the half containing them first and the other group second. This means that the more probable stimuli are located faster than the less probable ones, which tallies with the result found. Welford (1973) has produced a measure of "inspection time", and has used it subsequently (Welford, 1975 and Chapter 3 in this volume) to provide evidence in favour of the model by finding search strategies which give the measured RTs for assorted stimulus arrays. However, neither model can describe tasks in which RT is unaffected by N as has been found with letter-naming tasks and highly compatible vibrotactile (VT) stimuli.

(B) SUCCESSIVE INDIVIDUAL ELIMINATION

Luce (1960, 1963) produced a model of choice RT based on the choice axiom. This axiom can be summarized as follows: If pair-wise discrimination between a set of alternative responses is imperfect, then the probabilities of choice from a subset, R, are in the same ratio to each other as they are in the entire response set, and if one response is never preferred to another, then it will never be made and may be excluded. Additional to this axiom, Luce postulated that a subject successively rejects possible *responses* one at a time until only one is left. The RT is the sum of the constituent rejection times. This can be developed mathematically to show that if the individual rejection times follow a Gamma distribution, then

$$RT = A + B . \sum_j (-q_j \log q_j) \tag{5.2}$$

where q_j is the probability of the subject making response j. With negligible error rates, and stimulus i associated with response j, q_j will equal p_i and this equation reduces to the more usual form as in eqn (5.0). With all q_js equal it reduces to (5.1) as required.

This model has been criticized for its concentration on response effects to the exclusion of stimulus effects such as the more similar the stimulus set, the longer the RT, even with the same responses. Laming (1968) found experimentally that RT was not a linear function of $q_j . \log(q_j)$ and has more recently argued cogently that

> the choice axiom fails when there is a natural organization of the stimuli sufficiently salient to influence the choices made (Laming, 1977a,b).

Nor does the model account for the range of Bs obtainable with the same responses and stimuli, but with different S–R associates (e.g. Brainard, Irby, Fitts and Alluisi, 1962). It is, however, a useful attempt to tie choice RT in with other choice behaviour.

(c) CONTEMPORANEOUS COMPLETE IDENTIFICATION

An alternative to the successive elimination of groups or individual possibilities, but still using a complete criterion, occurs in a model by Rapoport (1959). It stems from one of the suggestions made earlier by Christie and Luce (1956). They suggested that choice between N alternatives could be described generally as involving N elementary decisions, taking place either serially or in parallel and they pointed out that either type of process could be specified by a directed graph, or Markov chain. Luce (1960) developed the strict serial alternative as detailed above while Rapoport (1959) favoured a strict parallel approach.

Rapoport assumed that choice RT consisted of processing all N possibilities completely (i.e. to a "yes" or a "no") and exhaustively (i.e. the response was made only after all N elementary processes had finished). Each elementary process is independent of the others, in that its duration is unaffected by the number of others present or whether they have finished, even if a completed one resulted in a "yes". The RT is thus the maximum of the N independent elementary process durations. If each such duration is drawn from an exponential distribution, which Rapoport suggested is well-founded neurologically, the mean RT varies with the logarithm of N.

Rapoport was one of the first to mention explicitly that the processing time in his model involves both stimulus recognition and response selection, and is influenced by factors which affect either component.

Laming (1966) described a very similar model in slightly different mathematical style. He developed his argument via the discrete approximation to the logarithmic function,

$$\log(M) \simeq \sum_{i=1}^{M} \frac{1}{r}$$

where M is a positive integer, which suggests that (5.1) can be rewritten as

$$RT = A + B \sum_{r=1}^{N} \frac{1}{r} \tag{5.3}$$

Using Hick's formulation that RT is proportional to $\log(N + 1)$ rather than the hybrid Hick-Hyman form of (5.1), this can be converted to

$$RT = A + B \sum_{r=1}^{N} \frac{1}{r + 1}. \tag{5.4}$$

Laming then generalized these two equations into

$$RT = A + B \sum_{r=1}^{N} \frac{1}{r + k}. \tag{5.5}$$

Obviously eqn (5.5) will give as good a fit to experimental data as the better of (5.3) and (5.4) for some value of k between 0 and 1, but Laming treated the more general case of $k \geq -1$. He developed the mathematical formula for a family of elementary process time distributions for which the maximum (i.e. the last of N parallel processes to finish) satisfies (5.5). If $k = 0$, the distribution is exponential as in Rapoport's version. Mathematical treatment for other values of k has been explored by Laming (1966) who also fitted RT variances predicted by the model to experimental data. Since the treatment is complex and the general principles are covered in the outline above, it will not be reproduced here. One point of interest in this model is the generalization parameter, k. Laming noted that it would probably be possible to produce a better fit to experimental data than either Hick's or Hyman's formulae give by selecting a suitable value for k in eqn (5.5). This point will be returned to later in the description of the new model proposed here.

3. Relative criterion models

These models embody the idea of processing on each trial as the sampling over time of evidence for the stimuli, forming tentative identities from each sample and assessing the accumulated evidence until one alternative gains sufficient support relative to the others. The terms "evidence" and "tentative identification" (*TI*) refer to different aspects of the decision process. *Evidence* is a loose concept referring to the value of the current imperfect internal representation of the stimulus and is a continuous variable, being either a direct neural representation of the stimulus or some simple transform of it. In contrast, a *TI* is formed in some models and is the best guess for the stimulus' identity based on the current sample of evidence. Effectively a *TI* labels the sample as being from one of the alternatives and thus takes only discrete values. Since the evidence is imperfect, a *TI* may not be correct. The criterion for decision is not absolute identity or binary information (yes/no) as it is for complete criterion models, but a value on a particular scale. All involve the collected evidence for each stimulus changing with time until the model's criterion is reached. Mathematically these can be represented or approximated by Markov chains, i.e. sequences of possible states which can be specified by the amount of evidence for all alternatives in the set, with absorption states, i.e. those at which a final decision is made, being defined by the response criterion. The major difference between the various models of this type is in the particular response criterion adopted.

(A) CRITERION: REPETITION OF *TI*

In these models, the first alternative which the processor produces as the *TI* in K successive samples is taken as correct. Audley (1960) and Kintsch (1963) have put forward models based on this criterion. Audley developed a general form for a range of K and produced the generating functions for $K > 2$ (Audley and Pike, 1965), while Kintsch restricted himself to treating $K = 2$, with the duration of each step to *TI* being distributed exponentially. Audley showed that this model predicts that error responses will be longer on average than correct responses, which is usually not so in choice reaction data.

The processing in the model may be described as follows. All alternatives have an initial count or score of zero. Successive *TI*s of the alternative given are produced and the corresponding score is incremented by 1. If it was zero, then the former *TI*s score is set to zero. Processing continues until a score accumulates to K, when the response is made. This only happens when K successive *TI*s are identical. The processor acts like a faulty memory, forgetting all previous evidence when the *TI* changes between samples.

(B) CRITERION: ONE ALTERNATIVE MORE LIKELY THAN CHANCE

One early model of this form was sketched briefly by Hick (1952b). In that model, all possibilities are imagined as comprising a range of sensory input divided into N states of equal probability, representing the *a priori* probability of any one state. If the probability of a state vanishing is fixed at τ/K for any instant at τ, the probability of a state lasting as long as τ msec is $e^{-\tau/K}$. When the input has stayed in one state for τ msec such that its probability of lasting that long, $e^{-\tau/K}$, becomes just less than the *a priori* probability, $1/N$, that state is chosen to initiate the response since the input was in that state for longer than would be expected from the *a priori* probability. The decision in this model is analogous to a statistical decision to reject a null hypothesis. Hick did not expand this outline, but others have since used the idea of a continuing statistical test as the decision mechanism.

(C) CRITERION: MOST EVIDENCE FROM A PRESET SAMPLE SIZE

Stone (1960) presented a model which draws an analogy between choice *RT* processing and a fixed sample size statistical decision. He assumed that the decision mechanism keeps a running total of successive samples of some transform of the data from each possible stimulus. With the criterion set for Q samples, then the duration of the decision process is Q times the time between samples, which is assumed to be constant for simplicity. The decision procedure is based on N running totals or accumulators such that the stimulus corresponding to the largest total at the criterion time is chosen.

Stone assumed that this decision is made after Q samples, where Q is set prior to the trial to the value which maximizes the subject's overall chance of success, as measured by the sequential probability ratio. Unfortunately this model has a major theoretical flaw. As the sample size is set prior to the start of the trial, the particular stimulus given can have no effect on the *RT* of that trial, which is not the case. For example, the probability of the given stimulus significantly influences its *RT*, as mentioned earlier.

Edwards (1965) replaced this fixed sample size feature with an assumption that the subject decides after each sample whether or not to take another. He adopted a Bayesian approach, taking explicit account of the costs and payoffs in the decision to stop or continue sampling. If the cost in terms of time (or other experimental penalties) is greater than the payoff for additional accuracy, the subject will stop and make the currently most favoured response. This approach is attractive, but the difficulties in assessing what are the costs and payoffs inherent in a typical *RT* task detract considerably from its usefulness.

(D) CRITERION: A PRESET NUMBER OF *TI*S

Another model is that of La Berge (1962). Rather than accumulating evidence from each sample, a *TI* is produced based on that sample, and this is tallied against the corresponding response. The criterion decision is that the first tally to reach a criterion total initiates its response and the sampling stops. This decision process is equivalent to a series of independent multinomial trials which continue until one outcome has occurred a preset number of times. From this model La Berge developed the relationship between RT and response probabilities for $N = 2$ into incomplete beta ratios. Laming (1968, p. 24) produced a further prediction from this model, namely that error latencies are longer than correct latencies, on which he found contrary evidence. However, reanalysis arising from a plausible simple suggestion can circumvent this apparent flaw and will be discussed in Section 6.

(E) CRITERION: SUFFICIENTLY MORE EVIDENCE FOR ONE ALTERNATIVE

The random walk model extensively developed by Laming (1968) from the sequential probability ratio test approach of Stone (1960) is best understood in the case for $N = 2$. The principles are the same for $N > 2$ and have been detailed by Laming (1968) but will only be given briefly here. On each trial, the subject takes a stream of evidence from the stimulus. This evidence is not veridical, and takes a continuous range of values distributed about the true identity along a hypothetical underlying dimension. The evidence in favour of each alternative is added to its current total and the first to get adequately more evidence than its opponents determines the response made.

For $N = 2$, two scores are initially zero. Each sample of the stimulus gathered in successive small time slices are converted to corresponding amounts of evidence in favour of S_1 and S_2, the two possible stimuli. These amounts are added to their corresponding scores. When a score exceeds the other by a predetermined amount, that response is initiated. The increment from each sample for S_1 is the logarithm of the probability that such a sample could occur given that S_1 is presented. Actually, Laming presented his model in terms of one score for $N = 2$, with each sample adding or subtracting an amount equal to the difference between the amounts added to S_1's and S_2's scores in this description. These approaches are conceptually equivalent, and the one presented here extends more readily to $N > 2$, as follows.

In general, N scores are kept, each incrementing from the samples by an amount specified as for $N = 2$, i.e. the logarithm of the probability that the sample came from a trial on which its stimulus was presented. A more rigorous description in more complex probability terms is given in Laming (1968).

Laming explored this model and found that it could explain a range of experimental results including the relationship between RT and p_is expressed in eqn (5.0). This has been developed into quite a comprehensive model, although it skirts the issue of $S-R$ compatibility which is of prime concern in this research.

4. Fast and slow distribution models

Falmagne (1965) and Kornblum (1969) have proposed theories of RT in which the RT on any trial is drawn from one of two distributions of times, one fast and one slow. The more general model is that of Falmagne. The subject is seen as learning to expect certain stimuli on each trial. Based on his expectancy he differentially prepares for the stimuli. If the stimulus presented is one for which he prepared, the RT is drawn from the distribution of fast times and, if not, from the slow distribution. The expectancy is set in part by the subjective assessed probabilities of the stimuli based on their recent relative frequencies.

Falmagne showed that this can account for speed-accuracy tradeoffs (RT decreases as error rate increases), the relationship between RT and $\log N$ (eqn 5.1), unequal stimulus frequencies ($RT_i < RT_j$ if $p_i > p_j$) and repetition effects (i.e. when repeated stimuli are responded to faster than alternations, see Chapter 4). In fact the model is derived in part from a study by Bertelson (1963) in which he demonstrated the repetition effect and found that S–R compatibility had more effect on alternations than on repetitions. This is a quite impressive list of successful matchings between theory and data, but leaves unexplained the source of the processing time difference beyond appealing to the idea of preparation. That is, the actual mechanics of identification as the expected stimulus or a particular other is not specified.

Kornblum (1969) used a similar framework for his model, replacing the concept of preparation with the specific effect of repetitions and gave a fuller description of the origin of the RT difference. The subject checks whether the stimulus on this trial is the same as that given on the previous one, and if so the RT is shorter than if the stimulus changes. This he attributed to the subject's not needing to process the stimulus fully if it was a repetition, because all the relevant checks and response selection mechanisms are still set for that stimulus. If the stimulus changes, however, this shortcut check fails, and the stimulus must be fully processed. Since the proportion of repetitions is confounded with the information metric, $H = \Sigma\,(-p_i \cdot \log p_i)$, as N varies, this model gives an alternative explanation of eqn (5.0). Kornblum showed that his analysis gave better fits to the data from experiments designed to unconfound repetition percentage and H than did models based on H. One difficulty with this model is that repetition effects are usually found for short response-stimulus intervals ($RSIs$), say less than 0.5 sec, although Kornblum (1973) listed some studies in which a repetition effect is still present at $RSIs$ of 10 sec and more. With longer $RSIs$ repetitions are sometimes slower than changes (Kirby, 1974), yet the relationship of eqn (5.1) still holds. Hawkins and his co-workers (Hawkins and Hosking, 1969; Hawkins, Thomas and Drury, 1970) failed to find any sequential effects in their data. These points preclude the differences in RT always being attributed to differential repetition/non-repetition RTs.

5. The need for a new model

(A) VERY HIGH COMPATIBILITY

Given the vast array of RT experiments, it is always possible to select an area which a particular model cannot describe adequately. If the area of discrepancy is important enough, a new model is needed. One such area is very high compatibility. Apart from the last two models mentioned, those reviewed above imply that some increase in RT with N must occur. This is not the case for some highly compatible or overlearnt RT tasks (Teichner and Krebs, 1974; Waugh and Anders, 1973; Conrad, 1962; Mowbray and Rhoades, 1959; Leonard, 1959). Models of the complete criterion type would need decision processes taking no time, or at least having zero variance for the models in Section 2.3, when RT is independent of N. For example, each step in Welford's successive dichotomization model must take zero time or else RT will increase with the number of steps which is proportional to $\log_2 N$. A step taking no time is difficult to envisage. Similarly an exponential distribution with zero variance has zero mean, so Rapoport's contemporaneous complete identification model becomes improbable when RT is independent of N. Indeed for a range of possible B values, a corresponding range of exponential distribution variances is required and, as B tends to zero, so must the variance and mean of the exponential distribution of elementary decision times. This is plausible except in the limit at zero. Luce's (1960) model, with N successive steps, fails under the same argument.

Similar arguments hold for models with relative criteria: no increase in processing time with N implies an infinitely fast sampling of evidence or formation of TIs, which is implausible and against the spirit of this type of model.

The models of Falmagne and Kornblum can account for this result in a *post hoc* fashion. For the former it is sufficient to say that preparation is maximal for all possibilities, and so the two assumed distributions are actually only one. Similarly if RTs to repetitions equal RTs for changed stimuli, Kornblum's model will predict no increase in RT with N. However without some *a priori* reason for suggesting that repetitions and changes are equal, the argument goes better in the other direction. That is, if RT does not increase with N, but the proportion of repetitions does, then repetition RTs must equal non-repetition RTs whatever underlying processing model is postulated.

In short, these models may handle tasks with different individual Bs, but they are not designed for tasks in which $B = 0$.

(B) EFFECTS OF STIMULI NOT PRESENTED

There is a second important area which existing models do not cover, namely the effects of latent stimuli. We define the latent stimuli on any trial as those which are alternatives in the task but which are not the one presented. Kornblum (1965) showed that RT for a particular stimulus and its response was affected by the nature of the response called for by a second (latent) stimulus. This effect is also clear in the independent results of Duncan (1977) and Smith (1977). Both compared RTs from two classes of task. In one class ("unmixed" tasks) the association between each stimulus and its response was the same for all possible stimuli. In the other class ("mixed" tasks) half of the stimuli had one association with their responses and the other half, another. Again comparison showed that the RT for the same S–R pair differed between the unmixed and mixed tasks, i.e. the latent stimuli affected the RT. The results of Smith (1977) will be given here in some detail as the model was developed to account for the pattern apparent in them. Differences between these results and those of Duncan (1977) will be discussed later.

Smith (1977) used VT stimuli delivered to the fingertips as they rested on the response keys. The twelve subjects did various combinations of the six tasks whose descriptions follow. These tasks were labelled $T1$ to $T6$. The basic difference between them was the stimulus-response associations for correct responses. Three types of mapping were used:

(i) *Compatible*: Each stimulus had to be responded to by pressing the key under the finger stimulated.

(ii) *Reflected*: The same finger on the other hand was correct; for example, a stimulus to the left index finger was responded to with the right index finger. The stimulus-response mapping was a reflection about the body midline.

(iii) *Shifted*: The correct response was described by shifting the stimulated position to the other hand and responded with, for example, the left index finger if the right little finger was stimulated.

The fingers, the stimuli to them, and responses by them are labeled 1–8 from right to left and referred to in this way.

The tasks in terms of their mappings were:

$T1$: all compatible;
$T2$: all reflected;
$T3$: half reflected, half compatible; that is, a left-hand stimulus had to be

reflected to give its correct response, and a right-hand stimulus had to be responded to with the stimulated finger;

T4: all shifted;

T5: half shifted, half compatible. Again, left-hand stimuli had to be shifted and right-hand stimuli were compatible with their correct responses; and

T6: responses were made in order from the rightmost to the leftmost cyclically, regardless of what stimulus was given. The stimulus sequence was designed so that each response was made to each stimulus an equal number of times.

T6 measured RT under conditions of stimulus uncertainty with response certainty. RT under these conditions was no shorter than in the compatible latencies from T1 (which were independent of N), and so were at some minimum level. Degree of choice ($N = 2$, 4 and 8) for T1–T5 was varied as a within subject factor. The comparisons of interest were within the trios T1, T2 and T3, and T1, T4 and T5, i.e. each mixed task with its constituent two unmixed tasks. Since the pattern of results is the same for each trio, only those from T1, T2 and T3 are given here. Firstly, the overall mean RTs were in the order $T1 < T3 < T2$. Comparing the stimuli with the compatible association in T1 (unmixed compatible) and T3 (mixed with reflected) revealed that RTs were longer in the mixed task. That is, the presence in T3 of latent stimuli with a more difficult association increased the RT on trials with the compatible S–R pairs. The equivalent comparison for the reflected stimuli, on the other hand, showed that RTs were *shorter* in the mixed task. That is, the presence of latent stimuli with an easier association decreased the RT for reflected S–R pairs. The third comparison, between the different associations in T3 showed that RTs to reflected S–R pairs were longer than the RTs for compatible S–R pairs, so the particular S–R association called for did influence RT. These three points held for 2, 4 and 8 choice conditions. Clearly the presence of latent stimuli with more difficult response associations increases, and with easier associations decreases RT. Interestingly the size of this increase or decrease was proportional to log N. A theory postulating a simple constant-duration decision of "which association" to use for the given stimulus is obviously inadequate to account for these data, but the model to be detailed later can do so.

(c) THE EFFECTIVENESS OF A DISCRETE STAGE APPROACH TO RT

A third consideration in developing a new model arises from the following review of the discrete stage approach to RT. In view of its conclusions, on the uncertain utility of assuming stages of processing, it seems opportune to attempt to develop a stage-free or parameteric model.

Early in the study of reaction time Donders (1868, see Koster, 1969) proposed a theory and method for investigating the structure of the *RT* process. He suggested that a choice reaction (Donders' *b* type) was composed of a series of subprocesses or stages each starting only after the previous one had finished. That is, the overall *RT* could be split into discrete amounts, each attributable solely to one of a succession of non-overlapping stages. In his review of choice *RT*, E. E. Smith (1968) suggested that the following four stages are present in a choice or *b* reaction:

(1) stimulus preprocessing,
(2) stimulus categorization,
(3) response selection, and
(4) response execution.

For consistency the following discussion will be in terms of these stages. To investigate them Donders used a set of three *RT* tasks differing as to which of the stages were assumed to be involved. The task in which all stages were present was the choice reaction consisting of several stimuli each with its own response to be made whenever it occurred. A selective or *c* reaction, which requires a single response to one of several stimuli and nothing to the others, Donders suggested, lacked a response selection stage but contained all others from *b*. In a simple or *a* reaction, a further stage, stimulus identification, is absent. In this discussion, to distinguish between the task and its *RT*, italicized letters will be used to denote the task and upper case for its *RT*. Under Donders' subtractive principle, the duration of stage (3), response selection, can be obtained by subtracting C from B, since *b* and *c* are differentiated only by its presence in *b* and absence in *c*. Similarly the stage time for stimulus identification is given by C–A.

In this framework, there is a qualitative difference between *a*, *b* and *c*. Other workers of the time did not accept this. Among these, Kulpë (1895) argued that the difference could be quantitative, noting that greater response preparedness was possible in a simple response than if a choice was called for. That is, subjects can set their motor readiness to a higher level when only one reponse is needed (*a* and *c*) than if several are possible (*b*) and higher still if that response can be executed as soon as any stimulation arises (Woodworth, 1938). Martius (1891, see Henmon, 1914, p. 29), noting that *RT* is shorter if the subject's attention is directed to responding, than if attention is to the stimulus, argued similarly: with a plurality of possible stimuli and responses, it is not possible to prime a response as fully as can be done in *a*. Further, Wundt (1883) held that the difference between *c* and *b* is not the presence of stage (3), since *c* involves not only stimulus identification but also a choice between movement and no movement. Cattell agreed and further felt that stages (2) and (3) were processed in parallel: as the nervous impulse from the stimulus excitation reached the brain it caused effects in two directions, one to a centre for perception, and the other to the muscle via a motor centre (Henmon, 1914, p. 9).

The stage approach provides a fair integration of many results on RT processing, and is intuitively attractive. Each stage can readily be understood as representing a particular aspect of RT processing and the effect of various factors on RT can be interpreted readily and logically by reference to their effect on one or more of the hypothetical stages (as reviewed by Sanders, 1977). Studies of perception with backward masking suggest that, to form an adequate impression of the stimulus, it needs to be presented for an appreciable though brief period—certainly for much shorter than a full RT—and the minimum adequate duration (Kahneman, 1968; Vickers, Nettelbeck and Willson, 1972) can be considered as measuring a stimulus preprocessing stage. Subjects usually become aware of the stimulus identity during processing and so a stimulus identification stage is plausible. They also make one response from all those possible, which suggests a response selection stage. The production of this selected response can be delayed under instructions until some subsequent signal, so a separate response execution stage can be created.

Other attributes of stages, especially their sequencing and seriality (order and non-overlapping) are more open to criticism. For example, whether stimulus identification takes place before response selection, as stage theories postulate, or in parallel, as Cattell suggested, is debatable. Both have found support: Coltheart (1972) put forward a model of word recognition in which the visual encoding and the naming process begin at the same point in time and Wood (1974) found results consistent with parallel processing of auditory and phonetic information in speech perception, while Sternberg (1969) supported a serial approach which will be discussed below. Although in most choice RT tasks, subjects' introspective reports suggest that stimulus identification is available to them before the identity of the response, this is not the case for vibrotactile (VT) tasks. Under conditions of spatial compatibility with VT stimuli subjects frequently say that they identified the stimulus at the same time as or after responding, which could imply parallel processing of stimulus identification and response selection. Although it cannot be shown that conscious recognition is equivalent to the end of processing the stimulus, it may be accepted as a working hypothesis for some interesting but tentative theoretical explanations. One may then speculate that the stimulus identity conceptually may itself be a "response", selected in parallel with the overt reaction. Usually stimulus identification, being highly compatible, is faster than other response selection and so appears to occur first; but in VT tasks, the two are about equally fast. If so, it is in highly compatible tasks that evidence in favour of parallel processing could be found.

Sternberg (1969) revived a modified and improved methodology to investigate stages of *RT*. He started by assuming that non-overlapping stages exist, each ideally having four properties:

(a) for a given input, the output is unaffected by factors influencing its duration,
(b) a stage should be functionally interesting, psychologically and qualitatively different from other stages,
(c) one stage can process only one signal at a time, and
(d) stage durations should be stochastically independent.

To discover such stages using Sternberg's method is conceptually simple. Given two factors (experimental variables) which individually influence choice *RT*, then if their joint effect on *RT* is additive, they affect different stages, but if they interact they influence at least one stage in common. This can be extended logically to more than two factors, and the patterns of interactive or additive joint effects determine the stage structure of the task. Starting with a set of *M* mutually additive factors, indicating *M* stages, a new factor which is additive with all *M* factors defines a new stage, and the nature of the factor gives insight into the functional nature of the new stage. This approach is called Sternberg's additive factor method.

However no *a priori* reason is offered for the existence of stages—Stone (1976, p. 297) refers to Sternberg's "presumption" of stages—although the approach has merit on the grounds that it is comprehensible and parsimonious. Nevertheless, the mathematics of the approach do not dictate or rely on the existence of stages. If factors are additive it may be inferred that they are affecting different, additive, parameters of the process, and if they interact an effect on a common parameter is likely, but to jump from this to the identification of parameters as discrete stages is not trivial. The alternative approach can be called the parameter approach and has the advantage that it avoids the drawback of discrepant results from closely related studies. For a discussion of such sets of studies see Blackman (1975), Pachella (1974) and Stanovich and Pachella (1977). Pachella (1974) reviewed a broad area of *RT* experiments, concluding against stage approaches and advocating the careful study of *RT per se*, which is essentially similar to the parameter approach discussed here. (He also noted that current models are poor if assessed on the criterion of being close analogies to actual events in processing.) Such results need a complex series of little stages under a stage approach, but under a parameter approach can be seen simply as implying the existence of a parameter, controlled by differences in the task, which interacts with at least one parameter affected by the other factors in the study. A first approximation to such a model will be developed later in this chapter.

Taylor (1976) also strongly criticized the additive factor method and put forward a viable alternative. He suggested that stages may overlap to a greater or lesser degree, even to the extent of being fully parallel. He developed these alternatives thoroughly in psychological and rigorous mathematical terms and advocated a more sophisticated but related analysis to probe the attributes of his redefined stages. As his meaning of "stages" eliminates the traditional concepts of seriality, stage independence and stochastic independence, a new term, "component" will be used for a Taylor-type stage. This leaves "stage" for the traditional Sternbergian idea. Since a component may start processing partial information from a previous component, the idea is more like a flow of information through the overall *RT* process. The difference can be seen in a bead-threading analogy. To thread a set of beads (stages) onto a cord under the stage approach, the needle must be passed completely through each bead before the next is tackled while, with a component approach, a second bead can be started on the needle before it is fully out of the previous one. This provides a less restricted outlook on *RT* processing.

Evidence of component overlap has been recently reported by Stanovich and Pachella (1977). Their experiment used the additive factors methodology to probe the stimulus categorization stage, via the factors of stimulus probability, stimulus contrast and S–R compatibility. Over a series of experiments they showed that stimulus contract and S–R compatibility interacted under-additively where this is defined as occurring "when a factor that shows processing has a larger effect on the faster levels of the other variable". This they demonstrate is most parsimoniously accounted for by the idea that "stages" overlap (i.e. are components in the current terminology), and they show that this makes sense of other data difficult to fit into a discrete stages framework. The approach is offered by them as an extension with the inference from under-additivity to components overlap adding precision to the investigation of *RT*s.

A further step from the stage viewpoint can be taken from the mathematical theorems of Townsend (1972, 1974, 1976) who has proved a high degree of equivalence between the reaction times produced under serial and parallel models. In brief, he has shown that any parallel processing model is indistinguishable from an appropriate serial model when considered on the basis of *RT*s. The reverse is not always true; that is, some serial models do not have equivalent parallel models, but a broad group of them do. Given this equivalence, the grounds for selecting a serial model as preferable to a parallel one cannot be firmly on the grounds of data alone, but usually reflects the experimenter's theoretical standpoint and must be justified on other grounds.

All in all, the picture is not as clear as some users of the additive factors method have presumed, as to either the definition of stages or their adequacy. Stone (1976, p. 297) mentioned this confusion in the use and definition of stages, referring to "our lack of clarity regarding the definition of stages" and Sternberg's "presumption" of stages. Sternberg (1969) was aware of some of the possible pitfalls, but hoped that experimental evidence would reveal an adequate path around them. Blackman (1975) and Sanders (1977), who both use the additive factors method, have separately noted that stages are sometimes insufficient as explanations without appealing to other concepts, but still offer the best current solution to a large body of RT data. Blackman (1975) reviewed some contradictory results with the factor of relative stimulus frequency, which gives additive effects in some tasks and interacts in others, with factors such as $S-R$ compatibility which are interpreted as affecting a stimulus processing stage. This led to a lack of consensus as to what stages were affected by these factors. However, in his own experiment, Blackman obtained consistent interpretable results, with additivity on not only means but also second and third cumulant statistics as would be predicted under a pure serial discrete stage model. This is a clear example of the method's power within a particular study. Between studies synthesis is more difficult.

Sanders (1977) holds the additive factors/stages view, but adds to stages (which comprise the *structure* of RT) a concept of *functional* factors which may affect structure in some tasks. He successfully rationalizes much of the additive factors data, mainly with the aid of the factor "practice": for well practised subjects seem to give consistent results between studies, with contradictory finding coming mainly from less practised subjects. He developed a stage model from his review of data and new experiments, but needed to appeal to concepts beyond stages. His functional factors are seen as selectively altering the stage structure, for example he suggested that "immediate arousal is not effective when the information flow involves the response choice mechanism". That is to say, a factor which he had previously argued caused a particular pattern of results sometimes applies and sometimes does not, as governed by a functional factor.

There is some reason to conclude that processing is not purely serial (or parallel) in all RT tasks or conditions but that the style of processing varies between these two extremes. Stages are obviously essential in some tasks, as in one used by Simon, Acosta, Mewaldt and Speidel (1976). They used several conditions, but the one most directly relevant here was essentially as follows: the stimulus was a tone, either high or low, with two keys for responding, each of which could be either green or red. Subjects were instructed to press the green key on hearing a high tone, while for a low tone, the red response was correct. However, the colour of the keys varied from trial to trial and in some conditions was set zero to 350 msec after the tone was given. Obviously the subject cannot start to select his response until the colours are set. This favours a stage processing situation, especially in the 350 msec delay condition where the subject could have processed the stimulus fully into its identity as one stage and be waiting for the response selection rule to be given before proceeding with the response selection as a discrete stage. This procedure forces stages onto the processing.

On the other hand, a partial advance information procedure used by Leonard (1958) makes overlap of stimulus identification and response selection probable. The subject faced six lights, arranged in an inverted V with three lights on each side. Responses were made by pressing one of six keys arranged in a 1–1 spatial correspondence with the lights, three in the left hand and three in the right. In one condition, half of the lights came on, either the left or the right three. After a brief period, one of these went off, specifying the particular response for that trial. The initial onset of three lights thus gave partial stimulus information which the subject could convert into partial response selection immediately, conceivably in parallel with further stimulus processing as it became possible. That is, the subject probably processed the partial stimulus information and then prepared the corresponding hand for responding while processing the complete stimulus information given by the light's offset. This overlap of components is one form of parallel processing.

Serial-parallel differences are also possible in more common choice *RT* tasks. If one adopts a simple processing model (Hick, 1952a) and considers a standard light-keys apparatus, one can conceive of parallel processing possibilities in a four choice condition that are not possible in a two choice version. One model explored by Hick assumes that subjects first decide in which half the stimulus occurs and then which half of that half and so on repeatedly, until the stimulus is identified precisely. So in a four choice condition, a subject may identify the stimulus as being in the left pair, and then as the leftmost of those. While this second identification step is proceeding, he may prepare the left hand for responding based on the result of the first step. Once again, overlap indicates parallel processing of items in different stages. This is not possible in the two choice—as soon as the stimulus is localized as left or right, it is completely specified and the response can be fully selected as a second stage, which is serial since no further stimulus processing is needed.

These analyses are hypothetical and are only included to indicate the range of serial-parallel possibilities. No attempt is made to find hard data supporting them, beyond noting their *prima facie* possibilities.

As can be seen from the above discussion, the issue is not clearcut, but it seems fair to conclude the stage approach should not be discarded *in toto* since it does allow sense to be made of much data, although it is sometimes faulty through oversimplicity, and therefore other approaches, such as the parameter one mentioned, should be developed. Stages have certainly widened our feeling of comprehension of *RT* processing and has proved to be an inspiration to a great deal of good research. The heuristic value of such a broad hypothesis seems to justify its continued use although not without qualification. In the words of Schwartz, Pomerantz and Egeth (1977) "Abandonment is too steep a price to prevent some possible misapplications." The recently suggested amendments to the additive factor method (Sanders, 1977; Stanovich and Pachella, 1977) provide possible qualifications which may increase the viability of a modified stage approach to *RT*. However, as already noted, arguments are being put forward that it is not necessary to postulate the existence of stages, at least under some circumstances. The most powerful of these appears to be the component approach of Taylor (1976), but as yet this lacks the vast array of research effort put behind the stage approach. The parameter approach which uses the additive factor method but infers additive or interacting parameters which may or may not be stages could also be useful but needs the development of a firm parametric model before more evaluation can be done. On the other hand, this approach can adopt all previous additive factor method results directly and use them to infer parameters just as the stage approach has inferred stages. The parameter approach's imprecision on the existence or otherwise of stages may prove to be an advantage, for it is possible that *RT* processing in some tasks has a dual nature, appearing as serial under some methods of analysis and parallel in other circumstances. This is in keeping with the theorems of Townsend (1976) and is analogous to the dual wave/corpuscular nature of light in the science of physics, where the form favoured reflects the methodology used. Certainly the chances are high that a model based on stages will be oversimplistic and inadequate to explain some tasks such as in the experiment described below.

(D) EXPERIMENTAL EVIDENCE FROM TASKS USING VIBROTACTILE STIMULI

Smith (1978) described a set of tasks that gave *RT*s which are difficult to explain as arising from serial stages. The experiment included a replication of Donders' *a*, *b* and *c* tasks and an extension to two related tasks which he called *x* and *t*. Vibrotactile stimuli to either index finger were used, with keypress responses by the same fingers. A paper tape punched with random equiprobable states 1 and 2 determined the stimulus sequence. Which of the two index finger stimuli was given and response required for a "1" or a "2" on the tape varied between the tasks as shown in Table 5.1.

The tasks a, b and c were the simple, choice and selective responses corresponding to those used by Donders. In the "crossed" task, x the correct response for either stimulus was pressing key 1, i.e. one stimulus required its compatible response but the other was crossed to the same key. For t the "temporal" task, every time a "1" occurred on the tape, stimulus 1 was given and response 1 required, but a "2" produced nothing—no stimulus was given. Thus t parallelled half of task b, with stimulus and response 1 occurring at equivalent times. These two tasks enabled an evaluation of two variables which might mediate the response preparedness concept used by Külpe and others (Külpe, 1895).

Table 5.1. A description of the five tasks used by Smith (1978) in terms of their two equiprobable states and the corresponding stimulus-response pairs. The symbol ϕ represents the null condition, i.e. no response or no stimulus. RT is in msec

	State "1"	RT	State "2"	RT
a	1–1	173	1–1	—
b	1–1	217	2–2	220
c	1–1	248	2–ϕ	—
x	1–1	173	2–1	192
t	1–1	208	ϕ–ϕ	—

In most b tasks RT is affected by the number of stimulus-response pairs, so that reducing the number of stimuli and responses from 2 and 2 in a b task to 2 and 1 in c and further to 1 and 1 in a would be expected to lower RT without postulating a change in the structure of processing. This does not hold in the highly compatible VT situation, for which choice RT is unaffected by the number of stimuli and responses (Leonard, 1959; Smith, 1978). Thus the effect of reducing the number of stimuli or responses in changing from b to c to a tasks can be assessed free from the possible confounding effects of compatibility.

Donders' stage analysis can be applied to x and t. The former needs neither stimulus categorization nor response selection, only detection of any stimulus and production of the one response. Since it has the same stages as a, its RT should equal that of a. Adopting the convention that upper case letters refer to the RT and lower case to the task, we have $X = A$ is the strict stage approach is correct. Similarly t only involves one stimulus and one response. It differs from a only in the temporal sequence of the stimulus and response, so again we could simplistically expect $T = A$. The overall order of RTs under stage theory would be $A = X = T < C < B$. The mean from ten subjects who did 308 trials on each task are given in Table 5.1. A Duncan's multiple range test on the stimulus-response pair, 1–1, common to all tasks identified three subsets with significant differences between the sets but not within, at the 0.05 level. Group 1 was A and X, group 2 was T and B, and group 3 was C. That is

$$A = X < T = B < C.$$

The most striking result is $B < C$, that is removing the response choice stage *increased RT*. A stage of negative duration is untenable. This result is unusual but not altogether unexpected, although using equivalent apparatus Broadbent and Gregory (1962) reported no significant difference between B and C. Perhaps the duration of the stimulus to be ignored was shorter than in Smith's experiment, which may result in a lengthening of RT by analogy with the finding that the more intense (possibly analogous to duration here) the stimulus to be ignored, the longer the c reaction time (John, 1966).

Other evidence comes from studies which have used naming digits presented visually, also a highly compatible task. Forrin and Morin (1966) found $B < C$ in such a task. Their c task used the digits 1–8 with subjects responding with "2" and "8" or with "2", "4", "7" and "8" to the corresponding stimuli and ignoring the rest. The b task controls used the stimuli corresponding to the two or four member response sets of the c condition, or all eight, and found that the 2, 4 and 8 choice Bs were each less than the 2- or 4-response Cs. Mowbray (1960) had subjects respond to one or all of 2, 4, 6, 8 or 10 numerals, and found that $B > C$ for 2, 4 and 6 stimuli but $B < C$ with 8 or 10.

The relationship between A, T and B in Smith's experiment goes against Donders' analysis because T would not be expected to exceed A, since both are forms of the simple reaction, nor should $T = B$ since t lacks the proposed stimulus identification in b.

In total the results are strongly contrary to the usual stage approach, but Külpe's broad idea of qualitative differences mediated by response preparedness gives a good fit to most of these data. Response preparedness should be higher for a and x than for t, b and c. This predicts that A and X are less than the rest, as was found.

The possible mediators of response preparedness can be evaluated from these data. Response inhibition (RI), i.e. the need to inhibit the particular measured response on some trials, is not well supported. It can explain $A = X$ since in neither is there ever a need to inhibit the one response to any stimulus, but RI is not present in t, yet $A < T$, and is present in b, yet $T = B$. The data do suggest that a form of temporal uncertainty (TU) is a major determinant of RT at this very high level of compatibility since $T = B$. That is, a simple and a choice task with matched occurrences in time of a given response have equal RTs. Additional confirmation comes from x, since $A = X$, and the one response is made with the same inter-response intervals in both a and x. Also, X and A are less than T and B, i.e. responses with more variable time of occurrence are slower than regular ones, as the TU principle predicts.

The finding, $B < C$, is an example of the latent stimulus principle which says that stimulus-response pairs not used on a particular trial affect the reaction time to the given stimulus, showing that the task must be considered as a whole and not just as a set of independent stimulus-response pairs. Smith (1977) suggested that the extent of the effect of the latent stimulus depends on its compatibility—the less compatible the more it lengthens RT. It seems likely that to suppress a highly compatible response to a VT stimulus is less compatible than to respond, while the reverse holds for less compatible taks in which RT does increase with N. This suggestion of differences in compatibility between responding and non-responding follows a similar argument by Brebner and Gordon (1964) who suggested that naming numerals is overlearnt (highly compatible) but naming selectively is not. A latent stimulus-response pair that is so compatible as to give no increase with N has the same effect as empty time ($B = T$), while the stimulus-response association of a VT stimulus to no response is less compatible and increases the RT ($B < C$). This experiment will be discussed again later.

(E) REQUIREMENTS OF A NEW MODEL

In consideration of these points, the model presented in Section 6 is designed to cover the following areas:

(i) RT is proportional to log N in general except that the slope relating RT and log N can be zero (i.e. RT is independent of N) for some tasks.

(ii) Whole-task effects. In general it is not sufficient to consider the RT of one S–R pair in a task as an index of processing since it is affected by other aspects of the task. In particular, latent stimuli will increase RT if they involve a more difficult S–R association and decrease it if they involve simpler ones.

(iii) Response-related effects. One element of this is the temporal uncertainty of each response as shown in the experiment described in 5(D). Speed/accuracy tradeoff is another aspect of response-related effects which should be covered.

(iv) Stimulus-related effects. The physical similarity between the stimuli affects the stimulus discriminability which in turn affects RT. Global stimulus probabilities control response probabilities and affect RT—stimuli with high probabilities have shorter RTs than those with low. Both of these points should be incorporated in the model if possible.

(v) Sequential effects in which a trial calling for the same response or using the same stimulus as the previous trial usually has a shorter RT, are important. Smith (1968) reviewed this effect and concluded that this was affected more by response than stimulus repetition. The main effect of repetitions can therefore be assigned to a response-related parameter.

(iv) Assumptions involving the existence of stages should be avoided.

6. A new model

(A) BRIEF DESCRIPTION

The model described here is a development of that presented previously by the author (Smith, 1977). The style of the model is strongly influenced by a perceptual recognition model developed by Vickers (1970), and is also related to La Berge's model (Section 3(D)) with TIs replaced by accumulating evidence as in Vickers' model.

In this *accelerating cycle* model, evidence from each of the N possible stimuli (in the form of internal stimulus excitation, being either "noise" or "signal plus noise") is transformed into excitation on the associated responses. This process continues until one of the responses accumulates a preset amount of evidence and is initiated. We define a "cycle" as a segment of time in which one unit (arbitrarily small) of total stimulus excitation is transformed into the corresponding responses. Since latent stimuli affect RT, each stimulus has a share of the time in each cycle as detailed below. The basic time taken to transform one unit of stimulus excitation, which is called the *association time*, reflects the strength of the association between that stimulus and its correct response. The association time is high for low compatibility and *vice versa*. In addition, it is assumed that cycle times get progressively shorter in successive cycles. That is, the more evidence that has been accumulated the faster the transformation; perhaps indicating increasing focussing of attention or dedication to the task, or increasing ease as transformation paths become better established—somewhat like a within-trial practice effect. It is this feature which gives the model its name.

The contribution of each stimulus to a cycle is determined by two factors, its association time and its proportion of the total excitation. Access to the processor is shared between the stimuli in accordance with the proportion of the overall excitation represented by each stimulus, as in the example below.

Once a stimulus has access, it will occupy the processor for the time needed to transform its excitation into its response, which is governed by its association time. Thus if there are two possible stimuli, S_1 and S_2, having 93 per cent and 7 per cent of the stimulus excitation, they will get 93 per cent and 7 per cent of the available access to the processor. In the case where the association times of the stimuli are 1 and 1.5 respectively, the basic cycle time will be $(0.93 \times 1) + (0.07 \times 1.5)$, i.e. 1.04 if stimulus S_1 is given, and $(0.07 \times 1) + (0.93 \times 1.5)$, i.e. 1.47 if S_2 is given.

The following is a mathematical development of the model consistent with this descriptive model.

(B) GLOSSARY OF TERMS

The following terms are useful in describing the model and are defined together for convenience.

It should be noted that most of these have only a transitory role, in that they are not present in the final equations of the model, but make the exposition of the model easier. N and α representing the number of alternatives and the S–R compatibility are the only parameters essential to the simple form of the model, with e and δ necessary in its extended form. The model therefore essentially has only four parameters.

1. N: the number of stimuli in use;
2. i: $i = 1, 2, \ldots, N$, a general stimulus set member;
3. j: the particular stimulus given on this trial;
4. k: $k = 1, 2, \ldots, M$, a general response set member;
5. m: the particular response made on this trial;
6. $r(i)$: a function specifying the S–R pairs of the task; for a correct response, $m = r(j)$;
7. $E(i)$: the initial excitation on stimulus i;
8. $e(i)$: the stimulus excitation. Scaled so that the total excitation is one unit;
9. q: the amount of excitation due to the signal;
10. u: the "noise" excitation;
11. $p(k, t)$: the response excitation of stimulus k at the time of t;
12. $\alpha(i)$: the association time for the mapping from i to $r(i)$;
13. $\delta(k)$: the response firing level for response k;
14. s: a variable representing cycles through the process of translating e into p;
15. $t(s)$: the duration of cycle s.

We assume two sources of excitation exist; q that due to the signal and u a measure of the neural and other noise unavoidable in the system. This noise is assumed to be independent of N and evenly distributed between the stimuli on average. That is, the greater N the less noise on any one stimulus. It can be conceived as being inherent in the transformation mechanism and thus independent of N. It is possible that noise has a beneficial purpose and is not merely a limitation of the system, as in the following explanation. The processor deals only with alternatives that have positive excitations and ignores those with zero excitations. In this way, the noise in the system maintains the N stimulus representations or S–R associations since only non-zero ones have access to the processor and thus noise indicates which stimuli are possible. All other conceivable stimuli not in the current task are at the zero level and do not get a share in the processing.

At the onset of the stimulus, the initial stimulus excitations are

$$E(j) = q + \frac{u}{N}$$

$$E(i) = \frac{u}{N} \qquad i \neq j \tag{5.6}$$

We can adopt arbitrary units for E but, for clarity in the following equations, it is simplest if we replace the Es with scaled excitations, $e(i)$, so that $\Sigma\, e(i) = 1$, i.e. $e(j) = E(j)/\Sigma\, E(i)$. Thus in the initial cycle, one unit of stimulus excitation is transformed into response excitation, which by definition takes one cycle. An equivalent but cumbersome alternative would be to replace all occurrences of $e(i)$ with $E(i)/\Sigma\, E(i)$. We shall return to this point later.

Every possibility gains access to the translation mechanism in each cycle, changing $e(i)$ units of excitation from stimulus to response excitation and in doing so adds to the cycle's duration in proportion to its association time, $\alpha(i)$, and its excitation level, $e(i)$. Less compatible S–R associations take longer as does the given stimulus (signal) relative to the latent ones (noise). The first cycle time equals $\Sigma\, \alpha(i)e(i)$, which is the sum of the individual alternative's times. As mentioned above, this process goes faster in each successive cycle, with the general cycle time at cycle s given by

$$t(s) = \frac{\Sigma\, \alpha(i)e(i)}{s}. \tag{5.7}$$

That the time taken in a cycle should vary inversely with the iteration variable, s, has at least two possible explanations. One is that time taken in a cycle by the transformation of a stimulus into its corresponding response is proportional to the constant association time, and the level of stimulus excitation stored in short term store. It is suggested that this falls off with iterations, and is given by $e(i)/s$. This fits at least qualitatively the fall off in neural reverberatory circuits with time. This, together with the assumption that each stimulus is serviced in an iteration, gives eqn (5.7).

A second approach is to link the α and $1/s$. Under this suggestion, the time to convert a unit of energy from stimulus into its response decreases with iterations within any trial. This would be like a within-trial practice effect; the task becoming faster as the neural pathways used become refreshed, more worn-in. Or, in attention terms, a gradual focusing of attention away from monitoring and other tasks and onto the translation process of that stimulus. Again, with each stimulus serviced in each iteration, this gives eqn (5.7).

This process continues until response m's criterion, $\delta(m)$, is reached in say x cycles and the RT is the sum, or more properly the integral, of the cycle durations. That is,

$$RT(j) = a + \int_{1}^{x} t(s)\, ds \qquad (5.8)$$

where a represents any small non-processing delays, e.g. those associated with the stimulus level rising to detectability or with the time from initiation of the response to its being registered by the apparatus. Substituting for $t(s)$ gives

$$RT(j) = a + \int_{1}^{x} \frac{\Sigma\, \alpha(i)e(i)}{s}\, ds$$

$$= a + \sum \alpha(i)e(i) . \log x \qquad (5.9)$$

since the mathematical definition of natural logarithms is

$$\log y = \int_{1}^{y} \frac{ds}{s}.$$

It now remains to find the value of x. For the latency to be proportional to $\log N$, x must be proportional to N. It is certain intuitively that x is proportional to N; a number of suggestions can lead to this. The simplest is that a constant amount of response excitation is allocatable on each cycle and that is shared equally between all N possibilities. This gives each $1/N$. However, this would have all responses reaching criterion together. A simple modification, weighting the $1/N$ with the stimulus excitation, corrects this, so that the increment in $\rho(i)$ is $e(i)/N$. Then at cycle s

$$\rho(k, s) = \int_1^s \frac{e(i)}{N} \, ds$$

$$= \frac{e(i)}{N} (s - 1). \tag{5.10}$$

So

$$\rho(m, x) = \frac{e(j)}{N} (x - 1). \tag{5.11}$$

But $\rho(m, x) = \delta(m)$ by the definition of x. Therefore

$$x = \frac{\delta(m) \cdot N}{e(j)} + 1. \tag{5.12}$$

Returning to eqn (5.9) and substituting for x,

$$RT(j) = a + \sum \alpha(i)e(i) \cdot \log\left[\frac{\delta(m) \cdot N}{e(j)} + 1\right]$$

$$= a + \sum \alpha(i)e(i) \cdot \log\left[\frac{\delta(m)}{e(j)}\left(N + \frac{e(j)}{\delta(m)}\right)\right]$$

$$= A + B \log\left[N + \frac{e(j)}{\delta(m)}\right] \tag{5.13}$$

where

$$A = a + \sum \alpha(i)e(i) \cdot \log \frac{\delta(m)}{e(j)}$$

and

$$B = \sum \alpha(i)e(i).$$

As the response criterion $\delta(m)$ increases relative to the stimulus excitation, $e(j)$, the value of $e(j)/\delta(m)$ tends to zero, while if $\delta(m)$ and $e(j)$ are equal, $e(j)/\delta(m) = 1$. We can assume that $\delta(m) > e(j)$, imposing the restraint that at least one iteration is needed to reach a response criterion, so that $e(j)/\delta$ ranges between 0 (low e, high δ) and 1 (equal e and δ): the model thus offers an explanation of why sometimes $\log(N)$ and sometimes $\log(N + 1)$ gives the better fit to experimental data. Low stimulus intensities (or more likely, discriminabilities) should give a better fit against $\log(N)$, while high intensities should be better fitted against $\log(N + 1)$. It does in fact appear that the stimulus intensities used by Hyman (1953) whose results are well fitted against $\log N$ were almost certainly less than those used by Hick (1952a) whose results are better fitted against $\log(N + 1)$. For the rest of this work we shall use $\log(N + D)$ where $D = e(j)/\delta(m)$.

The model also offers a partial explanation for the intercept, A, in eqn (5.1). The given expression for A shows that part of this is inherent in the process, and is time dependent on $\delta/e(j)$, which is needed for a decision to be reached. It also gives the intercept as varying with α. It is suggested below that α will decrease with practice, and therefore so will the intercept. Teichner and Krebs (1974), in a review of 59 visual choice reaction time studies, conclude that the intercept does in fact decrease with practice, and moreover is a function of the stimulus coding required.

If δ is constant across responses—i.e. no concentration or other biases exist—eqn (5.13) is independent of m. Hence the mean RT over all stimuli is given by

$$RT = A + \frac{\Sigma_j\Sigma_i\ \alpha(i)e(i)\,.\log(N + D)}{N}$$

$$= A + \frac{\Sigma\ \alpha(i)}{N}\,.\log(N + D) \tag{5.14}$$

as required.

(C) APPLICATION TO EXPERIMENT ONE

For an unmixed task in which the same S–R association holds for all stimuli, α will be independent of i, at least to a first approximation, and (5.14) becomes

$$RT = A + \alpha \log(N + D). \tag{5.15}$$

Thus an estimate of α for a particular S–R association is the slope of the regression line of $\log(N + D)$ on RT from a task using only that association. In addition, if $\alpha(i)$ depends only on the S–R association for that stimulus, we should expect that the same α would apply in a mixed task, as for the same association in an unmixed task. That is, for the mixed tasks described above, in which half the stimuli used one association and half another, the overall slope in (5.14) should be the mean of the two αs for the component S–R associations. The slope values calculated from the data in Table 5.2 for the compatible, reflected, and half reflected-half compatible tasks were 11,

125 and 75, respectively. The mean of the first two is 68, which is close to that of the mixed task. In addition, it would be expected that the calculated slope for a mixed task in which two stimuli map into each response as occurred here, would be lower than the simple mean of the αs incorporated in it, for $\rho(m)$ will have two increments (one signal and one noise) per cycle and so will reach criterion faster (lower x implies a shorter RT). This effect also occurred in the experiment of Section 5(D) as will be detailed later. Thus the result is acceptably near the value predicted by this model. An equivalent direct comparison for the other association, shifted, was not possible since some subjects who did the half shifted-half compatible task did task six instead of the compatible task so the relevant means came from different although overlapping subject groups.

Table 5.2. Mean choice RTs in msec for three related tasks, compatible, reflected and half reflected-half compatible as explained in the task. Each mean is taken over 196 trials from four subjects (from Smith, 1977)

	N		
	2	4	8
Compatible	227	240	248
Reflected	310	444	559
Half compatible-			
Half reflected	204	266	353

According to this model the effect of latent stimuli is proportional to their αs and their excitation levels, as can be seen from eqn (5.13). Consider one subset of stimuli with the same association in two tasks. For example, let the left half of the stimuli have an association time of α_1, and the right half, α_2, in the mixed task. We shall use the notation that $RT_{x,y}$ is the mean RT for stimuli with association α_x when α_y is the association time for the other, latent, half of the stimuli. Then the difference between the mean RT for the stimuli with α_1 in the mixed case, $RT_{1,2}$ and the equivalent mean from the unmixed case, $RT_{1,1}$ is

$$RT_{1,2} - RT_{1,1} = u(\alpha_2 - \alpha_1) \log(N + D) \qquad (5.16)$$

from eqn (5.13). This is positive if $\alpha_2 > \alpha_1$ (e.g. comparing reflected stimuli in mixed and unmixed tasks) but negative if $\alpha_2 < \alpha_1$ (e.g. compatible stimuli in mixed and unmixed tasks) and is proportional to log N which agrees with the result found.

Similarly the difference between RTs for different associations within a mixed task is given by

$$RT_{1,2} - RT_{2,1} = q(\alpha_1 - \alpha_2)\log(N + D) \qquad (5.17)$$

(where $RT_{1,2}$ is the RT when the given stimulus has an association time α_1 and the latent stimulus has association α_2, and *vice versa* for $RT_{2,1}$), which is proportional to log N and shows that the stimuli with the larger α have the larger RT, again in agreement with the data from this experiment.

(D) THE MODEL APPLIED TO THE EXPERIMENT OF SECTION 5(D)

All relationships between the RTs from the tasks in the experiment of 5(D) follow from this model. The temporal uncertainty principle is realized by assigning higher δs to responses with less regular occurrences, i.e. T, B and C than to regular responses, i.e. A and X_1. It takes longer to accumulate to a high δ, i.e. high δs give long RTs. Thus A and X_1 are less than T, B and C. In addition, the latent stimulus principle applies in x, b and c. The compatible VT response has been shown to have an α of zero, since RT in b does not increase with N, and so the effect of the latent stimulus in b, which is proportional to its α, will be zero. That is, it will have the same effect as no stimulus and no response. But this is what occurs in t. Hence $T = B$, as found.

The latent stimulus in c cannot have an α less than that for b, since α cannot be negative. Following this notion it is less compatible to ignore a highly compatible stimulus than to respond to it. That is, its α will be greater than zero, and it will increase the comparison RT, giving $B < C$. In addition, C will increase with the number of stimuli to be ignored, which is what Mowbray (1960) reported, when using a digit naming task.

For stimulus 1 in x, i.e. the compatible stimulus-response pair, $1 \rightarrow 1$, α will also be zero, but for the incompatible pair, $2 \rightarrow 1$, α will be greater than zero. This gives $X_1 < X_2$. The final relationship, between A and X_1 is more complex. On the basis of their αs they would be equal. The task x involves a latent stimulus with $\alpha > 0$, and so X_1 should be lengthened. Counteracting this, however, both stimuli are being transformed into the same response, which therefore accumulates excitation from both the signal and the noise stimuli. This results in that response's criterion being reached sooner than if the signal alone contributes to it, as noted above in the unmixed task. This reduces its RT. Since the increase due to the latent stimulus compensates for the decrease due to two sources of stimulation for one response, the result $A = X$ is consistent with the model.

(E) OTHER APPLICATIONS

In this section the points listed in Section 5(E) are discussed in relation to this model.

(i) Under this model, RT is proportional to $\log(N + D)$ where $0 \leqslant D \leqslant 1$ so its general form is in agreement with that area of results. Indeed, as noted above, the parameter D enables the two rival formulae of Hick and Hyman to be reconciled. This point will be returned to later.

The slope of the relationship is given by $\Sigma\ \alpha(i)e(i)$, which reduces to α for unmixed tasks. In its current form this model is not designed to predict what value α will have in a given task, although consistency is apparent for the same S–R association in different tasks in that the αs found for two particular S–R associations in unmixed tasks can be used to predict the overall slope, B, in the compatibility mixed task, as discussed above. A task which shows no increase in RT with N like the compatible VT task would have a measured association time of zero, which is not unacceptable in this theoretical framework, as it suggests that there is a complete association between the stimulus and its response and that no transformation is needed to convert the stimulus into its response. Given the directness of the relationship between a vibrating key and pressing that key, this is not implausible.

However, the introduction of latent stimuli with non-zero αs would induce a logarithmic increase with N in the RT even for stimuli with $\alpha = 0$, as shown in eqn (5.14) and as found in this experiment.

The effect of practice in reducing the slope, B, can be accounted for. As subjects become more practised at a particular S–R association, that association becomes stronger. Hence its α will be reduced with its B, possibly to zero as Mowbray and Rhoades (1959) found. Indeed, the explanation of α as association time would support this approach by analogy with paired-learning tasks and would be similar to the suggestion made by Welford (1968) that with practice the associations between stimulus and response become built in as a kind of transformation table.

(ii) Whole task effects are satisfactorily handled by this model in its use of latent stimuli as detailed at the end of Section 6(C).

(iii) Response-related effects can be mediated through the parameter δ. At the grossest level, getting the subject to concentrate on responses (set for responding) gives faster responses than if he concentrates on identifying the stimulus (Welford, 1971). This could correspond to a lowering of δ or an aggregation of noise to that stimulus so that its excitation would be larger than usual, with an attendant decrease in x as in eqn (5.12). Indeed, both mechanisms may occur together. Either possibility would result in more responses, correct and incorrect, being made with the speeded response. Such a response bias can be seen in the "2 choice with concentration on one stimulus" condition shown in Fig. 3.4. The number of responses with the faster response was 309 (296 correct, 13 errors) as against 288 (284, 4) with the other. This large increase in the number of errors for the faster response was not found in the four and eight choice.

A decrease in the specificity of the stimulus needed to make a response is often noticed when subjects adopt a bias towards quick responding. In extreme cases subjects waiting for a visual stimulus will respond to a loud sound. This suggests that the processor takes any extraneous stimulation and assigns it to be the favoured response, i.e. treats random excitation or noise as belonging to that response, and hence more frequently responds in error than is usual. If instructed to guard against such responses, but to respond quickly, subjects may compensate by raising their δ. This could account for the result reported by John (1966), where RTs in a Donders' c-task were longer the louder the stimulus to be ignored. That is, to avoid making errors of commission, they needed a higher δ in the loud stimulus condition than in the soft.

It was suggested in Section 5(D) that the different regularities of inter-response times for a particular response in experiment three were at least part of the reason for the pattern of RTs obtained for the various tasks, viz, the more regular the response, the shorter the RT. If we assume that in general a subject can prepare better for regular responses by reducing δ without making errors of anticipation as he might with irregular responses, these results follow from this model.

Speed-accuracy tradeoffs can also be accounted for via changes in the average response criteria, $\delta(k)$. If these are low, RTs will be short and it is more likely that the continuously varying noise will be large enough for an incorrect response to reach its low criterion before the correct response. This gives a higher error rate for low δs. Conversely, high criteria give long RTs and make it improbable that noise will be large enough for long enough to cause an error. The specific form of the relationship between the error rate and δ has not been developed and will be left for later research.

(iv) Stimulus related effects. As mentioned before unequal stimulus frequencies affect latencies, with more probable stimuli responded to faster than others (La Berge and Tweedy, 1964; and others). This model handles this at least qualitatively if it is assumed that the $1/N$ in eqn (5.10) is taken as a measure of some payoff function $p(j)$ for the stimuli. In the usual equal frequency choice task with no special instructions, all stimuli would have an equal payoff, $1/N$. If stimulus frequencies are unequal, the subject can obey the instruction to react as quickly as possible by changing this payoff to the probability of a signal. We can replace eqn (5.12) with

$$x = \frac{\delta(m)}{e(j)p(j)} + 1 \qquad (5.18)$$

where $p(j)$ is the payoff weighting given to stimulus j. This interpretation is reasonable in light of the explanation of eqn (5.12) given above. Replacing eqn (5.12) with eqn (5.18) gives shorter response latencies for larger $p(j)$ as required.

The effect of stimulus intensity in which higher intensity stimuli give shorter RTs is explicable. As stated above, the $e(i)$ were scaled arbitrarily so that $\Sigma\, e(i) = 1$. Consider the effect on $e(j)$, of increasing $E(j)$, the absolute stimulus excitation. In brief, as $E(j)$ increases, so does $e(j)$ to an asymptote of 1 as can be shown from eqn (5.6) and thus x decreases, from eqn (5.12). That is, fewer cycles are needed to reach criterion for the more intense stimulus since more signal excitation is transformed each cycle. This in turn means shorter RTs which is consistent with experimental results.

(v) Some features of sequential effects often noted in choice reaction times can be fitted with another assumption. If we assume that the stimulus and response excitation does not reset to zero immediately after a trial, but decays slowly, then repetitions of the same stimulus or response will be responded to more quickly, being as it were primed. Similar although lesser effects will be noted for successive trials in which the stimulus and response are not repeated but are in some way closely related. For example, a response by a different finger but on the same hand, will be faster than one by a finger on the other hand (Kirby, 1975). Also, long RSIs would give smaller sequential effects than would short RSIs, as has been found by Bertelson in 1961 and others subsequently.

(vi) Errors. Errors are made in this model either if one of the latent stimuli gets a large amount of noise or has a very small criterion which causes its response to reach criterion before the correct response does, or if the transformation mechanism uses a wrong association. The latter is hard to quantify and hopefully happens rarely in normal circumstances. Vickers (1970) has shown that error latencies in a two-choice task are faster than those of correct responses under a model like this if the response criterion is very low, which corresponds to a high error rate.

For less error-prone performance, a higher δ is needed and error latencies are then longer than correct responses *with the same* δ. At first sight it would appear that the accelerating cycle model fails on the same test that Laming rejected La Berge's *TI* accumulator model. However, although δ has been treated as constant across trials, it almost certainly varies. Within a block of trials, those on which δ is low will have a higher proportion of errors than will other trials with high δ. That is, errors will occur predominantly on trials with low δs, and correct responses on high δ trials. Hence the comparison between error and correct RTs is not between trials with equal δs, and since low δs give short RTs, errors will usually be faster than correct responses if δ varies, even though they are slower than correct responses with the same δ. So simply releasing the unlikely restriction that δ is constant, allows the model to fit the observed result that error RTs are usually shorter than correct RTs. This argument applies equally to error versus correct RTs in La Berge's model, and suggests that Laming's (1968) rejection of that model was not wholly fair, since a less restrictive interpretation which could explain the results he found, was possible.

(vii) This model has avoided the assumption of stages as advocated in the review in Section 5(c). Although it describes RT processing as a flow of evidence from stimulus to response, the flow is to be seen as embodying overlapping components, as favoured in the review. The degree of overlap may vary from complete to zero, depending upon the particular task, and so this model is not wholly inconsistent with a stage approach for some tasks. The accumulating process is that of a relative criterion model. Its viewpoint differs from similar models in that it considers equal amounts of evidence being accumulated in successively shorter cycles, rather than varying amounts of evidence being assessed in equal time slices.

It seems to cover a wide range of areas and to be capable of further extensions, for example in speed/accuracy tradeoffs or stimulus discriminability. It is an attempt to formulate a parameter model as an alternative to more conventional styles of model. Some of its assumptions and predictions were tested by Smith (1978), and will be mentioned briefly here.

7. Further experimental evidence

(A) "NOISE" IN CRT

Smith (1978) used a backward masked paradigm to measure the perceptual noise in a choice reaction task. His subjects faced a horizontal line of eight lights, with eight corresponding response keys under their fingers. They were told that one of the central 2 (or 4 or 8 under different choice conditions) lights would come on briefly, followed by all eight, masking all information. Their task was to press the key corresponding to the light which came on first. The time from the first stimulus' onset to the mask's onset varied randomly between 10 msec and 135 msec, plus a control of 2 sec. Plotting the percentage accuracy at each duration gave a cumulative normal curve for each degree of choice. Extending the argument developed by Vickers, Nettelbeck and Willson (1972), the standard deviation of these curves can be taken as a measure of the perceptual noise in the process. Smith used a least squares fitting technique to estimate the mean and standard deviation of the best fitting ogive, and found that the standard deviation for the 2, 4 and 8 choice conditions were equal. This supports the postulate of the accelerating cycle model that the magnitude of noise in the reaction process is independent of N.

(B) MIXING S–R ASSOCIATIONS IN CRT

The model makes predictions about RTs in mixed tasks, i.e. tasks with two or more distinct subgroups of S–R associations for different possible stimuli. Consider two tasks, P and Q, both of which have a single (different) rule, p and q, respectively, governing the mapping of a set of eight stimuli into eight responses such that the RT for P as a whole is less that RT for Q. If we now take four stimuli, say the left-hand four, and assign them responses according to rule p, and assign the others according to rule q, we create a new mixed task, R. The model predicts three relationships, namely

(1) RT for those stimuli under rule p will be less in P than in R which involves other less compatible S–R associations.
(2) In R, RT for the stimuli under rule p will be less than those under q.
(3) RT for those stimuli under rule q will be greater in Q than in R which involves other more compatible S–R associations.

These relationships were found in the experiments described in Section 5(B). However, Duncan (1977) found that all stimuli in similar mixed tasks with visual stimuli had longer RTs compared with the same associations in unmixed tasks. Smith (1978) investigated this discrepancy in a set of two experiments the first using eight VT stimuli and the second eight visual stimuli (a horizontal row of lights), but both with the same three tasks, a compatible or direct association (task D), incompatible or translated associations (T) and mixed compatible-translated associations (M) as detailed in Table 5.3. The three tasks D, T and M correspond to P, Q and R above. He found that the order of RTs was as predicted by the model for the VT stimuli in the first 200 trials—that is, from fastest to slowest, direct association in D, direct association in M, translated association in T. For the visual stimuli, this pattern was not apparent in the first 200 trials, but was found for the second 200. This suggests that an adequate degree of

Table 5.3 The S–R associations for the three tasks are listed, showing which response was correct for each stimulus. The stimuli are numbered 1–8 from left to right, as are the response fingers, for description only and were not used in the experiment

Task	Stimuli							
	Left hand				Right hand			
	1	2	3	4	5	6	7	8
D	1	2	3	4	5	6	7	8
T	4	3	2	1	8	7	6	5
M	4	3	2	1	5	6	7	8

practice before the model matches subjects' performance in mixed tasks. For highly compatible VT stimuli this can be achieved in under 200 trials while for the visual stimuli used it takes longer.

Duncan's experiment used vertical lines displayed on a screen, with the stimuli defined implicitly by the distance from a central fixation dot. This display may need more practice than the explicitly defined stimulus positions afforded by the lights used by Smith. Duncan also split the stimuli in the mixed task into inner versus outer sets in the mixed task, which again may have increased the task's difficulty. Duncan's results showed that the mixed task's RTs were decreasing faster than the two unmixed tasks, which trend if continued would have given the pattern found by Smith and predicted by the accelerating cycle model. Overall, it seems likely that the model can be applied correctly to mixed tasks after adequate practice has stabilized performance.

(c) SEQUENTIAL EFFECTS IN MIXED TASKS

Smith also looked at sequential effects in the visual tasks. A subject usually responds faster in choice reaction tasks if the current trial is similar to the previous trial, e.g. it has the same response. In this context, "similar" can be taken as being a repetition of the same stimulus-response association. The accelerating cycle model predicts that the repetition facilitation arises in part from residual excitation uncleared from the previous trial's processing which thus requires less excitation to be accumulated to reach its criterion and so is faster. On trials which are not repetitions, it is a latent stimulus-response which is primed and the time to transform this retards the correct response and is proportional to the previous stimulus' association time. In the accelerating cycle model, we should expect less retardation if the association time for the previous stimulus is short than if it is long. That is, repetition facilitation for the direct (faster) association is greater in the mixed task than in the unmixed task, but for the translated association it is less in the mixed task than the unmixed translation task. This was confirmed by the data; for the direct association: facilitation (measured by non-repetition RT minus repetition RT) was 26 msec and 62 msec in D and M, and for the translated association, 47 msec and 37 msec for T and M, respectively. Both comparisons were significant at the 0.01 level under related samples t-test. Thus the model's interpretation of sequential effects is supported by this experiment.

(d) HICK'S AND HYMAN'S FORMULAE

A feature of the model is that it subsumes both Hick's (1952a) and Hyman's (1953) formulations of the logarithmic relationship between RT and the number of alternatives. Equation (5.13) shows that RT is proportional to $\log(N + D)$, $D = e/\delta$, where e is a measure of signal to noise strength, and δ is the response criterion, with $0 < e/\delta < 1$. To test this prediction, Smith (1978) used a 2, 4 and 8 choice lights-keys choice reaction task with each subject performing under two conditions, accuracy (high δ) or speed (low δ). The other parameter, e, is determined by the display which was constant between conditions. D which is inversely related to δ should be larger with speed instructions (low δ) than with accuracy (high δ). He found that 7 out of the 8 subjects followed that prediction. This aspect of the model is thus supported.

8. Conclusions

The accelerating cycle model of CRT can satisfactorily explain a wide range of findings, including no increase in RT with N for highly compatible S–R associations, the latent stimulus principle, mixed task RTs and sequential effects, and resolves the difference between Hick (1952a) and Hyman (1953). The model is designed to be extended by adding further parameters to describe the precise effects of other variables. For example, once the effect of practice becomes determined in the context of the model, it can be included as an additional parameter with specified interactions with existing parameters. The accelerating cycle can thus be used as the basis for further RT research, at least until a better approach can be developed.

References

Audley, R. J. (1960). A stochastic model for individual choice behaviour. *Psychological Review* **67**, 1–15.

Audley, R. J. and Pike, A. R. (1965). Some alternative stochastic models of choice. *British Journal of Mathematical and Statistical Psychology* **18**, 207–225.

Bertelson, P. (1961). Sequential redundancy and speed in a serial two-choice responding task. *Quarterly Journal of Experimental Psychology* **13**, 90–102.

Bertelson, P. (1963). S–R relationships and RTs to new versus repeated signals in a serial task. *Journal of Experimental Psychology* **65**, 478–484.

Blackman, A. R. (1975). Test of the additive-factor method of choice reaction time analysis. *Perceptual Motor Skills* **41**, 607–613.

Brainard, R. W., Irby, T. S., Fitts, P. M. and Alluisi, E. A. (1962). Some variables influencing the rate of gain of information. *Journal of Experimental Psychology* **63**, 105–110.

Brebner, J. and Gordon, J. (1964). The influence of signal probability and the number of non-signal categories on selective response times. *Quarterly Journal of Experimental Psychology* **16**, 56–60.

Broadbent, D. E. and Gregory, M. (1962). Donders' B- and C-reactions and S–R compatibility. *Journal of Experimental Psychology* **63**, 575–578.

Christie, L. S. and Luce, R. D. (1956). Decision structure and time relations in simple choice behaviour. *Bulletin of Mathematical Biophysics* **18**, 89–112.

Coltheart, M. (1972). Visual information processing. *In* "New Horizons in Psychology", Vol. 2 (P. C. Dodwell, ed.). Methuen, London.

Conrad, R. (1962). Practice, familiarity and reading rate for words and nonsense syllables. *Quarterly Journal of Experimental Psychology* **14**, 71–76.

Donders, F. C. (1868). Die Schnelligkeit psychischer Prozesse. *Archiv für Anatomie and Physiologie und wissenschaftliche Medizin*, 657–681.
See Koster, W. G. (1969). On the speed of mental processes. *In* "Attention and Performance II" (W. G. Koster, ed.), *Acta Psychologica* **30**, 412–431.

Duncan, J. (1977). Response selection rules in spatial choice reaction tasks. *In* "Attention and Performance VI" (S. Dornic, ed.), pp. 49–61. Lawrence Erlbaum, Hillsdale, New Jersey.

Edwards, W. (1965). Optimal strategies for seeking information: Models for statistics, choice reaction times and human information processing. *Journal of Mathematical Psychology* **2**, 312–329.

Falmagne, J. C. (1965). Stochastic models for choice reaction time with applications to experimental results. *Journal of Mathematical Psychology* **2**, 77–124.

Forrin, B. and Morin, R. (1966). Effect of contextual associations upon selective reaction time in a numeral-naming task. *Journal of Experimental Psychology* **71**, 40–46.

Grice, G. R., Nullmeyer, R. and Spiker, V. A. (1977). Application of variable criterion theory to choice reaction time. *Perception and Psychophysics* **22**, 431–449.

Hawkins, H. L. and Hosking, K. (1969). Stimulus probability as a determinant of discrete choice reaction time. *Journal of Experimental Psychology* **82**, 435–460.

Hawkins, H., Thomas, G. B. and Drury, K. B. (1970). Perceptual versus response bias in discrete choice reaction time. *Journal of Experimental Psychology* **84**, 514–517.

Henmon, V. A. C. (1914). Professor Cattell's work on reaction time. *Archives for Psychology* **30**, 1–33.

Hick, W. E. (1952a). On the rate of gain of information. *Quarterly Journal of Experimental Psychology* **4**, 11–26.

Hick, W. E. (1952b). Why the human operator? *Transactions of the Society of Instrument Technology* **4**, 67–77.

Hyman, R. (1953). Stimulus information as a determinant of reaction time. *Journal of Experimental Psychology* **45**, 188–196.

John, I. D. (1966). Intensity of non-key stimuli in the Donders' C-type reaction. *Australian Journal of Psychology* **18**, 148–153.

Kahneman, D. (1968). Method, findings and theory in studies of visual masking. *Psychological Bulletin* **70**, 404–425.

Kintsch, W. (1963). A response time model for choice behaviour. *Psychometrika* **28**, 27–32.

Kirby, N. H. (1974). Sequential effects in serial reaction time. Unpublished thesis, University of Adelaide.

Kirby, N. H. (1975). Serial effects in an eight choice serial reaction task. *Acta Psychologica* **39**, 205–216.

Kornblum, S. (1965). Response competition and/or inhibition in two-choice reaction time. *Psychonomic Science* **2**, 55–56.

Kornblum, S. (1969). Sequential determinants of information processing in serial and discrete choice reaction time. *Psychological Review* **76**, 113–131.

Kornblum, S. (1973). Sequential effects in choice reaction time: A tutorial review. *In* "Attention and Performance IV" (S. Kornblum, ed.). Academic Press, New York.

Koster, W. G. (1969). On the speed of mental processes. *In* "Attention and Performance II" (W. G. Koster, ed.). *Acta Psychologica*, **30**, 412–431.

Külpe, O. (1895). "Outlines of Psychology". Sections 69, 70. MacMillan, New York.

La Berge, D. L. (1962). A recruitment theory of simple behaviour. *Psychometrika* **27**, 375–396.

La Berge, D. and Tweedy, J. R. (1964). Presentation probability and choice time. *Journal of Experimental Psychology* **68**, 477–481.

Laming, D. (1966). A new interpretation of the relation between choice reaction time and the number of equiprobable alternatives. *British Journal of Mathematical and Statistical Psychology* **19**, 139–149.

Laming, D. (1968). *Information theory of choice-reaction time*. Academic Press, London.

Laming, D. (1977a). A correction and a proof of a theorem by Duncan Luce. *British Journal of Mathematical and Statistical Psychology* **30**, 90–97.

Laming, D. (1977b). Luce's choice of axiom compound with choice reaction data. *British Journal of Mathematical and Statistical Psychology* **30**, 141–153.

Leonard, J. A. (1958). Partial advance information in a choice reaction task. *British Journal of Psychology* **49**, 89–96.

Leonard, J. A. (1959). Tactual choice reactions: I. *Quarterly Journal of Experimental Psychology* **11**, 76–83.

Luce, R. D. (1960). Response latencies and probabilities. *In* "Mathematical methods in Social Sciences", 1959 (K. J. Arrow, S. Karlein and P. Suppes, eds.), pp. 298–311. Stanford University Press, Stanford, Connecticut.

Luce, R. D. (1963). Detection and recognition. *In* "Handbook of Mathematical Psychology", Vol. 1 (R. D. Luce, R. R. Bush and E. Galanter, eds.), pp. 103–189. Wiley, New York.

Mowbray, G. H. (1960). Choice reaction times for skilled responses. *Quarterly Journal of Experimental Psychology* **12**, 193–202.

Mowbray, G. H. and Rhoades, M. V. (1959). On the reduction of choice reaction times with practice. *Quarterly Journal of Experimental Psychology* **11**, 16–23.

Pachella, R. G. (1974). The interpretation of reaction time in information processing research. *In* "Human Information: Tutorials in Performance and Cognition" (B. Kantowitz, ed.), pp. 41–82. Lawrence Erlbaum, Hillsdale, N.J.

Rapoport, A. (1959). A study of disjunctive reaction times. *Behavioral Science* **4**, 299–315.

Sanders, A. F. (1977). Structural and functional aspects of the reaction process. *In* "Attention and Performance VI" (S. Dornic, ed.), pp. 3–25. Lawrence Erlbaum, Hillsdale, N.J.

Schwartz, S., Pomerantz, J. and Egeth, H. (1977). State and process limitations in information processing. *Journal of Experimental Psychology: Human Perception and Performance* **3**, 402–410.

Simon, J. R., Acosta, E., Mewaldt, S. P. and Speidel, C. R. (1976). The effect of an irrelevant directional cue on choice reaction time: Duration of the phenomenon and its relation to stages of processing. *Perception and Psychophysics* **19**, 16–22.

Smith, E. E. (1968). Choice reaction time: An analysis of the major theoretical positions. *Psychological Bulletin* **69**, 77–110.

Smith, G. A. (1977). Studies of compatibility and a new model of choice reaction time. *In* "Attention and Performance VI" (S. Dornic, ed.). Lawrence Erlbaum, Hillsdale, N.J.

Smith, G. A. (1978). Studies of compatibility and investigations of a model of reaction time. Unpublished Ph.D. thesis, University of Adelaide.

Spencer, T. J. (1971). Encoding time from iconic storage: A single letter visual display. *Journal of Experimental Psychology* **91**, 18–24.

Stanovich, K. and Pachella, R. (1977). Encoding, stimulus-response compatibility and stages of processing. *Journal of Experimental Psychology: Human Perception and Performance* **3**, 411–421.

Sternberg, S. (1969). The discovery of processing stages: Extension of Donders' method. *In* "Attention and Performance II" (W. G. Koster, ed.), pp. 276–315. North Holland Press, Amsterdam.

Stone, G. (1976). On the circumspect pooling of reaction times. *In* "Knowing, Thinking and Believing" (L. Petrinovich and J. McGaugh, eds.). Plenum Press, New York.

Stone, M. (1960). Models for choice reaction time. *Psychometrika* **25**, 251–260.

Taylor, D. A. (1976). Stage analysis of reaction time. *Psychological Bulletin* **83**, 161–192.

Teichner, W. and Krebs, M. (1974). Laws of Visual Choice Reaction Time. *Psychological Review* **81**, 75–98.

Townsend, J. T. (1972). Some results concerning the identifiability of parallel and serial processes. *British Journal of Mathematical and Statistical Psychology* **25**, 168–197.

Townsend, J. T. (1974). Issues and models concerning the processing of a finite number of inputs. *In* "Human Information Processing: Tutorials in Performance and Cognition" (B. H. Kantowitz, ed.). Lawrence Erlbaum, Hillsdale, N.J.

Townsend, J. T. (1976). Serial and within-stage independent parallel model equivalence on the minimum completion time. *Journal of Mathematical Psychology* **14**, 219–238.

Vickers, D. (1970). Evidence for an accumulator model of psychophysical discrimination. *Ergonomics* **13**, 37–58.

Vickers, D., Nettelbeck, T. and Willson, R. (1972). Perceptual indices of performance: The measurement of "inspection time" and "noise" in the visual system. *Perception* **1**, 263–295.

Waugh, N. C. and Anders, T. R. (1973). Searching through long-term verbal memory. *In* "Attention and Performance IV" (S. Kornblum, ed.), pp. 363–377. Academic Press, New York.

Welford, A. T. (1960). The measurement of sensory-motor performance: survey and reappraisal of twelve years progress. *Ergonomics* **3**, 189–230.

Welford, A. T. (1968). "Fundamentals of Skill". Methuen, London.

Welford, A. T. (1971). What is the basis of choice reaction time? *Ergonomics* **14**, 679–693.

Welford, A. T. (1973). Attention, strategy and reaction time: A tentative metric. *In* "Attention and Performance IV" (S. Kornblum, ed.), chapter 2, p. 10. Academic Press, New York.

Welford, A. T. (1975). Display layout, strategy and reaction time: Tests of a model. *In* "Attention and Performance V" (S. Dornic and P. Rabbitt, eds.), pp. 470–484. Academic Press, London.

Welford, A. T. (1976). "Skilled Performance: Perceptual and Motor Skills". Scott, Foresman, Glenview, Illinois.

Wood, C. C. (1974). Parallel processing of auditory and phonetic information in speech perception. *Perception and Psychophysics* **15**, 501–508.

Woodworth, R. S. (1938). "Experimental Psychology". Methuen, London.

Wundt, W. (1883). Über Psychologische Methoden. *Philosoph. Studien* **10**, 1–38.

Chapter 6

The Single-channel Hypothesis

A. T. WELFORD

Craik (1948) in a now famous paper, noted that the course pursued when tracking a moving target did not follow the target motion smoothly, but showed a series of oscillations, implying that correction of misalignment between target and follower was not made continuously but at discrete intervals of about half a second. He pointed out that this could not be due to the misalignment having to build up to some critical value before the subject could detect it, because the intermittency was not reduced by magnifying the display. Nor could it be due to any motor limitation, since hand movements of the extent and nature required could be made very much more rapidly than two per sec. The effect, he concluded, must be in the central mechanisms of the brain.

Searching for a cause of the intermittency, Craik was led to consider the reasons for the reaction time between the presentation of a signal and the emergence of a response. He argued:

> We must . . . ask ourselves whether this delay is more likely to consist of the transmission-time of nerve impulses continuously travelling down an immensely long chain of nerve-fibres and synapses connecting sensory and motor nerves, or of a "condensed" time-lag occurring in one part of the chain. If the first hypothesis were correct, there would seem to be no reason why a continuous stream of incoming impulses should not evoke a continuous stream of motor ones. . . . If, on the other hand, the time-lag is caused by the building up of some single "computing" process which then discharges down the motor nerves, we might expect that new sensory impulses entering the brain while this central computing process was going on would either disturb it or be hindered from disturbing it by some "switching" system.
>
> These ideas can be tested to some extent by recording the human response to a series of discrete stimuli presented at various time intervals, to see whether there is a minimum interval within which successive stimuli cannot be responded to. Such an experiment is analogous to physiological investigations of the "refractory phase" of a nerve or synapse, as pointed out by Telford

215

(1931). The results of Telford and of the writer suggest a refractory period of about 0.5 sec, such that a stimulus presented within this interval after the preceding one is responded to later, or may be missed. (Craik, 1948, p. 147)

The use of the term "refractory phase" was unfortunate because the analogy is not really at all close. Apart from the gross difference of time-scale, the refractory phase of nerves is clearly a recovery phenomenon whereas the "psychological refractory period", as it has come to be called, is due to the time occupied by some central process of translating from stimulus to response. However, the idea of testing by experiments using discrete stimuli has been fruitful indeed, and has led to a vast literature. Much of this has been controversial because any one piece of evidence taken alone has been open to several different interpretations. Elimination of alternatives has involved an almost superhuman task of taking simultaneous account of a wide variety of data to produce a theoretical treatment which appears to be *sufficient* to cover the evidence without being *necessary* at any one point.

In this chapter an outline will be given of the theory which has come to be known as the *single-channel hypothesis*. This will be followed by an account of certain qualifications to the theory which have proved to be necessary. Alternative theories which have been proposed from time to time will then be briefly surveyed. Finally some important applications of the main theory will be discussed.

1. The effect of a signal during the reaction time to a previous signal

The first experiments designed to test Craik's ideas used a type of tracking task. The subject had to keep a pointer on a line drawn on a paper band which passed behind a narrow slit. From time to time the line abruptly changed position and the subject's reaction time (RT) to begin to follow it and movement time (MT) to reach the new position could be measured from the record of the pointer movements (Vince, 1948a, 1950). When a change of position was well separated in time from the previous change, RT averaged 250 to 300 msec. When, however, two changes ($S1$ and $S2$) occurred close together so that $S2$ came during $RT1$, $RT2$ was longer than normal. With one class of exceptions which will be discussed later, the lengthening could be roughly accounted for by assuming that the central mechanisms took the same time to deal with the data from both $S1$ and $S2$, but did not begin to deal with those from $S2$ until they had finished dealing with those from $S1$. In other words, data from $S2$ had to be held in some kind of store until the end of $RT1$ when the central mechanisms became free. The events envisaged are shown in Fig. 6.1 and the result can be expressed

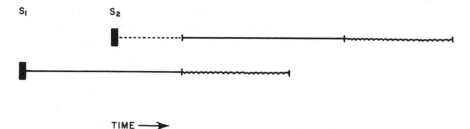

S₁   S₂

TIME ⟶

Fig. 6.1. Lengthening of reaction time to a signal which arrives during the reaction-time to a previous signal.
■ = Signal ——— = DT 〰〰〰 = MT ····· = time held in store.

in the equation

$$RT2 = RT1 + DT2 - ISI \qquad (ISI < RT1) \tag{6.1}$$

where *ISI* is the inter-signal interval between $S1$ and $S2$ and $DT2$ is the time taken to process the data from $S2$: this was taken in Vince's case to equal RT to a change of position well clear of others in time (Welford, 1952). Equation (6.1) implies that if $RT2$ were plotted against *ISI*, and $RT1$ had no variance, the result would be a line sloping at 45 degrees as shown by the solid line in Fig. 6.2. Since in any practical case $RT1$ always does have substantial variance, the actual plot expected would be as shown by the dotted line in Fig. 6.2.

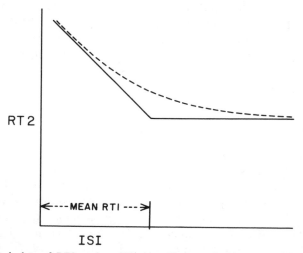

Fig. 6.2. Ideal plots of $RT2$ against *ISI* when $S2$ comes during $RT1$. The solid line shows the results expected if $RT1$ is exactly the same in all trials: the dotted line shows those expected when $RT1$ varies appreciably from trial to trial.

This result has been confirmed many times in subsequent experiments using lights or sounds as signals and key-pressing responses which make clearer-cut measures of RT possible than Vince was able to attain. Some of these experiments have followed Vince's in using a continuous stream of signals (Hick, 1948; Welford, 1959) but most have differed from hers in presenting discrete pairs of signals. The subject thus knew that in any one trial he would have only one signal in each of two classes. In these cases $DT2$ can be estimated by including in a series of trials some in which ISI is sufficiently long for all potential delays due to responding to $S1$ to be over well before $S2$ arrives. When $S1$ requires a two-choice reaction, an ISI of about 1 sec should be sufficient for this purpose. However several experiments using discrete signals have assumed that $DT2$ can be assessed by measuring the RT to $S2$ when it is given in a control series of trials from which $S1$ is omitted (e.g. Davis, 1956). This method is incorrect because, as was shown in Chapter 3, RT is shorter when only one signal has to be considered than when two or more may occur (E. Smith, 1967), even when signals are well separated in time (Gottsdanker et al., 1963; Salthouse, 1970; Brebner, 1977). The same principle can account for the finding in some experiments that $RT1$ increases slightly with degree of choice in $RT2$ (Karlin and Kestenbaum, 1968; M. Smith, 1969).

If this theory is correct, two results should follow. First, there should be a positive correlation between $RT2$ and $RT1$ for any one ISI. In studies in which this has been tested, substantial correlations have been found (Welford, 1967; Karlin and Kestenbaum, 1968). Second, any factor tending to lengthen $RT1$ should lengthen $RT2$ by approximately the same amount. This has been found to hold with variations in the intensity of $S1$, the degree of choice associated with it (M. Smith, 1967b) and the compatibility between $S1$ and $R1$ (Broadbent and Gregory, 1967). The increase of $RT2$ is sometimes a little less than might have been expected, but this could be due to complicating factors which will be discussed later.

(A) LOCATING THE EFFECT

The lengthening of $RT2$ is clearly not due to any sensory factors such as not being able to focus the eyes on two signals in quick succession, because it still occurs when $S1$ is visual and $S2$ is auditory or vice versa (Davis, 1957, 1959). Nor is it caused by the time required to execute $M1$, because it still occurs when $M1$ and $M2$ are made by different hands (e.g. Davis, 1956; Welford, 1959). Indeed $RT2$ is sometimes lengthened when $S1$ has merely to be observed and no response to it is required (Fraisse, 1957; Davis, 1959; Elithorn, 1961; Koster and Bekker, 1967) although this is not always so (e.g. Borger, 1963).

Davis suggested that delays in responding to $S2$ occur in these latter cases when some established response to $S1$ has to be inhibited or when there is difficulty in discriminating between $S1$ and $S2$. Some evidence for the latter view is provided by Rubinstein (1964) who found substantial delays when $S1$ (to which no response had to be made) was a large-field stimulus to one eye and $S2$ (which was responded to) was a similar stimulus to the other or when $S1$ and $S2$ were bursts of noise to different ears, but no delays when $S1$ was visual and $S2$ auditory or *vice versa*. More generally, it seems reasonable to suppose that delays occur insofar as data from $S1$ have to be processed even though no overt response is made. Nickerson (1967b) has shown that delays to $R2$ when no response is required to $S1$ are greater when it conveys information than when it can be ignored: when $S1$ indicated which of two keys to press when $S2$ arrived, delays were substantially greater than when $S1$ was neutral and the indication of which key to press came only with $S2$. The delays might have been longer still if $S1$ had not given part of $S2$'s information in advance (cf. Harrison, 1960). The complementary finding was made by Davis (1965) that no delays occurred when, instead of $S1$ being given, the subject himself pressed a "trigger" key which led after a variable ISI to the appearance of $S2$. This finding has, however, been both confirmed and challenged (Koster and Bekker, 1967; Kornblum and Koster, 1967). Some variability of result is perhaps to be expected since it may be difficult for the subject to ignore feedback from the triggering movement which, as will be seen later, may capture attention.

The lengthening of $RT2$ seems clearly to be due to delays somewhere in the central mechanisms, and appears to be fundamental in the sense that it is not eliminated by practice (Hick, 1948; Davis, 1956; Slater-Hammel, 1958; Gottsdanker and Stelmach, 1971). When attempting to pinpoint it within the central mechanisms it is important to note that many studies, from the earliest onwards, have shown what is implied in Fig. 6.1, that during the RT to one signal it is possible to execute the response to a previous signal, and also to receive and register a subsequent signal which comes and goes again before the RT is over. This is in line with the concept of separate stages concerned with *perception, choice of response* and *control of a motor programme* that was suggested by evidence discussed in Chapter 3, and implies that these three stages can work in parallel. Since, as has been noted in Chapter 3, the time taken by perception is usually short compared with that for choice of response, it is in this latter process that the main single-channel effects seem to lie, and it is the "computing process" in this stage that is protected from interference due to subsequent data by what Craik described as a "switching system" and will here be termed a *gate*. This gate is envisaged as shutting when data are fed through from the perceptual to the choice, or as we have termed it *translation*, stage, choice stage, and as opening again only when the computations in this latter stage have been completed.

(B) REFINEMENTS OF THE THEORY

If the gate acts in this way, however, a difficulty arises with eqn (6.1). Although it fits the facts reasonably well, it assumes that the time for which the single channel is occupied by data from $S1$ is equal to the whole of $RT1$, and takes no account of any time during which the perceptual mechanism may have been dealing with data from $S2$ in parallel which choice of response to $S1$. A possible solution of this difficulty is to assume that some minimum *feedback* from the responding action, indicating that execution of the response chosen has begun, is required to open the gate. Such feedback would take an appreciable time to become effective, and if this time approximately balanced the time taken to perceive $S2$, eqn (6.1) would appear to hold although the situation would be more accurately expressed:

$$RT2 = RT1 + FT(\text{min}) + DT2 - PT2 - ISI$$
$$((ISI + PT2) < (RT1 + FT\,\text{min}))\quad(6.2)$$

where $FT\,\text{min}$ is the time required for the minimum feedback to become effective and $PT2$ is the time taken to perceive $S2$. The relationships envisaged are shown in Fig. 6.3.

Some feedback of this kind almost certainly plays an important part in checking whether errors have been made: in copying activities such as rapid typing, feedback data seem to be compared with some trace of the input and any discrepancy alerts the subject to stop and discover where the error has occurred. Support for the view that feedback is necessary to clear the central mechanisms to deal with further input data comes for the "motor stuttering" observed with delayed visual feedback. A subject writing a word when he cannot see his hand directly but only via a television screen where its movements are shown after a delay of about 0.5 sec, will often repeat a letter, suggesting that the "orders" to write it go on being effective until visual feedback confirming that this has been done are received (Smith *et al.*, 1960). Similar results occur with delayed auditory feedback: for example Chase *et al.* (1961) found that subjects who had to repeat the sound "b" or

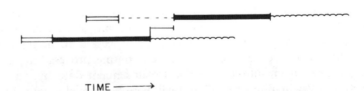

TIME ⟶

Fig. 6.3. Events envisaged when $S2$ arrives during $RT1$, in terms of eqn (6.2).
═══════ Detection of signal (PT). ▬▬▬▬▬ Choice and initiation of response (DT–PT).
────────── Detection of beginning or end of response (FT_{min}). ∿∿∿∿Execution of response
(MT). ── ── ── Signal held in store.

tap on a morse key in groups of three produced more sounds or taps than they should when feedback was delayed by about 0.25 sec. Again, Yates (1965) showed that delayed auditory feedback impaired the accuracy of Morse code operators, usually by causing them to insert extra dots or dashes. A further indication that some feedback is normally required to open the gate and that it takes time to do so is perhaps contained in the finding by Fraisse (1957), Davis (1959) and M. Smith (1967c) that delays found when no response is required to $S1$ are shorter than when a response is demanded—presumably in these cases the signal for clearing the translation mechanism comes from within the brain. More direct evidence that feedback which tallies with the orders given for action, is required to open the gate, comes from the finding by Rabbitt and Rodgers (1977) that if an error had been made in responding to a signal, a following response that would have been correct to the preceding signal was made relatively fast, as if the orders for giving that response had not been cancelled and were still operating, at least to some extent (Welford, 1979).

The scheme indicated in Fig. 6.3 and eqn (6.2) can explain two types of finding otherwise anomalous. First, increasing the degree of choice of the response to $S2$ from one to two does not raise $RT2$ as much when $S2$ comes during $RT1$ as would have been expected from the increase of $RT2$ when $S2$ is well after $RT1$ (Karlin and Kestenbaum, 1968). The time required to perceive $S2$ in a two-choice situation would almost certainly have been longer than in a simple one, so that more of the time required to deal with the data from $S2$ would have overlapped $RT1$. Second, lengthening of $RT2$ has been shown to be less than would be predicted from eqn (6.1) when $S1$ and $R1$ are highly compatible—a condition which has been noted in Chapter 3 as reducing the time required to translate from perception to response.

Confusion has often arisen between the functioning of the whole system and of the separate parts of it, especially regarding the extent to which separate signals or responses can be dealt with in parallel within the different stages. It seems clear that the translation and programme stages can produce complex responses and sequences which require simultaneous action by different effectors as when, say, playing an organ, both hands and feet may be involved. Laboratory experiments have shown that simultaneous responses by the two hands or by hand and voice are little slower than the corresponding single responses (Sanders, 1967; Schvaneveldt, 1969). The simultaneous responses are, however, coordinated in time so that they should be regarded as a single complex response rather than two separate ones.

As regards perception, the picture is not so clear (for a review see Triesman, 1966). Coordinated data arriving over different sensory modes, for instance the hearing of speech and sight of the speaker's lips, must be dealt with simultaneously rather than successively otherwise rapid and close coordination of such data would be impossible (Bernstein, 1970). There has, however, been considerable controversy as to whether, when a decision has to be made on two or more different features of an item, such as colour, shape and size, these are identified serially or simultaneously. Suppose, for example, a subject has to select from a series of shapes those which are *both* red *and* square. If the conjunctive decisions between red as opposed to other colours and between square as opposed to other shapes are made simultaneously, the overall time taken will roughly equal the time required to decide about colour alone or about shape alone, whichever is longer. Because of random variation in the time required to make decisions, the conjunctive decision will tend to take a little longer than this, but probably not much. If the decisions are made successively, the time to decide on both criteria will be the sum of the times required to decide on each criterion alone, in addition to the time required for any purely sensory processes or for the motor action of responding.

Similarly, the time taken by a subject to make the disjunctive decision, about whether a shape is *either* red *or* square, as opposed to neither red nor square, would, if decisions are simultaneous, lie between the times for the longer and shorter of the decisions about colour or shape taken singly, since sometimes one and sometimes the other would suffice. If the decisions are successive, the time would sometimes be that for one of the single decisions, sometimes that for the other, and sometimes the sum of both, again in addition to purely sensory or response times.

The evidence from studies in this area is not entirely clear, and the interpretation of published experiments is often difficult or impossible. Generally speaking, however, the evidence seems to indicate that decisions about different features of an object have, in many cases at least, to be made successively (e.g. Nickerson, 1967a; Posner and Mitchell, 1967). Perhaps analyses of two or more different criteria are in fact made simultaneously, but the one which first reaches a critical state triggers a decision, and by doing so closes the gate to the translation mechanism for a short time, so that decisions about other criteria are delayed. This would not happen if the critical states were reached almost simultaneously, since a single decision could then incorporate the data from all of them.

2. The effect of a signal during or shortly after the movement in response to a previous signal

Several experiments have shown that some lengthening of $RT2$ may also occur when $S2$ comes shortly after the end of $RT1$ (Vince, 1948a, 1950;

Welford, 1959; Ells, 1973; Williams, 1974; Wilke and Vaughn, 1976). Vince's results suggested that if $S2$ came during the initial 150 msec or thereabouts of $MT1$ dealing with the data from it was delayed until the end of this period (Welford, 1952). More recent results (Welford, 1959) where this point was examined in detail suggested that the delay was until the end of $MT1$. Probably the most plausible reason for the delay was given by Hick who suggested that

> The attention may be switched to that sensory field from which confirmation of the occurrence of the response is expected. Or alternatively, to avoid the teleological concept of "expecting confirmation", we may suppose that the attention is reflexly deflected by the inevitable stimulation of kinaesthetic or other receptors by the response. (Hick, 1948, p. 43)

If this is so, and if the data fed back have to be dealt with by the translation mechanism, perhaps being compared for correctness with processes there, feedback from the beginning of the response (FTb) would be expected to "capture" the translation mechanism for a brief period—in other words the response would be monitored. Any fresh signal from outside arriving after FTb had begun would be dealt with only after it had ended. $FTb1$ might or might not be the same as $MT1$: when it is, it may well be that MT is "tailored" to FTb rather than *vice versa*. The time taken by such monitoring presumably depends on the information conveyed by the feedback and will therefore, like reaction time, depend upon such variables as the frequency of the response as well as on its complexity.

The time relationships envisaged are expressed in the equation

$$RT2 = RT1 + DT2 + FTb1 - ISI$$
$$(RT1 < ISI < (RT1 + FTb1)) \quad (6.3)$$

Delays in responding to $S2$ have also been found when it comes shortly after the end of $MT1$, suggesting that the translation mechanism may become occupied for a further brief period at the termination of $MT1$, if no $S2$ has arrived by then. The time of occupation cannot be measured with certainty but has been estimated for Vince's experiments at about 150 msec (Welford, 1952) and for the present writer's (Welford, 1959) at about 200 msec—in each case a time similar to FTb. It seems reasonable to suppose that *any* "high point" of kinaesthetic, tactile or other stimulation arising during a response might capture the translation mechanism and that the end of a movement often provides such a high point. Alternatively, there may be some monitoring of the completion of each response which enables the subject to set himself in readiness for the next. The time relationships involved are set out in the equation

$$RT2 = RT1 + DT2 + MT1 + FTe1 - ISI$$
$$((RT1 + MT1) < ISI < (RT1 + MT1 + FTe1)) \quad (6.4)$$

where FTe is the time for which the translation mechanism is occupied by data fed back from the end of a response. The importance of the beginning and end of a movement appear to extend beyond the brief actions of key pressing or tracking. For example, Salmoni *et al.* (1976) found that lengthening of $RT2$ was greater when $S2$ came near the beginning or end of a movement of 1–2 sec than when it came nearer the middle.

If neither $RT1$, $FTb1$ nor $FTe1$ varied from trial to trial, the plot of $RT2$ against ISI would, according to eqns (6.1), (6.3) and (6.4), assume a saw-tooth form, starting high when ISI was short and falling at 45 degrees as in Fig. 6.2 until the end of $RT1$. Thereafter it would rise sharply to fall at 45 degrees until the end of $FTb1$, and would rise again at the end of MT1 to fall once more at 45 degrees to the end of $FTe1$. Variations in the times concerned will, however, always obscure this picture and tend to produce a gradual fall of $RT2$ as ISI increases up to a point some time beyond the end of $MT1$.

Confirmation that monitoring of the kind envisaged in eqns (6.3) and (6.4) does in fact occur and that it takes time is contained in the results of an experiment by Leonard (1953). His task could be presented in two ways. In the first, a lever had to be moved to the corner of a triangular guide corresponding to that of a signal light in a triangular display. On reaching this corner the light would go out and one of the other two come on, and so on. The task in the second condition was the same, except that with each light a second light came on which gave the subject foreknowledge of which light would be the next in the series. Performance in the second condition was faster than in the first, presumably because the advance signals enabled a decision to be made about the direction of each movement during the preceding movement. The important point in the present context is that the advance signals also seemed to prevent attention to feedback from the responding movements. Many subjects, to their surprise, found that with the second condition, in contrast to the first, they had little awareness of what they were doing—the movements seemed "automatic" and without conscious control. Similar results were found in a serial RT task in which keys had to be pressed in response to light signals. If each signal appeared immediately the response key to the last was *pressed*, RT was shorter than if the next signal came on when the key was *released*, and at the same time the subject seemed to lose awareness of what he was doing—as one put it, "the lights seem to be chasing you instead of you chasing them" (Welford, 1977). In the latter condition each response could be monitored, while in the former monitoring seemed to have been omitted.

Why the signals in the display should have taken precedence over the monitoring of responses is not easy to see, but these experiments are not alone in posing this problem. If eqn (6.1) holds, it seems clear that whenever

$S2$ comes during $RT1$ monitoring of $M1$ must either be cut out or deferred, otherwise $RT2$ would be lengthened by a delay to the end of $FTb1$ or oven $FTe1$ instead of to the end of $RT1$. Two possibilities appear to deserve consideration. First, Klein and Posner (1974) found that visual data tend to take precedence over kinaesthetic in gaining attention. Second, Davis (1956) and Marill (1957) in paired-signal experiments with simple key-pressing responses, found no lengthening of $RT2$ if $S2$ came after the end of $RT1$—it looked, in fact, as if the responses made by their subjects were not being monitored. This is plausible in that practice is likely to increase the accuracy of actions so that they do not need to be checked—in other words, the feedback will become redundant (Annett, 1966). The amount of practice needed before this state is reached is likely to increase with the complexity of the response. For simple actions such as those used by Davis and Marill, the practice possible within a normal laboratory experiment could well be sufficient. With more elaborate, graded actions, however, the practice required to do without monitoring would probably be much longer, and attained only by musicians, typists, industrial repetition workers, professional games players and others who exercise a skill over a number of years.

3. Supplementary theories

Two qualifications of the basic theory arise from the operation of principles, demonstrated in other areas of human performance, which interact with the processes of dealing with the signals in certain experimental situations. Both have the effect of making $RT2$ shorter than eqns (6.1)–(6.4) would predict.

(A) GROUPING OF SIGNALS AND RESPONSES

When ISI is less than about 100 msec reaction to $S2$ is sometimes delayed as eqn (6.1) predicts, but is often hardly delayed at all. When this is so, however, there are signs that $M1$ and $M2$ are coordinated: in some cases both are made simultaneously or $M2$ begins before $M1$ has finished; sometimes the responses are in the wrong order suggesting that the order of $S1$ and $S2$ has not been resolved. More often, temporal order seems to have been perceived correctly, but as a unitary pattern. In Vince's experiments, where $S2$ in effect cancelled $S1$, the total result with short ISI was sometimes that no response was made. In some cases the short $RT2$ is coupled with an $RT1$ which is longer than normal, suggesting that the subject has as his categories of response, not only $M1$ and $M2$ but also ($M1 + M2$) which, because it is rare, takes longer to produce (Hick and Welford, 1956). In other cases both $RT2$ and $RT1$ seem unusually short suggesting that, when both signals have appeared, the subject makes an undifferentiated, and therefore rapid, response to both. The different types of grouping effect have been illustrated by Halliday *et al.* (1960), by Kerr *et al.* (1963, 1965) and by Elithorn and Barnett (1967), although their evidence has to be taken with caution because they used *only* short *ISI*s (of up to 100 msec) and the subjects' whole strategy of performance may therefore have been different from that in experiments where a wider range of *ISI*s was presented.

The evidence suggests that when *ISI* is less than about 100 msec, *S*1 and *S*2 may in some way be treated together as a single *group*. The result is that, if grouped and ungrouped responses are not separated, the average *RT*2 is shortened (e.g. Slater-Hammel, 1958; Adams, 1962). In extreme cases it is actually shorter when *ISI* is very short than when *ISI* is a little longer, instead of falling continuously with increase of *ISI* in accordance with eqn (6.1) (Elithorn and Lawrence, 1955; Marill, 1957; Koster and Bekker, 1967). A further result of grouping is that the inter-response interval (*IRI*), that is the time from the beginning of *M*1 to the beginning of *M*2, is shorter than would be predicted from eqns (6.1)–(6.3). This fact, together with the fact that grouping tends to occur when *S*2 comes very shortly after *S*1 means that *IRI* will rise with *ISI* in the manner found by Kahneman (1973) reanalysing data by M. Smith (1969), instead of remaining the same until *ISI* becomes greater than *RT*1.

It must be emphasized that grouping of this kind is not a process confined to the conditions we have been discussing, but seems to be a common— indeed essential—feature of many high-speed performances. Bryan and Harter (1899) observed that Morse-code operators performed faster when they came to deal with "dots" and "dashes" in groups corresponding to words or phrases instead of letters. Craik (1948) pointed out that if a musician dealt with each note, or a typist with each letter, separately they would perform very much more slowly than they in fact do. The rates actually attained imply that the translation mechanism takes in data from whole musical phrases or words or even groups of words as single units and issues "orders to the effector stage in terms of correspondingly complex series of actions. Vince (1949) has demonstrated this point with experiments in which subjects had to tap a Morse key in response to dots on a paper band moving past a slit in a screen. She found the number of dots that could be reacted to accurately was very much higher if they appeared in groups of two, three or four than if they were presented singly.

Grouping in the context of reaction time appears to imply that the gate between perception and choice takes an appreciable time to close after the onset of *S*1. The time appears to average about 80 msec: signs of grouping are very frequent when *ISI* is less than this, and rare when it is greater. The time is comparable with that during which subjects have difficulty in discriminating the order of events (see Norman, 1967; Sternberg and Knoll, 1973) and over which backward-masking is likely to occur (see Kahneman, 1968), and it is tempting to assume that a common mechanism underlies all these cases. However, the time is probably also affected by a number of factors at present imperfectly understood: for example Kerr *et al.* (1963) found grouping to be less frequent when $S1$ and $M1$ were on the non-dominant side and $S2$ and $M2$ on the dominant than with the reverse order of sides, but that among grouped responses those where $RT2$ was especially short tended to follow the presentation of $S1$ to the dominant side.

Grouping might arise over a longer interval if the subject waited a brief time after $S1$ to see if any further signal arrived before committing himself to a response. This seems to have been done spontaneously in certain cases (e.g. Adams, 1962; Borger, 1963), and was clearly done by Sanders' (1964) subjects when instructed "to collect all perceptual data before any response is carried out" as opposed to completing $RT1$ "without taking any notice of $S2$." It would be especially likely to occur if subjects performed a long series of trials with the same ISI. Such waiting might occupy the central mechanisms for the period the subject decided to wait, during which both $S1$ and $S2$ could occur and therefore be dealt with together. Alternatively it might represent a postponement of closing the gate until $S2$ arrived. In the former case $RT1$ should be lengthened by the waiting time and $RT2$ should be the sum of the waiting time plus $DT2$ less ISI. In the latter case RT1 should rise with ISI while $RT2$ should remain roughly constant. The experimental evidence seems to favour the latter alternative (e.g. Sanders, 1964; Reynolds, 1966; Brebner, 1977), although processing of data from $S1$ appears to proceed during the waiting time because, if in some trials $S2$ is omitted altogether, $RT1$ may not be longer in these than it would be without waiting, even though it is so in the trials in which $S2$ occurs (Greenwald and Schulman, 1973)—a curious result which merits further study.

Although the main evidence of grouping comes from cases in which $S2$ has occurred early in the course of $RT1$ and is grouped with $S1$, a form of grouping between $S2$ and $Fb1$ seems also to occur when $S2$ comes shortly after the beginning of $M1$. In these cases not only is $RT2$ shorter than would be predicted by eqn (6.3), but $MT1$ tends to be longer than normal (Welford, 1959). It seems possible that such grouping may also occur when $S2$ comes shortly before the beginning of $M1$, in which case $RT2$ is longer than would be predicted by eqn (6.1) and at the same time $M1$ is lengthened. Grouping between $S2$ and Fe doubtless also occurs, but is difficult to detect with confidence since there is no overt response to be modified and the only indication is that $RT2$ is longer than predicted by eqn (6.3) or shorter than predicted by eqn (6.4).

(B) MODIFICATION OF RESPONSE

Several studies concerned with the single-channel hypothesis have examined the time taken to modify an action (Vince, 1948b; Hick, 1949; Poulton, 1950). The results appear to be consistent with eqns (6.1), (6.3) and (6.4), the equation applicable depending upon whether the modification depends upon an amending signal given during $RT1$, upon the beginning of $M1$ or upon its results. In some tracking experiments, however, modifications are occasionally made in a very much shorter time than these equations would predict—in about 100 msec as opposed to 200–300. It is perhaps reasonable to regard these as cases where an error has been made by the programme control mechanism rather than by the translation mechanism—the "orders" given by the latter have been correct, but have not been correctly carried out. Such modifications seem to imply a comparison of feedback from the moving member with the translation mechanism's orders, and correction without the issue of fresh orders. If this is true, modifications should take place in these cases without visual observation of the error concerned.

Some evidence supporting this view is provided by Rabbitt (1966b) who found in a serial choice-reaction task that errors could be detected and corrected even when no indication that they had occurred was given by the display, and that corrections were in most cases substantially faster than the corresponding accurate responses. However, although corrections in such cases often tend to be quicker than accurate responses (Rabbitt, 1966a; Rabbitt and Phillips, 1967) they may not be greatly so, suggesting that an error has occurred in the translation mechanism and that some of the work of selecting the response has therefore had to be done again. It is understandable that in these cases the correcting response should still be somewhat quicker: Rabbitt (1967) cites a study by Burns who showed that errors in choice-response tasks were not entirely random but were in part correct. They might, for example, in a four-choice task be in the correct pair but the wrong member of the pair. This is not the whole explanation because Rabbitt (1967) has shown that responses to errors may be faster even if they are quite different from correct responses. He used a choice-reaction task in which responses were given by keys under the several fingers of one hand. Whenever an error was made the subject had to depress keys under both thumbs. Rabbitt regarded this as an "anatomically awkward" response, but from what was said in Chapter 3 about the neurological control of the fingers, it might be regarded as relatively easy and thus understandably fast: while each finger would have to be depressed individually without moving the others, the thumbs could be depressed by a relatively gross rotation of the hands. It should be emphasized in passing that rapid correction of errors is by no means universal: in some cases it takes substantially longer than making a correct response (e.g. Adams and Chambers, 1962). We may surmise that in these cases there is not only recalculation of orders by the translation mechanism, but some review of the strategy of performance.

The corrections discussed by Rabbitt do not seem to involve any breach of the principle implied in eqns (6.1), (6.3) and (6.4). A clear breach does, however, seem to be shown by the results of an experiment by Vince on changing the *speed* of a response (Vince and Welford, 1967). These results suggest that an amending signal may sometimes get through the closed gate. Subjects were presented with vertical lines rising 1.5 in from a baseline on a paper band revolving on a kymograph drum behind a screen in which was a vertical slit 10 mm wide. The lines were spaced so as to appear at irregular intervals of 2–3 sec. One group (*A*) was told that as soon as a blue line appeared they were to draw a line of the same length in the slit and then return to the baseline, making the whole movement smoothly and without hurrying. After some practice they were told that occasionally a red line would appear, in which case they should make the movement as rapidly as possible. A second group (*B*) made their normal responses to the blue lines as rapidly as possible and their occasional responses to the red lines at leisure. A third group (*C*) were given the same instruction as group *A*, except that when a red line occurred they were to stop their movement and pause before returning to baseline.

The results are set out in Fig. 6.4, in a way suggested by Bertelson (1967). They consist of all cases in which $S2$ arrived during the reaction time to $S1$ and separate responses were made to both. Cases were excluded in which the response to the red line was wholly substituted for that to the blue—a kind of grouping effect which sometimes occurred when the interval between $S1$ and $S2$ was less than 100 msec. According to the hypothesis, the points for each group should lie on a straight line sloping at 45 degrees. Those for group *B* are in very fair agreement with prediction, and this was so for each of the subjects individually. The fact that the observed $RT2$s were rather too long when $S2$ came only a short time before the end of $RT1$ may have been due to monitoring of $M1$: $Fb1$ may have become grouped with $S2$ and thus lengthened $RT2$. The results for group *A* showed no systematic trend and this was again true for each subject individually. Two members of group *C* behaved like those of group *B*: their shorter mean reaction times are understandable in that the decision to stop a response is probably simpler than one to change its speed. The third subject in group *C* behaved like those in group *A*.

The results imply that a signal to speed up a movement, and in some cases one to slow it down, can become effective without the usual single-channel delay. They are in line with several previous results of step-tracking experiments in which a signal has occurred to make a movement to a target

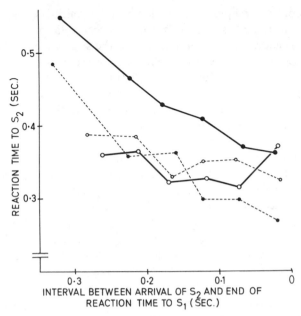

Fig. 6.4. Times taken to modify the speed of a response. Results of an experiment by Vince (Vince and Welford, 1967).
○———○ Group A (slow to fast): three subjects. ●———● Group B (fast to slow): three subjects. ○ – – ○ One subject in group C (slow to stop) whose performance resembled that of group A. ● – – ● Two subjects in group C whose performances resembled that of group B. Each point is the mean $RT2$ for a range of intervals between the arrival of $S2$ and the end $RT1$. The ranges (from right to left) in msec were 0–49, 50–99, 100–149, 150–199, 200–249 and 250 and over.

a given distance away and then, before the movement has actually begun, a second signal has called for the movement either to be extended to a target further away, or to be reversed and aimed at a target on the other side of the starting point. $RT2$ has in some of these cases been shorter than would have been predicted by eqn (6.1) (Vince, 1950; Gottsdanker, 1966; Brebner, 1968). Megaw (1970, 1974) who took detailed measures of acceleration and EMG records in a task of this type, showed that the shortening of $RT2$ was more apparent than real. The signal to extend or reverse a movement indeed became effective without the usual single-channel delay, but its effect was to intensify all the muscular actions involved in making the response, so that both agonists and antagonists contracted more vigorously than they otherwise would have done and therefore had effect a little sooner. The *timing* of the sequence of contractions was, however, unchanged. These results suggest that the decision process protected by the gate is the *initiation of a fresh pattern of action* or, to put it another way, the *changing of relations between input and output.* Thus a signal to bring other muscles into play is excluded, while signals conveying instructions merely to intensify the activity of those already in action can get through. The intensification in this case is perhaps attributable to an increase of general activation or arousal. If so, signals to intensify may be more effective than those to reduce activity because increases of arousal tend to be more rapid than decreases.

4. The theory and some suggested alternatives

To sum up the argument so far, the single-channel hypothesis as it now stands is that:

(i) Somewhere along the line of central mechanisms from sensory input to effector action there is at least one which deals with only one signal or group of signals and only one action or coordinated group of actions at a time.

(ii) Each of the three broad stages of the central mechanisms, concerned with the perception, translation from perception to action (choice of response) and the control of programmes of action, can deal with a signal or group of signals or an action or group of actions while other stages are dealing with others. In the experiments reported so far, the main limitation has been in the time required for choice of response, but it seems possible that any of the three stages might set the limits in certain circumstances. For example, perception might be limiting if fine discriminations were required, or execution of action if this had to be slow or very complex.

(iii) There is a "gate" between the perceptual and translatory stages which protects processes concerned with choice of response from interference by subsequent signals until action has been initiated. The gate takes an appreciable time to close after a signal has arrived, and a further signal arriving before it closes may be grouped with the one preceding to give rise to a coordinated response to both. The closing of the gate may be postponed by waiting to see if a further signal arrives. When an overt response is required, the opening of the gate occurs only after the receipt of some minimal feedback indicating that the response has begun.

(iv) Monitoring of responses may occupy the translation mechanism to the exclusion of dealing with further signals, especially for periods following the beginning and end of responses. Monitoring is, however, usually suppressed if a second signal has arrived before response to the first has begun.

(v) Signals to intensify response, and occasionally those to reduce it, can pass the gate without waiting for it to be opened, and can thus influence an ongoing response. They do not, however, affect the basic temporal pattern of the programme of actions constituting the response.

Several alternative theories that have been canvassed will be briefly discussion, showing in each case how far they account for the present author's (1959) data.

(a) An early suggestion was that there is a *refractory state*, independent of $RT1$ and $MT1$, following an event in some part of the chain of mechanisms leading from signal to response. Various periods ranging from 0.1 to 0.5 sec have been proposed. None of these gives a good fit to the data in that no one fixed interval will account for the observed delays both when $S1$ comes during $RT1$ *and* when it comes during $MT1$ (see Table 6.1a). Also if the refractory state started with the onset of $S1$, there would be no correlation between $(RT2 + ISI)$ and $RT1$, although a positive correlation might arise if the refractory state started with the initiation of $M1$. This theory has assumed an *absolute* refractory period. The alternative of a decaying *relative* refractory period does not yield quantitative productions. Such a theory is at first sight attractive in that it might be expected to link lengthening of $RT2$ with the course of average evoked potentials in the cortex. The two appear, however, to be independent (Boddy, 1972).

(b) Several authors have proposed that perception may be quantized into samples about a third of a second long, and Broadbent (1958) suggested that a subject begins a new sample when $S1$ arrives so that, when ISI is less than a third of a second, the data from $S2$ have to wait until a new sample begins. This theory makes fairly close predictions of $RT2$ in some cases but does not account for certain other features of the data. For example, it implies that when $S2$ comes during $RT1$, $RT2$ for any given ISI, or more generally $(RT2 + ISI)$, will be independent of $RT1$, whereas eqn (6.1) implies they will be correlated. It also suggests that when $S2$ comes during $MT1$, $RT2$ and $RT1$ will be positively correlated since short $RT2$ would be obtained if $RT1$ ended and $S2$ arrived before the end of the first sample, but $RT2$ would be much longer if $S2$ missed the end of the first sample and had to wait to be dealt with until the end of the second. Substantial correlations were in fact found by both Welford (1959) and by Borger (1963) when ISI was *less* than $RT1$, becoming very low when ISI was *longer* (see Table 6.1b). Also if intermittency is due to a division into fixed quanta, $RT2$ should be unaffected by the compatibility of $S1$ and its response: if on the other hand the single-channel hypothesis is correct, the incompatibility which lengthens $RT1$ should lengthen $RT2$ by the same amount. It was noted earlier that this has been found to occur (Sanders, 1967; Broadbent and Gregory, 1967).

(c) An alternative to the single-channel hypothesis that was persistently canvassed in the 1950s was that the delays in responding to $S2$ can be accounted for in terms of temporal uncertainty effects. Many studies have shown that when a warning precedes a signal by a foreperiod which varies

Table 6.1. Comparison of observed values of $RT2$ obtained by Welford (1959) with values predicted by several theories. All times are given in msec. In all cases $M1$ and $M2$ were made with different hands. Reversed and grouped responses have been omitted. $DT2$ has been taken as 282 msec—i.e. the mean RT to a signal coming 1 sec or more after the end of the movement made to the preceding signal

	S2 arrives during RT1		S2 arrives during MT1		Total discrepancy regardless of sign	Correlation $(RT2 + ISI) \times RT1$ for cases in which S2 came during RT1
	Mean	Predicted minus observed	Mean	Predicted minus observed		
Observed (±standard of mean)	458 (±15)		393 (±14)			$\tau = +0.473$ ($p < 0.001$)
Predicted						
(a) Refractory period of 0.5 sec after beginning of $M1$ before						
$M2$ can begin	613	+155	409	+ 16	171	0 or +
Ditto 0.327 sec†	458	0	292	−101	101	0 or +
Ditto 0.1 sec	303	−155	282	−111	266	0 or +
(b) Intake dealt with only at instant of S_1 and at intervals of $\frac{1}{3}$ sec thereafter	434	− 24	471	+ 78	102	0
(c) Temporal uncertainty	No quantitative predictions			0		
(d) $M1$ inhibits $M2$ so that $M2$ cannot begin until $M1$ has finished: eqn (6.5)	312	−146	282	−111	257	+
(e) Single-channel hypothesis: eqs (6.4) and (6.3)	413	− 45	356	− 37	82	+*

* More rigorous evidence for the single-channel hypothesis is a positive correlation between $(RT1–ISI)$ and $RT2$. τ in this case was found to be $+0.466$ ($p < 0.001$).

† The value of 0.327 sec was chosen to give the result most favourable to the theory when $S2$ came during $RT1$.

from one trial to the next, reaction to the signal is slower on those trials when the interval is very short—say 200 msec or less—than when it is somewhat longer: it is generally assumed, as was discussed in Chapter 1, that the subject makes some kind of preparation during the foreperiod but that the state of preparedness cannot be held at optimum level for more than a fraction of a second, so that the subject prepares for the mean or modal foreperiod and is less than fully prepared if the signal comes earlier. It has been held that lack of preparedness can account for the delays to $RT2$ in the experiments we have been discussing, although it seems equally plausible, *prima facie*, that the temporal uncertainty effects are, at least in some cases, due to single-channel delays caused by the warning capturing the channel.

Attempts to distinguish between these views consist of separating temporal uncertainty and single-channel effects. This has been done in two main ways. First, foreperiods varying from trial to trial have been presented over different ranges. For example, Drazin (1961) compared ranges of 2.0–4.0 sec with 1.0–3.0, 0.5–2.5, 0.25–2.25 and 0.125–2.125 sec. In all cases, reaction times were a little longer at the beginning of the range. The absolute lengthening—about 20 msec—differed little between the three higher ranges, all of which could be regarded as clear of single-channel effects. Results by other experimenters have been roughly similar (Klemmer, 1956; Karlin, 1959).

Second, conditions in which foreperiod or ISI varied from trial to trial have been compared with conditions in which they remained the same over a block of trials. It has already been noted that under the latter conditions reaction times to single signals may be suspiciously short, suggesting that the subject is responding to the warning rather than the signal itself. It has also been observed that when responses have to be made to two signals, $S1$ and $S2$, an ISI which remains the same over a block of trials favours grouping. However, both difficulties seem to have been avoided in some experiments by the use of instructions emphasizing fast reaction to $S1$, catch trials in which $S1$ or $S2$ is omitted, or by using choice instead of simple reactions. This second approach is illustrated in an experiment by Kay and Weiss (1961) whose subjects performed under several different conditions after considerable practice. In all cases a trial began by pressing a "ready" key. There followed after a 1, 2, 3 or 4 sec foreperiod a click ($S1$), and this was followed after an ISI of 25–1000 msec by a second click ($S2$). Their results are shown in Fig. 6.5. When both foreperiod and ISI were constant over a block of trials and no response was required to $S1$ (condition cc), the subject could in effect begin to react to $S2$ as soon as he pressed the "ready" key although occasional catch trials in which $S2$ was omitted would prevent him doing so completely before $S2$ arrived. Both temporal uncertainty and

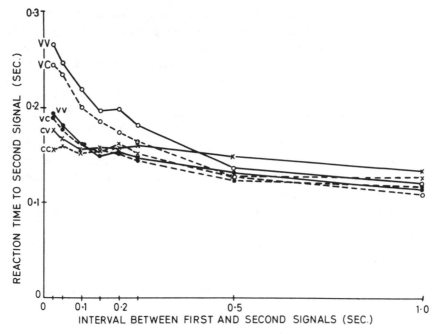

Fig. 6.5. Results of an experiment by Kay and Weiss (1961). The results are plotted as follows:

	Foreperiod	*ISI*	*Response to*
cc	Constant	Constant	S2 only
cv	Constant	Variable	S2 only
vc	Variable	Constant	S2 only
vv	Variable	Variable	S2 only
VC	Variable	Constant	S1 and S2
VV	Variable	Variable	S1 and S2

single-channel effects were thus excluded and, as expected, *RT* differed little with *ISI* up to 250 msec. The slight fall of *RT* with longer *ISI* perhaps indicates that 500 msec or so were required to take full advantage of the warning given by *S*1. With an irregular foreperiod (condition *vc*) *S*1 would convey more information and it would be expected that its full benefits would take longer to realize. It is therefore not surprising that in condition *vc RT* became longer with short values of *ISI*. The extra delays with irregular *ISI* (conditions *cv* and *vv*) were clearly small and well within the range of temporal uncertainty effects found by Drazin (1961). The difference between *RT*2 in conditions *VC* and *VV* in which a response had to be made to *S*1 was also within this range. Delays in these latter conditions were much greater than when no response was made to *S*1, and it is particularly important to note that delays were not abolished in condition *VC* when *ISI* was held constant: the delay here clearly cannot be accounted for in terms of temporal uncertainty. Similar evidence has been provided from experiments by Borger (1963), Creamer (1963) and Bertelson (1967).

A further indication that the delays in responding to $S2$ are not simply due to the effects of temporal uncertainty is the substantial correlation between $(RT2 + ISI)$ and $RT1$ shown in Table 6.1. Since temporal uncertainty due to varying ISI should have nothing to do with $RT1$, no correlation would be expected (Table 6.1c). An even clearer indication that temporal uncertainty effects cannot account for single-channel effects is provided by Sternberg (1969) who notes that the two effects are additive, implying that they are attributable to different stages in the central mechanisms, as discussed in Chapter 4.

(d) Elithorn and Lawrence (1955) seem to imply the suggestion that the results of experiments using pairs of responses made by different hands could be accounted for in terms of cortical or other central interaction. A somewhat similar suggestion appears to be made by Reynolds (1964, 1966) and by Herman and Kantowitz (1970) under the title "response-conflict theory". The fact that the central response to $S1$ in some way inhibits that to $S2$ is not in dispute—it is indeed the foundation of the single-channel hypothesis. The question is at what stage the inhibition occurs. One suggestion has been that the execution of $M1$ might block that of $M2$ (M. Smith, 1967a). If so, the lengthening of $RT2$ should depend on $MT1$ in such a way that in place of eqns (6.1) and (6.3) we could write

$$RT2 = RT1 + MT1 - ISI \qquad (DT2 < (RT1 + MT1 - ISI)) \quad (6.5)$$

This equation gives a very poor fit to the experimental data (see Table 6.1d). Herman and Kantowitz argue, however, that the conflict is not between overt responses but between central tendencies to response evoked by $S1$ and $S2$, and that the conflict affects $RT1$ as well as $RT2$. They suggest that the conflict should be greatest when $S2$ follows closely on $S1$, and that this is the cause of the lengthening of $RT1$ with short ISI. It has already been seen, however, that this lengthening can be well accounted for as a result of grouping. The serious problem with response-conflict theory as proposed by Herman and Kantowitz is that it yields no quantitative predictions except that the correlation between $(RT2 + ISI)$ and $RT1$ should be negative instead of positive as in Table 6.1. This would be so because they do not distinguish between grouped and ungrouped responses. If grouping occurs with short $ISIs$, as it usually seems to do, $RT2$ will tend to be shorter and $RT1$ longer than predicted by eqn (6.1). The rate of decrease of $RT2$ with ISI will therefore be less than the rate of increase of ISI itself, so that $(RS2 + ISI)$ will tend to rise with ISI while $RT1$ will tend to fall.

The predictions of the single-channel hypothesis shown in Table 6.1e give a better overall fit than any of the alternative theories although the times predicted are a little too short both when $S2$ comes during $RT1$ and when it comes during $MT1$. Part of the discrepancy may be attributed to the temporal uncertainty effects found by Kay and Weiss and by Drazin. Part was probably due to grouping of $Fb1$ with $S2$ in a few cases when it came just before the end of $RT1$: this would have produced long $RT2$s instead of the short ones predicted by eqn (6.1). Similar grouping may have occurred with $FTe1$ when $S2$ arrived close to the end of $M1$. The instances were too few to treat separately, but had they been omitted from the calculations the mean $RT2$s would certainly have been appreciably closer to those predicted.

5. Continuous performance

Bertelson (1966) in reviewing the single-channel hypothesis remarked

> It is easy to see what was so important in the intermittency idea. It was to open the way to an analysis of complex activities, whether apparently continuous of discrete, into basic decision units, each consisting of the choice of the adequate reaction for a particular sample of sensory input. (p. 156)

Craik (1948) assumed that the speed of a continuous performance such as tracking was limited by the times, firstly to observe and decide upon corrections for misalignments, and secondly to carry out the correcting actions—in short by the sum of the RTs and MTs involved. He observed, however, that correcting movements tended to run into one another as subjects became more practised and, as we have noted, subsequent work has shown that RT can overlap a previous MT. We should, therefore, rather say that, so long as MT is shorter than RT, the speed of a continuous performance will be limited by the decision times involved *plus* the times required to carry out any essential monitoring of responses—that is by the sum of RTs and essential FTs. This may be either greater or less than $(RT + MT)$ according to circumstances:

(a) When actions have to be carried out meticulously and the display is static, as for example when tracing carefully over a pattern, subjects may well monitor the ends of movements as well as any earlier significant points, as shown in Fig. 6.6(a), so that FTe will have to be added to $(RT + MT)$.

(b) When action does not have to be so precise, or when the display is changing so that misalignments are continually building up, FTe is likely to be cut out, and the speed of performance limited by $(RT + FTb)$ as shown in Fig. 6.6(b). For tracking, taking RT as 300 and FTb as 150 msec, as in Vince's (1948a) experiments, yields a correction rate of 1 per 450 msec which is close to the half second suggested by Craik, and in fact a better fit to

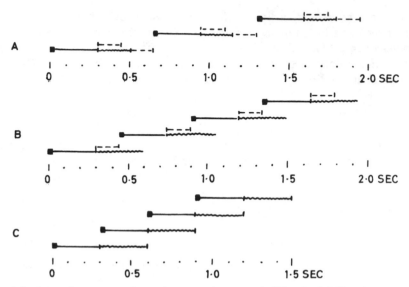

Fig. 6.6. Successive responses in continuous performance. A. When both *FTb* and *FTe* occur. B. When *FTb* occurs but not *FTe*. C. When all *FT* is cut out.

Vince's data. This figure is also consistent with the breakdown of high-speed tracking performance found when the track changes direction more than about twice per sec (Welford, 1958, pp. 86–96).

(c) When the display changes very fast even *FTb* may fail to capture the single channel. In tracking tasks this would follow from eqn (6.1) if misalignment built up so fast that there was always a substantial correction waiting to be made before the end of the *RT* to the previous observations. Speed of performance in this case would depend on *RT* alone as shown in Fig. 6.6(c). Accuracy in these circumstances would, however, tend to be low unless responses were very simple and ungraded, since any error made in one movement could not be corrected in the next, but only in the next but one. This type of performance seems to have been attained in the author's high-speed tracking experiments already mentioned: when the track was changing direction three times per sec, subjects maintained the correct *number* of changes, but accuracy was very poor compared with that attained with changes of two per sec or less.

In the type of tracking considered in Fig. 6.6, movements of the target are continuous so that for maximum performance the subject's actions would also have to be a continuous series. A different situation arises with step-tracking where the target movements are intermittent (e.g. Vince, 1948a, 1950) or when discrete signals for action occur in a continuous series with irregular *ISI*s. In these cases, overall performance at the task will depend not only upon the average number of signals that have to be dealt with in a given time, but also upon the regularity with which they occur: any bunching will tend to produce instantaneous rates which are higher than average, and may not allow enough time for all the signals to be dealt with before it is too late. The effects of bunching would best be studied by analysing a detailed record of the times at which each signal appeared and each response was initiated and completed, but in many cases this somewhat formidable exercise has not been possible. In these cases, however, predictions of overall performance can be made in terms of the single-channel model by assuming that the data from any particular signal will occupy the channel for a particular time, and that if the total time required for signals occurring within a particular period exceeds that available, responses will be delayed or omitted.

Klemmer and Muller (1969) have shown that reaction times to signals presented in a continuous series do not differ with the rate of presentation. Now if the time t required to deal with each signal is an unvarying quantity and all signals arrive at identical intervals i, every signal can be responded to so long as t does not exceed i. If it does, every alternate signal can be responded to so long as t does not exceed twice i, and so on. The relationship between response rate and signal frequency will take the form shown in Fig. 6.7. Any variability in t or i will quickly lead to smoothing of the "saw tooth" pattern and its replacement by a curve which is convex upward and asymptotic to a rate at which the subject's whole time is taken up in responding and there are no gaps during which he is waiting for a signal. The smoothing will be quicker still if he can not only respond to

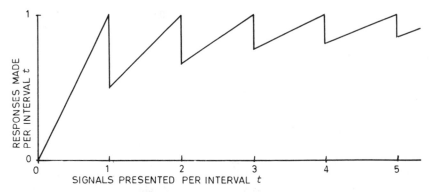

Fig. 6.7. Theoretical relationship between response rate and signal frequency when each signal takes a time t to deal with and has to be responded to immediately it appears or be missed. Signals are assumed to arrive at equal intervals of time.

signals immediately they arrive, but can also respond a little early or late. Such latitude can arise either when signals remain on view long enough to enable responses to be made at any time during an appreciable period, or if the subject is able to predict items or can hold them in running short-term memory, and for the present purpose all these are equivalent. The effects of different signal frequencies and degrees of latitude on frequency of response are shown in Table 6.2.

This approach yields very reasonable results when applied to data obtained in a series of experiments by Conrad (1951, 1954a,b). The subject's task was to respond by pressing a key or turning a knob each time one of a number of rotating pointers coincided with one of several irregularly spaced marks on the edges of dials. The number of signal sources was varied by using 2, 3 or 4 dials in different trials, and the signal frequency was independently varied by changing the speed at which the pointers rotated. An increase of either variable led to an increasing proportion of signals failing to secure a response. Conrad in a private communication has

Table 6.2. Probability of response (R) in paced task with differing signal rates and amounts of storage

$\bar{x}$	Without storage	With storage over 1 stage	With storage over 2 stages	With storage over 3 stages
0.1	0.909	0.995	0.9998	0.9999
0.2	0.833	0.982	0.998	0.9995
0.3	0.769	0.961	0.994	0.9992
0.4	0.714	0.934	0.986	0.997
0.5	0.667	0.904	0.973	0.992
0.6	0.625	0.870	0.953	0.982
0.7	0.588	0.836	0.928	0.966
0.8	0.556	0.800	0.897	0.941
0.9	0.526	0.765	0.862	0.909
1.0	0.500	0.731	0.824	0.870
1.1	0.476	0.698	0.784	0.826
1.2	0.455	0.666	0.745	0.781
1.3	0.435	0.636	0.707	0.737
1.4	0.417	0.607	0.670	0.694
1.5	0.400	0.580	0.635	0.654
1.6	0.385	0.555	0.602	0.617
1.7	0.370	0.531	0.572	0.683
1.8	0.357	0.509	0.544	0.553
1.9	0.345	0.488	0.518	0.524
2.0	0.333	0.468	0.494	0.499

indicated that the rate of responding was not limited by motor factors—subjects could respond much faster when they made responses in a predetermined pattern without regard to the display and, although subjects were allowed to use both hands, the intervals between responses were such that they could easily have made them with one hand alone. The limitation seems clearly to have been in the speed at which the central mechanisms could deal with the data from the signals and, perhaps, monitor the responses.

Crossman in a private communication has shown that Conrad's results can be fairly well fitted by assuming that subjects dealt with data at 4 bits per sec and responded whenever there was a long enough gap between one signal and the next in the series he used. The present writer obtained reasonable fits, shown in Fig. 6.8, to Conrad's data assuming constant t for

Table 6.2.—*cont.*

$\bar{x}$	Without storage	With storage over 1 stage	With storage over 2 stages	With storage over 3 stages
2.1	0.323	0.450	0.472	0.475
2.2	0.313	0.432	0.451	0.454
2.3	0.303	0.417	0.432	0.434
2.4	0.294	0.402	0.415	0.416
2.5	0.286	0.387	0.399	0.400
2.6	0.278	0.374	0.384	0.385
2.7	0.270	0.361	0.369	0.370
2.8	0.263	0.350	0.356	0.357
2.9	0.256	0.338	0.344	0.345
3.0	0.250	0.328	0.3330	0.3333

Use of this table.
1. To find R when time per item t, signal frequency and λ are known: the product of t and signal frequency gives $\bar{x}$ against which R may be read directly. For example, if $t = 0.5$ sec and signal frequency = 4 per sec, $\bar{x} = 2$ and R with storage over one stage ($\lambda = 1$) is 0.468: i.e. responses will be made to 0.468 of the signals presented, and the remaining 0.532 will be missed.
2. To find t when signal frequency, λ and R are known: find R in the appropriate λ column; divide the $\bar{x}$ corresponding to this by the signal frequency to obtain t.
3. To find signal frequency when t, λ and R are known: find R in the appropriate λ column; divide the $\bar{x}$ corresponding to this by t to obtain the signal frequency.
4. When λ is not known it may be inferred provided values of R are obtainable over a fairly wide range of $\bar{x}$. At high and very low values of $\bar{x}$, R is practically independent of λ provided at least one signal can be stored. If signal frequency, t and R can be calculated for one or both extremes, the λ may be chosen which gives the best fit for intermediate values.
  For values not given in the table interpolation is accurate enough for most purposes. When $\lambda = 2$ or more, R for values of $\bar{x}$ above 3.0 can be calculated approximately as $R = 1/\bar{x}$. The derivation of this table is described by Welford (1968, pp. 401–408).

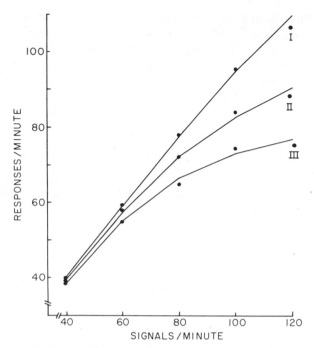

Fig. 6.8. Conrad's (1951) data fitted assuming that signals arrive at random intervals and that dealing with each takes an equal time t. It is also assumed that if the subject cannot deal with the signal at the instant it arrives it can wait, but that data from not more than two signals at a time can wait in this way—in other words the latitude (λ) in responding is two signals. I 2 dials, $t = 0.37$ sec. II 3 dials, $t = 0.59$ sec. III 4 dials, $t = 0.74$ sec.

any given number of pointers, random i and a latitude of two items. The treatment is the more plausible in that the values of t for 2, 3 and 4 dials give a good fit when the ratio 1:1.58:2 required by Hick's Law (eqn 3.1) for two-, three- and four-choice responses. The fit was found to be even better if it was assumed that latitude also varied with number of dials rising from 2 with two dials to 2.5 with three and 3 with four.

The model is obviously a gross over-simplification taking no account of possible grouping effects or of subtleties in the results such as the fact that at high signal frequencies many subjects neglected one dial, and missed all signals on it, for a minute or so at a time. Such a procedure could raise the rate of responding because the loss of potential responses to signals from the neglected dial could be more than offset by the shortening of t which would result from reducing the number of possible responses combined with the effective lengthening of i when signals on one of the dials was neglected. The assumption that t and i remained constant with signal speed would, however, then underestimate performance at high signal speeds.

(A) THE INTERACTION OF TWO SIMULTANEOUS TASKS

It has long been known that if the attempt is made to perform two tasks at the same time, the speed or accuracy of one or of the other or of both is likely to be lower than when the tasks are carried out separately. Early experiments in this field are those of Bornemann (1942) who paired mental arithmetic with a task in which the subject had to "dot" with a stylus through holes in a paper band passing over a drum, and of Mowbray (1952, 1953, 1954) whose subjects were required to report on data such as letters, digits, or prose passages presented either visually or aurally. He found that subjects could not deal adequately with two different streams of information, one presented to the eyes and one to the ears, at the same time. The limitation could obviously not have been sensory and, since subjects did not have to report until afterwards, it was not on the motor side. The effects seemed clearly to be the result of an overloading of some central mechanism, and it is reasonable to suppose that the impairment was due to the single channel being captured by data from one task at a time, to the exclusion of data from the other. Some evidence in favour of this view is Mowbray's finding that when the two tasks were of unequal difficulty, it was the easier that tended to suffer more. This is understandable if the more difficult task tended to occupy the single channel for longer periods than the easy: capture of the single channel by the more difficult task would mean the omission of a relatively large block of data from the easier task, whereas capture by the easier task would cause a relatively brief interruption of the more difficult task. Alternatively, the subject might try to maximize his overall performance by concentrating on the easier task and doing it well, in which case he would tend to do relatively better with the easy task. This may have been the reason why Brown et al. (1965) found that a tactile discrimination suffered more when paired with an easy visual discrimination than with a more difficult one—a result which is otherwise surprising in view of Mowbray's evidence.

From what has been said earlier in this chapter, it would be expected that the main interference between two tasks would result from their competing for the time of the translation mechanism. If so, interference will depend on the extent to which each task requires active choice of responses and on the compatibility between signals and responding actions. Results obtained by Noble et al. (1967) and by Trumbo et al. (1967) suggest this is the case. They paired tracking with a task in which the subject had either (a) to try to predict a series of numbers presented aurally at 3 sec intervals or (b) merely repeat them or (c) generate random numbers in response to clicks at 3 sec intervals. The first and third tasks clearly involved a more active choice of response than the second, and were shown to cause much more interference.

Tracking while performing the second task seemed little if at all different from tracking with no extra task added. Again Posner (1969) compared variability of movements between end-stops, between targets seen visually and between targets the positions of which had to be remembered. Of these the second and third, presumably involving more time by the translation mechanism than the first, were more disrupted by a concurrent task of keeping a sensitive key in a central position or even by the instruction to "think of something else".

(B) DIVISION OR ALTERNATION OF ATTENTION?

In most experiments in which two tasks have been presented together, one has been designated the primary task to which main attention has had to be given, and the other as the secondary task, to which attention is given only when it is not required by the primary. The primary task when given alone can be conceived as not occupying the single-channel fully, but as leaving some "spare capacity" into which the secondary task can be fitted. Performance is impaired when this spare capacity is insufficient for this to be done. There is some question whether the primary task occupies the single-channel *continuously* but not completely at any one instant, or whether occupation is *complete* but intermittent so that spare capacity is in the form of "gaps" during which the single-channel is free. With the former view the assumption is commonly made that the total capacity can be divided between both tasks which can, therefore, be dealt with in parallel. Allport *et al.* (1972) have argued that this can be done when the input channels are distinct (ear and eye) and the output channels are also distinct (voice and hands). They found that there was no noticeable interference between repeating a passage of prose as it was heard and either remembering pictures or playing a piano from a score. However, what has already been noted about the possibility of overlap between the activities of the perceptual, translatory, and programme-control stages of the central mechanisms, makes it reasonable to suppose that their subjects may have been rapidly alternating between the one task and the other.

A clear decision between the competing views requires a detailed examination of the timing of signals and responses in both primary and secondary tasks. A study by Fisher (1975a) in which this was done, clearly favoured the concept of alternation. As a primary task she used a five-choice serial reaction task in which each signal appeared 50 msec after the completion of the previous response. In the secondary task the signals were digits presented auditorily at random time intervals, which had to be responded to by adding 7 to whatever digit had been given. Both input channels and both output channels were thus distinct as in the cases studied by Allport and co-workers. Fisher found that on most occasions when a digit was presented, response to the immediately preceding primary signal was completed in normal time, as would be expected from eqns (6.1) or (6.3). Response to the next primary signal was however, delayed until after response had been made to the digit. Occasionally response was made to the digit without any response to a primary signal intervening, as might be expected if the digit appeared just as a primary response was ending and before a fresh primary signal had appeared. Occasionally also, responses to more than one primary signal would intervene between the secondary signal and its response, but in this case the reaction time to the secondary signal was longer than normal. Fisher (1975b) showed that the interdigitation of primary and secondary responses was capable of some modification at will: when the digit task was designated as primary and the five-choice as secondary, reactions to the digits without any intervening response to the five-choice task became more frequent. Further indications against parallel operation come from experiments by Oldfield (1976) who found that when visual signals were presented in a way which confined them each to one hemisphere and responses were produced from the same hemisphere, there was no evidence that the two hemispheres were able to handle separate reactions simultaneously.

One of the most compelling arguments against independent, parallel processing and at the same time in favour of the view that interdigitation of simultaneous tasks can be affected by skill comes from the fact that it seems impossible to carry out actions, say by the two hands, which are truly simultaneous without their being in some way coordinated and fitted into a common temporal framework. For example, in the well-known children's party trick of making tapping movements with one hand and circular motions with the other, the number of taps seems to be inevitably a multiple of the number of circles. Such coordination is a type of grouping and seems to enable a more elaborate performance to be carried out than would otherwise be possible. For example, Kalsbeek (1964) noted that subjects in double-task experiments tended to build up a rhythmic pattern of performance in which the two tasks were regularly interdigitated, and that when this was achieved, the impairment produced by combining the two tasks was reduced, implying presumably that they were no longer separate but had been combined into one more complex task. Further evidence is provided for tracking by Adams and Chambers (1962) and for serial reaction times by Dimond (1966), that responses in the two tasks tend to be coordinated and performance improves when the signals in one or both tasks come at regular intervals or are otherwise predictable. One wonders whether more detailed measurement of the repeating of prose and the piano playing in the experiments by Allport and co-workers mentioned earlier would have revealed that the two performances had been coordinated in time. This might have been the more likely since both were familiar tasks—the repetition obviously so, the piano playing because the subjects were experienced pianists. Results obtained by Kalsbeek and Sykes (1967) suggest that coordination is fostered by training, and that the scope for it is greatest when the total loading is moderate, as it appears to have been in the situation studied by Allport and co-workers.

(C) PROBLEMS OF MEASUREMENT

If the intermittency view is correct, the loads imposed by the primary and secondary tasks separately and together can in principle be calculated by methods similar to those used to provide the basis of Table 6.2 and Fig. 6.8—the problem becomes essentially one of queueing by signals from the two tasks for use of the translation mechanism.

An empirical index of loading in dual tasks had been proposed by Michon (1964, 1966; Michon and Van Doorne, 1967) on the basis of experiments in which the secondary task has been the tapping of a foot pedal at intervals of 0.5 to 1.0 sec which the subject attempts to keep as regular as possible. Michon noted that the interval between each tap and the next seemed to be a sensitive indicator of interference by the primary task, and suggested that tapping performance can be measured in terms of the average difference of each interval from the one preceding. Adapting his equation we may write:

$$\text{Tapping performance} = \sum_{1}^{N-1} \frac{(t_i \sim t_j)}{N-1} \times \frac{1}{\bar{t}} \qquad (6.6)$$

where t_i is each interval from the first to the $(N-1)$th taken in turn, and $\bar{t}$ is the mean interval. Michon proposes that

$$\frac{\text{Index of}}{\text{loading}} = \frac{\text{Difference between tapping performances with and without primary tasks}}{\text{Tapping performance without primary task}}. \qquad (6.7)$$

Accurate measurement will obviously be complicated if coordination of the two tasks is achieved, and may also be rendered difficult if the subject reacts to the greater load imposed when the two tasks are combined, by changing strategy. For example, Conrad (1956) in a study of telephone operators showed that the time taken per call decreased linearly with increase in the log frequency of calls coming in, although it is not clear how far this represented a true speeding up and how far a reduction of ancillary activities and is therefore an illustration of Parkinson's Law. More compelling evidence is provided by R. Brown (1957) who found that subjects in a plotting task made more plots under paced conditions than would have been predicted from their unpaced performances: detailed study of the results indicated that their approach had become more hurried and the extra speed was attained at some cost of accuracy. Despite these difficulties the dual task technique provides a potentially important means of assessing the load imposed by tasks for which direct measurement is not possible, and of showing up differences of loading which would otherwise be difficult to detect. Examples are driving a car (e.g. Brown and Poulton, 1961; I. Brown, 1962, 1965) or monitoring industrial process plants. It would be inappropriate to survey these studies here, but a summary has been given elsewhere (Welford, 1968) and the problems of the technique have been summarized and discussed by I. Brown (1977).

References

Adams, J. A. (1962). Test of the hypothesis of psychological refractory period. *Journal of Experimental Psychology* **64**, 280–287.

Adams, J. A. and Chambers, R. W. (1962). Response to simultaneous stimulation of two sense modalities. *Journal of Experimental Psychology* **63**, 198–206.

Allport, D. A., Antonis, Barbara and Reynolds, P. (1972). On the division of attention: a disproof of the single channel hypothesis. *Quarterly Journal of Experimental Psychology* **24**, 225–235.

Annett, J. (1966). A note on Davis's refutation of the expectancy hypothesis. *Quarterly Journal of Experimental Psychology* **18**, 179–180.

Bernstein, I. H. (1970). Can we see and hear at the same time? Some recent studies of intersensory facilitation of reaction time. *In* "Attention and Performance III" (A. F. Sanders, ed.), pp. 21–35. North-Holland Publishing Co., Amsterdam.

Bertelson, P. (1966). Central intermittency twenty years later. *Quarterly Journal of Experimental Psychology* **18**, 153–163.

Bertelson, P. (1967). The refractory period of choice reactions with regular and irregular interstimuli intervals. *In* "Attention and Performance I" (A. F. Sanders, ed.). North-Holland Publishing Co., Amsterdam.

Boddy, J. (1972). The psychological refractory period and vertex evoked potentials. *Quarterly Journal of Experimental Psychology* **24**, 175–192.

Borger, R. (1963). The refractory period and serial choice-reactions. *Quarterly Journal of Experimental Psychology* **15**, 1–12.

Bornemann, E. (1942). Untersuchungen uber der grad der geistigen beanspruchung. *Arbeitsphysiologie* **12**, 142–191.

Brebner, J. (1968). Continuing and reversing the direction of responding movements: some exceptions to the so-called "psychological refractory period". *Journal of Experimental Psychology* **78**, 120–127.

Brebner, J. (1977). The search for exceptions to the psychological refractory period. *In* "Attention and Performance VI" (S. Dornic, ed.), pp. 63–78. Erlbaum, Hillsdale, N.J.

Broadbent, D. E. (1958). "Perception and Communication". Pergamon Press, London.

Broadbent, D. E. and Gregory, Margaret (1967). Psychological refractory period and the length of time required to make a decision. *Proc. Roy. Soc. B.* **168**, 181–193.

Brown, I. D. (1962). Measuring the "spare mental capacity" of car drivers by a subsidiary auditory task. *Ergonomics* **5**, 247–250.

Brown, I. D. (1965). A comparison of two subsidiary tasks used to measure fatigue in car drivers. *Ergonomics* **8**, 467–473.

Brown, I. D. (1977). Dual task methods of assessing workload. *Ergonomics* **21**, 221–224.

Brown, I. D. and Poulton, E. C. (1961). Measuring the spare "mental capacity" of car drivers by a subsidiary task. *Ergonomics* **4**, 35–40.

Brown, Ruth A. (1957). Age and "paced" work. *Occupational Psychology* **31**, 11–20.

Brown, R. L., Galloway, W. D. and San Giuliano, R. A. (1965). Effects of time-sharing and body positional demands on cutaneous information processing. *Perceptual and Motor Skills* **20**, 1021–1026.

Bryan, W. L. and Harter, N. (1899). Studies on the telegraphic language. The acquisition of a hierarchy of habits. *Psychological Review* **6**, 345–375.

Chase, R. A., Harvey, S., Standfast, Susan, Rapin, Isabelle and Sutton, S. (1961). Studies on sensory feedback I: effect of delayed auditory feedback on speech and key tapping. *Quarterly Journal of Experimental Psychology* **13**, 141–152.

Conrad, R. (1951). Speed and load stress in sensori-motor skill. *British Journal of Industrial Medicine* **8**, 1–7.

Conrad, R. (1954a). Missed signals in a sensorimotor skill. *Journal of Experimental Psychology* **48**, 1–9.

Conrad, R. (1954b). Speed stress. *In* "Symposium on Human Factors in Equipment Design" (W. F. Floyd and A. T. Welford, eds.), pp. 95–102. H. K. Lewis & Co. for the Ergonomics Research Society, London.

Conrad, R. (1956). Performance of telephone operators relative to traffic level. *Nature* **178**, 1480–1481.

Craik, K. J. W. (1948). Theory of the human operator in control systems II. Man as an element in a control system. *British Journal of Psychology* **38**, 142–148.

Creamer, L. R. (1963). Event uncertainty, psychological refractory period, and human data processing. *Journal of Experimental Psychology* **66**, 187–194.

Davis, R. (1956). The limits of the "psychological refractory period". *Quarterly Journal of Experimental Psychology* **8**, 24–38.

Davis, R. (1957). The human operator as a single channel information system. *Quarterly Journal of Experimental Psychology*, **9**, 119–129.

Davis, R. (1959). The role of "attention" in the psychological refractory period. *Quarterly Journal of Experimental Psychology* **11**, 211–220.

Davis, R. (1965). Expectancy and intermittency. *Quarterly Journal of Experimental Psychology* **17**, 75–78.

Dimond, S. J. (1966). Facilitation of performance through the use of the timing system. *Journal of Experimental Psychology* **71**, 181–183.

Drazin, D. H. (1961). Effects of foreperiod, foreperiod variability, and probability of stimulus occurrence on simple reaction time. *Journal of Experimental Psychology* **62**, 43–50.

Elithorn, A. (1961). Central intermittency: some further observations. *Quarterly Journal of Experimental Psychology* **13**, 240–247.

Elithorn, A. and Barnett, T. J. (1967). Apparent individual differences in channel capacity. *In* "Attention and Performance I" (A. F. Sanders, ed.). North-Holland Publishing Co., Amsterdam.

Elithorn, A. and Lawrence, Catherine (1955). Central inhibition—some refractory observations. *Quarterly Journal of Experimental Psychology* 7, 116–127.

Ells, J. G. (1973). Analysis of temporal and attentional aspects of movement. *Journal of Experimental Psychology* 99, 10–21.

Fisher, Shirley (1975a). The microstructure of dual task interaction. 1. The patterning of main-task responses within secondary-task intervals. *Perception* 4, 267–290.

Fisher, Shirley (1975b). The microstructure of dual task interaction. 2. The effect of task instructions on attentional allocation and a model of attention-switching. *Perception* 4, 459–474.

Fraisse, P. (1957). La période réfractoire psychologique. *Année Psychologique* 57, 315–328.

Gottsdanker, R. (1966). The effect of superseding signals. *Quarterly Journal of Experimental Psychology* 18, 236–249.

Gottsdanker, R., Broadbent, L. and Van Sant, C. (1963). Reaction time to single and to first signals. *Journal of Experimental Psychology* 66, 163–167.

Gottsdanker, R. and Stelmach, G. E. (1971). The persistence of psychological refractoriness. *Journal of Motor Behavior* 3, 301–312.

Greenwald, A. G. and Schulman, H. G. (1973). On doing two things at once: II. Elimination of the psychological refractory period effect. *Journal of Experimental Psychology* 101, 70–76.

Halliday, A. M., Kerr, M. and Elithorn, A. (1960). Grouping of stimuli and apparent exceptions to the psychological refractory period. *Quarterly Journal of Experimental Psychology* 12, 72–89.

Harrison, J. S. (1960). Psychological refractoriness and the latency time of two consecutive motor responses. *Research Quarterly* 31, 590–600.

Herman, L. M. and Kantowitz, B. H. (1970). The psychological refractory period effect: only half the double-stimulation story? *Psychological Bulletin* 73, 74–88.

Hick, W. E. (1948). The discontinuous functioning of the human operator in pursuit tasks. *Quarterly Journal of Experimental Psychology* 1, 36–51.

Hick, W. E. (1949). Reaction time for the amendment of a response. *Quarterly Journal of Experimental Psychology* 1, 175–179.

Hick, W. E. and Welford, A. T. (1956). Comment on the paper "Central inhibition: some refractory observations" by Alick Elithorn and Catherine Lawrence. *Quarterly Journal of Experimental Psychology* 8, 39–41.

Kahneman, D. (1968). Method, findings, and theory in studies of visual masking. *Psychological Bulletin* 70, 404–425.

Kahneman, D. (1973). "Attention and Effort". Prentice-Hall, Englewood Cliffs, New Jersey.

Kalsbeek, J. W. H. (1964). On the measurement of deterioration in performance caused by distraction stress. *Ergonomics* 7, 187–195.

Kalsbeek, J. W. H. and Sykes, R. N. (1967). Objective measurement of mental load. *In* "Attention and Performance I" (A. F. Sanders, ed.). North-Holland Publishing Co., Amsterdam.

Karlin, L. (1959). Reaction time as a function of foreperiod duration and variability. *Journal of Experimental Psychology* 58, 185–191.

Karlin, L. and Kestenbaum, R. (1968). Effects of number of alternatives on the psychological refractory period. *Quarterly Journal of Experimental Psychology* 20, 167–178.

Kay, H. and Weiss, A. D. (1961). Relationship between simple and serial reaction times. *Nature* 191, 790–791.

Kerr, M., Mingay, Rosemary and Elithorn, A. (1963). Cerebral dominance in reaction time responses. *British Journal of Psychology* **54**, 325–336.

Kerr, M., Mingay, Rosemary and Elithorn, A. (1965). Patterns of reaction time responses. *British Journal of Psychology* **56**, 53–59.

Klein, R. M. and Posner, M. I. (1974). Attention to visual and kinesthetic components of skills. *Brain Research* **71**, 401–411.

Klemmer, E. T. (1956). Time uncertainty in simple reaction time. *Journal of Experimental Psychology* **51**, 179–184.

Klemmer, E. T. and Muller, P. F. (1969). The rate of handling information: key pressing responses to light patterns. *Journal of Motor Behavior* **1**, 135–147.

Kornblum, S. and Koster, W. G. (1967). The effect of signal intensity and training on simple reaction time. *In* "Attention and Performance I" (A. F. Sanders, ed.). North-Holland Publishing Co., Amsterdam.

Koster, W. G. and Bekker, J. A. M. (1967). Some experiments on refractoriness. *In* "Attention and Performance I" (A. F. Sanders, ed.). North-Holland Publishing Co., Amsterdam.

Leonard, J. A. (1953). Advance information in sensori-motor skills. *Quarterly Journal of Experimental Psychology* **5**, 141–149.

Marill, T. (1957). The psychological refractory phase. *British Journal of Psychology* **48**, 93–97.

Megaw, E. D. (1970). Response factors and the psychological refractory period. Unpublished Ph.D. Thesis, University of Birmingham.

Megaw, E. D. (1974). Possible modification to a rapid on-going programmed manual response. *Brain Research* **71**, 425–441.

Michon, J. A. (1964). A note on the measurement of perceptual motor load. *Ergonomics* **7**, 461–463.

Michon, J. A. (1966). Tapping regularity as a measure of perceptual motor load. *Ergonomics*, **9**, 401–412.

Michon, J. A. and Van Doorne, H. (1967). A semi-portable apparatus for the measurement of perceptual motor load. *Ergonomics* **10**, 67–72.

Mowbray, G. H. (1952). Simultaneous vision and audition: the detection of elements missing from overlearned sequences. *Journal of Experimental Psychology* **44**, 292–300.

Mowbray, G. H. (1953). Simultaneous vision and audition: the comprehension of prose passages with varying levels of difficulty. *Journal of Experimental Psychology* **46**, 365–372.

Mowbray, G. H. (1954). The perception of short phrases presented simultaneously for visual and auditory reception. *Quarterly Journal of Experimental Psychology* **6**, 86–92.

Nickerson, R. S. (1967a). Categorization time with categories defined by disjunctions and conjunctions of stimulus attributes. *Journal of Experimental Psychology* **73**, 211–219.

Nickerson, R. S. (1967b). Psychological refractory phase and the functional significance of signals. *Journal of Experimental Psychology* **73**, 303–312.

Noble, M., Trumbo, D., and Fowler, F. (1967). Further evidence of secondary task interference in tracking. *Journal of Experimental Psychology* **73**, 146–149.

Norman, D. A. (1967). Temporal confusions and limited capacity processors. *In* "Attention and Performance I" (A. F. Sanders, ed.). North-Holland Publishing Co., Amsterdam.

Oldfield, S. R. (1976). Hemisphere and attentional effects on the transmission of somatosensory information. Unpublished Thesis, Australian National University, Canberra.

Posner, M. I. (1969). Reduced attention and the performance of "automated" movements. *Journal of Motor Behavior* **1**, 245–258.

Posner, M. I. and Mitchell, R. F. (1967). Chronometric analysis of classification. *Psychological Review* **74**, 392–409.

Poulton, E. C. (1950). Perceptual anticipation and reaction time. *Quarterly Journal of Experimental Psychology* **2**, 99–112.

Rabbitt, P. M. A. (1966a). Errors and error correction in choice-response tasks. *Journal of Experimental Psychology* **71**, 264–272.

Rabbitt, P. M. A. (1966b). Error correction time without external error signals. *Nature* **212**, 438.

Rabbitt, P. (1967). Time to detect errors as a function of factors affecting choice-response time. *Acta Psychologica* **27**, 131–142.

Rabbitt, P. M. A. and Phillips, Shirley (1967). Error-detection and correction latencies as a function of S–R compatibility. *Quarterly Journal of Experimental Psychology* **19**, 37–42.

Rabbitt, P. and Rodgers, B. (1977). What does a man do after he makes an error? An analysis of response programming. *Quarterly Journal of Experimental Psychology* **29**, 727–743.

Reynolds, D. (1964). Effects of double stimulation: temporary inhibition of response. *Psychological Bulletin* **62**, 333–347.

Reynolds, D. (1966). Time and event uncertainty in unisensory reaction time. *Journal of Experimental Psychology* **71**, 286–293.

Rubinstein, L. (1964). Intersensory and intrasensory effects in simple reaction time. *Perceptual and Motor Skills* **18**, 159–172.

Salmoni, A. W., Sullivan, S. J. and Starkes, Janet L. (1976). The attention demands of movements: a critique of the probe technique. *Journal of Motor Behavior* **8**, 161–169.

Salthouse, T. (1970). Human performance as a function of future demands. *Perceptual and Motor Skills* **30**, 327–336.

Sanders, A. F. (1964). Selective strategies in the assimiliation of successively presented signals. *Quarterly Journal of Experimental Psychology* **16**, 368–372.

Sanders, A. F. (1967). Some aspects of reaction processes. *In* "Attention and Performance I" (A. F. Sanders, ed.). North-Holland Publishing Co., Amsterdam.

Schvaneveldt, R. W. (1969). Effects of complexity in simultaneous reaction time tasks. *Journal of Experimental Psychology* **81**, 289–296.

Slater-Hammel, A. T. (1958). Psychological refractory period in simple paired responses. *Research Quarterly* **29**, 468–481.

Smith, E. E. (1967). Effects of familiarity on stimulus recognition and categorization. *Journal of Experimental Psychology* **74**, 324–332.

Smith, Marilyn C. (1967a). Theories of the psychological refractory period. *Psychological Bulletin* **67**, 202–213.

Smith, Marilyn, C. (1967b). Reaction time to a second stimulus as a function of intensity of the first stimulus. *Quarterly Journal of Experimental Psychology* **19**, 125–132.

Smith, Marilyn C. (1967c). The psychological refractory period as a function of performance of a first response. *Quarterly Journal of Experimental Psychology* **19**, 350–352.

Smith, Marilyn C. (1969). The effect of varying information on the psychological refractory period. *Acta Psychologica* **30**, 220–231.

Smith, W. M., McCrary, J. W. and Smith, K. U. (1960). Delayed visual feedback and behavior. *Science* **132**, 1013–1014.

Sternberg, S. (1969). The discovery of processing stages: extensions of Donders' method. *Acta Psychologica* **30**, 276–315.

Sternberg, S. and Knoll, R. L. (1973). The perception of temporal order: fundamental issues and a general model. *In* "Attention and Performance IV" (S. Kornblum, ed.), pp. 629–685. Academic Press, New York.

Telford, C. W. (1931). The refractory phase of voluntary and associative responses. *Journal of Experimental Psychology* **14**, 1–36.

Treisman, Anne M. (1966). Our limited attention. *Advancement of Science* **22**, 600–611.

Trumbo, D., Noble, M. and Swink, J. (1967). Secondary task interference in the performance of tracking tasks. *Journal of Experimental Psychology* **73**, 232–240.

Vince, Margaret A. (1948a). The intermittency of control movements and the psychological refractory period. *British Journal of Psychology* **38**, 149–157.

Vince, Margaret A. (1948b). Corrective movements in a pursuit task. *Quarterly Journal of Experimental Psychology* **1**, 85–103.

Vince, Margaret A. (1949). Rapid response sequences and the psychological refractory period. *British Journal of Psychology* **40**, 23–40.

Vince, Margaret A. (1950). Some exceptions to the psychological refractory period in unskilled manual responses. Medical Research Council Applied Psychology Research Unit Report No. 124/50.

Vince, Margaret A. and Welford, A. T. (1967). Time taken to change the speed of a response. *Nature* **213**, 532–533.

Welford, A. T. (1952). The "psychological refractory period" and the timing of high-speed performance—a review and a theory. *British Journal of Psychology* **43**, 2–19.

Welford, A. T. (1958). "Ageing and Human Skill". Oxford University Press for the Nuffield Foundation. (Reprinted 1973 by Greenwood Press, Westport, Connecticut).

Welford, A. T. (1959). Evidence of a single-channel decision mechanism limiting performance in a serial reaction task. *Quarterly Journal of Experimental Psychology* **11**, 193–210.

Welford, A. T. (1967). Single-channel operation in the brain. *Acta Psychologica* **27**, 5–22.

Welford, A. T. (1968). "Fundamentals of Skill". Methuen, London.

Welford, A. T. (1977). Serial reaction-times, continuity of task, single-channel effects and age. *In* "Attention and Performance VI" (S. Dornic, ed.), pp. 79–97. Erlbaum, Hillsdale, New Jersey.

Welford, A. T. (1979). Comment on the paper "What does a man do after he makes an error? An analysis of response programming" by P. Rabbitt and B. Rodgers. *Quarterly Journal of Experimental Psychology* **31**, 539–542.

Wilke, J. T. and Vaughn, S. C. (1976). Temporal distribution of attention during a throwing task. *Journal of Motor Behavior* **8**, 83–87.

Williams, L. R. T. (1974). Effects of number of alternatives on the psychological refractoriness of an extended movement. *Journal of Motor Behavior* **6**, 227–234.

Yates, A. J. (1965). Effects of delayed auditory feedback on morse transmission by skilled operators. *Journal of Experimental Psychology* **69**, 467–475.

Chapter 7

Reaction Time and the Study of Memory

D. McNICOL and G. W. STEWART

Although some of the earliest experiments on memory used reaction time as a measure (Cattell, 1886, 1897; Jung, 1919), there was a long period when its use was quite neglected. There were good reasons for this neglect. First, too little had been achieved in understanding what reaction time measured. Second, research had concentrated on questions about how information was encoded and stored, and the study of errors rather than time seemed a better way of obtaining answers. As the other chapters of this book show, much more is now known about the processes which determine a reaction time than was known ten or twenty years ago. Also, the present interest in retrieval has reinstated reaction time as a measure of memory processes.

If you ask people questions about information they have in memory, the time needed to answer should reflect the act of retrieval. By making changes in the stored information, or in the type of answer required to the question, the time needed to reply may be lengthened or shortened, and these variations in reaction time may be useful in testing ideas about how retrieval works. Of course this is too simple a statement of the relationship between retrieval and reaction time, as the reaction time may reflect many other operations such as the time needed to understand the question, or to execute a response, once it has been decided which response to make. Experimenters try to hold such variables constant, or vary them in such a way as to separate their contributions to reaction time from that of the retrieval process. The first modern-day studies of retrieval by measuring reaction time were those of Sternberg (1966, 1969a,b). He presented a short list of items to be remembered, following them by a single item (the probe) which was either a member or a non-member of the list. Subjects responded to the probe by pressing one of two keys to indicate whether it was a list member or not. This was the *item recognition task*. With it one could change the stored information by increasing or decreasing the length of the list to be memorized, and one could change the type of response required by using a probe which was either a member or a non-member of the list. The effects these changes had on reaction time are shown in Fig. 7.1. For each extra item added to the list, reaction time increased by a constant amount.

From this simple experiment Sternberg first concluded that retrieval involves an item by item search through the list, with each item requiring the same average time to be matched with the probe. This explains why reaction time increases linearly with list length. As the slope of the reaction time function is 38 msec this must be the amount of time needed to compare a single memory item with the probe. The intercept of the function, in this case about 400 msec, must reflect the time needed to execute all other processes, such as encoding the probe and organizing a response. Second, he reasoned, all items in the list must be examined, both when positive and negative probes are presented; that is, the search is *exhaustive*. This conclusion may run counter to the intuition that a decision about a positive probe ought to be able to be made by searching the list until a matching item is found, and then stopping searching to make a response. This is called a *self-terminating* search. However this cannot be what is happening. If it

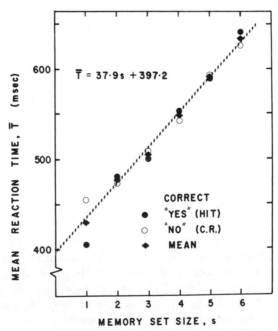

Fig. 7.1. Reaction time to positive and negative probe items, plotted as a function of memory set size, and fitted with a linear function. (From Sternberg, 1969a)

were, only half the items in the list would, on average, need to be examined before encountering the probe, and the reaction time function for positive probes should have a slope half that of the function for negative probes, as illustrated in Fig. 7.2.

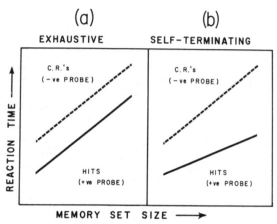

Fig. 7.2. Linear reaction time functions for positive and negative probes expected by two serial search models: (a) the exhaustive search, which predicts that the functions will be parallel, and (b) the self-terminating search which predicts that the slope of the positive function will be half that of the negative function.

Sternberg had provided a simple paradigm for investigating retrieval, and from the results of his experiments, provided a simple model of the process—an exhaustive serial scan of the memorized list, followed by a YES–NO decision. This simple experiment with its apparently straightforward conclusion was immensely enticing to other memory researchers. The lid was off Pandora's Box and it would soon be apparent that the straight line functions of Fig. 7.1 were open to a bewildering array of alternative explanations. One purpose of this chapter is to examine the more important models of retrieval to see if any is a fair description of how human memory works. With so many contenders, this sifting of models is likely to become confusing unless it is realized that they are all variations of three basic types. Figure 7.3 gives a rough classification of retrieval models. It is not complete, and Taylor (1976) discusses many other variants not depicted here.

The general types are serial, parallel and direct access models, the first of which has already been introduced. Serial models assume that the *n* items in a memorized list queue up to be compared with the probe one at a time. Parallel models assume that all the *n* list members are simultaneously compared with the probe, each item racing against the others to have its processing completed. Direct access models propose that only the probe

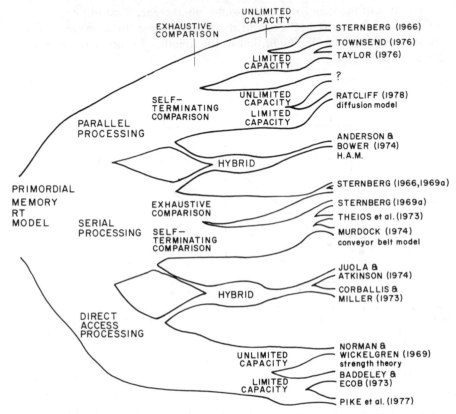

Fig. 7.3. A classification of retrieval models discussed in this chapter according to whether they involve serial, parallel, or direct access processing, exhaustive or self-terminating searches, and have limited or unlimited processing capacity.

item is examined. It is as if all possible items that might be presented in the memory task are represented by an orderly set of units, that is in some kind of lexicon where any item can be looked up directly without having to scan through the other items. When a list is presented, its items' units have their strengths increased, so that they stand out from the remainder of memory. When a probe is presented, its representation in the lexicon is examined to see if its strength is above the average level.

There are many variations of the three basic model types. Frequently these arise from proposals that retrieval is exhaustive as opposed to self-terminating, or has limited as opposed to unlimited capacity. The exhaustive versus self-terminating distinction has already been encountered in Sternberg's examples of serial searches, but the idea is also applicable to a parallel search. In this case all n items being processed simultaneously may have to be completed before the search ends, so that the search is parallel and exhaustive, and its duration dependent on the slowest of the n processes. Alternatively, processing may continue only until the item which matches the probe has been identified, so that the duration of a self-terminating parallel search is the time needed to deal with this single critical item.

Retrieval mechanisms may also have a limited capacity for handling information. This is most easily illustrated by considering that the n items in a parallel search are competing for the attention of the process which matches them with the probe. If the process has unlimited capacity, the time needed to match an individual item should be unaffected by the number of competitors. If capacity is limited, the more items being processed, the longer the completion time for each of them. The same idea can be applied to serial and direct access models. Taylor (1976) discusses limited and unlimited capacity serial models, but they will not be dealt with here, as serial models which have been seriously applied to data generally assume that processing times for individual items are unaffected by list length. Discussion of limited capacity direct access models will be deferred until later in this chapter. It should be noted at this point, however, that the linear relationship between memory set size and reaction time depicted in Fig. 7.1, can result from all three basic models, under certain conditions.

As Fig. 7.3 shows, it is also possible to have a retrieval model which includes more than one of these three main types. Atkinson and Juola (1974) have proposed that we first try to access a probe's memorial representation directly but if this fails, we discover it by a serial search. In their Human Associative Memory model (HAM), Anderson and Bower (1974) suggest that several serial searches race against one another. Hybrid models often give a better fit to data than do their basic components, but this flexibility is purchased at the price of extra complexity. While the Atkinson and Juola hybrid will be discussed in the section on direct access in this chapter, HAM will not. Ratcliff and Murdock (1976) have some interesting comments to make about HAM's abilities as a retrieval model.

So much for an overview of retrieval theories. Before trying to evaluate them it is useful to know the main experimental paradigms used in this area of research. The item recognition paradigm has already been mentioned. It normally yields low error rates (5 per cent or less, although we will encounter studies where they go much higher) and seems particularly suitable for studying retrieval over the short term. The prememorized list paradigm resembles the item recognition task in that it produces low error rates, and studies reaction time as list length is varied. It requires fairly thorough learning of an n-item list, followed by a test of $2n$ items, half being from the original list, and half being lures. Repeated tests may be given after list learning to study the effect of increasing the subject's familiarity with both list members and lures (Atkinson and Juola, 1974).

A second technique for studying retrieval over the long term is the study-test paradigm developed by Murdock and his co-workers (Murdock, 1974; Murdock and Anderson, 1975; Murdock, Hockley and Muter, 1977; Ratcliff and Murdock, 1976). A study list of 16 to 64 items is presented once, followed by a test list where the n study items are mixed with n lures. The variable of major interest is lag, the number of other study and test items intervening between an item's presentation in the study list, and its ocurrence in the test list. Responses are made in the form of judgements of confidence that test items were members of the study list, and up to 20 per cent errors can occur in the high confidence categories.

Lag is also the independent variable of major interest in the third method of studying long-term retrieval. This is the continuous recognition memory paradigm used by Okada (1971) where a series of items is presented, and after each presentation the subject must judge if this was its first or a repeated occurrence in the list. Each item therefore serves as a negative and as a positive probe at different times, and may be tested several times in the latter role to examine repetition effects. Depending on lag length, error rates may be as high as 20 per cent in this task.

A satisfactory theory of memory retrieval ought to be able to explain the results obtained in each paradigm, item recognition, prememorized list, study-test and continuous recognition memory. Most theories fall far short of this standard, being designed by their authors with only one paradigm in mind. As our aim is not to find models for particular paradigms, but for the retrieval processes revealed by them, we have sometimes extended someone's paradigm-specific model to data that its author had not intended it to explain. In such cases we have indicated where the original model stopped and where the extensions started, to avoid putting unpalatable words in the mouths of some theoreticians.

1. Serial search models

(A) THE ITEM RECOGNITION PARADIGM

1. *Evidence favouring an exhaustive serial search*
Sternberg's (1966, 1969a) exhaustive serial search has been the model most favoured for accounting for the results of the item recognition task. The model's apparent simplicity, coupled with the many successful replications of Sternberg's basic findings that reaction time increases linearly with

memory set size, and at the same rate for positive and negative probes, explain its popularity. Contradictory data have had a hard time getting recognized, but some experiments which have not found the expected results of linearity and parallelism will be discussed presently.

Sternberg (1969a) used two variants of the item recognition task, the *fixed set* procedure, where the memory set is held constant from trial to trial, and the *varied set* procedure, where a new set of items is presented on each trial. Reaction time functions were the same with both procedures, so that it appeared that serial scanning was used in retrieval both with familiar and unfamiliar sets of items. Similarly, the fact that the shapes of reaction time functions are unaffected by the type of item used, suggests that serial scanning is used generally in retrieval, and not only with sequentially presented items, such as digit strings. Both verbal and non-verbal items, presented sequentially or simultaneously in a spatial array, give the familiar linear and parallel functions (Sternberg, 1975). Gould (1973) has also supported the sequential scanning hypothesis for spatially presented information with eye-movement data, and Lehtiö and Kauri (1973) have obtained reaction time data supporting the idea that people match fragments of a picture to their memory of its whole by a sequential process.

There is also an impressive amount of evidence showing that the basic findings of the item recognition task can be replicated with different populations of subjects. Estimates of search rates from the slopes of reaction time functions for the normal college student population are in the range of 30 to 40 msec. Similar slope values have been found for children (Hoving, Morin and Konik, 1970) and alcoholics (Checkosky, cited in Sternberg, 1975). In these experiments only the intercept varied from one group to another, but not the memory search rate. However, the slopes of functions for retardates (Harris and Fleer, 1974) and older people (Anders, Fozard and Lillyquist, 1972) were steeper than those for normal children and young adults. It would be tempting to conclude that the longer scanning times were the result of older people and retardates having more noisy memory traces but, excepting the case of retardates, where errors were also found to be higher than for normals, this conclusion is not justified. Changes in processing rates could occur simply through subjects adopting a more cautious criterion for each decision in the scan, a strategy typical of older people in many discrimination tasks (Welford, 1964) and this possibility could only be ruled out by showing that errors and reaction time increase together.

Another point worth considering is whether the serial scanning model is applicable only to unpracticed subjects performing an unfamiliar task, or is also typical of highly practiced performance. Anyone familiar with Mowbray and Rhoades (1959) study of choice reaction time (see Chapters 3 and 5) would wish to know whether practice on the item recognition task decreases set size effects in a similar fashion. Kristofferson (1972a) and Ross (1970) found decreased slopes and intercepts as a result of practice, but Kristofferson (1972b) obtained intercept changes only after extensive practice. The studies reporting the slope changes used the same items for the memory set in all trials, while in the second Kristofferson study, which found no slope change, the set was changed from trial to trial. There seem to be two possible interpretations of these results. Either repeated presentation of the same list of items changed the way in which it was encoded in memory, so that its items could be accessed more rapidly, or increasing familiarity with the list resulted in lowered caution, and hence more speed in searching longer lists. Such changes are not exclusive of one another, and feature prominently in models to be reviewed later in the chapter. In any case, practice on the item recognition *task* does not reduce set size effects, although practice on the same *list* may.

2. Serial position effects in the item recognition task

Turning now to data which may contradict the exhaustive serial model, the first objection to be discussed is that the model is invalidated by experiments which have discovered that the speed of a response to a positive probe is related to its serial position in the memory list. Although Sternberg (1966, 1969a) found no relationship between reaction time and serial position, a number of studies have since reported that responses to items occurring later in the list are faster than those to items in early positions. Sometimes there is also a primacy effect, with the first couple of items giving faster reaction times than those following, but the most marked serial position effect is a recency one. Figure 7.4 shows typical recency and primacy effects for the serial positions in the item recognition task. The data are from Corballis, Kirby and Miller (1972), and other examples may be found in Burrows and Okada (1971) and Kennedy and Hamilton (1969). At first glance it seems difficult to reconcile these findings with an exhaustive serial scan which, as it assumes all items are searched, should predict flat serial position curves for reaction time. Although it was once believed that this was a vulnerable point in Sternberg's model, Townsend (1974) and Taylor (1976) have pointed out that the model can handle serial position effects if it is assumed that items in some positions are more discriminable than others, and that the time needed to make a positive match between an item and the probe is proportional to its discriminability.

3. Non-linear and non-parallel reaction time functions

Experiments which have failed to replicate the basic findings of linearity and parallelism of the reaction time functions for positive and negative probes are

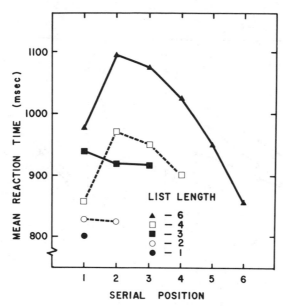

Fig. 7.4. Reaction time plotted as a function of serial position for various list lengths in the item recognition task. The functions show a primacy effect for position 1 at list lengths 4 and 6, and recency effects over the other positions at all list lengths. (From Corballis *et al.*, 1972)

a more serious threat to the exhaustive serial model. A number of studies have reported non-parallel functions, but few have shown that the negative probe function has a slope twice that of the positive function, as predicted by the self-terminating serial search model considered by Sternberg (1966). The exceptions are studies by Klatzky and Atkinson (1970), Klatzky, Juola and Atkinson (1971), and Sternberg (1969a). Data from the first of these three studies are shown in Fig. 7.5. All the experiments are characterized by the subject being required to make a more complex decision about the probe than a simple YES-NO classification of its presence or absence in the memory set. Thus it is possible to believe that while a simple match can be achieved by a fast automatic scan of the whole list, followed by a single YES-NO decision, a more complex match may require a decision after each item, making the scan slower, and self-terminating.

However, not all reports of non-parallel functions seem explicable as non-automatic self-terminating searches. Figure 7.6 shows data from Corballis *et al.* (1972) who found that the slope of the positive function was greater than that of the negative function, the opposite to the type of slope difference predicted by a self-terminating search. Scan rates estimated from the slopes were 40.5 msec/item for positive probes, and 27.3 msec/item for negative

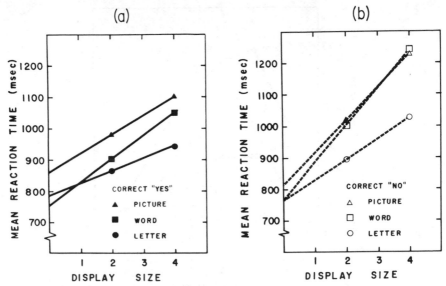

Fig. 7.5. Item recognition data where the slopes of the positive ("Yes") functions are nearly half those of the negative ("No") functions, as predicted by the serial self-terminating search. The task involved presentation of a list of letters followed by a probe which was (a) a letter which might match one of those in the list (Condition L); (b) a word, whose first letter might match a letter in the memory list (Condition W); or (c) a picture, whose name might begin with one of the letters in the memory list (Condition P). (From Klatzky and Atkinson, 1970)

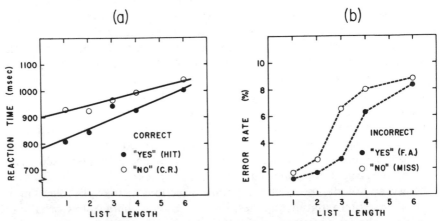

Fig. 7.6. Item recognition data which do not show the parallel reaction time functions predicted by the exhaustive serial search model. (a) Linear reaction time functions for correct responses where the slope of the positive (Yes) function is greater than that of the negative (No) function. (b) Error percentages showing that both misses and false alarms increase as a function of list length. (From Corballis *et al.*, 1972)

probes, which are in the ranges normally associated with the fast automatic process. Why are the data in Fig. 7.6 so different from the typical item recognition results shown in Fig. 7.1? Are they important evidence against exhaustive serial scanning, or are they an aberration which can be deemed so rare as to not trouble the general rule of parallel functions? To answer this question it is worth noting another major difference between the Corballis et al. (1972) data and Sternberg's (1966) results. The original Sternberg experiments which found linear and parallel reaction time functions had low error rates (about 2 per cent), which did not vary with memory set size.

Figure 7.6 shows that in the Corballis and co-workers' study, both misses and false alarms increased as the memory set increased, with the former being somewhat more prevalent than the latter. Other studies confirm that non-parallel, and even non-linear, reaction time functions are associated with moderate error rates which increase with set size. Burrows and Okada (1974), Corballis and Miller (1973), Pike, Dalgleish and Wright (1977) and Wingfield and Branca (1970) have reported changing error rates and non-parallel functions, while non-linearities are to be found in the data of Aubé and Murdock (1974), Banks and Atkinson (1974) and Swanson and Briggs (1969). The Aubé and Murdock (1974) data are presented in Fig. 7.7 as an illustration of non-linear functions. Notice also that both misses and false alarms increased with set size in this experiment.

4. Error-prone serial scanning

Although Sternberg developed his serial scanning model to account for error-free performance, the studies just described suggest that the scanning model should be extended to include scans where moderate error rates could occur. In this discussion we introduce the notion of a *sub-decision*, which is the operation carried out on each memory list item during the fast automatic scan to determine whether it matches the probe or not. If a match is made, a register is incremented and, after all items have been examined, a YES decision about the probe is made if it is found that the match register had been incremented. Note that the sub-decisions about individual memory list items in the automatic and exhaustive scan are not equivalent to the decisions made about each item in the self-terminating scan as they do not stop the search process, but merely provide information for the final decision. Now consider what might happen during the scan if there was a chance of the probe being positively matched with a memory set item which did not correspond to it (i.e. a false alarm), or of it failing to be matched to its corresponding item in the memory set (i.e. a miss). If a correct NO response is to be made to a negative probe after the search is completed, it is necessary that no false alarms occur in any of the matches; i.e. a correct NO implies that all n sub-decisions in the matching process be correct rejections.

If an incorrect NO response is made to a positive probe, this implies that the $n - 1$ sub-decisions about the non-corresponding items in the memory set were correct rejections, and that the single decision about the match of the probe to its corresponding memory item was a miss. Thus the time needed to make a correct NO response will be the time needed to make n correct rejections of the memory set items, while the time for an incorrect NO will be the time to make $n - 1$ correct rejections and one miss.

YES responses are more complicated to predict because they can arise from many different patterns of sub-decisions. For example, a correct YES (or a

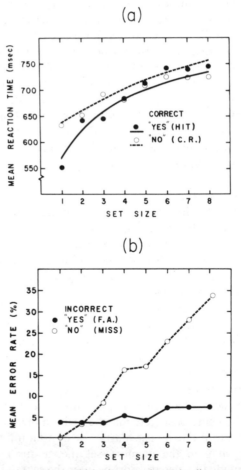

Fig. 7.7. Item recognition data which do not show the linear reaction time functions predicted by the exhaustive serial search model, and where misses and false alarms increase as a function of memory set size. (From Aubé and Murdock, 1974)

hit) will occur, either if the probe is correctly matched with its corresponding memory item, or if one or more false alarms is made to the $n - 1$ non-
corresponding items. An incorrect YES will similarly occur when between 1
and n false alarms are made in the sub-decisions about a negative probe. If
the probabilities of making sub-decision misses and false alarms do not
change with variations in memory set size it should be easy to see that
increasing the length of the memory list will increase the risk of at least one
sub-decision false alarm being made during the scan. Thus the longer the
list, the more incorrect YES responses and the fewer incorrect NO responses
should be made. However this prediction is contradicted by the error data
given in Figs 7.6 and 7.7 which show that both types of error increase with
list length.

The error-prone scanning model can also make predictions about reaction time. It is possible to derive expressions for total reaction time in terms
of the probabilities and times of correct and incorrect YES and NO responses,
but the main properties of the model can be illustrated without doing this.
Remember first, that we have seen that as list length increases, there is an
increased likelihood of one or more sub-decision false alarms occurring
during the scan. Consequently, the time needed to make this type of error
response will play an increasing role in determining the reaction time for YES
responses at longer list lengths. Assume firstly that sub-decision errors take
up more time than sub-decision correct responses, but that a false alarm
takes the same time as a miss, and a hit takes the same time as a correct
rejection. The model will then predict that incorrect YES and NO responses
will take longer than correct YES and NO responses, which agrees with most
data on error reaction times in the item recognition task (Biederman and
Stacy, 1974; Pike et al., 1977; Ratcliff, 1978). The presence of increasing
numbers of slow sub-decision false alarms at longer list lengths will also
mean that the reaction times of correct YES responses should rise more
rapidly with list length than those of correct NO responses, which result only
from the faster sub-decision correct rejections. However this prediction is at
variance with the results in Fig. 7.6 which show that the slope of the positive
probe function is less than that of the negative probe function. The correct
slope changes could be obtained from the error-prone scan by assuming that
sub-decision errors are executed more rapidly than sub-decision correct
responses, but then the model would conflict with the finding that error
responses are usually slower than correct responses.

Perhaps the error-prone scanning model could be made to make correct
predictions about error rates and reaction time functions by assuming that
the speed of a sub-decision false alarm differs from that of a miss, or that a
hit takes a different length of time from a correct rejection, or that the
probabilities of sub-decision errors change as a function of memory set size

and serial position. The authors have explored these possibilities but have been unable to arrive at a combination which gives a generally satisfactory account of item recognition data with moderate error rates. It appears that although the exhaustive serial scanning model gives a good account of error free performance in the item recognition task, it cannot be easily extended to cope with error-prone performance.

5. *Self-terminating serial search*

The evidence so far suggests that the type of self-terminating search depicted in Fig. 7.2 only applies to special situations where the decision required about the probe is so complex that it cannot be deferred until the list has been completely scanned, but must be made after each item has been examined.

Outside these special cases, a different type of self-terminating search needs to be proposed to account for the linear and parallel functions normally found in the item recognition task. Taylor (1976) lists several possibilities, but the one which has received most attention is a model by Theios, Smith, Haviland, Traupman and Moy (1973) which is capable of making the necessary predictions of parallelism and linearity. Besides differing from the Sternberg exhaustive model by proposing that the search is self-terminating, the Theios *et al.* (1973) model has two other important differences. First, it assumes that the search need not be restricted to the n items in the memory set. Memory may be considered as having a buffer containing the most recently presented items. Normally the most recent item will occupy position 1 in the buffer, the next most recent item will be in position 2, etc. so that while the n memory list items may occupy the earliest buffer positions, other items from earlier trials may also be present in later positions. Thus if the task requires memory of digit lists, and if the memory set "7284" has just been presented, the state of the buffer, from most to least recent item may be:

$$\underline{4\ 8\ 2\ 7}\ 1\ 3\ 9\ 6\ 0\ 5,$$

where the positions of the six non-members of the memory set have their buffer positions determined by their recency of presentation in previous trials.

The model's second assumption is that memory is always searched until an item has been found to match the probe. This applies both to positive and negative probe presentations. Thus in the above example, if the positive probe "2" is presented, three items in the buffer must be searched before attaining a match, while if the negative probe "9" is presented, seven items must be scanned, these including the four memory set items plus three non-members. On average, then, presentation of a positive probe will require $n/2$

items to be searched, while presentation of a negative probe will involve an average scan of $n + m/2$ items, where m is the number of non-members of the memory set. The example above used digits as the memory items so $n + m$ will always sum to 10. If a range of values is now chosen for n it is easy to see that $n/2$, the expression for the reaction time to a positive probe, and $n + m/2$, the expression for the reaction time to a negative probe, both increase linearly with n, and at the same rate. Although self-terminating on both positive and negative probes, the model is able to produce the linear and parallel functions expected by the exhaustive version.

What can be said against the self-terminating model? Among other criticisms, Sternberg (1975) drew attention to experiments by Lively (1972) and Lively and Sanford (1972) where the fastest correct reaction time to both positive and negative probes was shown to increase with memory set size. To see why this should be an embarrassment to the self-terminating model, and to illustrate a point about reaction time data which will become more important later in this chapter, a simple example will be given about how the reaction time distributions of two models behave as memory set size is increased.

First, consider the self-terminating search, and imagine that an experiment has been conducted where n has ranged from 2 to 4, and with trials arranged to that each serial position in the memory set has been probed equally often at each set size. When $n = 2$, half the scans for positive probes will terminate after one item of the memory set has been searched, and on the other 50 per cent of occasions, two items will need to be searched to discover a match. The reaction time distribution, which is depicted in Fig. 7.8, will therefore consist of two equally likely components, one where one unit of time is needed to get a match and the other where two units of time are required. If n is increased to 3, Fig. 7.8 shows that the reaction time will have three components, representing the units of time needed to obtain a match when the search terminates on the first, second or third serial position. Similarly, a list of length four will have four reaction time components.

Second, consider a simple version of the exhaustive serial search where each item in the list requires a constant time to be scanned, and where a decision is made after the scan is complete. As Fig. 7.8 shows, the reaction time distribution will always comprise one component as n increases, this being the number of units of time to scan the entire list. Now compare the distributions predicted by the two models. Mean reaction time, M, increases linearly for both models, but notice that the range of reaction times increases with n for the self-terminating version, but not for the exhaustive version. Also note that the fastest reaction time, L, remains constant for the self-terminating model, but increases with n for the exhaustive model. This explains the relevance of Lively's (1972) and Lively and Sanford's (1972) finding about minimum reaction time, and illustrates the point that although two models may make identical predictions about changes in mean reaction time as a function of *n*, they may often be distinguished by comparing some other statistics of the reaction time distribution; in the case of Fig. 7.8's examples by a measure of variance or of minimum latency.

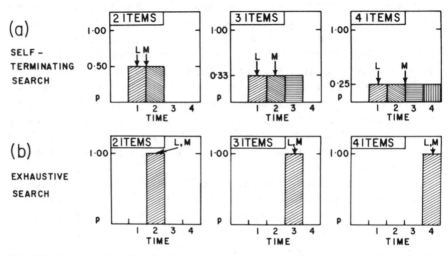

Fig. 7.8. Reaction time distributions to positive probes predicted (a) by a self-terminating serial search, and (b) by an exhaustive serial search. Changes in *L* minimum latency, and *M* mean latency, are shown as a function of set size for both models. It has been assumed that items are scanned at a constant rate.

To do justice to both the exhaustive and self-terminating models it should be pointed out at once that the examples in Fig. 7.8 are far too simple. For a start, there are good reasons to suppose that items do not require a constant amount of time to be processed and that therefore the mean time to search a list is not the sum of a set of constant times, but the sum of the average times needed to match the memory items with the probe. This will have no effects on predictions about the way that mean latency varies with *n*; the mean time to arrive at a decision is simply the sum of the mean times needed to process the items. However if two distributions are added together, their sum will not only have a mean equal to the sum of the means of the component distributions, but also a variance equal to the sum of their separate variances. Hence, if the processing times of individual items are variable, the exhaustive scanning model will predict that reaction time variance will increase linearly with *n*, subject to certain assumptions being satisfied about the independence of the processing operations (Sternberg, 1969b).

From the evidence reviewed so far it would seem that either an exhaustive or a self-terminating serial search could account equally well for the basic data of the item recognition task, with the exhaustive model doing better in accounting for changes in minimum latency. On the other hand, the self-terminating model gives a convincing explanation for the recency effects revealed by plotting reaction time against serial position, as the self-terminating scan of the buffer begins with the most recently presented items and proceeds to the least recently presented ones.

(B) THE STUDY-TEST PARADIGM

1. *Basic findings and the conveyor belt model*
When retrieval of items from lists longer than the 2 to 6 items normally used in the item recognition task is considered, the results do not favour a serial exhaustive search. In the study-test paradigm a study list may contain from 16 to 64 items, and is followed by a test list of the *n* study items, plus another *n* new items. Retrieval is usually tested by asking the subject to indicate his confidence on a six-point scale that the item was either new or old (e.g. Murdock, 1974; Murdock and Anderson, 1975; Ratcliff and Murdock, 1976), and recording the time taken to make this judgement. Usually only reaction times in the highest confidence categories for YES and NO responses are considered in the data analysis. The reason for this will be clear when the theory behind the paradigm is explained, but no biases seem to be introduced by eliminating all but the most confident responses (Murdock, Hockley and Muter, 1977).

Initially it seemed that reaction time was determined by one variable in the task, the lag (i.e. the number of intervening study and test items) between an item's presentation and the occurrence of its probe. Murdock's (1974) data, shown in Fig. 7.9, demonstrate a strong linear relationship between lag and reaction time to old items from the study list. Also, as far as new items in the list are concerned, reaction time is a linear function of test list position. This suggested to Murdock that when a probe is shown, subjects scan backwards through all the items presented so far, both test and study items, until either a match is found to a positive probe or, in the case of a negative probe, the beginning of the list is reached. The search process is serial, being self-terminating for positive probes and exhaustive for negative probes.

Why must the scan include both the study list and the test list? According to Murdock, this is the way this form of memory works. Items are like suitcases being deposited on a conveyor belt, with each new piece of

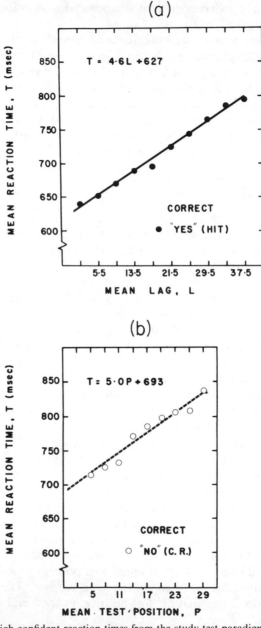

Fig. 7.9. Mean high confident reaction times from the study-test paradigm, fitted with linear functions. (a) "Yes" responses to study list items, plotted as a function of lag between an item's presentation in the study list, and its occurrence in the test list. (b) "No" responses to new items in the test list, plotted as a function of test list position. (From Murdock, 1974)

information being placed serially into memory as it arrives, and with previously presented items receding into the distance. The only way to get to these earlier items is to move sequentially over all those which have arrived after them. The complete conveyor belt model is a little more complicated than this, however. The confidence judgement procedure used by Murdock (1974) and Murdock and Dufty (1972) showed that high confidence YES and NO responses were made more rapidly than low confidence responses. This led Murdock to consider the possibility that the items in memory may have to be scanned more than once before either a convincing match or mismatch to the probe can be found. The reason for this may lie in the fact that memory traces are noisy, so that the search process is likely to yield false alarms to negative probes, and misses to positive ones, just as in the standard signal detection task. Thus, by analogy to the Signal Detection model, criteria will have to be set such that a YES response is made to a probe if the evidence favouring a match exceeds an upper criterion, k_Y, while a NO response is made if all the mismatches yield evidence falling below a lower criterion, k_N. The detection model is depicted in Fig. 7.10, and it is assumed that on the first scan of the list k_{Y1} and k_{N1} are set stringently and will give fast, low error, high confidence responses. If the criteria for making high confidence responses are not met, they are relaxed, by moving them closer together, say to k_{Y2} and k_{N2}, and the list is rescanned. This procedure, which is flow-charted in Fig. 7.10, may be repeated for each confidence level on the rating scale, and it is easy to see that at each level more errors will occur and the response will be slower than at the preceding level. These predictions were confirmed by Murdock and Anderson (1975). To simplify data analysis usually only responses made on the first scan of the list (i.e. high confidence responses) are considered.

Not only do errors increase as the confidence in a response decreases, but both misses and false alarms become more prevalent the longer the lag for a positive probe, or the later the test position for a negative one. Using Murdock's analogy, the items on the conveyor belt become less distinct as they recede into the distance. Notice, however, that it does not seem that more time is taken to compare a probe with an old indistinct item than it does to compare it with a new distinct one. If that were the case, reaction time should be a positively accelerating function of lag, but Fig. 7.10 shows that the relationship is linear, indicating a constant rate of inspection, and the price paid for a constant rate is an increase in errors.

Until this point the discussion has assumed that lag alone determines the reaction time and error rate to positive probes, and that we can ignore the fact that a lag of a given length can be composed of different proportions of study and test items. However, when Murdock and Anderson (1975) averaged reaction times over study positions to get out functions to positive

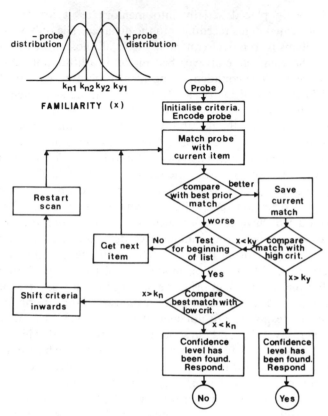

Fig. 7.10. The conveyor belt model. Strength distributions with criteria corresponding to confidence categories, and a flow chart of the stages leading to a decision about the probe.

probes, or averaged over test positions to get input functions, they obtained a pair of linear functions with different slopes. The scanning rate of the study list was estimated at 4.2 msec/item, while that of the test list was slower, being 6.5 msec/item. Moreover, Murdock and Anderson (1975) found that the slopes of output position functions varied as a function of the length of the study list, from 1.3 msec/item for a 64-item list to 6.3 msec/item for a 16-item list. This suggests that the longer the memory list, the faster it will be scanned. Ratcliff (1978, Fig. 10) also found non-linear study-position/reaction-time functions which generally showed that study items near the beginning and end of a list were responded to more rapidly than those in the middle of the list. These additional complications are not critical evidence against the conveyor belt model, but it can only predict them at the expense of extra assumptions.

2. *Confidence judgements and reaction time*

Although other evidence could be advanced which generally supports the conveyor belt analogy, and the idea of serial scanning in the study-test paradigm (see Murdock *et al.*, 1977), some of the contradictory evidence suggests strongly that no serial scanning model is a good description of memory retrieval. First, however, a specific difficulty for the conveyor belt model will be discussed because it suggests a potentially useful technique for discriminating between different types of retrieval model.

Figure 7.10 shows that for the conveyor belt, the list scanning process (the loop labelled "Get next item") is nested inside the process which sets the confidence levels (the loop labelled "shift criteria inwards") so that the reaction time to a probe will be a function of the number of items to be scanned in the inner loop multiplied by the number of criterion shifts made in the outer loop. It is easy to see an alternative way by which confidence judgements could enter into the retrieval process by assuming that the items are scanned only once, and the results of this scan are then evaluated to determine the confidence level of the response. (It is assumed that loss of distinctiveness of the items in memory may often yield evidence which does not clearly favour either a YES or NO decision, much as in Signal Detection Theory's rating scale task.) In this case the confidence judgement process occurs after all scanning has been carried out. Now consider how reaction time might change in the various confidence categories for probes which occur in later and later positions in the test list. Obviously for both types of model, reaction time in both Sure and Unsure categories will increase for later test positions as there will be more test items to scan before the study list is reached. But in the case of the conveyor belt, lower confidence levels will show a greater slowing of reaction time than higher confidence levels for later test positions. This is because the lower confidence levels involve more than one scan of the items and, as was pointed out above, test position and confidence level combine multiplicitively to determine reaction time. This prediction is shown in the first panel of Fig. 7.11.

On the other hand, if the confidence judgement is made after all scanning is complete, no interaction between test position and confidence level should occur. Reaction time should increase uniformly over all confidence levels for probes later in the test series. This prediction is shown in the second panel of Fig. 7.11.

The third panel in Fig. 7.11 shows what Murdock *et al.* (1977) actually found. There is an interaction between test position and confidence level, but it shows that high confidence responses become slower for later test positions while low confidence responses take about the same amount of time at all test positions, the opposite effect to that predicted by the conveyor belt model. These results are not at all easy to explain and will be

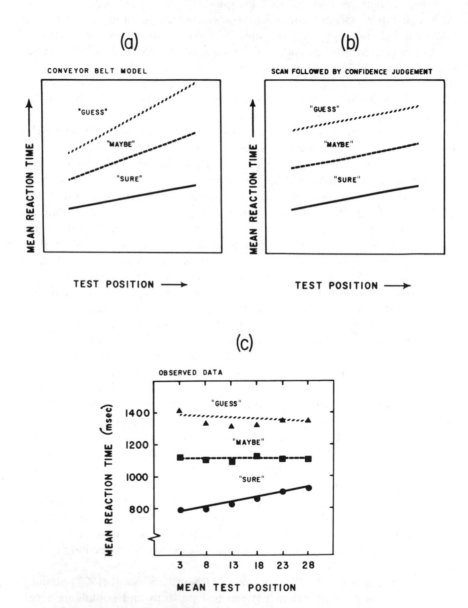

Fig. 7.11. Reaction times of high and low confidence judgements as a function of test list position in the study-test paradigm. (a) The pattern of reaction times expected by the conveyor belt model, where the scanning process is nested inside the process which determines confidence level. (b) The pattern of reaction times expected if confidence is determined after all scanning has been completed. (c) Observed data from Murdock *et al.* (1977).

referred to again to see if they can be accounted for by other retrieval models. Murdock and his co-workers have shown that confidence latency judgements are easy to collect in memory retrieval tasks, and it is likely that they could prove a useful source of information in testing retrieval theories. However, only a few experimenters have taken advantage of the procedure.

3. Reaction time distributions

In discussing the item recognition paradigm it was pointed out that other statistics of the reaction time distribution besides its mean may prove useful in discriminating amongst different types of retrieval model. Sternberg's (1969b) additive factors method, described in Chapters 3 and 5, shows how reaction time analysis may be carried out at three different levels; predictions about mean reaction time only, predictions about higher moments around the mean, such as variance, skew and kurtosis, and predictions about the entire form of the reaction time distribution. Although it may often seem desirable to work at a more complex level of analysis than that of mean reaction time, practical problems often stand in the way of doing this. The calculation of the mean requires obtaining Σx, the sum of the set of scores, while variance, skew and kurtosis require the sums Σx^2, Σx^3 and Σx^4, respectively. The higher moments, involving the sum of higher powers of the scores, have larger standard errors, so while the data may show a clear relationship between mean reaction time and the experimental variables, it may become disappointingly random at the level of skew, or even the variance. Ratcliff (1979) has discussed this problem quite fully, and has some practical suggestions to make about measures for describing the shape of a reaction time distribution.

To partially overcome this problem, Ratcliff and Murdock (1976) first looked for a theoretical distribution which would approximate the shapes of normally obtained reaction time distributions. Such a distribution would have to be bell-shaped, but positively skewed, and have a lower limit of zero. From several candidates they decided upon the distribution which is the convolution of the normal and exponential distributions. For readers unfamiliar with the concept of convolution, it is easiest to understand by imagining a reaction process which has two stages. Stage 1, illustrated in Fig. 7.12, produces reaction times which conform to a negative exponential distribution. (This stage might correspond, say, to the time needed to match a probe with a memory set item.) When Stage 1 is completed, Stage 2 commences. The times taken to complete the second stage are normally distributed, as illustrated in the second panel of Fig. 7.12. The total reaction time will be the sum of the two stage times, so that the total reaction time distribution will be the sum, or convolution, of the two stages' distributions. This is illustrated in the third panel of Fig. 7.12, and it can be seen that the

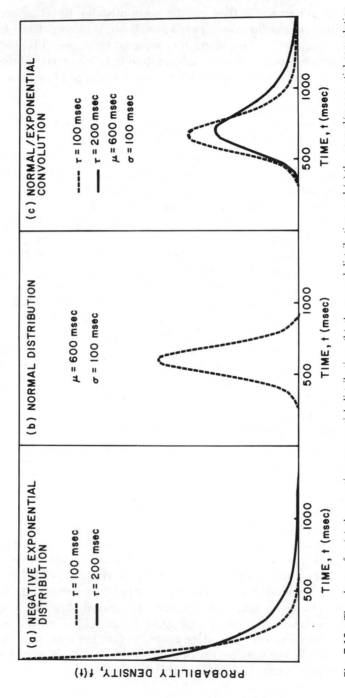

Fig. 7.12. The shapes for (a) the negative exponential distribution, (b) the normal distribution, and (c) the normal/exponential convolution.

normal/exponential convolution is described by three parameters, μ and σ, which are the mean and standard deviation of the normal component, and τ, the mean (sometimes called the time constant) of the exponential component. The meaning of these parameters can be understood by seeing what happens to the reaction time distribution as each is changed. An increase in μ will result in the whole reaction time distribution being shifted up along the X-axis, while an increase in σ will spread the distribution out. Changing either of these parameters therefore shifts both the lower and upper ends of the reaction time distribution. Increasing τ however, causes a shift in the upper (slower) region of the distribution, while leaving the lower (faster) region largely unchanged. Thus τ resembles the third central moment normally used to measure skew.

Having found a way of characterizing the most important features of a reaction time distribution, the next step was to relate the parameters μ, σ and τ to models of retrieval. There are two ways of doing this. First, we might take the illustration of the normal and exponential distributions as the sum of two successive reaction stages seriously, and look for separate stages in retrieval which might have normally and exponentially distributed processing times. Second, we might treat the convolution simply as a distribution of convenience, which gives a good fit to an observed distribution, and provides three useful measures of performance. Ratcliff and Murdock (1976) mainly used the second strategy to test several retrieval models, but at present discussion will be restricted to serial scanning models, particularly the conveyor belt.

The most obvious prediction about the reaction time distribution made by the conveyor belt, or any other serial scanning model, is the one illustrated in Fig. 7.8, namely that increasing the number of items to be scanned will shift the entire reaction time distribution up the X-axis. In terms of the parameters of the convolution distribution, μ should increase with both lag and test position. It does not, as Fig. 7.13 shows. The value of μ remains constant, but τ increases, showing that the increase in mean reaction time at later test positions is due to a buildup of very slow latencies, but that the lower end of the reaction time distribution, which contains fast latencies, does not shift. This result, which has been replicated several times by Ratcliff and Murdock (1976), and by Ratcliff (1978), is embarrassing for any model which proposes that retrieval requires a serial scan of the study and test lists. No doubt modifications could be made to serial models to incorporate this result, but it would be nicer to find a theory which predicted such an important fact naturally.

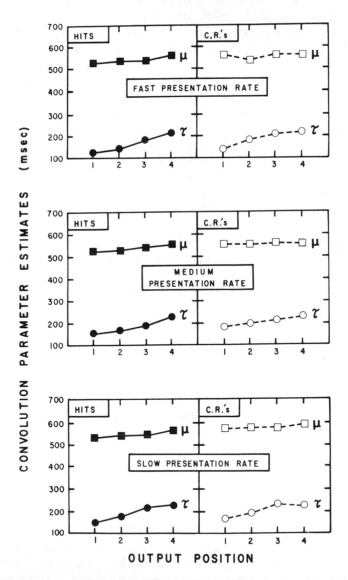

Fig. 7.13. Changes in μ and τ, the parameters of the normal/exponential convolution obtained by fitting the distribution to reaction times from the study-test task. Note that μ remains constant over output (test) position, indicating that the fast end of the reaction time distribution is not affected by changing the output position of a probe, while τ increases as a function of output position, showing that the slow end of the reaction time distribution is becoming even slower. (From Ratcliff and Murdock, 1976)

(c) THE PREMEMORIZED LIST PARADIGM

1. *Slopes of reaction time functions*

In experiments from this paradigm subjects normally learn a list of items until they are able to recall them correctly on two successive trials. One or more test periods are then conducted where subjects make YES-NO decisions about items in test lists containing the *n* items from the memory list plus a number of new items. In such an experiment Burrows and Okada (1975) had subjects learn lists of 2, 4, 6, 8, 10, 12, 16 or 20 words, and then measured retrieval by presenting a test list containing the *n* memory items plus *n* lures. In Experiment 1, a list of new words was learned before each test, so that during the experiment there was no repeated probing of memory list items. In Experiment 2, only one list was learned, and its memory items were probed on more than one testing occasion. Negative probes were always changed from one test to the next. The results of the experiments are shown in Fig. 7.14, fitted either by a pair of linear functions, or by a logarithmic function. Clearly, no simple serial search model will account for these results. Two general possibilities which involve scanning could be considered. The first, which would give some meaning to the logarithmic fit, is that longer lists were scanned more rapidly than shorter lists (an effect similar to that noticed by Ratcliff and Murdock (1976) in the study-test paradigm). This might occur if the scan did not proceed item by item, but involved a search process where, say, half the memory items in the list were eliminated first as not matching the probe, then half the remainder were eliminated in the second match, etc. This resembles an information theory model of list scanning proposed by Briggs and Swanson (1970). The second possibility is that retrieval involves two processes, one which is dependent on list length, and one which is not. The list length dependent process if more likely to be used with short lists of up to eight items, while longer lists require the process which is independent of *n*. Burrows and Okada (1975) tentatively identified the processes with short and long term memory searches, as their first linear function applied over the 7 ± 2 range associated with the memory span.

Before accepting the proposition that data from the pre-memorized list paradigm differ from those of the item recognition task, in that they need to be fitted by bilinear and logarithmic functions, it should be remembered that some of the item recognition data have also shown a curvilinear relationship between list length and reaction time, and for values of *n* well within the normal memory span. Remembering that those experiments were also characterized by a positive correlation between list length and number of errors, it is worth asking whether the same correlation occurs in the Burrows and Okada data. It does, as has been shown by Ratcliff (1978, Fig.

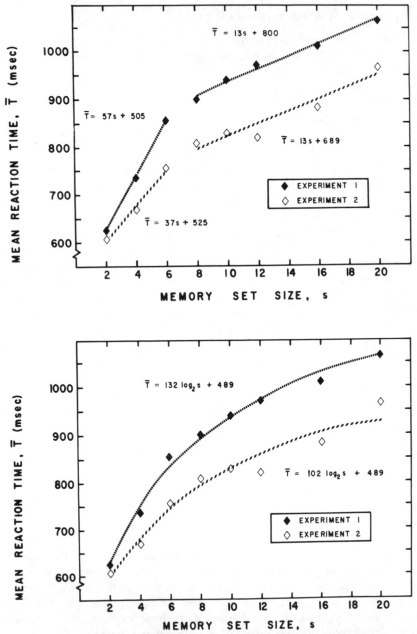

Fig. 7.14. Reaction time as a function of memory list length for the prememorized list task. Data for positive and negative probes have been combined, and fitted either by a pair of linear functions, or by a logarithmic function. (From Burrows and Okada, 1975)

17), so perhaps we should seek an explanation of the relationship between the curvilinearity of the reaction time function and error rate, rather than try to develop a model for subspan and supraspan memory retrieval.

2. *Probe repetition effects*

The procedure used by Atkinson and Juola (1972, 1974), Fischler and Juola (1971) and Juola, Fischler, Wood and Atkinson (1971), has provided extra information about reaction time changes when probe items are repeated on successive tests. In their task a memory list is followed by the first test which may contain 25 per cent of the items from the memory list, plus an equal number of lures. In test 2, all the test 1 items are repeated, plus another 25 per cent of the memory list items and an equal number of new lures. In tests 3 and 4 the same procedure is repeated; all the probes presented on the previous test are given again, plus additional memory list items and new lures. The basic findings of the task are shown in Fig. 7.15. The upper section of Fig. 7.15 shows changes in reaction time and errors to memory list items and lures over successive testing sessions. It can be seen that repeated probing with memory list items decreases their reaction times and reduces misses, while repetition of lures increases their reaction times and raises the false alarm rate. The lower section shows how reaction time is affected by list length and probe repetition. The first test is shown in the left panel, and in the right panel the function has been averaged over all subsequent tests with repeated probes. The functions are roughly linear, but not parallel, with both slopes and intercepts being changed by probe repetition.

Atkinson and Juola's (1974) explanation for these results will be discussed later when direct access models are described. It involves a two-stage model, one stage involving a serial search of the memory list, and hence accounting for the linear relationship between list length and reaction time, and another stage involving direct access, and accounting for the probe repetition effects. However, it does not seem that the data in Fig. 7.15 could easily be explained by a model which involves only scanning. Three ways in which probe repetition could affect reaction time in a serial model are as follows:

(i) Repeating a probe may speed up its encoding prior to the scan. Thus the intercepts for both positive and negative functions should decline, but the slopes should not change.

(ii) Repeated scans of the same list may either facilitate or interfere with subsequent scanning, so-called scanning residue effects (Murdock *et al.*, 1977; Muter and Murdock, 1977). Thus the slopes for positive and negative probe functions should be both either increased or decreased.

(iii) The decision process after the scan may be biased by probe repetition

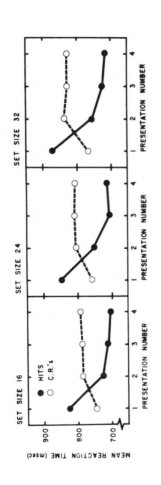

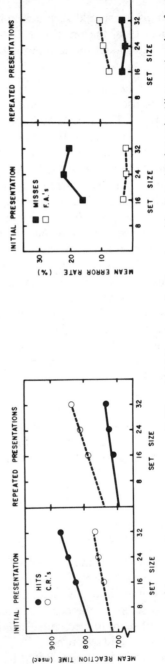

Fig. 7.15. Probe repetition effects in the prememorized list task. (a) Correct reaction times to positive (target) and negative (distractor) probes after 1, 2, 3 or 4 presentations, for lists of 16, 24 or 32 items. (b) Reaction times and error rates to positive and negative probes as a function of list length, for the initial presentation of a probe, or for repeated presentations. (From Juola and Atkinson, 1974)

so that YES responses are made more quickly, and NO responses more slowly. Thus the intercept of the YES function should decline, and that of the NO function should increase, and the slopes should remain the same.

None of these possibilities, or combination of them, predicts the results in Fig. 7.15. If a scanning model is to account for them, it would seem to need the inclusion of some other retrieval process.

(D) THE CONTINUOUS RECOGNITION MEMORY PARADIGM

In this task a list of items is presented and, after each, the subject judges whether or not it had occurred previously in the list. On its first presentation, therefore, an item serves as a negative probe; on subsequent presentation it is a positive probe. Okada (1971) used words as the memory items, and varied the number of intervening words between an item's first and second presentations. The time to respond YES to a repeated probe is plotted as a function of lag between its first and second presentations in Fig. 7.16.

A serial scanning account of the continuous recognition memory task might resemble the conveyor belt model's description of the study-test paradigm, by supposing that on the presentation of an item, the list is searched by a backward scan until either a match is found to a repeated item, or the beginning of the list is found without matching a new item. Okada (1971) discussed other variations of serial scanning, but like the

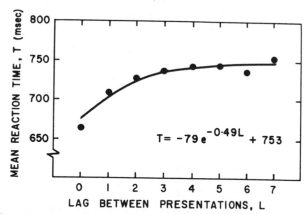

$$T = -79\,e^{-0.49L} + 753$$

Fig. 7.16. Data from the continuous recognition memory task. Correct reaction times to old items plotted as a function of lag between their initial and subsequent presentations fitted by an exponential function. Also shown are the reaction times for correct rejections, misses, and false alarms. (From Okada, 1971)

example given, they all predict that reaction time should be a linear function of lag, providing the items are searched at a constant rate. As it is not, it must follow either that the scan accelerates as more items are searched, or that retrieval does not involve a serial scan. Okada (1971) favoured a direct access interpretation of his results, which will be discussed in the section dealing with that class of model. The data from this paradigm do not favour any simple serial model.

(E) OVERVIEW OF SERIAL MODELS

The main strength of serial models is that they account for the linear relationship between memory set size and reaction time, particularly in the item recognition paradigm where the positive and negative functions are frequently parallel and error rates are low. Sternberg's (1966) serial exhaustive model is an attractively simple explanation of these data, although Theios et al.'s (1973) self-terminating model is a plausible alternative. Even in the study-test paradigm, the linear functions obtained by plotting latency against lag fit easily with the notion of serial scanning. However, as soon as other data are considered, such as the effects of moderate error rates, reaction time statistics besides the mean, and confidence judgements, serial scanning models encounter difficulties. When other paradigms are considered, such as the prememorized list and continuous recognition memory tasks, examples of non-linear reaction time functions are found. Serial models can explain many of these data if they are complicated to incorporate non-constant scanning rates, or other stages in the retrieval process such as direct access or short-term/long-term memory distinctions. However, the types of additions which must be made to accommodate a serial model to the data vary from task to task, so that it becomes difficult to discern any general theory of retrieval based on serial scanning. The former generality and simplicity having been lost, it is worth looking for another perspective on the problem of retrieval.

2. Parallel search models

(A) SIMPLE PARALLEL MODELS AND THE ITEM RECOGNITION TASK

Getting a serial model to predict changes in reaction time as a function of memory set size is a relatively simple matter. As the items are scanned one after another, total reaction time is just the sum of the n durations needed to process the items. In a parallel model things are a little more complicated as the n processing operations are being carried out simultaneously, and the total time will depend on whether a decision is made as soon as the process which matches the probe is complete (self-terminating version), or only after all n items have been completed (exhaustive version). To account for the bulk of the data from the item recognition task, a model must be able to predict roughly linear increases in reaction time as a function of memory set size for values of n up to about 20. Also, the slopes of positive and negative functions ought not to be too dissimilar. Taylor's (1976) review of parallel processing models shows that most self-terminating versions usually predict very different slopes for positive and negative probes so attention will first be restricted to parallel exhaustive models. It will also be assumed that there is some variability in the time needed to process a single item, so that the processing time for a memory item can be considered as a random drawing from some distribution of possible processing times. The time needed to process n such items completely will therefore correspond to the largest (i.e. slowest) of n random drawings from the distribution of possible processing times. The bigger n becomes, the longer the total time, because as the size of the sample is increased, the greater the likelihood of randomly drawing large values for the processing times of some items.

To test whether this conception of parallel processing adequately describes the linear increase in reaction time with set size frequently observed in the item recognition task, we need to know how the value of the largest of n random drawings increases as a function of n. There are two ways of getting an answer to this question. The obvious method is to hope that the underlying distribution from which the random drawings are being taken can be specified, and then that the distribution of its largest value, as a function of n, can be derived. The second method is to stick to properties of parallel processes which do not depend on specifying the distribution of processing times. Sternberg (1966, 1975) used the second approach to reject parallel models in favour of the exhaustive serial model. Gumbel (1958, Section 3.1.8) has shown that for any continuous distribution which has a mean and a variance (some distributions are deficient in these respects) the mean largest value of n random drawings increases more slowly than $\sqrt{(n/2)}$ times the standard deviation of the initial distribution. Thus reaction time should be a negatively accelerating function of memory set size, but Sternberg (1966) found that his obtained reaction time functions grew more quickly with set size than this relationship allows.

However, not all parallel models have this property, and by specifying the underlying distribution of processing times it is possible to arrive at exhaustive parallel models which closely mimic the behaviour of Sternberg's (1966) exhaustive serial model. This has been the approach adopted by Townsend (1974) and Taylor (1976). Their models have many common features, and as Taylor's is mathematically simpler, it will be used as the example here. The underlying distribution of processing times may be specified on theoretical grounds, or may be chosen simply for convenience. Because it is frequently difficult to derive an expression for the mean maximum value of n random samples from most distributions, the distribution of convenience approach has generally prevailed. In most cases, the exponential distribution (see Fig. 7.12) is used. Gumbel (1958) has shown that if n random drawings are taken from an exponential distribution with a time constant of τ, then the mean maximum value of the sample, M_{max}, is given by the expression:

$$M_{max} = \frac{1}{\tau} \sum_{i=1}^{n} \frac{1}{i}. \tag{7.1}$$

If this formula is taken as the mean time to process n memory items in parallel, τ can be considered as the rate at which each is processed.

As it stands, eqn (7.1) is not quite what is needed. If some arbitrary value of τ is chosen, and M_{max} is plotted as a function of n, it will be found to be negatively accelerating. This might be appropriate for fitting results from those experiments where reaction time has been found to be a curvilinear function of set size, but for the parallel model to cope with linear reaction time functions, some plausible way must be found to modify eqn (7.1) so that M_{max} rises more rapidly as n increases. This can be done by making τ, the rate parameter, contingent on n, so that the processing rate of individual items declines as the number of items being processed increases. This modification is plausible if it is assumed that the retrieval system has a limited capacity for processing items, and that this capacity is shared amongst the n memory items. Taylor's (1976) way of expressing a capacity limitation is to set $\tau = P/n$, where P is the total available capacity, and n is the number of items competing for it. Thus eqn (7.1) becomes:

$$M_{max} = \frac{n}{P} \sum_{i=1}^{n} \frac{1}{i}. \tag{7.2}$$

If an arbitrary value of P is chosen, and M_{max} is plotted as a function of n, it will be found that the function is almost linear on n. Perfect linearity can be obtained by substituting Townsend's (1974) expression for τ in eqn (7.1), so that the limited capacity exhaustive parallel model with exponential processing times exactly mimics Sternberg's (1966) serial exhaustive model in its predictions about mean reaction time.

Using a distribution of convenience rather than one which has some theoretical or empirical support raises the question of how dependent the parallel model's predictions are on the choice of the exponential. Sternberg (1975) has criticized this choice on theoretical grounds, but from a practical point of view the model's predictions are not greatly altered by choosing another distribution, so long as only mean reaction time is considered. The exponential distribution is very asymmetrical, but if the expression for the mean maximum value of n random drawings from a symmetrical distribution is substituted in eqn (7.2), M_{max} still increases almost linearly with n. The distribution used for this purpose was the logistic, whose shape closely resembles that of the normal distribution, and for which there is a convenient expression for M_{max} (Gumbel, 1958). The shape of the function relating the variance of the maximum value of the reaction time to n is greatly affected by the choice of a distribution, however, so that it is meaningless to make predictions about this statistic until a model can be developed which strongly specifies a particular distribution of processing times. Such a model will now be described.

(B) THE DIFFUSION MODEL

Ratcliff (1978) has proposed that memory retrieval takes place by a parallel search which is self-terminating for positive probes, and exhaustive for negative ones. His theory differs from most others in that it begins by describing how a probe is compared with the memory items, and from this a specification of the reaction time distribution follows. His analogy to retrieval is resonance; the probe is like a tuning fork with a particular frequency which, when it vibrates, produces sympathetic vibrations from other tuning forks (memory items) with similar frequencies. The more similar the probe is to a memory item, the stronger the resonance, and this serves as the evidence for deciding whether or not a satisfactory match has been found.

The second important part of Ratcliff's model is how the evidence is used to make a decision about the probe. The output of the resonance process for each item is assumed to drive a random walk (see Chapter 5 for a description of the random walk) towards one of two boundaries which, when crossed, terminate the match for that item with either a YES or a NO decision. The crossing of a single positive boundary terminates the entire search of the memory items with a YES decision, while a NO decision occurs after the random walks for all n memory items terminate at their negative boundaries. The retrieval theory therefore resembles many models of simple discrimination (Link and Heath, 1975; Pike, 1973; Stone, 1960; Vickers, 1970) where a decision about a stimulus is based on accumulation of evidence about how it is to be classified, and where the reaction time reflects the duration of this evidence accumulation process. The theory differs from other random walk processes in that they (e.g. Link and Heath, 1975) have considered the random walk as a series of steps resulting from a set of discrete samples of evidence, whereas the memory theory is based on a continuous random walk, or diffusion process (Feller, 1964, XIV.6).

The time to respond YES correctly to a positive probe or incorrectly to a negative probe will therefore depend on two factors; the rate at which the random walk diffuses towards the positive boundary, and the distance between the starting point of the random walk and the positive boundary. The time for a NO response will depend on three things: rate of drift towards the negative boundary, distance of the starting point from the negative boundary, and the number of memory items whose random walks must terminate at the negative boundary before a NO decision can be made. Figure 7.17 illustrates some of these factors. Obviously the rate of drift depends on the resonance level produced in matching the probe with a memory item, while the relationship between the starting point z and the two boundaries, 0 and a, reflects the degree of bias towards either a NO or a YES response.

To specify the drift rate of the random walk, the theory assumes that the resonance levels for memory list members and non-members can be represented by two normal distributions with means u and v, respectively, and with a common standard deviation, η. The distributions, called the relatedness distributions, are located on a continuum which runs from strong relatedness (when the probe closely matches a memory item) to strong unrelatedness (a strong mismatch), with a zero point which represents the state of affairs when the evidence neither favours a match nor a mismatch. The relatedness distributions are analogous to the signal and noise distributions of Signal Detection Theory, and the asymptotic discriminability, d', is simply $(u - v)/\eta$.* The zero point on the relatedness continuum is like the criterion of Signal Detection Theory.

If fluctuations in the resonance level produce relatedness values exceeding the zero point, the random walk will move towards the positive boundary, while fluctuations below the zero point will drive it towards the negative boundary. The point at which the boundary is crossed, which represents the duration of the random walk, will vary randomly from trial to trial depending on the fluctuations in resonance, so that for a particular setting of the random walk boundaries and a relatedness distribution with a particular mean and standard deviation, there will be a distribution of times to

---

* The term "asymptotic d'" is used to distinguish it from the observed d' which would be found in the normal way from the hit and false alarm rates. As the observed hits and false alarms, and therefore the observed d', are the result of the action of the diffusion process on the relatedness distributions, they will be a function both of the relatedness parameters, u, v and η, and of the random walk parameters, z and a. The asymptotic d' assumes that the random walk parameters have been held constant, and are thus only a function of u, v and η. This measure can therefore only be calculated after the values of u, v, η, z and a have been estimated from the data.

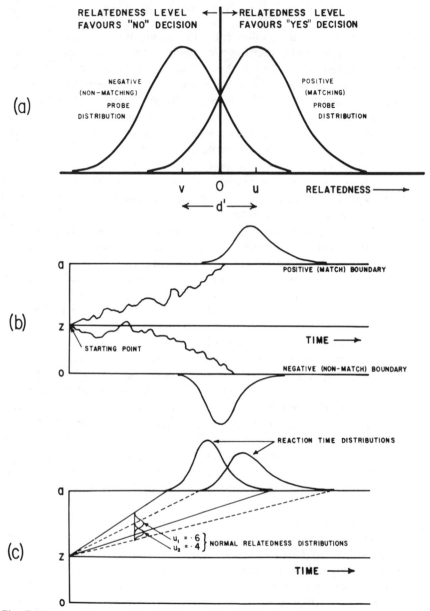

Fig. 7.17. Some features of the diffusion model. (a) The relatedness continuum, showing the zero point, which serves the same function as the criterion in Signal Detection Theory, and the two relatedness distributions for probes which either match or do not match items in memory. (b) Examples of random walks which start at z, and terminate at a or 0, the positive and negative boundaries. As the starting point is closer to the negative boundary, No responses will, on the average, be faster than Yes responses. (c) Changes in the reaction time distribution brought about by shifting the relatedness distribution along the relatedness continuum. As the relatedness mean declines from u_1 to u_2, the upper tail of the reaction time distribution becomes smaller. (Adapted from Ratcliff, 1978)

complete the random walk, as illustrated in the bottom section of Fig. 7.17. Thus the diffusion model predicts the entire form of the reaction time distribution, in terms of z and a, the random walk boundary parameters, and u and η, the relatedness distribution parameters for positive probes, or v, η and n (memory set size) for negative probes. Also, as is common in reaction time models, a constant, T_{ER}, must also be included when fitting the model to real data, to account for those parts of the reaction process, such as encoding the probe or making a response, which occur in addition to the retrieval of the information. The prediction of error rates and latencies follows naturally from the theory as the probability of the random walk terminating at the wrong boundary, and the time taken to do so, are both able to be expressed in terms of the model's parameters.

Testing of this model required consideration of other statistics of the reaction time distribution besides the mean. Previously, accumulator models for simple discrimination have been evaluated by Vickers (1970) and Vickers, Caudrey and Willson (1971) by testing predictions about higher moments of the reaction time distribution such as variance, skew and kurtosis. Ratcliff's approach was similar, except that he used the convolution method of Ratcliff and Murdock (1976) described earlier in this chapter. An observed distribution of reaction times was fitted to the normal/exponential convolution to obtain observed values of μ, σ and τ. The diffusion model was then used to predict μ, σ and τ values from its own parameters and these were then compared with the observed values to see how well they accounted for the data. The model was applied to data from the four experimental paradigms discussed in this chapter; item recognition, study-test, prememorized list and continuous recognition. In each case it did moderately or very well in accounting for the basic data. Ratcliff (1978) should be consulted for details of these tests; here we will sketch the major factors which seem to govern performance in the tasks according to the diffusion model.

When applied to data from the item recognition task, the diffusion model showed that the approximately linear and parallel reaction time functions were attributable to two factors; the increase in the number of parallel processes needing to be completed before a NO decision could be made and a decrease in discriminability of memory set items as set size was increased. This latter factor which was largely responsible for the linear increase in reaction time to positive probes, also accounted for serial position effects in the data, with early items in the list showing the greatest discriminability decreases and reaction time increases, as set size grew larger.

Two types of change were also responsible for the variations in reaction time as a function of study list and test list position in the study-test paradigm. Presenting a study item in an early study position, or a late test position, caused a drop in its relatedness value, making it more like a negative probe, while when negative probes were presented in later test positions, their relatedness values were increased, making them more like positive probes. These changes gave a net decrease in discriminability which, in turn, was responsible for the increases in reaction time with longer lags or later test positions. By looking at Fig. 7.17 and imagining the effects of shifting a relatedness distribution on the projection of its reaction time distribution, it should be apparent that shifting the distribution mean closer to the zero point will move the lower portion of the distribution up slightly, while the upper regions will be stretched considerably. This explains why μ remains constant and τ changes with lag and test position, the fact which proved so difficult for scanning models like the conveyor belt.

In addition to the changes in relatedness, reaction time is also increased by the random walk boundaries being moved farther apart for later test positions, as if subjects were trying to offset the decrease in discriminability by setting a more cautious criterion for a response. This speed-accuracy trade-off, coupled with the shifts in the relatedness distributions, adequately accounted for the major results in the study-test paradigm, including the linear reaction time functions, error rates and shapes of the reaction time distributions.

Similar changes in relatedness and in speed-accuracy trade-off allowed the diffusion model to account for the Burrows and Okada (1975) prememorized list data in Fig. 7.14. The means of the relatedness distributions were closer together for longer lists with the asymptotic d' dropping from 5.3 for a 2-item list to 4.8 for a 10-item list, and remaining constant thereafter. Also as list length increased, the random walk boundaries moved further apart, much as in the study-test paradigm, again indicating an attempt to compensate for increased errors due to decreased discrimination. Ratcliff (1978) also noted that the diffusion process could account for the probe repetition data of Atkinson and Juola (1974) which is illustrated in Fig. 7.15. Multiple presentations of either a positive or a negative probe will increase its relatedness, so that the distributions for repeated probes are moved up closer to the positive boundary of the random walk. This is tantamount to inducing a bias towards a YES response, and should result in more rapid correct YES responses to repeated than to non-repeated probes, but to slower correct NO responses to repeated lures. False alarms should also increase with probe repetition while misses should decrease, which is what happens.

In the three experimental paradigms so far considered, there is a clear distinction between the study and test phases of the experiment, and subjects are aware of the amount of information which must be held in memory. This makes it possible for them to shift the positions of the random walk boundaries to compensate for discrimination decreases brought about by lag or list length effects. As the continuous recognition memory task has no separate test phase, and as its lags are of unpredictable lengths, such speed-accuracy tradeoff strategies should not be possible, and the diffusion model was able to fit the Okada (1971) data, assuming only that the relatedness of positive probes declined as a function of lag.

1. Confidence judgements

Ratcliff (1978) briefly mentioned that the confidence judgement procedure of the study-test paradigm might be incorporated into the diffusion model by considering that subjects set deadlines, so that if the random walk exceeds a criterion time, the response would be made at a lower level of confidence. At first glance this seems to be a plausible way of thinking about confidence judgements, as low confidence responses are generally less accurate and have slower latencies than high confidence responses. Difficulties occur for the idea if one considers the changes in reaction time for high confidence responses in the study-test task at longer lags, or later test positions. As items become less discriminable, high confidence latency increases, due largely to a lengthening of the upper tail of the distribution. However, if a deadline is operating, these long latencies should be being assigned to a lower confidence category so that as high confidence judgements are slowed down we should observe progressive truncation of the upper tail of their reaction time distribution. There is no indication in the Ratcliff and Murdock (1976) or Ratcliff (1978) data that this happens.

Perhaps confidence is not determined by the length of the reaction time but by the clarity of the evidence being provided by the relatedness distributions. In Signal Detection Theory, the criterion, which corresponds to the zero point on the relatedness continuum, is not fixed but can have its position varied to establish different levels of stringency for making a YES or NO response. In Signal Detection Theory's rating scale task, the subject is assumed to hold several such criteria simultaneously, these representing confidence levels. It would thus be possible either to have a diffusion process where the criterion on the relatedness distribution varied from trial to trial to give a range of confidence levels over the entire experiment, or one where several criteria were held simultaneously on every trial, each having its own random walk corresponding to a particular confidence level.

(C) OVERVIEW OF PARALLEL MODELS

Although parallel search models have been less frequently studied than serial models, there are many indications that they are as capable as the serial models in accounting for the data of the various experimental paradigms. In their simplest forms, parallel models can mimic the behaviour of the serial models in the item recognition task, producing both linear and parallel reaction time functions. However, like the serial models, they fail to say anything about errors and the shape of the reaction time distribution. It is comparatively easy to produce curvilinear reaction time functions with a simple parallel model, by altering the relationship between the rate parameter, τ, and the experimental variable (e.g. memory set size), but some theoretical basis would be needed for the rate change to make this an interesting feature of a model.

Ratcliff's (1978) parallel model, based on the diffusion process, is a much more impressive attempt at incorporating error and reaction time distribution data from several paradigms into a single retrieval theory. Much existing data is explained by plausible assumptions about changes in item discriminability and in the setting of the boundaries for the random walk process. The model has close affinities with some current psychophysical theories about discrimination times, which should please those who believe that theories should not only extend over a variety of experimental paradigms within one area of psychology, but should also find their counterparts in other areas. The general conclusion which seems able to be drawn from the diffusions model's applications is that factors such as list length and lag alter item relatedness, and change the value of the asymptotic d'. To compensate for variations in error rates brought about by this discrimination change, subjects adopt different degrees of caution for making a response by moving the boundaries of the random walk process to give a speed-accuracy trade-off. One question should be asked about the model: that is whether it owes its explanatory power to the fact that it involves parallel rather than serial or direct access processing, or to the incorporation of the random walk which determines the decision? The answer to this question may be clearer after some direct access models have been described.

3. Direct access models

(A) STRENGTH THEORY

The diffusion process was one example of how signal detection concepts about item discriminability can be combined with a decision process which determines the latency. Strength Theory is another example. It appeared as a memory model in Norman and Wickelgren (1969), and since then has either been considered as a model in its own right (Murdock, 1974; Murdock and Dufty, 1972; Ratcliff and Murdock, 1976), or as a stage in a hybrid model of retrieval (Atkinson and Juola, 1974; Corballis and Miller,

1973). The general features of the model are shown in Fig. 7.18. Items which have been learned are assumed to receive an increment of strength relative to unlearned items and the traces for both learned and unlearned items are assumed to be noisy. When a probe is presented, its corresponding memory item is accessed directly and its trace strength compared with a fixed criterion value, k. The distributions of trace strength for the memorial representations of positive and negative probes are shown in the left section of Fig. 7.18; strengths lying above the criterion lead to YES responses, while those below the criterion lead to NO responses. If the strength distributions are assumed to be normal, the distance between their means, d', and the position of the criterion, k, may be obtained from the hit and false alarm probabilities by the standard signal detection procedures.

Latencies of responses are assumed to be negatively correlated with the absolute distance of the probe's trace strength from the criterion, as illustrated by the strength-latency function in Fig. 7.18. It is frequently assumed that this function is a pair of negative exponentials, with the same time constant, as depicted in the figure, but other functions could be used (Pike, 1973; Pike and Ryder, 1973).

The model has been criticized by Pike (1973) and Pike and Ryder (1973) as a general model for discrimination times on a variety of grounds,

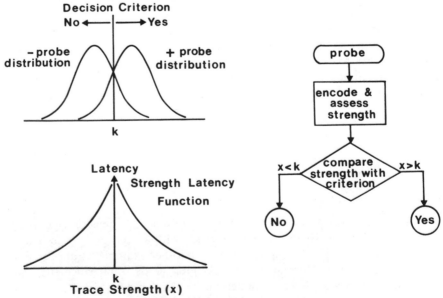

Fig. 7.18. Strength Theory. Strength distributions and the criterion, the strength latency function, and a flow chart of the stages leading to a decision about a probe.

particularly because of its predictions about the relative sizes of latencies for hits, misses, false alarms and correct rejections under different levels of response bias. Murdock and Dufty (1972) have also noted that although Strength Theory predicts that reaction time variability should be smaller for errors than for correct responses, this is not true in fact. Finally, as it stands, Strength Theory makes no predictions about changes in reaction time as a function of memory set size. To do so it requires one of two modifications. Either it must be incorporated as part of a multistage retrieval model, where another stage bears the burden of predicting set size changes (the strategy used by Atkinson and Juola, 1974, and Corballis and Miller, 1973), or it must be assumed that the strength distributions change in a way to make members of the memory set less discriminable from non-members as set size increases (the strategy used by Baddeley and Ecob, 1973).

1. *The item recognition task*

Baddeley and Ecob (1973) have proposed what amounts to a limited capacity direct access model, by assuming that strength values of memory set items approach those of non-members of the set as n increases. Specifically, the means of the positive and negative strength distributions are $+P/n$ and $-P/n$, where P is capacity and n is the number of items in the memory list. Incorporating this assumption into Strength Theory allows it to predict the commonly found linear and parallel reaction time functions of the item recognition task. This model can also explain why items which occur more than once in the memory set give faster responses when probed than those which occur once only (Baddeley and Ecob, 1973). According to the simple exhaustive serial scanning model, repeated items should yield the same reaction times as non-repeated items, as in both cases the whole memory list must be scanned. However, according to Strength Theory, multiple presentations of an item will increase its trace strength and thus lower its latency. (Some parallel models also predict faster responses to repeated than to non-repeated items, Ratcliff, 1978.)

Corballis and Miller (1973) have suggested an alternative Strength Theory model for the item recognition task. This involves two stages; a scan which primes the memory list items so that they have their trace strengths incremented for a short period of time, followed by direct access of the probe, whose strength is evaluated to give a YES–NO decision. The priming scan is thus responsible for the linear increase in reaction time with set size, while the direct access process accounts for recency effects over serial positions on the grounds that the most recently presented items will generally have the greatest strengths and hence the shortest latencies. Neither this account, nor that of Baddeley and Ecob (1973) explain why many reaction time functions from the item recognition task are not parallel and sometimes not linear. Corballis and Miller (1973) proposed that non-parallel functions may arise from multiple scans of a list prior to a decision being made about the probe. It is as if the priming scan sometimes fails to elicit an appropriate level of trace strength for the direct access stage to make a clear YES or NO decision and, when this happens, another scan is made. Resemblances to the conveyor belt are obvious and we again encounter the idea that speed is traded for accuracy during retrieval. Another way of incorporating speed-accuracy trade-off in the Strength Theory model which includes no scanning stage will be discussed presently.

2. The study-test paradigm

It is known that discriminability of the memory trace, as measured by d', declines exponentially with the lag between an item's presentation and test (Wickelgren, 1970; Wickelgren and Norman, 1966). Using this fact, along with Strength Theory's assumption that latency is exponentially related to strength, Murdock (1974) was able to fit the data in Fig. 7.9 to Strength Theory, and discovered that it was capable of predicting a linear relationship between latency and lag. However, having fitted the latency data, he then used the parameters so obtained to predict error rates, and discovered that while the observed hit rate declined from 0.99 to 0.80 over a lag of 40 items, Strength Theory predicted a drop of 0.93 to 0.16. If Strength Theory is fitted to the latency data, it will predict too rapid a decline in errors as lag increases, or if it is fitted to the error data it will predict too sharp an increase in reaction time. It cannot fit both error and latency data with a common set of parameter values.

In addition to this weakness, Strength Theory also has difficulties in accounting for the confidence judgement data in Fig. 7.11. Figure 7.19 illustrates how confidence is incorporated into Strength Theory by partitioning the strength continuum into regions where low strength values correspond to low confidence, and high strength values to high confidence. It follows from this that high confidence responses should produce the faster latencies, as Murdock and Dufty (1972) have shown. Also, Fig. 7.19 shows how latency will change in the confidence categories as the mean of the strength distribution declines. As the figure shows, the latency distribution is obtained by plotting latencies from the strength/latency function against corresponding probabilities for the strength distributions. A decrease in mean strength from μ_2 to μ_1 will shift the mean latency of sure responses from M_{S1} to M_{S2}, and the mean of unsure responses from M_{U1} to M_{U2}. The $M_{U2} - M_{U1}$ difference exceeds the $M_{S2} - M_{S1}$ difference. For the study-test paradigm, where an increase in test position reduces an item's strength, the theory predicts a pattern of reaction times similar to that in Fig. 7.11a, but not to the pattern of the obtained data in Fig. 7.11c.

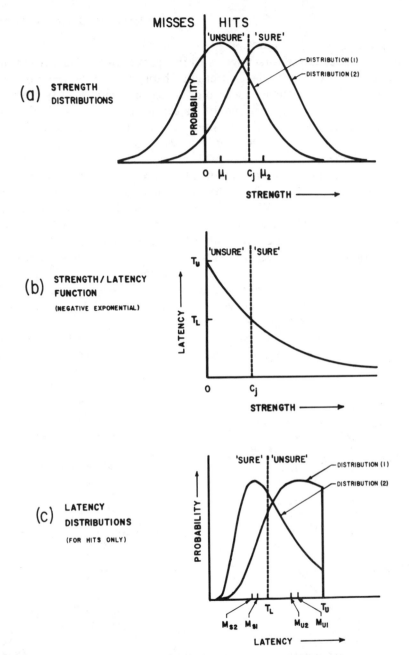

Fig. 7.19. Strength Theory's predictions about high and low confidence reaction times. (a) The strength continuum with criteria for Sure and Unsure categories, and distributions showing low average strength values (mean = μ_1) or high average strength values (mean = μ_2). (b) The strength/latency function. (c) Reaction time distributions for hits formed by plotting the latency from (b) against its probability from (a) for each point along the strength continuum.

3. *The prememorized list paradigm*

The major application of direct access to this paradigm has been Atkinson and Juola's (1974) model, where Strength Theory and serial scanning are combined. Items are assumed to be represented in memory in two ways: first in a form where their representations can be accessed directly (lexical memory) and, second, in order of presentation where serial scanning is necessary for their retrieval (the event/knowledge or E/K store). The E/K store has affinities with Tulving's (1972) episodic memory. When a list of items is presented for memory, each member's lexical entry has its strength (familiarity) incremented and, at the same time, a copy of the item is recorded in the E/K store. When a probe is presented, its lexical representation is first accessed directly and its familiarity value compared with two criteria, as shown in Fig. 7.20. If familiarity exceeds the upper criterion, k_Y, no further processing is done, and a rapid YES response is emitted. Similarly, if familiarity is less than k_N, a rapid NO response ensues. If the probe's familiarity lies between the criteria, a list scan is needed. For well learned lists, this scan is normally assumed to be error free and exhaustive with items scanned at a constant rate α, as shown in Fig. 7.20.

Mean reaction time will therefore be the result of a probabilistic mixture of short latencies from Stage 1 decisions, which will be independent of list

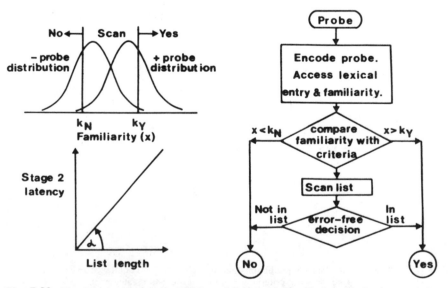

Fig. 7.20. The Atkinson and Juola (1974) model. Strength (familiarity) distributions and the criteria for Stage 1 familiarity testing; the latency/list length function for Stage 2 scanning; and a flow chart of the stages leading to a decision about a probe.

length, and of longer latencies arising from Stage 2, which will be linearly related to list length. In general, the model does a good job of explaining the data generated by Atkinson, Juola and their co-workers (e.g. Atkinson and Juola, 1972, 1974; Fischler and Juola, 1971; Juola et al., 1971). The effects of probe repetition illustrated in Fig. 7.15 are interpreted by the model as arising from increasing familiarity values for the lexical representations of repeated probes. This would enable more fast Stage 1 decisions to be made about repeated positive probes and, as the scanning stage would be used less frequently for these items, the slope of the positive probe reaction time function should decline. As repetition of negative probes should increase their familiarity, this would mean that they would frequently yield familiarity values above k_N, but below k_Y, thus increasing the use of the scanning process, and hence increasing the slope of the negative probe reaction time function. These are the changes depicted in Fig. 7.15.

The major problem for the Atkinson and Juola model concerns its predictions about error latencies. For a well learned list, errors can arise only from Stage 1 familiarity testing but not from the Stage 2 scan. Therefore, error latencies should be faster than correct latencies. Although some studies support this prediction (e.g. Juola et al., 1971, Experiment 1), errors are generally slower than correct responses (e.g. Homa and Fish, 1975; Pike et al., 1977). Pike et al. (1977) also considered the possibility that slow errors might occur in the Stage 2 list scan in experiments where the list is not learned thoroughly. For example, the list in the E/K store may have items deleted from it, thus giving rise to misses, or may have items added to it, thus causing false alarms. As false alarms occur when the list has been augmented by the addition of non-members, it is easy to see how their latencies would be longer than those for correct responses. But as misses occur when the list has been shortened, the implication is that their latencies will be shorter than those for correct responses. This pattern of error latencies was not found in the data of Pike and co-workers which showed that both misses and false alarms took more time than hits and correct rejections.

4. The continuous recognition memory paradigm

The only application of Strength Theory to this task has been by Okada (1971) who suggested that the curvilinear relationship between lag and reaction time, illustrated in Fig. 7.16, would be expected if memory items were accessed directly and if their strengths, which determine reaction time, declined exponentially with lag. This relationship in itself is not a strong test of Strength Theory, so Okada (1971) conducted a second experiment in which items were presented three times in the memory list. Thus the item should be judged as a new one on its initial presentation, and should be judged as old on the second and third presentations. The item series was arranged to give a variety of lags between the second and third presentations, the purpose of this being to test Strength Theory's prediction that the repetitions of the item would increment its strength so that it would be responded to faster on its third than on its second occurrence. Moreover, if the lag between presentations 2 and 3 was short, the net strength of the item should be higher and its reaction time shorter than if the lag was long. Responses were quicker to items presented for the third than for the second time, but the length of the lag between the second and third presentations had no affect on reaction time. Thus Strength Theory's predictions were not entirely borne out.

5. *Summary of strength theory*

Strength Theory is clearly inadequate as a model for memory retrieval, although as Baddeley and Ecob (1973) have shown, it can make appropriate predictions about increases in reaction time with list length by assuming that memory items become less discriminable as the list gets longer. There are similarities between Strength Theory and the diffusion model in this respect. Also, Strength Theory does have something to say about errors, confidence judgements and speed-accuracy trade-off. This is because it incorporates Signal Detection ideas about noisy memory traces and a response criterion which, Ratcliff and Murdock (1976) suggest, are largely responsible for Strength Theory's successes. Although attempts to remove some of the theory's deficiencies by accompanying it with other retrieval stages have not been completely satisfactory, it still merits further consideration. A modification to it, which involves multiple observations of items in memory, will now be discussed.

(B) THE RECRUITMENT PROCESS AND DIRECT ACCESS

By assuming that item discriminability declines as list length increases, and that subjects attempt to compensate for this by sampling more evidence from the memory trace prior to a response, Pike *et al.* (1977) have developed a direct access model of retrieval which accounts for many of the basic data in the item recognition task. Their idea of direct access differs from that of a store where each item is represented in its own memory location, and where retrieval involves testing the strength of the contents of that location. Instead they propose a wholistic store similar to that of Anderson (1973), Cavanagh (1976) and Murdock (1977), where the items in a list are encoded as sets of features summed together in a common location in memory. Thus there is no separate representation of each item in the memory trace, but the trace is an agglomeration of all the information in the list.

Retrieval involves encoding the probe as a set of features, and correlating it with the memory trace of the list, rather in the manner that engineers use Fourier analysis to detect the presence of a particular frequency in a complex sound. The strength of the correlation is the evidence on which a YES–NO decision is made, serving the same role as the resonance level of memory to the probe in Ratcliff's (1978) diffusion model. Because the memory trace is noisy, the output of the correlation process will vary randomly so that, like the diffusion process or like Strength Theory, there will be distributions of strengths for members and non-members of the memory set. This model supposes that these distributions are normal with a distance between their means of d' (like the asymptotic d' of the diffusion model) and a variance of S^2. A cut-off is set between the distribution means so that strength levels falling above it are counted as evidence in favour of a YES decision to a probe, while those below count in favour of NO. Increases in n, memory set size, change discriminability by increasing the variance of the two strength distributions according to the relationship $S^2 = n$. This is similar to the limited capacity assumption in Baddeley and Ecob's (1973) strength model.

Although the model so far resembles standard Strength Theory, its proposal about how reaction time enters the picture is not. Strength Theory assumes that the probe's strength level is sampled once, and that this then determines the speed of the response. In the model put forward by Pike and co-workers there are two counters, $+$ and $-$, and the strength distribution is sampled over a period of time with the $+$ counter being incremented whenever the strength level exceeds the cut-off, and the $-$ counter being incremented whenever the strength level falls below it. Sampling ceases with a YES response if the $+$ counter achieves a value of k before the $-$ counter does, or with a NO response if the $-$ counter wins the race. This is the recruitment process first suggested by LaBerge (1962), although the version proposed by Pike et al. (1977) is one of continuous rather than discrete sampling as described by Pike (1973). The critical count value, k, in the recruitment process, thus plays a similar role to the random walk boundaries in the diffusion model.

Pike et al. (1977) argue that subjects in the item recognition task adopt stricter values of k as n increases, to reduce errors likely to arise from the increase in S^2. It is this speed-accuracy trade-off which is responsible for the linear increase in reaction time with memory set size and for the fact that positive and negative reaction time functions are parallel to one another. However, the functions may become non-linear or non-parallel if k is not increased sufficiently as n rises, and functions of these types will occur along with error rates which increase as a function of n, which, as was described earlier, is what is frequently observed.

In their own experiments, Pike *et al.* (1977) demonstrated that errors did increase with n, resulting in a linear fall in the observed d', as set size increased. Also error reaction times were invariably slower than those of correct responses, which is to be expected of the recruitment process when it is not subjected to extreme bias (Pike, 1973). Biasing the process towards a YES response, which could be achieved by setting a smaller value of k for the $+$ counter than for the $-$ counter, would result in more rapid YES than NO responses, and more false alarms than misses. Thus the model is capable of accounting for the probe repetition effects reported by Atkinson and Juola (1974). Although the model has not been formally fitted to data from the various experimental paradigms, as Ratcliff (1978) has done for the diffusion process, Pike *et al.* (1977) have noted that it not only gives a good description of results from the item recognition and prememorized list tasks, but is compatible with the non-linear lag-latency function, and the slower error reaction times reported by Okada (1971) in the continuous recognition memory task.

The recruitment and diffusion processes are close relatives and there are yet other accumulator processes which might be substituted for them in a retrieval model (Vickers, 1970; Vickers *et al.*, 1971; Pike, 1966). Ratcliff (1978) pointed out that the diffusion process predicts an increase in positive skew of the reaction time distribution as the random walk boundaries are moved farther apart, while the recruitment model predicts a decline in skew as k is increased (Pike, 1973, Table 2). The former prediction appeared more compatible with Ratcliff's own data, but he noted that there is still too little data on which to reject one model and accept the other. Although it might be interesting, from a psychophysical point of view, to discriminate between the models, in the context of memory retrieval theories it might be better to emphasize their similarities, and to contrast them with other ideas of how reaction time enters into the retrieval process.

The Pike *et al.* (1977) memory model also differs from that of Ratcliff (1978) in that it proposes that memory is interrogated by direct access rather than a parallel search. How important this difference will turn out to be is hard to say, but one suspects that both models owe their explanatory powers more to their use of the Signal Detection idea of a noisy memory trace and to an evidence accumulation decision process than to anything peculiar either to parallel as opposed to direct access processing. No doubt this question will be explored in the future, and it would be interesting to know how well a direct access diffusion process would fit the data from the experimental paradigms so impressively modelled by the parallel processing version.

Concluding remarks

Present-day theories of memory retrieval began with the concept of a memory trace where items were clearly represented, and equated reaction time with the search which matched items in the trace with a probe item. Now, the evidence suggests that the trace is noisy, and reaction time reflects a gradual accumulation of evidence in favour or against the probe corresponding to part of the trace. The linear increases in reaction time with memory set size, which were originally seen as strong evidence for a serial search, have since been shown to be as compatible with parallel searches or direct access. Although this alone was an insufficient reason for abandoning a serial model, accumulating evidence of non-linear reaction time functions, particularly in association with moderate error rates, has proved difficult to fit into the framework of a serial model. Considerations of other experimental paradigms, such as the study-test, prememorized list and continuous recognition memory tasks, plus more detailed information about the shapes of reaction time distributions, have made a serial processing account of memory even more complicated.

However, looking at the same facts from a different point of view, such as parallel processing or direct access, has offered some hope of a return to the simplicity which seemed to prevail when Sternberg (1966, 1969a) presented his results and explanation of the item recognition task. The most important new insight, illustrated in the accounts by Pike *et al.* (1977) and Ratcliff (1978), is that retrieval involves sampling evidence from an ambiguous memory trace in an attempt to discover whether it contains some relevant information. The degree of noise in the trace apparently depends on factors known to memory researchers for a long time; interference due to the number of other items in the list, or to the lag between an item's presentation and testing. Thus theories of retrieval based on reaction time measures begin to make contact again with an older memory literature where the emphasis was on interference, forgetting and errors.

The process by which the trace continues to be examined to discover its contents, seems to resemble closely that involved in a simple discrimination task with noisy stimuli. Evidence for or against alternative decisions is accumulated by repeated sampling from the trace until a satisfactory criterion for responding has been reached. Gains in accuracy are brought at the expense of more time in sampling, although it is not clear how much freedom we have in manipulating this speed-accuracy trade-off. In the item recognition, study-test and prememorized list tasks, adjustments may be made to the time spent sampling, but they are frequently inadequate in holding error rates constant, while in the continuous recognition memory task, errors rise unchecked because the task offers no feedback to the subject for controlling them. Retrieval theories which emphasize concepts such as trace discriminability and speed-accuracy trade-off have their affinities with psychophysical models for discrimination, particularly those which make use of Signal Detection ideas coupled with multiple observations of the sensory evidence (Pike, 1973). In fact these concepts seem to contribute more to a model's ability to explain facts about retrieval than does specifying that memory is interrogated by direct access or by a parallel search of its contents.

ACKNOWLEDGEMENTS

We are grateful to Siu Chow, Roger Ratcliff and Alan Welford for their comments on earlier versions of this chapter. This chapter underwent drastic revision while the first author was on study leave at Bennet B. Murdock's laboratory in the Psychology Department, University of Toronto, and we acknowledge that the approach of Murdock and his group to the study of memory has strongly influenced the way in which we wrote this chapter.

References

Anders, T. R., Fozard, J. L. and Lillyquist, T. D. (1972). Effects of age upon retrieval from short-term memory. *Developmental Psychology* **6**, 214–217.
Anderson, J. A. (1973). A theory for the recognition of items from short memorized lists. *Psychological Review* **80**, 417–438.
Anderson, J. R. and Bower, G. H. (1974). "Human Associative Memory". Hemisphere, Washington, D.C.
Atkinson, R. C. and Juola, J. F. (1972). Search and decision processes in recognition memory. Paper presented to the conference on Developments in Mathematical Psychology. University of Michigan.
Atkinson, R. C. and Juola, J. F. (1974). Search and decision processes in recognition memory. *In* "Contemporary Developments in Mathematical Psychology" (D. H. Krantz, R. C. Atkinson, R. D. Luce and P. Suppes, eds.), Vol. 1. W. H. Freeman, San Francisco.
Aubé, M. and Murdock, B. B., Jr. (1974). Sensory stores and high-speed scanning. *Memory and Cognition* **2**, 27–33.
Baddeley, A. D. and Ecob, J. R. (1973). Reaction time and short-term memory: Implications of repetition effects for the high-speed exhaustive scan hypothesis. *Quarterly Journal of Experimental Psychology* **25**, 229–240.
Banks, W. P. and Atkinson, R. C. (1974). Accuracy and speed strategies in scanning active memory. *Memory and Cognition* **2**, 629–636.
Biederman, I. and Stacy, E. W., Jr. (1974). Stimulus probability and stimulus set size in memory scanning. *Journal of Experimental Psychology* **102**, 1100–1107.
Briggs, G. E. and Swanson, J. M. (1970). Encoding, decoding, and central functions in human information processing. *Journal of Experimental Psychology* **86**, 296–308.

Burrows, D. and Okada, R. (1971). Serial position effects in high-speed memory search. *Perception and Psychophysics* **10**, 305–308.

Burrows, D. and Okada, R. (1974). Scanning temporally structured lists: Evidence for dual retrieval processes. *Memory and Cognition* **2**, 441–446.

Burrows, D. and Okada, R. (1975). Memory retrieval from long and short lists. *Science* **188**, 1031–1033.

Cattell, J. McK. (1886). The time taken up by cerebral operations. *Mind* **11**, 220–242. Reprinted *In* "Psychological Research", J. McK. Cattell: Man. of Science, Vol. 1. The Science Press, Lancaster, Pennsylvania, 1947.

Cattell, J. McK. (1897). Experiments on the association of ideas. *Mind* **12**, 68–74. Reprinted *In* "Psychological Research", J. McK. Cattell: Man. of Science, Vol. 1. The Science Press, Lancaster, Pennsylvania, 1947.

Cavanagh, P. (1976). Holographic and trace strength models of rehearsal effects in the item recognition task. *Memory and Cognition* **4**, 186–199.

Corballis, M. C. and Miller, A. (1973). Scanning and decision processes in recognition memory. *Journal of Experimental Psychology* **98**, 379–386.

Corballis, M. C., Kirby, J. and Miller, A. (1972). Access to elements of a memorized list. *Journal of Experimental Psychology* **94**, 185–190.

Feller, W. (1964). "An Introduction to Probability Theory and its Applications", Vol. 1. Wiley, New York.

Fischler, I. and Juola, J. F. (1971). Effects of repeated tests on recognition time for information in long-term memory. *Journal of Experimental Psychology* **91**, 54–58.

Gould, J. D. (1973). Eye movements during visual search and memory search. *Journal of Experimental Psychology* **98**, 184–195.

Gumbel, E. J. (1958). "Statistics of Extremes". Columbia University Press, New York.

Harris, G. J. and Fleer, R. E. (1974). High speed memory scanning in mental retardates: Evidence for a central processing deficit. *Journal of Experimental Child Psychology* **17**, 452–459.

Homa, D. and Fish, R. (1975). Recognition reaction time in long-term memory as a function of repetition, lag, and identification of positive and negative search sets. *Journal of Experimental Psychology. Human Learning and Memory* **104**, 71–80.

Hoving, K. L., Morin, R. E. and Konik, D. S. (1970). Recognition reaction time and size of the memory set: A developmental study. *Psychonomic Science* **21**, 247–248.

Jung, C. G. (1919). "Studies in Word-association". Moffatt, New York.

Juola, J. F., Fischler, I., Wood, C. T. and Atkinson, R. C. (1971). Recognition time for information stored in long-term memory. *Perception and Psychophysics* **10**, 8–14.

Kennedy, R. A. and Hamilton, D. (1969). Time to locate probe items in short lists of digits. *American Journal of Psychology* **82**, 272–275.

Klatzky, R. L. and Atkinson, R. C. (1970). Memory scans based on alternative test stimulus representations. *Perception and Psychophysics* **8**, 113–117.

Klatzky, R. L., Juola, J. F. and Atkinson, R. C. (1971). Test stimulus representation and experimental context effects in memory scanning. *Journal of Experimental Psychology* **87**, 281–288.

Kristofferson, M. W. (1972a). Effects of practice on character-classification performance. *Canadian Journal of Psychology* **26**, 540–560.

Kristofferson, M. W. (1972b). When item recognition and visual search functions are similar. *Perception and Psychophysics* **12**, 379–384.

LaBerge, D. (1962). A recruitment theory of simple behaviour. *Psychometrika* **27**, 375–396.

Lehtiö, P. and Kauri, T. (1973). An experiment in memory scanning. *In* "Attention and Performance IV" (S. Kornblum, ed.). Academic Press, New York.

Link, S. W. and Heath, R. A. (1975). A sequential theory of psychological discrimination. *Psychometrika* **40**, 77–105.

Lively, B. L. (1972). Speed/accuracy trade off and practice as determinants of stage durations in a memory search task. *Journal of Experimental Psychology* **96**, 97–103.

Lively, B. L. and Sanford, B. J. (1972). The use of category information in a memory search task. *Journal of Experimental Psychology* **93**, 379–385.

Mowbray, G. H. and Rhoades, M. V. (1959). On the reduction of choice-reaction times with practice. *Quarterly Journal of Experimental Psychology* **11**, 16–23.

Murdock, B. B., Jr. (1974). "Human Memory: Theory and Data". Erlbaum, Potomac, Maryland.

Murdock, B. B., Jr. (1977). Convolution and correlation in perception and memory. *Paper presented to the Conference on Memory, Uppsala University, June 20–24.*

Murdock, B. B., Jr. and Anderson, R. E. (1975). Encoding, storage and retrieval of item information. *In* "Theories in Cognitive Psychology: The Loyola Symposium" (R. L. Solso, ed.). Erlbaum, Hillsdale, New Jersey.

Murdock, B. B., Jr. and Dufty, P. O. (1972). Strength theory and recognition memory. *Journal of Experimental Psychology* **94**, 284–290.

Murdock, B., Hockley, W. and Muter, P. (1977). Two tests of the conveyor-belt model for item recognition. *Canadian Journal of Psychology* **31**, 71–89.

Muter, P. and Murdock, B. B., Jr. (1977). A search for scanning residue in recognition memory. *Bulletin of the Psychonomic Society* **10**, 66–68.

Norman, D. A. and Wickelgren, W. A. (1969). Strength theory of decision rules and latency in short-term memory. *Journal of Mathematical Psychology* **1**, 336–350.

Okada, R. (1971). Decision latencies in short-term recognition memory. *Journal of Experimental Psychology* **90**, 27–32.

Pike R. (1966). Stochastic models for choice behaviour: Response probabilities and latencies of finite Markov chains. *British Journal of Mathematical and Statistical Psychology* **19**, 15–32.

Pike, R. (1973). Response latency models for signal detection. *Psychological Review* **80**, 53–68.

Pike, R., Dalgleish, L. and Wright, J. (1977). A multiple-observations model for response latency and the latencies of correct and incorrect responses in recognition memory. *Memory and Cognition* **5**, 580–589.

Pike, R. and Ryder, P. (1973). Response latencies in the yes/no task: An assessment of two basic models. *Perception and Psychophysics* **13**, 224–232.

Ratcliff, R. (1978). A theory of memory retrieval. *Psychological Review* **85**, 59–108.

Ratcliff, R. (1979). Group reaction time distributions and an analysis of distribution statistics. *Psychological Bulletin*, (in press).

Ratcliff, R. and Murdock, B. B., Jr. (1976). Retrieval processes in recognition memory. *Psychological Review* **83**, 190–214.

Ross, J. (1970). Extended practice with a single-character classification task. *Perception and Psychophysics* **8**, 276–278.

Sternberg, S. (1966). High-speed scanning in human memory. *Science* **153**, 652–654.

Sternberg, S. (1969a). Memory-scanning: Mental processes revealed by reaction-time experiments. *American Scientist* **57**, 421–457.

Sternberg, S. (1969b). The discovery of processing stages: Extensions of Donders' method. *In* "Attention and Performance II" (W. G. Koster, ed.). North-Holland, Amsterdam.

Sternberg, S. (1975). Memory scanning: New findings and current controversies. *Quarterly Journal of Experimental Psychology* **27**, 1–32.

Stone, M. (1960). Models for choice reaction time. *Psychometrika* **25**, 251–260.

Swanson, J. M. and Briggs, G. E. (1969). Information processing as a function of speed versus accuracy. *Journal of Experimental Psychology* **81**, 223–229.

Taylor, D. A. (1976). Stage analysis of reaction time. *Psychological Bulletin* **83**, 161–191.

Theios, J., Smith, P. G., Haviland, S. E., Traupmann, J. and Moy, M. C. (1973). Memory scanning as a serial self-terminating process. *Journal of Experimental Psychology* **97**, 323–336.

Townsend, J. T. (1974). Issues and models concerning the processing of a finite number of inputs. *In* "Human Information Processing: Tutorials in Performance and Cognition" (B. H. Kantowitz, ed.). Erlbaum, Potomac, Maryland.

Tulving, E. (1972). Episodic and semantic memory. *In* "Organization of Memory" (E. Tulving and W. Donaldson, eds.). Academic Press, New York.

Vickers, D. (1970). Evidence for an accumulator model of psychophysical discrimination. *Ergonomics* **13**, 37–58.

Vickers, D., Caudrey, D. and Willson, R. (1971). Discriminating between the frequency of occurrence of two alternative events. *Acta Psychologica* **35**, 151–172.

Welford, A. T. (1964). The study of ageing. *British Medical Bulletin* **20**, No. 1, 65–69.

Wickelgren, W. A. (1970). Multitrace strength theory. *In* "Models of Human Memory" (D. A. Norman, ed.). Academic Press, New York.

Wickelgren, W. A. and Norman, D. A. (1966). Strength models and serial positions in short-term recognition memory. *Journal of Mathematical Psychology* **3**, 316–347.

Wingfield, A. and Branca, A. A. (1970). Strategy in high-speed memory scanning. *Journal of Experimental Psychology* **83**, 63–67.

Chapter 8

Reaction Time in Personality Theory

JOHN M. T. BREBNER

We saw in Chapter 1 that reaction time studies originated with Bessel's interest in comparing the transit reaction time of different astronomers. From that early beginning the use of reaction time measures in the study of individual differences has grown, flourished and contributed to our understanding in broad areas including ageing, intelligence and mental retardation, and abnormal conditions such as schizophrenia. Studies in these areas are surveyed in other chapters. However, throughout the history of personality theorizing, it has been uncommon until recently to find measures of reaction time cited in support of any *theory* of personality. This is because most theorists have been concerned with behaviour in interpersonal situations rather than individual differences in responsiveness to physical stimuli. The handful of exceptions who do study the performance capabilities of the individual as well as interpersonal behaviour have, however, been enormously influential and have generated a large number of testable hypotheses and a vast research literature. The theorists in question who share as part of their work an interest in the individual's responsiveness to changes in the physical environment are Cattell in America, Eysenck, Gray and Claridge in England, and Teplov and Nebylitsyn in Russia. The differences between these theorists are much more evident than any similarities which exist, yet it is arguable that there is one portion of their work in which they are on common ground—that is the study of extraversion. This short chapter outlines a simple model of extraversion which is an amalgamation of the relevant parts of the several theories and describes the results of some reaction time studies which are consistent with that model.

309

1. Previous attempts to account for extraversion

(A) EYSENCK'S REACTIVE INHIBITION EXPLANATION

Reactive inhibition is a concept which was invoked by Hull (1943) to explain the extinction and spontaneous recovery of conditioned responses. In the Hullian model, reactive inhibition is a negative drive—a drive not to respond—which builds up as a function of the amount of work done, but dissipates spontaneously as a function of time. Hence, once a conditioned response has been established and the unconditioned stimulus is withdrawn, reactive inhibition will build up incrementally with each conditioned response to the application of the conditioned stimulus. If the time between responses is too short for reactive inhibition to dissipate entirely, it will accumulate until it is stronger then the excitatory potential of the conditioned response which will, in consequence, be extinguished. After the spontaneous dissipation of reactive inhibition over time, the conditioned response recovers spontaneously.

Eysenck (1955, 1957) adopted reactive inhibition as the process underlying behavioural differences between introverts and extraverts, arguing that the latter generated reactive inhibition more quickly and dissipated it more slowly than the former. The results of various early studies lend support to this view (e.g. Franks, 1956) although some others produced equivocal results (e.g. Brebner, 1957). Nevertheless, over the years, evidence has accumulated supporting the idea that, at least in some circumstances, extraverts appear to generate response-mediated inhibition faster than introverts (see Eysenck, 1967).

(B) THE TEPLOV—NEBYLITSYN STRENGTH-SENSITIVITY EXPLANATION

Teplov and his successor Nebylitsyn have followed up that part of Pavlov's theory which is concerned with the strength of the excitatory process. Pavlov (1935) saw individual differences deriving from three properties of the nervous system which he described as *strength*, *balance* and *mobility*. The strength of a nervous system is gauged by the weakness and duration of the central excitatory process produced when any given stimulus is applied. A weak nervous system produces a much greater central excitatory state for any given stimulus, and continues to do so over more repeated applications of the stimulus. The balance of the nervous system refers to the relative strength of excitatory and inhibitory processes, and mobility to the system's capacity to change the strength of these processes and to switch between them.

A number of studies of individual differences carried out within the Pavlovian model have produced results bearing some similarity to the differences observed between introverts and extraverts. For example, the finding that people with strong nervous systems have higher sensory thresholds (Nebylitsyn, Rozhdestventskaia and Teplov, 1960) can be compared with similar findings for extraverts (see Mangan, 1972). These parallel results have been interpreted by some to link the concept of strength of the nervous system to extraversion (Eysenck, 1966; Mangan, 1972), although it is conceded that the relationship is liable to be complex.

The evidence from reaction time studies concerning differences between strong and weak nervous systems is somewhat inconsistent and probably depends on the precise experimental methods used in the reaction time tasks, as well as on the techniques used to measure strength of the nervous system (Mangan and Farmer, 1967). Nebylitsyn (1960) showed that the reaction time of strong nervous system individuals was relatively longer at weak intensities of both auditory and visual stimuli, than that of weak nervous system people, but that as intensity was increased this difference disappeared. Zhorov and Yermolayeva-Tomina (1972), however, found faster reaction times for extraverts and no overlap between them and introverts although the reduction in reaction time as stimulus intensity was increased was greater for the introverts. It is tempting to speculate upon the times observed in these experiments. Figure 8.1 is adapted from the auditory reaction time data of Nebylitsyn and Zhorov and Yermolayeva-Tomina and shows good agreement for the extravert-strong nervous system subjects, but considerably faster *RT*s from Nebylitsyn's weak nervous system subjects than the introverts of Zhorov and Yermolayeva-Tomina's study. This could be due to different response strategies in the two studies, or to unexplained methodological differences—for instance, signal duration is not given by Zhorov and Yermolayeva-Tomina, and introverts might check the presence of a signal before responding if signal duration allowed. It is also possible that extraverts correspond to the strong group better than introverts to the weak, at least on what is measured by simple reaction time.

(C) AROUSAL EXPLANATIONS

Slightly different explanations of differences between introverts and extraverts in terms of arousal level have been advanced by Welford (1965), Eysenck (1967) and Claridge (1967). All suggest that extraverts are in a state of chronic underarousal and tend to seek stimulation in order to reach and maintain a higher level of arousal. Extraverts have been described as "stimulus hungry" on the basis of this theory and, again, a body of evidence has been adduced which supports this view (Eysenck, 1967). Recently also Eysenck and Zuckerman (1978) have shown that "sensation seeking" scale scores are positively related to extraversion but not to neuroticism.

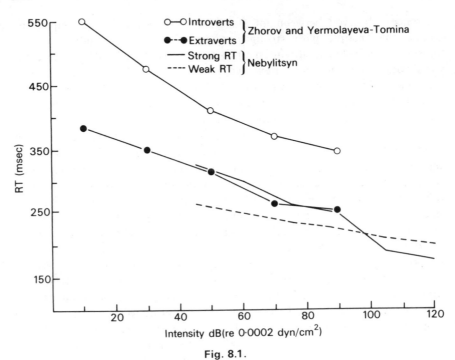

Fig. 8.1.

Moreover, the functional losses which are evident with overarousal, and which on this theory are expected to affect introverts at lower levels of stimulation, and the weak nervous system's proneness to go into so-called "transmarginal" inhibition have been related together. In the Pavlovian system transmarginal inhibition is related to the top level of stimulus intensity at which the nervous system produces the strongest response. Beyond that top capability the strength of a response decreases as the excitatory state gives way to an inhibitory one the function of which is to protect the system from overstimulation. The weaker the nervous system the weaker the intensity of stimulation producing transmarginal inhibition.

The relationship between strength of nervous system and arousal has been investigated by Gray (1964) who translated the neo-Pavlovian strength-sensitivity model of individual differences into an explanation in terms of the arousability of the individual. Gray (1964) avoided equating extraversion with strength of the nervous system. In a subsequent article, however, in which he reviews a number of relevant Russian and Western studies (Gray, 1967), he concluded that the notion of extraversion-introversion and strength of the nervous system as identical merited serious consideration.

Thus, arousal has been used to explain extraversion by Welford (1965), Eysenck (1967) and Claridge (1967), to explain strength of the nervous system by Gray (1964), and extraversion and strength-sensitivity have been compared directly by Gray (1976) and Eysenck (1966).

(D) CATTELL'S "CORTERTIA" (CORTICAL ALERTNESS) FACTOR

Cattell, like Eysenck and Nebylitsyn, uses factor analysis to identify the main features of personality, and includes measures of reaction time among his objective data. The factor with which these measures are most frequently associated is Cortertia or cortical alertness (see Cattell and Warburton, 1967, p. 463). Cattell describes this factor as arousability, not arousal level, and states that it maintains a characteristic level in an individual's waking life (Cattell, 1972). In the same article he suggests that Cortertia and strength of the nervous system may be inversely related. Cortertia is not identified as introversion-extraversion which emerges as a different factor in Cattell's work but nevertheless, like the other theorists mentioned, Cattell sees the possibility that they are studying the same thing in their several ways, and his own suggestion is very close to Gray's re-interpretation of the neo-Pavlovian model.

2. A simplified model

Starting with the view that the data bases underpinning each of the several interpretations above were sufficiently good that it was unlikely that any one theory could be judged to be correct at the expense of the others, a simplified way of amalgamating these major positions was sought. To this end, it was proposed (Brebner and Cooper, 1974) that the central mechanisms are capable of being to varying extents in one of two possible states, excitation or inhibition, and that either state could be induced by the demands for stimulus analysis (S-excitation or S-inhibition), or for response organization (R-excitation or R-inhibition). It was emphasized that the overall state is affected by all stimulation and response demands, not only those given some arbitrary significance. It was also suggested that, while perceiving any stimulus is itself a response, and any overt response creates a set of stimuli which are fed back from it, the feedback from responses should be regarded as stimuli. Excitation may be considered as the tendency to continue that activity—whether stimulus analysis or response organization—and inhibition as the tendency to discontinue it.

Extraverts, it was argued, produce relatively greater R-excitatory potential for any given S-state, and are "geared to respond". Introverts, on the other hand, produce relatively stronger S-excitation and are "geared to inspect".

This simple model incorporates the reactive inhibition explanation in the feedback link and feedback-mediated S-inhibition would build up faster for extravert subjects. Such a build-up of inhibition would be opposed by R-excitation generated by the organization of responses, but with rapidly repeated responses S-inhibition would come to predominate. Since introverts generate greater S-excitation for a given level of stimulation, strength-sensitivity explanations also fit the model. To include the concept of transmarginal inhibition it is only necessary to accept that there is an upper limit to S-excitation which, because of their greater sensitivity to stimulation, will be reached with lower stimulus intensities by introverts than extraverts.

It is probably also useful to conceive of response organization as applying only to voluntary responses. Involuntary responses, such as salivation, may require an organizational process of their own, but since these effects are largely prescribed by the stimulus applied, they should probably be classed under stimulus analysis effects. Reaction time experiments are one way of bridging the gap between involuntary and voluntary responses by controlling expectancy, muscle tension, choice, the stimulus-response relationship and so on. Having greater S-excitation, introverts are expected to produce stronger involuntary responses.

Arousability explanations are encompassed by the model through the assumption that while stimulus effects are more excitatory for introverts, response organization produces greater excitation than stimulus analysis in extraverts. Response organization will, therefore, be more effective in maintaining a high arousal level in extraverts. If response possibilities are low extraverts, in comparison with introverts, will require more intense and more rapidly varying stimulation to generate a given level of S-excitation.

This way of amalgamating the main points of the major theories gives rise to predictions of differences in the performance of introverts and extraverts as well as predictions of no difference. In some tasks, for example, a given performance level may be maintained through S-excitation in introverts but R-excitation in extraverts. This does not mean that the model can explain *any* effect observed, only that similar effects can arise in different ways, and that accurate prediction is a function of the degree to which all stimulus analysis and response organization requirements are controlled.

(A) EXTRAVERSION AND S-INHIBITION

Some predictions from the simplified model have been tested using reaction time methods. The prediction that under extremely low response demands and with low requirements for stimulus analysis, R-excitation would be insufficient to maintain arousal and S-inhibition would become relatively higher in extraverts, was tested in a simple reaction time task (Brebner and Cooper, 1974). It was hypothesized that, under these conditions, the performance of extraverts but not introverts would deteriorate. A visual stimulus to respond—the onset of small neon lamp—occurred regularly every 18 secs. The student subjects sat in a reclining position in a dental chair holding the response key. The same experimental method was used twice. In both cases the first 9–10 mins at the task was treated as a "settling-in" period and the results during this period disregarded. In the first experiment 100 reaction times were provided by each subject, in the second, using different subjects, 150 were recorded.

The specific predictions were that extraverts would miss more signals than introverts and produce relatively slower reaction times as time on the task increased. The mean reaction times in the first and second halves of both experiments are shown in Fig. 8.2. Although the correlation between numbers of signals missed and extraversion score was significant in both experiments: $+0.53$ ($p = 0.05$) in experiment 1, and $+0.69$ ($p < 0.01$) in experiment 2, it can be seen from Fig. 8.2 that the predicted slowing of mean

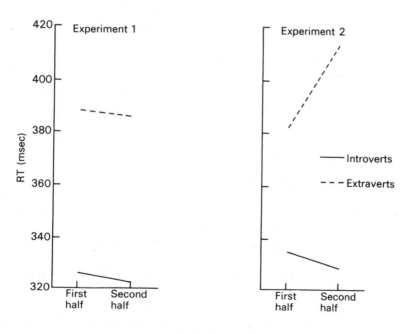

Fig. 8.2.

reaction times for the extravert group occurred only in experiment 2. The fact that this only occurred in the longer of the two experiments was interpreted to mean that the effect was not due to any difference in characteristic arousal level, which would have been evident at the beginning of the task, but to a more gradual build-up of S-inhibition in the extraverts but not the introverts.

(B) EXTRAVERSION AND R-EXCITATION

A further experiment (Brebner and Flavel, 1978) employed a different form of simple reaction time task to investigate the complementary hypothesis from the model that R-excitation is stronger for extraverts than it is for introverts.

In this experiment there were three conditions with different proportions of catch-trials: in Condition A, 10 per cent; in Condition B, 40 per cent; and in Condition C, 70 per cent. The signal was the digit "1" shown on a Nixie tube, and it was responded to by pressing a Morse key. In the catch trials, no signal was given. The interval between trials—either signal or catch-trials—was 2.3 secs. A pre-test without catch-trials was performed by all subjects. Under these conditions it was predicted that:

(i) Extraverts generating relatively more R-excitation should show a stronger tendency to respond in the absence of the signal and thus make more commissive errors.

(ii) Since R-excitation is a function of response rate which is inversely related to the proportion of catch-trials, both speed and accuracy would be affected more for extraverts as the catch-trial rate increased.

(iii) Rather less confidently it was suggested that "if in the present experimental situation responding is sufficiently frequent to build up S-inhibition through feedback stimulation" an effect akin to "involuntary rest pauses" might be observed among the extravert subjects.

The first two hypotheses were confirmed as Table 8.1 shows.

There was no statistically significant mean difference of reaction time between the two groups on the pre-test which was performed without any catch-trials. In the experimental conditions, however, extraverts were faster than introverts when the response rate was highest but slightly slower on average at the lowest response rate.

Since there were only three cases of not responding to a signal in the whole experiment, the "involuntary rest pauses" suggested in prediction 3 could not be assessed from failures to respond. However, the mean length of runs of reaction times in which latency decreased progressively was scrutinized. The expected effect would be for extraverts' reaction times to be

Table 8.1.

(1) Number of commissive errors			
Condition	A	B	C
Extraverts	42	44	11
Introverts	0	0	0
(2) Mean RT			
Condition	A	B	C
Extraverts	289	328	344
Introverts	313	321	337

No statistical test was considered necessary to show the difference in errors between the two groups. For the extraverts the difference in errors across the three conditions is significant, $\chi^2 = 21.1$, d.f. $= 2$, $p < 0.01$.

The interaction between personality type x conditions is significant, $F = 8.5$, $p < 0.01$.

progressively shorter with faster response rates, due to the generation of R-excitation, but less frequent longer reaction times should occur when feedback mediated S-inhibition was strong enough to oppose R-excitation. Only in Condition B did the mean length of such runs of accelerating reaction times tend to be longer for the extraverts, and this effect failed to reach significance.

Overall, however, these experimental results support the view that R-excitation is greater in extraverts in accordance with the simplified model.

(C) EXTRAVERSION AND THE TENDENCY TO RESPOND RATHER THAN INSPECT

A third experiment tested the prediction drawn from the model that if extraverts generate R-excitation and introverts S-excitation, then in a situation where it is possible either to inspect or respond, extraverts should tend to respond and introverts to inspect (Brebner and Cooper, 1978).

To separate the tendencies to inspect or respond it is necessary that response rates be independent of stimulus changes. The method of achieving this employed a slide projector controlled by a PDP 8L computer which could be operated by a response button held in the subject's hand. To avoid any specific interests of subjects affecting results, and to try to cover the range from "boring" to "interesting", five sets of colour slides were used: (1) blank slides; (2) random dot patterns; (3) Adelaide streets (with little human interest); (4) buildings (taken from an architectural series and also with little human interest); (5) foreign tourist attractions. The subjects were instructed that they could look at the slide showing, or press the button to move to the next one, but that the experiment was controlled by the computer which would be randomly "on" or "off" when they pressed the button. It was explained that if the button was pressed during an "off" period the slide would not change, and that the slide could not change unless the button was pressed.

The first slide was presented the first time the response button was pressed. Thereafter, subjects operated under a variable ratio "reinforcement" schedule such that to change a slide could require 2, 8 or 16 responses or, regardless of the number of responses made, the slide would only be changed by the first response made 50 seconds or more after the presentation of the current slide. The design was balanced so that equal numbers of the five types of slide were used with each schedule.

The predictions made were:

(i) extraverts would have shorter inspection times before attempting to change the slide.
(ii) extraverts would respond more frequently even though responding did not always produce a new slide.
(iii) that extraverts, generating excitation from responding, should tend to respond at an accelerating rate.

The first prediction was borne out with extraverts showing much shorter inspection times (see Fig. 8.3).

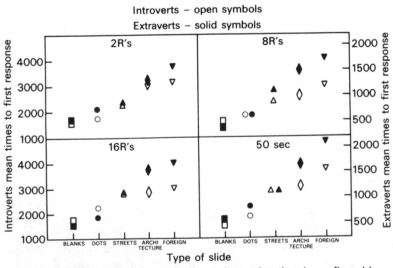

That extraverts show much shorter inspection time is confirmed by ANOVA (F = 9·5, p <0·01)

Fig. 8.3. Note: different scales for internals and externals.

The second prediction that extraverts would respond more frequently, was also confirmed as Table 8.2 shows.

Finally, the third prediction, that extraverts would show a tendency to accelerate in their responses, was tested by comparing the proportion of runs in which reaction times became progressively faster. Again in line with the prediction, extraverts' average proportion of accelerations was 26.7 per cent compared with introverts' 13.5 per cent, and the difference between the groups was statistically significant.

Given that the simplified model is a deliberate attempt to amalgamate the main points of the major theories, it is perhaps not surprising that even the new predictions it gives rise to have so far been confirmed experimentally. But to some extent the predictive accuracy derives from the requirement, inherent in the model, to consider all stimulus analysis and response organization demands acting upon the individual, and the sensitivity of the particular effect under study to them.

Whether this simplified model of introversion-extraversion will continue to be useful in the future or not remains to be seen. In the present context, however, these experiments may serve to show the role reaction time experiments can play, along with other objective measures, in trying to resolve matters of very general interest in the field of personality.

Table 8.2.

	Mean number of responses	Mean response rate
Introverts	394	13.3 secs
Extraverts	874	4.4 secs

On a one-tailed t-test extraverts are shown to respond significantly more rapidly ($t = 2.49$, d.f. 16, $p < 0.01$).

References

Brebner, J. (1957). An experimental investigation of the relationship between conditioning and introversion-extraversion in normal subjects. Unpublished M.A.(Hons.) thesis, University of Aberdeen.

Brebner, J. and Cooper, C. (1974). The effect of a low rate of regular signals upon the reaction times of introverts and extraverts. *Journal of Research in Personality* **8**, 263–276.

Brebner, J. and Cooper, C. (1978). Stimulus- or response-induced excitation. A comparison of the behavior of introverts and extraverts. *Journal of Research in Personality* **12**, 306–311.

Brebner, J. and Flavel, R. (1978). The effects of catch-trials on speed and accuracy among introverts and extraverts in a simple *RT* task. *British Journal of Psychology* **69**, 9–15.

Cattell, R. B. (1972). The interpretation of Pavlov's Typology, and the arousal concept, in replicated trait and state factors. *In* "Biological Bases of Individual Behavior" (V. D. Nebylitsyn and J. A. Gray, eds.). Academic Press, London, New York.

Cattell, R. B. and Warburton, F. W. (1967). "Objective Personality and Motivation Tests", pp. 463–464. University of Illinios Press, Urbana.

Claridge, G. S. (1967). "Personality and Arousal". Pergamon Press, Oxford.

Eysenck, H. J. (1955). A dynamic theory of anxiety and hysteria. *Journal of Mental Science* **101**, 28–51.

Eysenck, H. J. (1957). "The Dynamics of Anxiety and Hysteria: an Experimental Application of Modern Learning Theory to Psychiatry". Routledge and Kegan Paul, London.

Eysenck, H. J. (1966). Conditioning, introversion-extraversion and the strength of the nervous system. Proceedings of the 18th International Congress of Psychology, Ninth Symposium, pp. 33–45.

Eysenck, H. J. (1967). "The Biological Basis of Behavior". Chas. C. Thomas, New York.

Eysenck, S. and Zuckerman, M. (1978). The relationship between sensation-seeking and Eysenck's dimensions of personality. *British Journal of Psychology* **69**, 483–487.

Franks, C. M. (1956). Conditioning and personality: a study of normal and neurotic subjects. *Journal of Abnormal and Social Psychology* **52**, 143–150.

Gray, J. A. (1964). Strength of the nervous system and levels of arousal: a reinterpretation. *In* "Pavlov's Typology" (J. A. Gray, ed.). Pergamon Press, Oxford.

Gray, J. A. (1967). Strength of the nervous system, introversion-extraversion, conditionability and arousal. *Behavior Research and Therapy* **5**, 151–169.

Hull, C. L. (1943). "Principles of Behavior". Appleton-Century-Crofts, New York.

Mangan, G. L. (1972). The relationship of strength-sensitivity of the visual system to extraversion. *In* "Biological Bases of Individual Behavior" (V. D. Nebylitsyn and J. A. Gray, eds.). Academic Press, London, New York.

Mangan, G. L. and Farmer, R. G. (1967). Studies of the relationship between Pavlovian properties of higher nervous activity and Western personality dimensions. The relationship of nervous strength and sensitivity to extraversion. *Journal of Research in Personality* **2**, 101–106.

Nebylitsyn, V. D. (1960). Reaction time and the strength of the nervous system. *Dokl. Acad. pedag., Nauk, RSFSR* **4**, 93–100.

Nebylitsyn, V. D., Rozhdestventskaia, V. I. and Teplov, B. M. (1960). Concerning the interrelation between absolute sensitivity and strength of the nervous system. *Quarterly Journal of Experimental Psychology* **12**, 17–25.

Pavlov, I. P. (1935). General types of higher nervous activity in animals and man. Reprinted in "Selected Works" Moscow: Foreign Languages Publications Office, 1955.

Welford, A. T. (1965). Stress and achievement. *Australian Journal of Psychology* **17**, No. 1, 1–11.

Zhorov, P. A. and Yermolayeva-Tomina, L. B. (1972). Concerning the relation between extraversion and the strength of the nervous system. *In* "Biological Bases of Individual Behavior" (V. D. Nebylitsyn and J. A. Gray, eds.). Academic Press, London, New York.

Chapter 9

Relationships Between Reaction Time and Fatigue, Stress Age and Sex

A. T. WELFORD

Reaction time has been shown to covary with several factors in normal everyday life, and has sometimes been used as an index of these. Consideration will be given here to certain important areas in which relevant research has been done: fatigue, stress, age and sex. The third of these has generated a very substantial literature which makes it possible to measure changes with age in many of the areas surveyed in previous chapters. The others have been less thoroughly studied in terms of reaction time, although extensively considered from other points of view, and treatment here will therefore be relatively brief.

1. Fatigue and stress

Performance at a wide variety of tasks in known to deteriorate if it is continued for a long time under pressure for speed, but to recover after a period of rest or of different activity (for a review see Welford, 1968). It is also known to deteriorate under certain conditions which appear to tax the subject's capacities (for a review see Broadbent, 1971). These effects of fatigue and stress respectively have been assessed by various measures of performance including, in some cases, reaction times. A number of studies which appear to offer leads in these areas will be outlined here. From what has been said in previous chapters, reaction times, especially choice reaction times, would appear able often to provide more sensitive and precise measurements of changes in performance resulting from fatigue and stress than have been employed hitherto.

321

(A) FATIGUE

One of the most frequently observed fatigue effects is the slowing of sensory-motor performance. It is often suggested that this may be due to muscular fatigue, but there is no doubt that central factors are often, and probably mainly, involved. An indication is contained in the results of an experiment by Singleton (1953) who used a serial choice-reaction task. Subjects sat in a chair and pushed a joystick from a central position along slots in four directions in response to four lights, one corresponding to each of the slots. As soon as the subject reached the end of the correct slot the light went out, and on his return to the centre another came on, until 64 responses had been completed. Three variations of the task were presented. They were, in ascending order of difficulty: (i) "Direct" with the joystick having to be pushed in the direction which corresponded to the position of the light; (ii) "180 degrees" with the joystick pushed in the opposite direction to the light; and (iii) "270 degrees" with the joystick pushed away in response to the left light, to the left for the bottom light, and so on. The times per response gradually lengthened during each run but, as can be seen from Fig. 9.1, the lengthening was much more in time spent at the centre, that is in deciding which way to move, than in the actual execution of movements. Moreover, this lengthening increased with the difficulty of the condition, implying that the fatigue effect became greater as the demands of the central task rose.

Complementary indications that central and muscular fatigue are different phenomena is contained in results obtained by Kroll (1973) who found that the reaction time to extend the right knee in response to a light signal was not affected by exercizing the muscles concerned to a point at which their strength had been substantially reduced. Most research subsequent to Kroll's which has separated premotor and motor components of reaction time has confirmed his result which showed that neither time was affected, although examples have been found where the one but not the other is lengthened (Hanson and Loftus, 1978; Stull and Kearney, 1978). All these studies have measured reaction time after the exercise concerned has ceased. It has been known since the turn of the century that central fatigue effects are minimized under these conditions as opposed to those where measurements of performance are made while the fatiguing task is being done, so that the techniques of these experiments must be regarded as insensitive and their results therefore inconclusive.

Long-continued repetitive performance tends to become not only slower but also less regular. To some extent irregularity may be more apparent than real: the distributions of times for individual cycles of repetitive tasks tend to be skew, with a tail of long times and with a variance increasing with the mean; so that any overall slowing will increase the variance and the

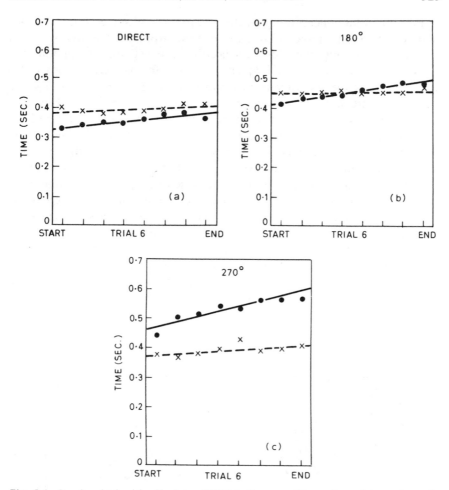

Fig. 9.1. Results obtained by Singleton (1953) in three conditions of a serial reaction task. The results shown are for the sixth trial of 64 reactions under each of the 3 conditions. Each point is the mean for 8 reactions by 10 subjects. The dots and solid lines are for times between the end of one movement and the beginning of the next, with the joystick in a central position, and are essentially reaction times. The crosses and broken lines are for the movement times from centre to end of slot and back.

number of what seem to be unusually long times. It has, however, been suggested by Bills (1931) that irregularity is due rather to occasional "blocking". That is to say, every now and than a short gap appears in an otherwise rapid performance, and the frequency of such gaps increases when the task is continued for a long time. On this view, the greater part of the distribution might be only a little affected, but there should be a marked increase in the size of the tail.

Bills based his conclusion upon the performance of subjects in tasks such as alternate addition and subtraction of three from a list of digits, colour naming, substituting letters for digits according to a code or giving opposites of words. He found that the frequency of times for individual items which exceeded twice the subject's average time increased during 7 min of work. His results are not very convincing and could probably have been due to simple slowing, but much clearer evidence has been obtained by Bertelson and Joffe (1963) using a serial choice-reaction task. The subjects in this were required to press one of four keys in response to the figures 1 to 4 shown in random order on a "Nixie" tube. Each response brought on the next figure. Samples of reaction times were scored at the second minute of work and at the end of 30 min. No change was found in the averages of the shortest or the median reaction times, but there was a marked increase in the average of the longest. The percentage of "blocks" (defined as reaction times longer than twice the mean, excluding responses in which errors were made) rose rapidly during the first 5 min of work and slowly thereafter. More important, there was a clear tendency for reaction time and errors to rise during the responses immediately before a block and to fall immediately after, as shown in Fig. 9.2.

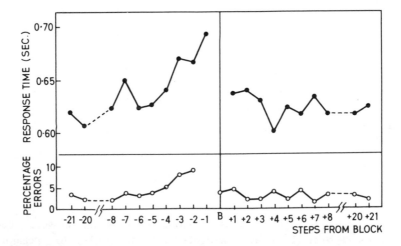

Fig. 9.2. Response times and errors made before and after a "block", in a serial reaction experiment by Bertelson and Joffe (1963). The graph was constructed by taking for each of 28 subjects the last 11 blocks observed (and not immediately associated with an error) during 30 min work and plotting the mean reaction times and errors for the first to eighth reactions before and after the block. The twentieth and twenty-first reactions before and after are also shown as an indication of reactions well clear of a block.

The results are consistent with the view that some kind of fatigue effect builds up gradually over a series of responses and is dissipated by the block. It should be noted that on this view there are two fatigue effects involved: a short-term effect dissipated at each block and a longer-term effect causing a rise in the frequency of blocks. The longer-term effect could perhaps be regarded as due to recovery during a block being not quite complete, so that the time taken to build up the next block is shorter than it would otherwise have been.

The cause of such blocking is not clear. Perhaps the most obvious suggestion is that some part of the sensory-motor mechanism becomes momentarily inoperative, although saying this does little more than restate the phenomenon. Whatever the cause, the main effect is short-lived compared with muscular fatigue, and it is perhaps for this reason that, while such effects show in the actual performance which causes the fatigue, they can seldom be detected in any other performance undertaken subsequently—the change of task and the inevitable brief gap in performance while the change is made are enough to dissipate most of the fatigue effect.

(b) STRESS

Broadly speaking, the effects of conditions used to study stress under laboratory conditions can be interpreted as having been of one or both of two types. First, noise, pain, discomfort and other sensory stimulation may capture attention momentarily and thus cause interference with performance in accordance with the single-channel principle discussed in Chapter 6. As a result, reactions may be more or less frequently delayed and the smooth flow of continuous performance may be interrupted (Broadbent 1971). In line with the single-channel hypothesis, Woodhead (1964) who showed her subjects two multi-digit numbers and then required them to subtract the second from the first, found that a sudden burst of noise while the numbers were being presented reduced the accuracy of performance, but did not do so if it occurred while the subtraction was being done—a time when the *gate* described in Chapter 6 was presumably closed against further perceptual input. The second type of effect can be attributed to raising or lowering of the subject's level of *arousal* (for reviews see Welford 1973, 1976 ch. 7). Sensory stimulation such as loud noise to which the subject has not habituated, changes, conflicts, challenges, physical or mental effort, pressure for speed, and various incentives all tend to raise arousal level, while quiet conditions, uneventful monotony, relaxation, idleness and lack of aim tend to lower it. Loss of sleep appears to be variable and often anomalous in its effects because, while the resulting drowsiness is a sign of lowered arousal, this may be partly compensated, or even over-compensated, by the effort to keep awake (Wilkinson 1965).

Relationships between arousal and performance have been summed up in the "Inverted-U Hypothesis" which states that performance rises from low levels of arousal until some optimum is reached: thereafter as arousal increases further, performance declines. Arousal is plausibly regarded as causing some general activation of the cortex which makes cells there readier to fire and so increases sensitivity and responsiveness. If so, the relationships between arousal and performance can be represented in Signal-Detection Theory terms as shown in Fig. 9.3. At low arousal levels as in Fig. 9.3A, there will be few correct detections but also few false ones and the value of β will be high. Increase of arousal will expand both the "Noise Alone" and the "Signal plus Noise" distributions roughly in proportion. As this happens the number of correct detections will increase and so will the number of false ones. Up to the point shown in Fig. 9.3B the former will increase faster than the latter, so that the net effect will be to improve performance. Beyond this point, as shown in Fig. 9.3C, false detections will increase faster than correct ones so that performance will deteriorate. Throughout, d' would change comparatively little, the main effect of increasing arousal would be to lower β. As envisaged in Fig. 9.3, under-arousal, optimum and over-arousal are three phases along a continuum. There is probably also a fourth phase which occurs with very high arousal levels: if the cells of the cortex are not only made more sensitive but are in

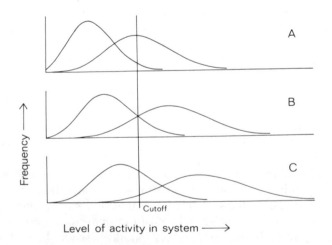

Fig. 9.3. Distributions of "Noise Alone" (left hand curve) and of "Signal-plus Noise" (right hand curve) for three levels of arousal: low (A), optimal (B) and high (C).

some cases actually fired, the noise will increase more than the signal, and this will lead to a fall of d' and all the signs of a lowered signal-to-noise ratio in the brain.

Reaction times appear to behave in a manner which is broadly consistent with this scheme:

(a) In "vigilance" tasks where subjects have to watch for faint, brief, infrequent signals over substantial periods of time—up to 2 hours or more—correct detections become fewer after about 20 min. The deterioration of performance is reasonably regarded as due to lowered arousal because false detections also become fewer. Over the same period, reaction time to those signals that are detected tends to increase (for reviews see Buck, 1966; Davies and Tune, 1970). When signals are stronger or of longer duration, detections do not decline with time, but reaction times still tend to become longer. The results suggest that the lowered arousal level means that a longer time is required to accumulate data to the critical level required to trigger a response, and that this is the cause of the longer reaction times.

(b) A study by Freeman (1933) of the effects of induced muscular tension produced results which are consistent with the scheme proposed here and are difficult to account for otherwise. Electric shocks of various measured strengths were delivered to the subject's right middle finger, and both the latency and the extent of the reflex movements were recorded. The shocks were given in pairs and the subject had to respond with the left hand to indicate whether the second member of the pair was equal to or stronger than the first. The experiment was performed under three conditions: (i) "normal" with the subject sitting in a chair, (ii) with the subject "relaxed" by methods advocated by Jacobson (1929) and (iii) with "tension" induced by a somewhat complex arrangement which made it necessary to tense the trunk muscles in order to maintain balance. The results are shown in Table 9.1 from which it can be seen that with increase of tension from the "relaxed" through the "normal" to the "tension" condition, the latency of the reaction to shock and the discrimination reaction-time shortened and the finger movements became greater, all of which would be expected from the facilitation due to increased activation. The accuracy of discrimination rose from the "relaxed" to the "normal" condition but fell again to the "tension" condition. In short, the increased tension made performance faster but at the expense of accuracy. This is what would be expected if it produced increased arousal in the manner envisaged in Fig. 9.3.

A somewhat different relationship between reaction time and effort was obtained by Levitt and Gutin (1971) who measured five-choice reaction times under various conditions of work-load on a treadmill. They found that reaction times were shorter with a load producing a heart rate of 115

Table 9.1. Effects of relaxation and of induced muscular tension on reactions. Data from Freeman (1933). Each entry is the mean of 20 readings from each of 9 subjects

	Relaxed	Normal	With induced muscle tension
Muscle-tonus in quadriceps (arbitrary units)	− 29.1	+ 18.2	+ 64.9
Reaction time to shocks delivered to right middle finger (msec)	401	259	247
Extent of finger withdrawal to these shocks (mm)	10.3	28.0	27.5
Time taken to discriminate whether second shock of pair was equal to or stronger than first (msec)	634	442	355
Accuracy of this discrimination (%)	65	97	69

beats per min than under resting conditions, but with loads producing higher heart rates they became longer again. Movement times, declined steadily with increasing load. Since heart rate is a recognized index of arousal, it appeared that high levels of arousal lengthened reaction times while a moderate level shortened them. Similar results were obtained by Sjöberg (1975) who measured two-choice reaction times at various work loads on a bicycle ergometer. He found reaction time to be shortest at a heart rate of 120 beats per min. A further similar fall and rise of simple reaction time was found by Freeman (1940) with transition from states of relaxation to mental tension and effort, with arousal measured by palmar skin resistance: as resistance fell so did reaction time up to a point, but thereafter reaction time rose again. These several results perhaps indicate that, at the high levels of effort used, either arousal became so high that the fourth phase mentioned above was reached at which there is a disproportionate increase of neural noise, or that the effort drew attention away from the reaction task, thus producing interference effects of the kind discussed at the end of Chapter 6.

(c) Nettelbeck (1973) found that reaction times in the discrimination task used by Vickers *et al.* (1972) and described in Chapter 2 of this Volume, were somewhat less for subjects scoring highly on the Taylor Manifest Anxiety Scale. Scores on this scale are commonly taken as an indicator of the degree to which an individual reacts to stress, and are presumably therefore related to arousal level under stressful conditions. Nettelbeck's results imply that his experiment was sufficiently stressful to produce a noticeable effect on the reaction times of highly anxious subjects. In a further experiment (Nettelbeck, 1972) he found that giving painful electric shocks at random intervals during the testing session did not increase reaction time but did reduce accuracy—a result somewhat similar to that obtained by Freeman (1940), Levitt and Gutin (1971) and Sjöberg (1975), and implying a disproportionate increase in the level of neural noise in the central mechanisms.

(**d**) Several experiments have shown that electric shocks given when reaction times are slow, lowers mean reaction time and shifts the whole distribution downwards (e.g. Johanson, 1922; Botwinick *et al.*, 1958a; Weiss, 1965). Johanson also found that the incentive of telling the subject after each reaction how he had done produced a similar although smaller effect.

Three further points about the effects of fatigue and stress on reaction times may be noted briefly. First, the studies outlined make it clear that it is not sufficient to look only at mean reaction times, but is necessary also to examine variability, accuracy and the characteristics of the signals used. Second, in many tasks both fatigue and stress occur together so that it is often difficult to separate their effects and decide which is causing any observed change of performance. The evidence makes it reasonable to suppose however, that the effect of fatigue should be a change of d' in cases where this can be measured, while the effects of stress should be mainly on β except at very high levels, when d' also may be affected. Third, Schmidtke (1976) practised subjects at a choice reaction task until the differences of reaction time between degrees of choice from 12 to 36 became very small as in the experiment by Mowbray and Rhoades (1959) mentioned in Chapter 3. He found that after intensive mental work, times were lengthened and once more rose linearly with the logarithm of degree of choice—the fatiguing effects of the mental work had negated the benefits of practice.

2. Age

The results of several studies of reaction time over a wide range of ages are summarized in Table 9.2. It can be seen that pursuit, simple and choice reaction times all shorten from childhood through adolescence to the twenties. Thereafter they tend to lengthen again, slowly until the fifties or sixties then more rapidly in the seventies and beyond. The change in the sixties and seventies is probably even more rapid than some of the results in Table 9.2 suggest: it is difficult to require people at later ages to act as subjects in experiments and those who volunteer are likely to be reasonably

Table 9.2. Examples of reaction times for various age groups. All times in msec. In several cases the figures have been read off graphs and the last digit is therefore liable to be inaccurate

Author	Task	6–9	10–14	15–19	20–29	30–39	40–49	50–59	60–69	70–79	80+	Notes
Pursuit reaction												
Miles (1931)	Stop rotating pointer at mark	154	98	63	61	69	74	89	97	127	134	Times measured are mean absolute errors
Simple reactions												
Galton (1899)	Press key to light			187	182	181	190	186	206	205		Subjects were visitors to a health exhibition who paid a small fee to be tested. Figures calculated from those given by Koga and Morant (1923).
	Press key to sound			158	154	158	159	157	167	174		
Miles (1931)	Release key to sound	323	243	222	203	203	207	203	203	267	263	
	Lift foot to sound	329	271	228	209	213	220	217	236	278	288	
Goldfarb (1941)	Raise finger to light and move to press key short distance away			376	321	334	366	387				Age groups: 18–24, 25–34, 35–44, 45–54, 55–64.
Fieandt *et al.* (1956)	Press button to light		228		201	201	217	212	217	245	353	Age groups: 11–14, 21–24, 29–36, 39–47, 49–56, 69–79, 80–88.
Pierson and Montoye (1958)	Lift hand to light	354	302	265	263	281	295	337	344	323		Age groups: 8–9, 10–14, 15–20, 21–30, 31–40, 41–50, 56–65, 66–75, 76–85.
Hugin *et al.* (1960)	Flex left foot to touch on right foot	247	210		178	177	184	192	214	222	229	Age groups: 3–9, 10–19, 20–29, etc. until 80–98. Responses measured from muscle action potentials.
Hodgkins (1962)	Release key to light	343	222	225	203	214	240	253		307		Age groups: 6–7, 12–13, 15–17, 18–21, 22–38, 39–54, 55–69, 70–84. Subjects all females.
Choice reactions												
Goldfarb (1941)	As above but 2-choice			394	380	395	436	451				Same subjects as for simple reactions.
	As above but 5-choice			429	418	432	472	495				
Noble *et al.* (1964)	4-choice: Males	467	386	252	245	268	296	345	430	582		Oldest age group 71–84.
	Females	507	374	277	287	316	346	388	467	538		Oldest age group 72–87.

fit and to feel they will make a good showing. Data about changes from young adulthood onwards are much fuller than about changes in childhood and the teens. The reason presumably is that theories of development in the earlier years have seldom been interested in speed of performance, whereas this has been a central concern in middle and old age because the early aim of research was to assess the potential of older people for employment. It is, therefore, with the adult years that the present discussion will be mainly concerned. Studies in this field have been thoroughly reviewed (Welford, 1977a) and it will be possible here to concentrate on principles rather than details.

It is now well recognized that changes of reaction time during adulthood are essentially due to changes in the central mechanisms of the brain or in the strategies of performance. Slowing of processes in the sense organs and falling speed of nerve conduction with age account for what is almost always a negligible proportion of the whole reaction time, and the proportional change of reaction time with age does not differ with the sense organ stimulated. Nor is much of the change with age due to time taken to activate the muscles (Weiss, 1965; Botwinick and Thompson, 1966), except when the responding action requires considerable force such as jumping with the whole body (Onishi, 1966). There is some discrepancy of evidence about whether age changes in simple reaction times are greater or less than in reflex times, but the more recent evidence is that they are greater (Magladery et al., 1958; Feinberg and Podolak, 1965). The slowing seems to be fundamental and not due to such factors as reduced motivation. For instance, as mentioned earlier, giving electric shocks for slow reactions causes subjects to react faster, but no consistent tendency has been shown for speeding up to be greater among the old than among the young (Botwinick et al., 1958a; Weiss, 1965). The slowing is too great to be explained entirely by the tendency of older people to sacrifice speed for accuracy in terms of eqn (3.8) (Salthouse, 1979).

As regards choice reaction times, the main question has been whether age affects the slope relating reaction time to degree of choice, or whether it adds a constant at all degrees—that is whether it increases a or b in eqn (3.5). The evidence is equivocal. The earliest results, those of Goldfarb (1941) shown in Table 9.2, show slight average rises of both a and b with age, although they are not entirely consistent. Crossman and Szafran (1956) who repeated part of Crossman's card-sorting experiment which was the basis of Fig. 3.2, found no sign of a rise of b—in fact a slight fall—and virtually no change of a from the twenties to the forties, but a substantial rise of a between these and a group aged 50–80. Their results are shown in Table 9.3. The rise could not have been due to slowness in handling the cards, because the groups did not differ in the time they took to deal alternately onto two piles. An age

Table 9.3. Values of a and b obtained for different age groups in the equation: Reaction Time $= a + b \log_2 n$, where $n =$ the number of equiprobable choices or its equivalent. Time constants in msec

Author	Range of choices	Younger group age range or mean age	a	b	Older group age range or mean age	a	b
Change greater in a than in b							
Crossman and Szafran (1956)	2, 4, 8	20–49	50*	295	50–80	580*	215
Botwinick et al. (1960)	2, 4, 6, 8, 10	19–35	510†	188	65–81	745†	242
Szafran (1966a)	3, 5, 8	32.3			47.7		
Without subsidiary task			272	85		288	82
With subsidiary task			393	89		447	87
Change greater in b than in a							
Griew (1959a, 1964)	2, 4, 8	20–28	288	73	48–62	307	94
Suci et al. (1960)‡	1, 2, 3, 4	17–38	323	179	60–70	387	302
Talland and Cairnie (1960)	1, 2	20–40	253	80	65–75	309	114
					77–89	328	215
Morikiyo et al. (1967)	2, 4, 8	Teens	209	191	Forties	191	233
		Twenties	199	193	Fifties	216	234
		Thirties	205	207			

* Card sorting task: dealing time deducted.
† Card sorting task: dealing time not deducted.
‡ These results are also well described by the equation: Reaction Time $= K \log_2 (n + 1)$ with $K = 300$ msec, for the younger subjects and 410 for the older.

effect predominently in *a* was observed in a further card-sorting task by Botwinick *et al.* (1960), whose results are also shown in Table 9.3. A rise in *a* but not in *b* was also found in Szafran (1966a) in a conventional reaction time task in which subjects pressed microswitches in response to neon lights. The regressions he found are shown in Table 9.3 both for straightforward choice tasks and for when these were accompanied by a subsidiary task involving short-term retention or making statements under conditions of delayed auditory feedback.

On the other hand, several experiments have shown proportionately greater rises of *b* than of *a* with age. These results too are shown in Table 9.3:

(i) Griew (1959a, 1964) had his subjects respond to lights arranged in a semicircle on a board some 3 ft away by moving a stylus from a central disc to the corresponding one of a 5 in radius semicircle of discs. The reaction time measured was from the appearance of the light to the raising of the stylus from the centre disc.

(ii) Suci *et al.* (1960) used a task in which subjects responded by speaking nonsense syllables on the disappearance of one or more of four lights.

(iii) Talland and Cairnie (1961) compared two-choice manual reactions to red and green lights with simple reactions to the green light only.

(iv) Morikiyo *et al.* (1967) tested factory workers with a task in which they responded by pressing keys under their fingers to numerals shown on a Nixie tube.

In order to understand and reconcile the conflict of evidence it is necessary to consider what appear to be certain fundamental causes of slowing of performance with age.

(A) CAUSES OF THE LENGTHENING OF REACTION TIME WITH AGE

Most, perhaps all, slowing of performance with age can be attributed either directly or indirectly to a fall of signal-to-noise ratio in the brain. Well-known changes in the sense organs obviously imply that the signals from them to the brain will be weaker, and the progressive loss of brain cells that occurs with age and various trends, such as to poorer cerebral blood flow, will mean that signals from one part of the brain to another will also be weaker. There is, in addition, evidence that increased random activity in the sensory systems and brain raises the "neural noise" level (Crossman and Szafran, 1956; Gregory, 1959, 1974, pp. 167–215). Vickers *et al.* (1972) reanalysing data by Botwinick *et al.* (1958a) measured this noise in terms of their model set out in Chapter 2. Botwinick and co-workers had recorded times taken to discriminate the longer of two parallel lines exposed for either

0.15 or 2.0 sec. With the brief exposures, the increase of time as the percentage difference between the lines fell from 20 to 1 was about the same for subjects aged 18–35 and 65–79 years, but the older group were less accurate. On the basis of the errors made, Vickers and co-workers calculated that the average standard deviations of the noise were about 0.21 degree of visual angle for the older subjects and about 0.14 for the younger. With the longer exposure, the increase of reaction time as the discrimination became finer was greater for both groups, but more so for the older, while the accuracies of both were equal. The calculated noise level was about 0.10 degree for each. It thus appeared that when a signal of longer duration was available, subjects accumulated data from it and thereby averaged out some of the noise. By averaging over a longer time, the older were able to attain the same accuracy as the younger.

A lowering of the signal-to-noise ratio with age would mean an increase in the ratio C/E in eqn (3.6) and, as indicated in eqn (3.7), would lead to a rise of choice-reaction time by an approximately equal amount for all degrees of choice. It would thus appear as an increase of a, in line with the results obtained by Crossman and Szafran (1956), Botwinick et al. (1960) and Szafran (1966a). The difference between these results and the others shown in Table 9.3, in which there was a greater rise of b than of a with age, can perhaps be attributed to differences in the effective duration of the stimuli. In all cases where the main age effect was in b the signal could be viewed by the subject continuously until he was ready to respond, and he could therefore accumulate data until he had attained an adequate confidence level. The conditions thus resembled those of Botwinick et al. (1958b) using a long exposure. On the other hand, in the card-sorting tasks used by Crossman and Szafran and by Botwinick et al. (1960) where the age effect was mainly in a, the conditions required the subject, in order to make his response, to look away from the display towards the area where the card was to be placed. In these cases, therefore, his inspection of the display was likely to be brief and the conditions would be like those of a brief signal in the study by Botwinick et al. (1958b). The situation in Szafran's case is unclear because he does not state the conditions of his experiment in detail, but it seems likely from his description that the signals he used were brief.

Two further results are anomalous, but appear to be special cases. The first is a card sorting experiment by Rabbitt (1964b) using cards each of which bore a single letter in one of nine positions. Comparing two- and four-choice conditions and age groups of 17–25 and 68–82 years he found the main age effect was in b. The task appears, however, to have required much closer scrutiny of the cards than in other card sorting experiments where the main age change was in a. The second anomalous case is that of a more normal reaction time experiment by Deupree and Simon (1963) in which the age effect was not reduced by brief exposure as opposed to exposure terminated by the response. Their short exposure—59 msec—was, however, too short to be fully effective at the low intensity they used: Vickers *et al.* (1972) have shown that exposures less than about 100 msec pose special problems.

Signal-to-noise ratio appears to be fundamental to other types of cause which have been suggested for the lengthening of reaction time with age.

(a) There is evidence that cardiovascular impairments which might reduce cerebral circulation and thus signal-to-noise ratio are associated with slowing of several types of performance, both motor and intellectual, and that the likelihood of these impairments increases with age (e.g. Birren and Spieth, 1962; Spieth, 1964, 1965; Simonson, 1965; Simonson and Anderson, 1966; Botwinick and Storandt, 1974). With regard to the parameters of choice reaction time, Szafran (1966b), using the task already mentioned, found that in addition to the rise of *a* with age, there was also a rise of *b* among subjects showing cardiac deficiency after exercise. Similarly Abrahams and Birren (1973) found that both *a* and *b* were higher among subjects judged to be predisposed to coronary heart disease by Friedman's Standard Situation Interview.

(b) Several studies have shown that physical fitness, which might be expected to improve signal-to-noise ratio, tends to lower reaction time, and it has been suggested that some of the slowing with age is due to older people tending to be less fit. Results are conflicting. Spirduso (see Stelmach and Diewert, 1977) found differences of reaction time associated with amount of exercise normally taken to be greater among older adults than among young, but Botwinick and Storandt (1974) found the reverse. In neither case could differences of exercise account for the whole age effect.

(c) It is sometimes argued that older people fail to realize their full capacities because they are out of practice at the type of task set in the laboratory, and that sufficient practice would equate the performances of old and young: lack of practice might imply weaker signals within the brain. However, Noble *et al.* (1964) whose results are shown in Table 9.2 found that when they plotted the changes of reaction time over 16 blocks of 20 trials, the asymptotes to which the times were tending showed essentially the same pattern of age changes as did the means.

(d) Hicks and Birren (1970) have surveyed relationships between age changes in psychomotor performance and the symptoms of various kinds of brain deficiency which might be expected to lower signal-to-noise ratio, and several authors, especially Obrist (1965), Surwillo (1961, 1963, 1964) and Mankovsky and Belonog (1971), have studied relationships between changes of EEG and performance with age. Surwillo has shown a close correlation between reaction time, both simple and choice, and the frequency of the alpha-rhythm, and has argued that the slowing of this can account for the lengthening of reaction time with age. He suggests that the alpha rhythm can be used as a kind of metric for reaction times, implying that it consists of "modules" of about 0.1 sec. This suggestion has obvious affinities with the concepts of "inspection time" discussed in Chapters 2 and 3.

(e) Lowered signal-to-noise ratio could indirectly impair ability to prepare reactions, hold states of readiness or formulate expectations. In line with this view, lengthening of reaction time when foreperiods or inter-signal intervals are relatively short, tends to be greater among older subjects (Botwinick et al., 1957, 1959; Brinley and Botwinick, 1959; Brebner and Szafran, 1961; Botwinick and Brinley, 1962). It has also been shown that when subjects have to guess which will be the next signal in a choice-reaction task, the older tend to guess less accurately (Sanford and Maule, 1973). Further evidence is provided by Morris and Thompson (1969) who found that the slowing of heart rate while waiting for a signal, commonly taken as an indicator of preparation, was less among older subjects than among younger, implying that older subjects do not prepare so *intensively* as young. In line with this view, Loveless and Sanford (1974) found that older subjects failed to show an anticipatory electrocortical potential between a warning and a signal to respond. Also, Rabbitt (1964a) found that a warning which conveyed information such as that one of four out of a possible eight responses would be called for, shortened reaction times for younger but not older subjects.

(f) Signal-to-noise ratio can, as was discussed earlier in this chapter, be affected by *arousal level*, and it is sometimes suggested that older people are less aroused than younger. This, however, appears unlikely. Surwillo and Quilter (1965) showed that although the latency of the galvanic skin response, commonly taken as a measure of arousal, was longer for older than for younger subjects, there was no relationship between this and reaction time. A similar lack of correspondence has been found for EEG measures of arousal and reaction time by Thompson and Botwinick (1968), while Surwillo (1969), who did find relationships in some individuals, found they were unrelated to age. More generally, the evidence about whether older or younger people show higher arousal levels is equivocal (Valk and Groen, 1950; Surwillo, 1965): an amphetamine-like drug "Meretran", which would be expected to raise arousal level, was found to make action more vigorous but not to increase its speed in a group of elderly men (Kleemeier et al., 1956). Again, the effects of monotonous conditions which, as was noted earlier, tend to lower arousal, differ little between young and old (Griew and Davies, 1962; Davies and Griew, 1963; Kemp, 1973), and any individual changes of vigilance under these conditions do not appear to be related to speed of reaction (Surwillo and Quilter, 1964).

Further, if arousal were important, reactions should be faster and age changes less in continuous tasks which should produce greater arousal than in discontinuous tasks. In fact, the reverse appears to be true. In a two-choice task using light signals and key-pressing responses, all age groups were faster when each signal followed 2 sec after the completion of the previous response than when it followed immediately, and the slowing with age between subjects in their late teens or twenties and their grandparents aged 67–87 was found to average 24 per cent in the former conditions and 36 per cent in the latter (Welford, 1977b). Members of a middle generation—parents of the younger subjects—showed results which resembled those of their sons or daughters: evidently the age changes were substantial only after the age of about 60.

(g) A plausible interpretation of the last result, and also of the slowing of reaction time among older subjects when the interval between warning and signal is very short, is that some after-effect, increasing with age, of the processes concerned with the decision to respond or the observation of the warning, continue for a brief period and act as noise, blurring any decision process which follows shortly after (Welford, 1965). Such after-effects could be expected to impair performance less when the following response is the same as the one just made: they should rather facilitate it since the processes for its initiation would already be operating to some extent. If this is the correct explanation of the disproportionate rise of reaction time with age in continuous tasks mentioned in the last paragraph, repetition effects should have increased with age in these. However, scrutiny of the results revealed no such tendency. Instead, the older showed *less* tendency than the young to repetition effects and greater tendencies to alternation effects.

(h) A more likely reason for the slower performance of older people in continuous tasks appears to lie in a greater tendency to monitor their responses. As noted in Chapter 6, while such monitoring is in progress, immediate attention cannot be given to new signals. There is considerable evidence that older people tend to look more at what they are doing (Szafran, see Welford, 1958, pp. 129 *et seq.*), are more cautious in reacting (Korchin and Basowitz, 1957; Botwinick, 1966; Craik, 1969) and tend, other things being equal, to sacrifice speed for accuracy (Brown, see Welford, 1958, pp. 65 *et seq.*). These tendencies are often regarded as signs of some change with age unrelated to others, but it seems more parsimonious to regard them as reactions to lowered signal-to-noise ratio which would increase the risk of error. This, as we have seen, can be compensated for to some extent by gathering extra data. Some of these tendencies are doubtless deliberate—the result of previous errors—but in the present author's experiments discussed in (f) and (g) above they appeared to be automatic.

As already noted, both younger and older subjects were slower when the next signal was given on the *release* of the key used for the previous response than when there was a 2 sec interval. Surprisingly, however, the times when the next signal arrived on *pressing* the key for the previous response were intermediate between the other two. For the youngest subjects, reaction times in this last condition approached those with the 2 sec interval after release, while for the oldest they approached the times taken when the next signal came immediately on release of the previous key. This could be accounted for by an indication contained in the results that the older subjects took longer than the young to perceive the signals, especially those that were repetitions of those given immediately before. If this were so, feedback from the beginning of the previous response would be likely to capture the single channel more frequently among older subjects because processing of the data from the new signal would not proceed fast enough for it to capture the channel first. The relationships envisaged are shown in Fig. 9.4 in the same terms as those of Fig. 6.3.

What appears to be an interesting parallel to these results in a different context has been obtained by Rabbitt and Rogers (1965) who compared times for movement to one of two alternative end points, one further away than the other in the same direction, with times for return movements to a single end point. They found that, when making the former movements, subjects aged 19–29 could overlap the time required to make the choice between alternatives with the initial stages of the movement. Subjects aged

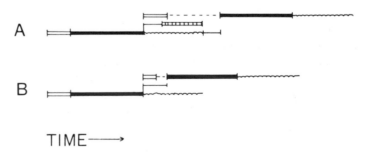

Fig. 9.4. Events envisaged when a new signal arrives simultaneously with the beginning of the response to a previous signal. A. When the beginning of the response takes less time to detect than the new signal, monitoring of the response delays reaction to the new signal. B. When the beginning of the response takes more time to detect than the new signal, reaction to the new signal suppresses monitoring of the response.
========= Detection of signal
———— Choice and initiation of response
———— Detection of beginning or end of response
ʇʇʇʇʇʇ Monitoring of response
ᘽᘽᘽ Execution of response
– – – – Signal held in store

63–76 appeared less able to do this, seemingly because they needed to monitor their movements more closely and were unable to combine this with making choices. A similar parallel is contained in the results obtained by Rabbitt and Birren (1967) whose subjects responded to regular, continuous sequences of signal lights in different positions by pressing corresponding keys thus: 1, 2, 1, 2, 1, 2 . . ., or 1, 2, 3, 4, 3, 2, 1, 2, 3, 4. . . . They found that subjects aged 60–81 were slower and less accurate than those aged 17–28, especially with the 4-item sequence, but were less affected by occasional deviations from the regular pattern. It seemed that younger subjects programmed and monitored the regular series as wholes, whereas the older tended to react to and monitor each signal individually.

(B) CONTINUOUS PERFORMANCE

The foregoing experiments raise the question of what age changes are observed in continuous performances of the type reviewed in Chapter 6. Studies of tracking have shown that the speed with which changes in direction of the track can be followed accurately falls with age from the thirties onwards, whether or not the changes can be seen in advance (Welford, 1958, pp. 86 et seq.). There seem to be no additional age effects when tracking is combined with reacting to occasional signals in a dual-task situation. Griew (1958a), whose subjects were required to respond by pressing a key as quickly as possible to the sound of a buzzer given at irregular intervals while they were tracking, found that tracking performance was about equally impaired by the distracting task in two groups of subjects aged 24–31 and 42–50. The two groups also showed very similar reaction times to the buzzer given apart from the tracking task. It seemed as if the performance at the double task could be adequately accounted for in terms of performance at the tracking and the reaction time tasks separately, and that there was no additional handicap to the older subjects from combining them.

Similar indications, using different tasks, were obtained by Talland (1962) who presented subjects with three tasks: (A) working a manual counter held in the non-dominant hand, (B) picking up beads, one at a time with tweezers held in the dominant hand, from a bowl of red beads and transferring them to another bowl, and (C) doing the same with blue beads mixed with an equal number of yellow beads. Each task was done singly, and also A was combined with B and with C. The older subjects performed more slowly than the younger. The percentage differences with age for B and C, both with and without A were, however, closely similar: the main change with age when the tasks were combined was in A implying, first, that subjects gave priority to B and C, and second that older subjects had less capacity to spare for A. The tendency for a relatively easy task such as A to suffer more than a difficult one when they are combined has been noted in Chapter 6 in connection with results obtained by Mowbray (1953).

(C) RELATIONSHIPS BETWEEN SIGNALS AND RESPONSES

Incompatibility between signals and responses exaggerates the changes with age in many types of performance which not only become slower but also less accurate, indicating that the effects are not fully compensated for by spending extra time. Certain factors such as ability to conceptualize relationships and to manipulate data in the abstract, which exert relatively little limitation in the twenties, appear to have much greater effects in later middle and old age. Evidence will be discussed here under the two headings used in Chapter 3.

Spatial transpositions
Simon and Wolf (1963), who measured two-choice reactions with display lights rotated at various angles from 0 to 180 degrees relative to response keys, found that times became longer as the angular discrepancy become greater, and that older subjects were slower than younger, but that there was no disproportionate increase of reaction time with age as the angle increased. However, different results were obtained by Griew (1964) in an extension of a study discussed earlier in which subjects had to move a stylus to one of several disks indicated by signal lights. Instead of requiring that the response to each light was to touch the disk in the corresponding position, response to the leftmost lisht was by touching the disk corresponding to the rightmost light, and so on. He found that reactions were not only slower in this latter condition but tended to become disproportionately so with age. The regressions of reaction time upon degree of choice for 2, 4 and 8 choices were $296 + 127 \log_2 n$ msec for subjects aged 20–28 years and $301 + 171 \log_2 n$ for those aged 48–62. The increases in the slope b of eqn (4.5) over the straightforward condition were 74 and 82 per cent respectively. Percentage changes of a were $+3$ and -2 respectively.

Two other studies support Griew's by showing greater proportional differences with age. One of these compared the reaction times in the discontinuous and continuous tasks already discussed (Welford, 1977b) with those of the same subjects when the relationships between signals and keys were reversed so that lights on the left were responded to with the right hand and *vice versa*. With this relationship the changes of reaction time between the young subjects and their grandparents were 43 per cent for the discontinuous and 39 per cent for the continuous task, as against 22 and 32 per cent, respectively, with direct relationships. It is interesting to note that in this case the percentage effects of incompatibility and continuity did not summate, and that the disadvantage of incompatibility to the older subjects was a little less in the continuous than in the discontinuous task. Why this was so is not clear.

The results of the other study by Kay (1955) are shown in Table 9.4. Kay used two boxes, one containing twelve light bulbs and the other twelve keys, one for each bulb. One of the bulbs was on, and the subject's task was to press the key corresponding to it, whereupon the bulb went out and another lit up, and so on through a series in which the various bulbs lit in random order. Performances were compared (a) with the lights immediately above the keys, (b) with the lights 3 feet away across a table, and (c) with the lights 3 feet away and the box turned through 180 degrees. The percentage changes of time taken with age from the combined 15–24 and 25–34 year age groups to the 65–72 group were 15 for (a), 25 for (b) and 56 for (c).

Symbolic translations
An important comparison of ten-choice reaction times with several different types of symbolic translation between signals and responses has been provided by Birren *et al.* (1962). The apparatus used in these experiments was modelled on that used by Kay. It can be seen from Table 9.5 that the percentage increase of time taken by the older subjects was about 27 for straightforward choices and about 50 for choices involving symbolic translation between signal and response. The percentage increase for tasks involving colour coding was somewhat higher. Why this was so is not clear, but it is well recognized that colour coding is inefficient in that only about eight different hues can be distinguished both reliably and quickly (see Miller, 1956).

The increase with age of about 50 per cent was similar to that found by Kay (1954) for a symbolic translation using the same apparatus as in his experiment already described. In the present case, as well as the two boxes, one of lights and one of keys, there was a card with numbers 1–12 in random order placed as shown on the left of Fig. 9.5. The subject was given typewritten instructions:

"(i) Think of the lights as being numbered 1–12 from the left.
(ii) When the light goes on, decide which number it is.
(iii) Find the number on the card.
(iv) The correct key to hit is the key in line with the number on the card."

The results are shown in the column headed "Condition 1" of Table 9.6.

The other condition of Kay's experiment, the results of which are shown under the column headed "Condition 2" of Table 9.6, indicate that adding a symbolic translation to a spatial transformation produces a far greater age

Table 9.5. Ten-choice reaction times (sec) obtained by Birren *et al.* (1962)

Tasks	Age range (years) 18–33	60–80	Percentage difference
Compatible conditions:			
1. Signal lights numbered randomly. Response buttons with some numbers in corresponding positions	0.64	0.81	27
2. Same with different random order	0.58	0.73	26
Arrangements requiring symbolic translation between signal and response:			
3. Lights numbered randomly, buttons numbered in order	1.04	1.58	52
4. Both lights and buttons numbered randomly	1.42	2.14	51
5. Same as 3 but with letters instead of numbers	1.05	1.59	51
6. Same as 4 but with letters instead of numbers	1.51	2.22	47
7. Lights numbered randomly. Buttons with symbols to be matched to numbers with code cards	2.88	4.34	51
8. As 4 but with syllables instead of numbers	1.29	1.87	45
9. As 8 but with words instead of syllables	1.33	1.92	44
10. As 4 but with colours or pairs of colours instead of numbers	1.74	3.38	94
11. As 4 but with one of 5 colours together with letter X or Y instead of numbers	1.53	2.84	86

Table 9.4. Mean times and errors per response in a spatial transposition task by Kay (1955). Times in sec. Errors shown in brackets

Age range	Conditions					
	a		b		c	
15–24	0.76	(0)	1.28	(0.18)	2.53	(0.30)
25–34	0.80	(0)	1.26	(0.14)	2.88	(0.34)
35–44	0.78	(0)	1.29	(0.13)	2.55	(0.28)
45–54	0.81	(0)	1.25	(0.15)	2.86	(0.35)
55–64	0.85	(0)	1.49	(0.12)	3.10	(0.26)
65–72	0.90	(0)	1.58	(0.08)	4.22	(0.27)

Table 9.6. Mean times and errors per response in a symbolic translation task by Kay (1954). Times in sec. Errors shown in brackets

Age range	Conditions			
	1		2	
15–24	2.82	(0.06)	4.24	(0.20)
25–34	2.71	(0.07)	5.58	(0.43)
35–44	3.10	(0.13)	6.86	(0.68)
45–54	2.71	(0.13)	8.74	(1.18)
55–64	3.69	(0.18)	11.47	(1.68)
65–72	4.24	(0.16)	22.27	(2.40)

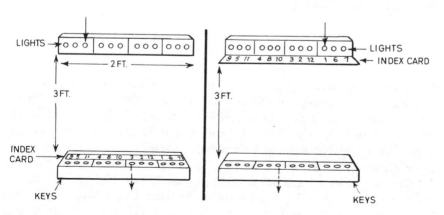

Fig. 9.5. Layout of apparatus in an experiment by Kay (1954). The left-hand arrangement requires a symbolic translation to relate each light to its corresponding key. The right-hand arrangement requires both a symbolic translation and a spatial transposition.

effect than the sum of the two effects separately. This was achieved by moving the card to the position shown on the right of Fig. 9.5. The instructions were the same, so that the subjects had not only to find the correct number on the card, but also to align across the three-foot gap in a manner similar to that required in condition (b) of Kay's (1955) experiment. The percentage rise of time from the combined 15–24 and 25–34 year age groups to the 65–72 age group which had been 25 for condition (b) and 53 for condition 1 was no less than 353 for condition 2. Similar results were obtained in a replication of Kay's experiment by Ross et al. (1960).

A further example of what can be broadly regarded as symbolic translation is provided in a card-sorting task by Botwinick et al. (1960). Cards had to be sorted into slots marked with sample cards such as the 7 of clubs or the 4 of diamonds. Subjects were told to "match the cards by number and colour if the number is even, but if the number is odd, then match number and opposite colour". The difference between a group aged 19–35 and one aged 65–81 averaged 62 per cent, whereas with a straightforward sorting by number it averaged 45 per cent. Sorting time was found to shorten with practice, but the rate of improvement did not differ with age.

Subjects of different ages might, however, come closer to equality after massive amounts of practice or long familiarity which had resulted in the relationships being thoroughly "built into" their memories as, for instance, in the case of letters and digits discussed in Chapter 3. Results obtained by Schonfield and Robertson (1968) are perhaps in line with this view. They found that a group of subjects aged 60–90 years responded faster to digits— a familiar class of symbol—displayed on a screen by pressing keys bearing the same digits, than they responded to unfamiliar symbols by pressing keys bearing the same symbols.

(D) STAGES BETWEEN SIGNAL AND RESPONSE

It has already been noted that if reaction time is divided into portions before and after the beginning of muscle action, the percentage change in the former tends to be greater than in the latter unless substantial muscular effort is required (Weiss, 1965; Botwinick and Thompson, 1966; Onishi, 1966). As regards attempts to separate identification and choice similar to those discussed in Chapter 3, Donders' c-reaction was studied by Surwillo (1973) who presented a series of tones, either 250 or 1000 cps in random order, and required subjects to respond to the higher while ignoring the lower. The need to discriminate between the tones made reaction time longer than in the simple reaction situation when only one tone was used, but the rise was roughly proportional with age—about 16 per cent in the simple case and 19 per cent in the disjunctive, between the ages of 30 and 70 years.

Of studies using the technique of mapping several signals onto the same response, Griew (1958b) compared the times taken to lift a stylus from a plate in response to 1 or any of 2, 4 or 8 light signals. Subjects aged 19–26 showed little difference of time with 1, 2 or 4 signals but an appreciable rise with 8. Those aged 52–59 showed a marked rise from 1 to 2 but little thereafter. The mean differences of reaction time between the two groups were 9 per cent when there was one light and 19 per cent with more than one. It seems as if the older subjects were less able to refrain from paying attention to which signal had occurred, despite the fact that it was irrelevant. Support for this view was obtained by Rabbitt (1965) who, using the same task as in his study mentioned in Chapter 3 (Rabbitt, 1964a), had subjects sort cards according to letters printed on them. He found that the time taken by older subjects rose more than that of younger when irrelevant letters were added to the cards. However, in another card-sorting task (Rabbitt, 1964b) he found that, although the rise of time taken with age increased with the number of stimuli calling for any one response, it was much less than that associated with increase in the number of different responses to be made; implying that the perceptual factors were less important than those concerned with choice of response.

A further study by Griew (1959b) suggests that the tendency of older people to attend to irrelevant information is similar to their tendency, noted by Botwinick et al. (1958b), to inspect incoming data for a longer time before making a decision, and that shortening exposure time so that extra data cannot be accumulated, tends to bring the performances of older and younger closer together. Griew repeated his (1958b) study but with signals lasting only 150 msec instead of remaining until the response was made. The age difference with more than one signal in use was only 1.5 per cent as opposed to 19 per cent in the former experiment.

Some evidence that both identification and choice are affected to a roughly equal extent with age is provided by Naylor (1973) and his associates who compared the times taken to *recognize* a digit 1–9 shown tachistoscopically, with the reaction time to press one of nine keys in *response* to a digit. The recognition times were 355 and 450 msec respectively for groups aged 18–28 and 65–75 years—a difference of about 27 per cent. The reaction times were 1075 and 1360 msec, respectively. Deducting the recognition times from these we obtain 720 and 910 msec for choice and initiation of response—an age difference of 26 per cent. The implications are that the identification times are shorter than the corresponding times for choice and initiation of response, but that the percentage change with age is the same for both.

(E) RELATIONSHIPS BETWEEN REACTION TIME AND MOVEMENT TIME

It was noted earlier that in the card-sorting experiment by Crossman and Szafran (1956), older subjects took substantially longer to sort cards according to colour or number, but very little longer to deal them. In line with this, experiments in which the responses have been key-pressing or other similar movements have shown that changes with age in the times taken to make these have usually been small and not related to reaction times (Botwinick and Thompson, 1966; Welford, 1977a). When responses involve more substantial movements, however, changes with age are more systematic and tend to be greater than for the corresponding reaction times. For example, Pierson and Montoye's (1958) subjects, whose reaction time results are shown in Table 9.2, had, when a light appeared, to raise the hand from a microswitch and thrust it forward with a full arm movement over a distance of about a foot. The changes of movement time were a fall of about 63 per cent from age 10 to 20 followed by a rise of about 74 per cent to age 60, whereas the corresponding changes of reaction time were both about 27 per cent. Again Birren *et al.* (1962) whose data have been given in Table 9.5, where it was seen that the rise of reaction time from a group aged 18–33 to one aged 60–80 was 27 per cent, found a rise of movement time of about 46 per cent.

A comparison of the relationship between reaction time and the nature of the responding movement is available from the results obtained by Miles (1931) also shown in Table 9.2. The changes of reaction time for releasing a key to a sound signal from the youngest age group (6–9) to the twenties was a fall of 59 per cent and from the twenties to the seventies a rise of 32 per cent. The corresponding changes when response was by lifting the foot instead of the hand were virtually identical—57 and 33 per cent. Similarly Singleton (see Welford, 1958, p. 99) who, as noted in Chapter 3, found that the reaction times before responses consisting of a single 18 in movement were some 5 per cent shorter than before a double movement of 18 in out and back to starting point, found no systematic change in this percentage in any decade between the twenties and the sixties. The rises between these ages were 27 and 26 per cent in reaction times preceding single and double movements, respectively.

(F) SEX DIFFERENCES IN RELATION TO AGE

Several studies have been concerned with the question of whether trends with age differ between the two sexes. Probably the most complete is that by Noble *et al.* (1964) whose results have been shown in Table 9.2. It can be seen that males show shorter reaction times than females in every age group except the 10–14 and the oldest (71–84). The tendency for females to have longer reaction times is broadly supported by the other results summarized in Table 9.7, which show that the trend is the same whether the response is to light or sound (Bellis, 1933), or is by pressing or releasing a key (Engel *et al.*, 1972), and is the same at different educational levels among older subjects (Botwinick and Storandt, 1974). Botwinick and Thompson (1966), who divided premotor from motor time by taking EMG records, found that the whole of the sex difference lay in the premotor time, implying that control rather than muscular factors were involved. Further results obtained by Noble *et al.* (1964) indicated that the sex difference of slower reaction times by females was not abolished by practice, and a subsequent study by Botwinick and Thompson (1967) who compared men and women in two age groups, 18–35 and 67–92, produced the same result.

Some support for the lack of sex difference found in the early 'teens by Noble and co-workers might be suggested by the virtual equality found by Botwinick and Storandt (1974) for their subjects in the twenties, although other studies of subjects both in the 'teens and twenties have shown females to be slower. If the result by Noble and co-workers is not due to an accident of sampling it may perhaps reflect a tendency for girls to mature more quickly than boys in the early 'teens.

The finding by Noble and co-workers that in their oldest group the women had shorter reaction times than the men is supported by Botwinick and Brinley (1962), although this may have been an artefact because their older women were, on average, about eight years younger than their older men and they expressed doubts about whether their samples were fully comparable in other ways. The results are certainly not supported by those of Botwinick and Thompson (1966) who found their older women to be slower. The conflict may well reflect the need for extreme care in sampling above the age of about 70. Speed of performance tends to decline rapidly during the few months before death. This fact, coupled with the tendency for women to live longer than men could mean that in any institutional or strictly representative sample, the older women would be on average fitter than the men and therefore likely to have shorter reaction times. On the other hand it is possible that in a sample recruited essentially on the basis of willingness to be tested, men might be equally as fit as the women since only those feeling reasonably fit would volunteer. The oldest subjects studied by Noble and co-workers appear almost certainly to have been from a rest home for the elderly, so that the women might be expected to be fitter than the men. The subjects of all the other studies were volunteers and in all except that of Botwinick and Brinley (1962), which has already been noted as questionable, the women were slower.

Why females should tend, on average, to have longer reaction times is not

Table 9.7. Reaction times obtained in experiments which compared men and women. All studies are of simple reaction times. All times in msec. Several results have been read off graphs so that the last digit is liable to be incorrect.

Author	Task		Teens	20s	30s	40s	50s	60s	70s	Notes
Bellis (1933)	Press key to light	Men	240	220	260	270	380			Scores are means of best five readings by each subject.
		Women	320	260	340	360	440			Published results are given to nearest 1/100 sec. only.
	Press key to sound	Men	230	190	240	250	370			
		Women	310	200	300	300	420			
Botwinick and Brinley (1962)	Lift finger to light									Foreperiods were 0.5 to 15 sec
	Regular foreperiods	Men		209					262	Age groups 18–27, 61–80
		Women		217					257	
	Irregular foreperiods	Men		234					293	
		Women		243					279	
	Lift finger to sound									
	Regular foreperiods	Men		171					207	
		Women		180					198	
	Irregular foreperiods	Men		195					228	
		Women		205					220	
Botwinick and Thompson (1966)	Lift finger to sound									Premotor times. Motor times differed little with either age or sex.
	Regular foreperiods	Men		184					241	Age groups men 19–32, 68–87.
		Women		201					305	women 18–35, 69–84.
	Irregular foreperiods	Men		223					280	
		Women		238					309	
Engel et al. (1972)	Press key to sound	Men		227				233		Age groups 20–30, 55–65.
		Women		242				286		
	Release key to sound	Men		227				236		
		Women		232				282		
Botwinick and Storandt (1974)	Release key to sound									Age groups men 20–28, 64–74.
	Higher education	Men		204					240	women 21–26, 66–73.
		Women		202					256	Age groups men 65–74.
	Lower education	Men							259	women 65–73.
		Women							292	

clear. There seems to be no obvious way in which the trend could result from the different roles played by the sexes in normal, everyday life. Part of it might be due to the fact that cigarette smoking tends to shorten reaction time (Myrsten and Andersson, 1973) coupled with the likelihood that at the time the studies were made, women smoked somewhat less than men. Apart from such a possibility, it is hard to resist the conclusion that the trend is due to some fundamental biological factor. For example, women's average brain weight is less than men's, and this could imply less powerful signals within the brain and consequent slower build-up to critical levels.

References

Abrahams, J. P. and Birren, J. E. (1973). Reaction time as a function of age and behavioral predisposition to coronary heart disease. *Journal of Gerontology* **28**, 471–478.

Bellis, C. J. (1933). Reaction time and chronological age. *Proceedings of the Society for Experimental Biology and Medicine* **30**, 801.

Bertelson, P. and Joffe, Rachel (1963). Blockings in prolonged serial responding. *Ergonomics* **6**, 109–116.

Bills, A. G. (1931). Blocking: a new principle in mental fatigue. *American Journal of Psychology* **43**, 230–245.

Birren, J. E., Riegel, K. F. and Morrison, D. F. (1962). Age differences in response speed as a function of controlled variations of stimulus conditions: Evidence of a general speed factor. *Gerontologia* **6**, 1–18.

Birren, J. E. and Spieth, W. (1962). Age, response speed, and cardiovascular functions. *Journal of Gerontology* **17**, 390–391.

Botwinick, J. (1966). Cautiousness in advanced age. *Journal of Gerontology* **21**, 347–353.

Botwinick, J. and Brinley, J. F. (1962) Aspects of RT set during brief intervals in relation to age and sex. *Journal of Gerontology* **17**, 295–301.

Botwinick, J., Brinley, J. F. and Birren, J. E. (1957). Set in relation to age. *Journal of Gerontology* **12**, 300–305.

Botwinick, J., Brinley, J. F. and Robbin, J. S. (1958a). The effect of motivation by electrical shocks on reaction-time in relation to age. *American Journal of Psychology* **71**, 408–411.

Botwinick, J., Brinley, J. F. and Robbin, J. S. (1958b). The interaction effects of perceptual difficulty and stimulus exposure time on age differences in speed and accuracy of response. *Gerontologia* **2**, 1–10.

Botwinick, J., Brinley, J. R. and Robbin, J. S. (1959). Maintaining set in relation to motivation and age. *American Journal of Psychology* **72**, 585–588.

Botwinick, J., Robbin, J. S. and Brinley, J. R. (1960). Age differences in card-sorting performance in relation to task difficulty, task set, and practice. *Journal of Experimental Psychology* **59**, 10–18.

Botwinick, J. and Storandt, Martha (1974). Cardiovascular status, depressive affect, and other factors in reaction time. *Journal of Gerontology* **29**, 543–548.

Botwinick, J. and Thompson, L. W. (1966). Components of reaction time in relation to age and sex. *Journal of Genetic Psychology* **108**, 175–183.

Botwinick, J. and Thompson, L. W. (1967). Practice of speeded response in relation to age, sex, and set. *Journal of Gerontology* **22**, 72–76.

Brebner, J. and Szafran, J. (1961). A study of the "psychological refractory phase" in relation to ageing. *Gerontologia* **5**, 241–249.

Brinley, J. F. and Botwinick, J. (1959). Preparation time and choice in relation to age differences in response speed. *Journal of Gerontology* **14**, 226–228.

Broadbent, D. E. (1971). "Decision and Stress". Academic Press, London.

Buck, L. (1966). Reaction time as a measure of perceptual vigilance. *Psychological Bulletin* **65**, 291–304.

Craik, F. I. M. (1969). Applications of signal detection theory to studies of ageing. *In* "Decision Making and Age" (A. T. Welford and J. E. Birren, eds.), pp. 147–157. Karger, Basel.

Crossman, E. R. F. W. and Szafran, J. (1956). Changes with age in the speed of information intake and discrimination. *Experientia Supplementum* **4**, 128–135.

Davies, D. R. and Griew, S. (1963). A further note on the effect of aging on auditory vigilance performance: the effect of low signal frequency. *Journal of Gerontology* **18**, 370–371.

Davies, D. R. and Tune, G. S. (1970). "Human Vigilance Performance". Staples Press, London.

Deupree, R. H. and Simon, J. R. (1963). Reaction time and movement time as a function of age, stimulus duration and task difficulty. *Ergonomics* **6**, 403–411.

Engel, B. T., Thorne, P. R. and Quilter, R. E. (1972). On the relationship among sex, age, response mode, cardiac cycle phase, breathing cycle phase, and simple reaction time. *Journal of Gerontology* **27**, 456—460.

Feinberg, R. and Podolak, E. (1965). Latency of pupillary reflex to light stimulation and its relationship to aging. *In* "Behavior, Aging and the Nervous System" (A. T. Welford and J. E. Birren, eds.). C. C. Thomas, Springfield, Illinois.

Fieandt, K. von, Huhtala, A., Kullberg, P. and Saarl, K. (1956). Personal tempo and phenomenal time at different age levels. Reports from the Psychological Institute, No. 2. University of Helsinki.

Freeman, G. L. (1933). The facilitative and inhibitory effects of muscular tension upon performance. *American Journal of Psychology* **45**, 17–52.

Freeman, G. L. (1940). The relationship between performance level and bodily activity level. *Journal of Experimental Psychology* **26**, 602–608.

Galton, F. (1899). On instruments for (1) testing perception of differences of tint and for (2) determining reaction time. *Journal of the Anthropological Institute* **19**, 27–29.

Goldfarb, W. (1941). An investigation of reaction time in older adults and its relationship to certain observed mental test patterns. Teachers College Contributions to Education, No. 831. Columbia University, New York.

Gregory, R. L. (1959). Increase in "neurological noise" as a factor in ageing. *Proceedings of the 4th Congress of the International Association of Gerontology, Merano 1957, Vol. 1*, pp.314–324.

Gregory, R. L. (1974). "Concepts and Mechanisms of Perception". Charles Scribner's Sons, New York.

Griew, S. (1958a). A note on the effect of interrupting auditory signals on the performance of younger and older subjects. *Gerontologia* **2**, 136–139.

Griew, S. (1958b). Uncertainty as a determinant of performance in relation to age. *Gerontologia* **2**, 284–289.

Griew, S. (1959a). Complexity of response and time of initiating responses in relation to age. *American Journal of Psychology* **72**, 83–88.

Griew, S. (1959b). A further note on uncertainty in relation to age. *Gerontologia* **3**, 335–339.

Griew, S. (1964). Age, information transmission and the positional relationship between signals and responses in the performance of a choice task. *Ergonomics* **7**, 267–277.

Griew, S. and Davies, D. R. (1962). The effect of aging on auditory vigilance performance. *Journal of Gerontology* **17**, 88–90.

Hanson, Cheryl and Loftus, Geraldine K. (1978). Effects of fatigue and laterality on fractionated reaction time. *Journal of Motor Behavior* **10**, 177–184.

Hicks, L. H. and Birren, J. E. (1970). Aging, brain damage, and psychomotor slowing. *Psychological Bulletin* **74**, 377–396.

Hodgkins, Jean (1962). Influence of age on the speed of reaction and movement in females. *Journal of Gerontology* **17**, 385–389.

Hugin, F., Norris, A. H. and Shock, N. W. (1960). Skin reflex and voluntary reaction times in young and old males. *Journal of Gerontology* **15**, 388–391.

Jacobson, E. (1929). "Progressive Relaxation". University of Chicago Press.

Johanson, A. M. (1922). The influence of incentive and punishment upon reaction-time. *Archives of Psychology*, No. 54.

Kay, H. (1954). The effects of position in a display upon problem solving. *Quarterly Journal of Experimental Psychology* **6**, 155–169.

Kay, H. (1955). Some experiments on adult learning. *In* "Old Age in the Modern World" Report of the 3rd Congress of the International Association of Gerontology, London 1954, pp. 259–267. Livingstone, Edinburgh.

Kemp, B. J. (1973). Reaction time of young and elderly subjects in relation to perceptual deprivation and signal-on versus signal-off conditions. *Developmental Psychology* **8**, 268–272.

Kleemeier, R. W., Rich, T. A. and Justiss, W. A. (1956). The effects of alpha-(2-piperidyl) benzhydrol hydrochloride (Meratran) on psychomotor performance in a group of aged males. *Journal of Gerontology* **11**, 165–170.

Koga, Y. and Morant, G. M. (1923). On the degree of association between reaction times in the case of different senses. *Biometrika* **15**, 346–372.

Korchin, S. J. and Basowitz, H. (1957). Age differences in verbal learning. *Journal of Abnormal and Social Psychology* **54**, 64–69.

Kroll, W. (1973). Effects of local muscular fatigue due to isotonic and isometric exercise upon fractionated reaction time components. *Journal of Motor Behavior* **5**, 81–93.

Levitt, S. and Gutin, B. (1971). Multiple choice reaction time and movement time during physical exertion. *Research Quarterly* **42**, 405–410.

Loveless, N. E. and Sanford, A. J. (1974). Effects of age on the contingent negative variation and preparatory set in a reaction-time task. *Journal of Gerontology* **29**, 52–63.

Magladery, J. W., Teasdall, R. D. and Norris, A. H. (1958). Effect of aging on plantar flexor and superficial abdominal reflexes in man—a clinical and electromyographic study. *Journal of Gerontology* **13**, 282–288.

Mankovsky, N. B. and Belonog, R. P. (1971). Aging of the human nervous system in the electroencephalographic aspect. *Geriatrics* **26** (8), 100–116.

Miles, W. R. (1931). Measures of certain human abilities throughout the life span. *Proceedings of the National Academy of Science* **17**, 627–633.

Miller, G. A. (1956). The magical number seven, plus or minus two: some limits on our capacity for processing information. *Psychological Review* **63**, 81–97.

Morikiyo, Y., Iida, H. and Nishioka, A. (1967). Age and choice reaction time. *Journal of Science of Labour* **43**, 636–642.

Morris, Joanna D. and Thompson, L. W. (1969). Heart rate changes in a reaction time experiment with young and aged subjects. *Journal of Gerontology* **24**, 269–275.

Mowbray, G. H. (1953). Simultaneous vision and audition: the comprehension of prose passages with varying levels of difficulty. *Journal of Experimental Psychology* **46**, 365–372.

Mowbray, G. H. and Rhoades, M. V. (1959). On the reduction of choice reaction times with practice. *Quarterly Journal of Experimental Psychology* **11**, 16–23.

Myrsten, Anna-Lisa and Andersson, Karin (1973). Interaction between effects of alcohol intake and cigarette smoking. *Reports from the Psychological Laboratories*, No. 402. University of Stockholm.

Naylor, G. F. K. (1973). The anatomy of reaction time and its relation to mental function in the elderly. *Proceedings of the Australian Association of Gerontology* **2**, 17–19.

Nettelbeck, T. (1972). The effects of shock-induced anxiety on noise in the visual system. *Perception* **1**, 297–304.

Nettelbeck, T. (1973). Individual differences in noise and associated perceptual indices of performance. *Perception* **2**, 11–21.

Noble, C. E., Baker, B. L. and Jones, T. A. (1964). Age and sex parameters in psychomotor learning. *Perceptual and Motor Skills* **19**, 935–945.

Obrist, W. D. (1965). Electroencephalographic approach to age changes in response speed. In "Behavior, Aging and the Nervous System" (A. T. Welford and J. E. Birren, eds.), pp. 259–271. C. C. Thomas, Springfield, Illinois.

Onishi, N. (1966). Changes of the jumping reaction time in relation to age. *Journal of Science of Labour* **42**, 5–16.

Pierson, W. R. and Montoye, H. J. (1958). Movement time, reaction time, and age. *Journal of Gerontology* **13**, 418–421.

Rabbitt, P. M. A. (1964a). Ignoring irrelevant information. *British Journal of Psychology* **55**, 403–414.

Rabbitt, P. M. A. (1964b). Age and time for choice between stimuli and between responses. *Journal of Gerontology* **19**, 307–312.

Rabbitt, P. M. A. (1965). An age-decrement in the ability to ignore irrelevant information. *Journal of Gerontology* **20**, 233–238.

Rabbitt, P. and Birren, J. E. (1967). Age and responses to sequences of repetitive and interruptive signals. *Journal of Gerontology* **22**, 143–150.

Rabbitt, P. M. A. and Rogers, M. (1965). Age and choice between responses in a self-paced repetitive task. *Ergonomics* **8**, 435–444.

Ross, S., Vicino, F. L. and Krugman, A. D. (1960). Effects of position in a display on problem-solving ability in aged subjects. *Journal of Gerontology* **15**, 191–194.

Salthouse, T. A. (1979). Adult age and the speed-accuracy trade-off. *Ergonomics*, **22**, 811–821.

Sanford, A. J. and Maule, A. J. (1973). The concept of general experience: Age and strategies in guessing future events. *Journal of Gerontology* **28**, 81–88.

Schmidtke, H. (1976). Disturbance of processing of information. In "Psychological Aspects and Physiological Correlates of Work and Fatigue" (E. Simonson and P. C. Weiser, eds.). C. C. Thomas, Springfield, Illinois.

Schonfield, D. and Robertson, Elizabeth A. (1968). The coding and sorting of digits and symbols by an elderly sample. *Journal of Gerontology* **23**, 318–323.

Simon, J. R. and Wolf, J. D. (1963). Choice reaction time as a function of angular stimulus-response correspondence and age. *Ergonomics* **6**, 99–105.

Simonson, E. (1965). Performance as a function of age and cardiovascular disease. *In* "Behavior, Aging and the Nervous System" (A. T. Welford and J. E. Birren, eds.), pp. 401–434. C. C. Thomas, Springfield, Illinois.

Simonson, E. and Anderson, D. A. (1966). Effect of age and coronary heart disease on performance and physiological responses in mental work. Proceedings of the 7th International Congress of Gerontology, Vienna, pp. 333–336.

Singleton, W. T. (1953). Deterioration of performance on a short term perceptual-motor task. *In* "Symposium on Fatigue" (W. F. Floyd and A. T. Welford, eds.), pp. 163–172. H. K. Lewis & Co. for Ergonomics Research Society, London.

Sjöberg, H. (1975). Relations between heart rate, reaction speed, and subjective effort at different work loads on a bicycle ergometer. *Journal of Human Stress* **1**, 21–27.

Spieth, W. (1964). Cardiovascular health status, age, and psychological performance. *Journal of Gerontology* **19**, 277–284.

Spieth, W. (1965). Slowness of task performance and cardiovascular diseases. *In* "Behavior, Aging and the Nervous System" (A. T. Welford and J. E. Birren, eds.), pp. 366–400. C. C. Thomas, Springfield, Illinois.

Stelmach, G. E. and Diewert, G. L. (1977). Aging, information processing and fitness. *In* "Physical Work and Effort" (G. Borg, ed.), pp. 115–136. Pergamon Press, Oxford.

Stull, G. A. and Kearney, J. J. (1978). Effects of variable fatigue levels on reaction-time components. *Journal of Motor Behavior* **10**, 223–231.

Suci, G. J., Davidoff, M. D. and Surwillo, W. W. (1960). Reaction time as a function of stimulus information and age. *Journal of Experimental Psychology* **60**, 242–244.

Surwillo, W. W. (1961). Frequency of the 'Alpha' rhythm, reaction time and age. *Nature* **191**, 823–824.

Surwillo, W. W. (1963). The relation of simple response time to brain-wave frequency and the effects of age. *Electroencephalography and Clinical Neurophysiology* **15**, 105–114.

Surwillo, W. W. (1964). The relation of decision time to brain wave frequency and to age. *Electroencephalography and Clinical Neurophysiology* **16**, 510–514.

Surwillo, W. W. (1965). Level of skin potential in healthy males and the influence of age. *Journal of Gerontology* **20**, 519–521.

Surwillo, W. W. (1969). Relationship between EEG activation and reaction time. *Perceptual and Motor Skills* **29**, 3–7.

Surwillo, W. W. (1973). Choice reaction time and speed of information processing in old age. *Perceptual and Motor Skills* **36**, 321–322.

Surwillo, W. W. and Quilter, R. E. (1964). Vigilance, age, and response-time. *American Journal of Psychology* **77**, 614–620.

Surwillo, W. W. and Quilter, R. E. (1965). The influence of age on latency time of involuntary (galvanic skin reflex) and voluntary responses. *Journal of Gerontology* **20**, 173–176.

Szafran, J. (1966a). Age differences in the rate of gain of information, signal detection strategy and cardiovascular status among pilots. *Gerontologia* **12**, 6–17.

Szafran, J. (1966b). Age, cardiac output and choice reaction time. *Nature* **209**, 836.

Talland, G. A. (1962). The effect of age on speed of simple manual skill. *Journal of Genetic Psychology* **100**, 69–76.

Talland, G. A. and Cairnie, Jean (1961). Aging effects on simple, disjunctive, and alerted finger reaction time. *Journal of Gerontology* **16**, 370–374.

Thompson, L. W. and Botwinick, J. (1968). Age differences in the relationship between EEG arousal and reaction time. *Journal of Psychology* **68**, 167–172.

van der Valk, J. M. and Groen, J. (1950). Electrical resistance of the skin during induced emotional stress. *Psychosomatic Medicine* **12**, 303–314.

Vickers, D., Nettelbeck, T. and Willson, R. J. (1972). Perceptual indices of performance: the measurement of "inspection time" and "noise" in the visual system. *Perception* **1**, 263–295.

Weiss, A. D. (1965). The locus of reaction time change with set, motivation, and age. *Journal of Gerontology* **20**, 60–64.

Welford, A. T. (1958). "Ageing and Human Skill". Oxford University Press for the Nuffield Foundation. (Reprinted 1973 by Greenwood Press, Westport, Connecticut).

Welford, A. T. (1965). Performance, biological mechanisms and age: a theoretical sketch. *In* "Behavior, Aging and the Nervous System" (A. T. Welford and J. E. Birren, eds.), pp. 3–20. C. C. Thomas, Springfield, Illinois.

Welford, A. T. (1968). "Fundamentals of Skill". Methuen, London.

Welford, A. T. (1973). Stress and performance. *Ergonomics* **16**, 567–580.

Welford, A. T. (1976). "Skilled Performance: Perceptual and Motor Skills". Scott Foresman, Glenview, Illinois.

Welford, A. T. (1977a). Motor performance. *In* "Handbook of the Psychology of Aging" (J. E. Birren and K. W. Schaie, eds.), pp. 450–496. Van Nostrand Reinhold, New York.

Welford, A. T. (1977b). Serial reaction times, continuity of task, single-channel effects and age. *In* "Attention and Performance VI" (S. Dornic, ed.), pp. 79–97. Erlbaum, Hillsdale, New Jersey.

Wilkinson, R. T. (1965). Sleep deprivation. *In* "The Physiology of Human Survival" (Ed. O. G. Edholm and A. L. Bacharach). London, Academic Press, pp. 399–430.

Woodhead, Muriel M. (1964). The effect of bursts of noise on an arithmetic task. *American Journal of Psychology* **77**, 627–633.

Chapter 10

Factors Affecting Reaction Time:
Mental Retardation, Brain Damage,
and Other Psychopathologies

T. NETTELBECK

1. Introduction

This chapter is principally a selective review of reaction time (RT) studies in mental retardation done since Baumeister and Kellas (1968a) reviewed the literature to that time. RT research into brain damage and mental illness is also included for comparison purposes, although these areas have been reviewed elsewhere more recently: the reader is referred to Hicks and Birren (1970) and King (1975) for RT with brain damage, and to King (1969, 1975) for the effects of different mental disorders on various measures of psycho-motor activity, including RT. Nuechterlein (1977) has reviewed RT studies into schizophrenia.

Towards the end of the nineteenth century, J. McK. Cattell, E. Kraepelin, A. Oehrn and others sought to develop exact measures of sensation and discrimination, assuming that laws governing more complex mental processes would emerge from an understanding of elementary functions. Simple RT was among the measures explored at that time, on the grounds that it ought to reflect the speed with which an organism could make decisions governing adaptability. Slowed RT was reported among various psychotic categories (Wells and Kelley, 1922), but no systematic attempt was made to follow up this finding for some time. Early attempts to evaluate the relevance of RT to intellectual functioning failed to establish its predictive validity with the samples of college students and children selected. Although there was some evidence that "dull" children had slower RTs than "average or bright" children, results on the whole were thought to be disappointing (Wissler, 1901).

On the other hand, pioneer work by A. Binet to devise a more general

355

mental test appeared from the outset to be much more promising (Sharp, 1898–99). Binet argued that the properties of highly complex intellectual and emotional activity would not necessarily be derived from the study of more simple mental processes. Instead, he sought a direct measure of the capacity of the individual to cope with complex situations. Following the early success of Binet's test and the subsequent widespread development of mental tests of all kinds, interest declined in the use of *RT* to study mental activity.

However, most procedures for assessing individual differences in mental functioning are not intended to reveal the aetiology of such differences. Nor do they aim at unravelling the processes and strategies applied by mentally retarded or disturbed persons to even relatively simple tasks and situations. Rather they furnish an indication of the consequences of various cognitive deficiencies for complex activities. To date at least clinical opinion aided by mental tests has not established a precise system for identifying mental disabilities. A wide variety of categories are in common use but there is considerable overlap between them and widespread doubt concerning the reliability with which they are applied (Nathan and Harris, 1975; Finkel, 1976). Although broad categories such as "mental retardation", "organic brain syndrome", "personality disorder", "neurosis", "schizophrenia", or "psychotic disturbance" provide a rudimentary organization, they are too arbitrary to provide a satisfactory basis for the formulation and distribution of professional services to disabled persons.

Following the researches of Shakow and his associates into schizophrenia (Huston, Shakow and Riggs, 1937; Shakow, 1946) and of Scott (1940) into mental retardation, there has been a resurgence of interest in *RT* as an index of the brain's biological efficiency. Technological advances now enable more complex aspects of *RT* to be studied and to be measured very precisely. In contrast to the more general mental tests, *RT* appears to be relatively independent from socio-cultural influences. Its potential advantage for the study of mental function, therefore, is that it might provide a relatively straightforward means of objectively investigating individual and group differences inferred to be relevant to more complicated forms of behaviour.

(A) AVERAGE *RT* AND VARIABILITY

A very large body of evidence makes it clear that virtually all psychopathological conditions are accompanied by slower and more variable *RT*, whether simple or choice tasks are employed, and irrespective of the modality of either stimulation or response. Furthermore, the extent of slowing covaries with clinical estimates of the condition's severity.

A negative relationship is most usually found between *RT* and performance on intelligence tests when a wide range of measured intelligence is involved. The degree of correlation may be reduced, or even disappear, among samples with average and and above-average intelligence, and occasionally only weak relationships have been reported where a narrow range of retardation was involved. However, when compared with non-retarded, retarded persons almost always have slower RTs (Baumeister and Kellas, 1968a).

RT is more variable among retarded than non-retarded persons, both between different individuals and as far as individual performance is concerned Baumeister and Kellas, 1968b, 1968c; Dugas and Baumeister, 1968; Weaver and Ravaris, 1970; Caffrey, Jones and Hinkle, 1971; Nettelbeck and Brewer, 1976). Distributions of RT for retarded subjects are more positively skewed, encompassing a wider range of slower responses. The fastest reactions of retarded subjects do not in any case generally approach the fastest found in non-retarded, but it is the larger proportion of much slower responses that is mainly responsible for the longer average RTs found among retarded persons. Thus, inconsistent behaviour rather than an intrinsic general slowness may largely cause the poorer performance of retardates in sensory-motor tasks (Baumeister, 1968).

Some recent work has examined differences of RT and other indices of psychomotor capability with different degrees of handicap. For example, Weaver and Ravaris (1972, 1974) found substantial differences on tests that included simple and serial RT between two large groups of subjects previously classified as either mildly retarded (IQ scores ranged from 52 to 67) or moderately retarded (IQ from 36 to 51), and that about 66 per cent of subjects could be classified correctly on the basis of these tests. RTs of retarded subjects were also slower than those of hospitalized mentally ill patients drawn from a variety of diagnostic categories.

The wide diversity of neurological disorders encompassed by the term "brain damage" makes generalizations about the RT of persons so categorized difficult. Research has frequently been based on relatively small numbers, and has been hampered by the difficulties of describing experimental participants adequately. However, Miller (1970) has convincingly shown that more complex tasks involving up to eight signal alternatives are very effective for distinguishing brain damaged from uninjured subjects and, in general, RT can provide an index of dysfunction, despite the fact that on occasions quite specific and severe brain lesions may not result in any significant reduction in simple RT (Talland, 1965).

Slowed performance is usually accompanied by increased variability in both simple and complex tasks, and is a function of the severity of damage (King, 1965; Bruhn, 1970; Bruhn and Parsons, 1971). In this regard, Olbrich (1972) has noted that the rate at which damage develops appears to be more critical than the size or location of lesions. Changes in RT following minor psychosurgery or chemical or electrical intervention may be temporary, but the extent of transitory slowing is correlated with the severity of treatment (King, 1965, 1975). Sectioning the corpus callosum slows RT to a marked extent, although other psychomotor and intellectual activities may remain unaffected. Frontal lobectomy results in slower RT than non-frontal surgery. Where damage is diffuse, as for example with multiple sclerosis, RT can be slowed less than when definite localized pathology is involved.

Results from a few recent studies suggest that RT might provide an index of cerebral damage localized within one hemisphere. Dee and Van Allen (1973) compared patients with lesions restricted to either hemisphere with persons free from cerebral disease in a series of RT situations involving 1, 2, 3 or 4 possible stimulus lights. These were arranged in a semi-circle in front of the subject who responded by first releasing a "home" key, then depressing a key adjacent to the stimulus. Thus, RT could be partitioned into two components: (1) the time required to detect and identify the presence of a signal ("decision time"); (2) the time required to make a movement that turned off the signal ("movement time").

As predicted by Hick's Law (Chapter 3, pp. 74–78) average decision RT in all groups slowed as alternatives increased. Zero intercepts of the straight lines best fitting these RT data were about the same for both brain damaged groups, but considerably higher than for control subjects. This, as noted in Chapters 3, 4 and 9, can be accounted for in terms of lower "signal strength" or higher criteria for response in the brain damaged groups. Slopes for the non-damaged and right hemisphere damaged groups were parallel, but a steeper slope for subjects with left hemisphere lesions confirmed that their capacity to make decisions of this kind was reduced considerably. Left hemisphere patients also made more errors when responding. Movement times were slower for both brain damaged groups than for control subjects and slowest among subjects with left hemisphere damage.

Karp, Belmont and Birch (1971) measured the speed of vocal reactions to mild electric currents on the forearms, comparing persons with damage restricted to the right cerebral hemisphere, and persons handicapped by various musculo-skeletal injuries, but without disorder in the central nervous system. The same experiment was repeated by Belmont, Handler and Karp (1972), but using auditory stimulation. For both sensory modalities, RT among subjects with a damaged right hemisphere was abnormally long following contralateral stimulation, whereas ipsilateral stimulation produced similar results in the brain damaged and control groups.

Although damage restricted to a single cerebral hemisphere delays sensory-motor processing relevant to effector mechanisms on the contralateral side of the body, such effects usually accompany general slowing. Dee and Van Allen's brain damaged subjects were slower over all, so that injury to any part of the brain can produce general effects in RT. Benton and Joynt (1959) also found that RTs for both hands were relatively slower among persons with localized lesions, although RTs contralateral to the damaged hemisphere were affected more than those made with the ipsilateral hand.

Epilepsy has usually been found to result in a marked increase in RT, responding becoming slower with the clinically assessed severity of behavioural disorder (King, 1962; Bruhn, 1970). However, the extent to which intellectual functioning contributes to this is not clear since IQ and disease appear to be confounded in most research to date (Wagenaar, 1975). Lengthening of RT has been shown to correlate strongly with paroxysmal events on EEG records, so that RT may have potential value for monitoring the effects of anti-convulsant medication (Solis, 1974). At least one study using mentally retarded epileptic subjects (IQ scores between 50 and 70) suggests that parietal lobe dysfunction together with inadequate connections between brain hemispheres via the corpus callosum may be contributory factors (Sylvester and Roy, 1971).

Hicks and Birren (1970) have reviewed RT studies relevant to Parkinsonism. Although the results of simple RT are contradictory, all studies employing more complex tasks have found slower and more variable RT among such subjects.

The general findings from RT research involving the different forms of mental illness are much the same as described for mental retardation and brain damage. The greater number of studies in this area have been concerned with aspects and types of schizophrenia (Shakow, 1972) and, as will be discussed later on, much of this work has gone beyond a simple demonstration that such disorders are accompanied by slower and more variable RTs.

Persons suffering from chronic (i.e. long-term) schizophrenia show the most marked psychomotor slowing and a considerable literature suggests that RTs of schizophrenics can reliably be distinguished from those of normal controls, psychoneurotics and mildly retarded persons. However, more severe levels of mental retardation, including Down's syndrome, are characterized by RTs as slow as those found among chronic schizophrenics (King, 1969, 1975). Although chronic schizophrenics have usually been found to be slower than the acutely ill, there is evidence of considerable overlap between the RTs of reactive patients (i.e. those with a better prognosis for recovery) and process patients (cases where the disease is thought to be caused by organic disorder and for whom recovery is unlikely). Similarly, overlapping distributions of RTs have been found with paranoid and non-paranoid groups, and even between schizophrenics and persons with non-schizophrenic disorders, including depression, personality disorders and anxiety reactions (Nuechterlein, 1977). Nevertheless, RT can be sensitive to the severity of disorder, even within the acute category. Thus, Zahn and Carpenter (1976, as reported by Nuechterlein, 1977) found that RT reliably discriminated between acute schizophrenics who subsequently improved during four months of hospitalization and those who did not.

It may be that the diagnostic reliability of RT can be improved by using it in conjunction with techniques other than the simple and choice tasks so widely applied. For example, Cancro, Sutton, Kerr and Sugerman (1971) have reported that prediction of hospitalization for reactive schizophrenic cases is significantly improved where trials measuring RT to a tone are preceded by a trial in which the stimulus is a light. Bruder, Sutton, Babkoff, Gurland, Yozawitz and Fleiss 1975) found that simple RTs of manic-depressive patients to a brief auditory click were improved significantly by the presence of a second less intense click following the first at an interval of 15 msec, whereas RTs of schizophrenics remained unchanged.

In summary, RT may provide a useful diagnostic procedure for estimating the severity of disorder, for monitoring the effects of medication, and for distinguishing long-term schizophrenia from most other forms of psychopathology, excepting moderate to severe mental retardation or severe brain damage. Comparing contralateral and ipsilateral RTs can help establish whether brain damage is predominantly in, or restricted to, one hemisphere. However, it is clearly also the case that diffuse forms of damage can result in similar RT outcomes. As Nuechterlein (1977) has pointed out, the value of the RT method is limited when identifying those individuals for whom early intervention might accomplish most—namely less severe cases of disorder. Whether positively skewed distribution of RT are found for psychopathological conditions other than mental retardation does not appear to have been explored systematically. This should be done since measures of central tendency do not reliably distinguish between RT distributions associated with various disorders. At this stage, RT procedures cannot provide a substitute for mental testing backed by clinical judgement, although there is certainly a role for measures of psychomotor performance, including RT, as an adjunct to tests of psychological functioning.

2. Information processing and mental disorder

In recent years, much RT research has been directed towards an understanding of the nature of the various disorders, rather than towards attempts at classification. The trend has been to try and identify the locus of deficit in terms of those components of the *RT* process responsible for the overall slower performance.

Difficulties of interpretation arise because different workers have begun from different theoretical viewpoints, adopting procedures that reflect these. Furthermore, with the notable exception of the work concerned with schizophrenia begun by Shakow about 50 years ago (Shakow, 1972), very little research has been formulated within a systematic framework and pursued in the long term. Nevertheless, problems of interpretation notwithstanding, some advances have been made, and some conclusions can be drawn.

Berkson (1960a,b,c) appears to have been the first to try to determine in a series of experiments which particular mechanisms contributing to the speed of *RT* cause slower performance among retarded persons. He concluded that intelligence is not related to factors governing the speed of stimulus identification nor to the planning of the response. Instead, he argued that slower *RT*s were due to motor components responsible for "initiating and executing" movement. It is not altogether clear which aspects of motor functioning Berkson intended to implicate. However, his conclusion has commonly been taken to mean that the slower performance of retarded persons on simple perceptual-motor tasks can be accounted for almost entirely by factors associated with motor disability. Dingman and Silverstein (1964) supported this explanation.

Several writers, however, have argued that the tasks used in these researches required some degree of perceptual-motor coordination in terms of stimulus discrimination, response selection and the guidance of movement (Baumeister and Kellas, 1968a; Groden, 1969; Nettelbeck and Brewer, 1976; Lally and Nettelbeck, 1977). As discussed later, evidence points also to the importance of variables which affect attention.

The main variables on which research has been done will be considered in turn.

(A) STIMULUS INTENSITY

Compared with that of normals, *RT* of retarded subjects is usually changed disproportionately by the intensity of the reaction stimulus, although this interaction between IQ and intensity has not always been found (Baumeister and Kellas, 1968a). It is also not clear to what extent those interactions found have been increased by "floor effects"—that is, average *RT*s of non-retarded subjects are in any case closer to some optimum level than those of retardates.

Intensity factors appear to influence expectancy and attention, so that *RT* depends on the particular experimental arrangements that precede response, as will be discussed later. However, research has not yet succeeded in specifying why these influences produce the effects they do. Some of the findings can be summarized as follows:

(i) Simple *RT*s of retarded and non-retarded subjects become faster and variability in individual *RT* decreases as signal intensity is increased above threshold levels. The relationship is not linear. Among non-retarded subjects *RT* approaches an asymptote at higher levels of intensity, but as yet no work involving retarded participants has explored the nature of the *RT* function for a wide range of stimulus intensities.

(ii) Increasing the intensity of the warning stimulus in a simple *RT* task results in slower *RT* among retarded subjects, apparently because of an interaction with the reaction stimulus, so that the perceived intensity of the latter is reduced (Baumeister and Kellas, 1968a). The same outcome has been obtained by presenting the warning stimulus without interruption until the reaction stimulus occurs (Baumeister and Kellas, 1968a; Baumeister and Wilcox, 1969), although at least one earlier study has reported the opposite result (Terrell and Ellis, 1964).

(iii) The effects of intensity on *RT* are not only influenced by the range of stimulation selected, but by the order in which the subject encounters different intensity values. Quite different and sometimes conflicting outcomes have been reported for different experiments, depending on whether stimuli were presented within blocks of equal strength or random order (Baumeister and Kellas, 1968a; Kellas, 1969a; Kellas and Baumeister, 1970). Kellas (1969a) has demonstrated that it is not simply the case that retarded subjects are more susceptible to the arousing properties of stronger stimulation. He presented stimuli at different intensities in random order. *RT* was faster at higher levels of intensity, the effect being more marked among retarded subjects (mean IQ 58). However, contrary to expectations if more intense prior stimulation produced an arousing effect, *RT* to the weakest stimulus (30 dB) was significantly *slower* following a signal of 90 dB than when the preceding trial involved either 60 or 30 dB. At this stage no single explanation has emerged that can successfully encompass all available data.

(iv) The influence of both intensity and interval between warning and stimulus appears to depend on the nature of the response required: Kellas (1969b) found that the influence of these factors on the variability of *RT* was greater when the response was to press, than when it was to release a key.

(B) DISCRIMINATION *RT*

In several recent experiments the discrimination model outlined in Chapter 2 has been applied to the investigation of perceptual sensitivity and its influence upon *RT* among mentally retarded young adults. Subjects judged which of two lines of markedly different length and side by side was the shorter, responding by pressing one of two keys. The stimulus lines were covered after a varying period of time by a second figure that provided no information about the discrimination required, and therefore served as a backward mask. It was assumed that this procedure limited the registration of sensory input to the time between stimulus and mask onsets. It was argued that if the discrimination required only a single inspection, the stimulus duration at which performance was virtually free from error provided a measure of "inspection time" (λ), and that λ should be independent of the speed with which a response is registered.

Nettelbeck and Lally (1976) have reported correlations of -0.92 and -0.89 between IQ scores and two separate estimates of λ obtained from ten young adult subjects. IQ ranged from 47 to 119, seven subjects having scores below 85. Subsequently, Lally and Nettelbeck (1977) obtained a correlation of -0.80 between IQ and λ, using a sample of 48 subjects whose IQ scores ranged from 57 to 138. These correlations were considerably influenced by the markedly different performances of non-retarded and retarded subjects, and the strength of association between IQ and λ among the latter. The index did not, however, discriminate between a group of average intelligence (IQ 90 to 115) and one of above average (IQ 116 to 130). On average, λ was about 100 msec for the non-retarded and 200 msec for the retarded subjects.

Results obtained by Nettelbeck and Lally (1979) suggest that longer λ is not attributable to a slower rate of perceptual development. Average estimates from four groups of children (7, 8, 9 and 10 years old) having average intelligence were 147, 142, 137 and 139 msec, respectively. These values were very close to the mean of 130 msec found in this study for a sample of university students, whereas that for young retarded adults (mean IQ 69) of the same chronological age was 256 msec.

With respect to the children in this study, the outcome is at variance with the limited experimental work that has been done with children on tasks involving tachistoscopic recognition and visual search. Here, findings have generally been taken to mean that speed of perceptual processing increases with age. As pointed out by Wickens (1974), however, available data can be interpreted in terms of learning effects, rather than as due to changes in central limitations. Nettelbeck and Lally's (1979) finding of very similar perceptual speeds among normal adults and children as young as seven years supports this proposal. Furthermore, the form of RTs at the different stimulus exposure durations suggested that non-retarded adults and children were doing the task in similar ways, although overall RT was much slower among the children. The average pattern of RTs among retarded subjects was different, however, as discussed below.

The general pattern of RT among non-retarded subjects in these studies, including where children have been tested, can be summarized as follows: mean, variability and positive skewness of RT for correct responses have increased as the stimulus figure was exposed for shorter durations. RTs for errors have been significantly slower than for correct responses and particularly so when the probability of error was very low, that is, at long stimulus exposure durations. Among retarded subjects, on the other hand, means and standard deviations of correct RTs have been relatively constant, irrespective of the time for which the stimulus figure was exposed. On occasions, mean RT in this group has actually been faster than that among non-retarded subjects—usually at shorter stimulus durations. Incorrect RTs have been somewhat slower, but not markedly different from correct, and skewness scores have been consistently lower than those found among non-retarded subjects. A small number of individuals have not conformed to this general trend, the pattern of their RTs resembling more closely those made by non-retarded persons. However, in by far the majority of cases functions relating RTs for correct responses to stimulus duration have been well defined by flat straight lines.

In short, RTs from retarded subjects in these experiments have revealed trends opposite to those usually characterizing mental retardation—namely, slower responding, and more variable, more positively skewed distributions of responses. These findings raise questions concerning the "demand characteristics" that define the experimental task for the different comparison groups. The validity of the comparison of retarded and non-retarded samples rests on the assumption that subjects in different intelligence groups do not differ systematically in the way in which they approach the discrimination involved—for example, with regard to motivation or understanding. Yet these results suggest that retarded and non-retarded subjects are using different strategies.

This suggestion receives support from an interpretation of the data in terms of Vickers' accumulator model set out in Chapter 2. This predicts patterns of RT like those among non-retarded subjects when decisions follow the accumulation of high levels of information. Where insufficient evidence is obtained from one inspection of sensory input, accumulation continues until the criterion is reached by sampling non-informative, "noise-produced" differences between the objectively equal lines in the masking figure. At the shorter stimulus exposures samples will result in minimal additions to stored information, so that accumulation to criterion must take longer. Thus, the shortest exposures give rise to the longest RTs, but with RT becoming faster and less variable as stimulus duration is extended.

When the likelihood of making an error is high, incorrect RTs are at least as slow as correct, there being little difference between the weight of evidence accumulated favouring one alternative or another. As the probability of error falls, however, incorrect RTs become still longer, errors only occurring as a consequence of "noisy" observations, and hence prolonged sampling sequences. Thus, errors are slower than correct responses when criteria are higher.

Patterns like those seen in the retarded group, however, are predicted by Vickers' model where subjects adopt criteria that are considerably lower. Functions are less steep because fewer observations are required, even when the probability of error is high. The lower the criterion adopted, the more similar RTs for incorrect and correct responses become, and the sequence of inspections preceding the decision becomes shorter. Distributions of RT show less variability and are less skewed since decisions are being based on consistently fewer inspections and there is consequently less opportunity for very long times.

What causes these RT differences in this task is not clear. The RT behaviour of non-retarded subjects seems counter intuitive, it being less efficient in one sense to continue sampling in the absence of hard evidence. Whether this is a strategy reflecting adaptively successful behaviour in the more usual situation in which viewing time is not limited remains to be determined; an answer to this question might also help establish why retarded subjects respond as they do.

Results from unpublished studies indicate that it is not a simple case of retarded subjects not trying as hard as non-retarded, adopting lower criteria and sacrificing accuracy for speed. Encouraging subjects to slow their reactions, or to withold a response until a decision has been considered carefully, does not influence the estimates of λ obtained to any marked extent. Nor does it seem likely that poor concentration or lower focal awareness can account for the outcome; the eye-surround on the tachistoscope used in the experiments and the isolated experimental situation should reduce extraneous distractions. Subjects have been very carefully trained and instructions were designed to maximize preparatory set. Furthermore, most subjects participated with enthusiasm, showing every indication that they had understood what was required and that they were trying hard to do it.

Dr N. O'Connor has suggested (personal communication) that retarded subjects may have sometimes responded to the detection of the presence of the stimulus figure—leading to simple rather than discriminative RT. Certainly, their RT patterns suggest that these subjects have failed to process input on a significant proportion of trials with short stimulus exposure. This would seem to imply an insufficiently formulated plan directing sampling in a coherent fashion rather than a deficient sampling mechanism, since any such impairment should result in slower RT, not faster RT as found in these experiments.

(C) DISCRIMINATION FACTORS IN CHOICE REACTIONS

Using an eight-choice task in which stimulus lights were either close—directly above the corresponding response key—or distant—2.8 m from the response keys—Nettelbeck and Brewer (1976) found that when compared with non-retarded, RTs of mildly retarded young adults (mean IQ 68) for ring and middle fingers were disproportionately slower than those for index and little fingers. When stimulus lights were at a distance from the subject, RT differences between retarded and non-retarded participants were further increased for all responses except those made with the little fingers. However, RTs among retarded subjects were substantially faster with all fingers for trials in which the stimulus light was the same as in the immediately preceding trial. Such a "repetition effect" (see Chapter 4) was also found in the non-retarded group, but the savings made were appreciably less. Thus, retarded subjects were very dependent upon certain critical features in the experimental situation, in particular lights which were either at the ends of the display, or next to a midline between the fourth and fifth lights, or lights which were repetitions of the preceding stimulus.

Subsequent experiments replicated these results, establishing that they could not be attributed to peripheral motor factors. A comparison of the RTs for the different fingers in a series of two choice tasks established that any differences due to motor difficulties were only minor (Brewer, 1978).

Since response requirements remained unchanged in the distant condition, the only change to the stimulus display being to move it away from the subject, RT differences between distant and close conditions should be attributable to perceptual factors. Taken together, the results suggest that the slower RTs found in the retarded group were due in part to a slower average rate of accumulating information among these subjects, rather than to some general non-specific slowness which would have added a constant time factor to every finger.

Brewer and Nettelbeck (1977) have demonstrated that retarded young adults (mean IQ 69) in an eight choice task benefit from a centre line dividing the row of eight lights into two rows of four. Among non-retarded subjects, RTs to lights in the middle of the display were little affected when the centre line was removed. However, reactions of retarded subjects made with the index and middle fingers were slowed substantially and became more variable. RTs to repeated stimuli were faster, confirming that repeated stimulus-response sequences aided responding, even when the midline was absent, although the advantage of both the midline and a repetition trial together was greater than that obtained from either cue by itself.

With the midline removed, reactions by retarded subjects with the index fingers were slower as the distance of the stimulus in the ongoing trial from that in the preceding trial increased. This "proximity" effect was also found in the non-retarded group but was not nearly as marked. The results suggest that in the absence of the centre line retarded subjects relied more on the position of the previous stimulus and its associated response when locating stimuli in the middle of the array. Thus, even in a task in which the stimulus-response relationships are quite direct, mildly retarded subjects are very reliant upon the presence of readily available perceptual cues. This suggests that their longer RTs were not simply due to an impaired ability to focus on relevant aspects of the stimulus situation, a conclusion supported by Silverman's (1975) demonstration that retarded adults (mean IQ 58) are able to take advantage of stimulus redundancy.

Zeaman and his associates (Zeaman and House, 1963; Fisher and Zeaman, 1973; Zeaman, 1973) have shown that differences between retarded and non-retarded subjects in discrimination are due to retardates taking longer to learn what are the relevant dimensions of the task (e.g. aspects such as position, shape, or colour.) Once attention is drawn to these, learning rates are much the same as found among normals. The tests used in this work, however, have been very simple. As far as choice RT is concerned, retarded subjects are still slower to respond, even when apparently making use of aspects in the task that improve performance significantly. As yet, no research has systematically explored the effect of sustained practice on the RT of retarded subjects, but it is probably over-optimistic to suppose that emphasizing critical perceptual cues will permit retarded persons to overcome all problems that they encounter when learning new concepts.

Discrimination is involved not only between different stimuli but also between different responses. Results from a study by Kirby, Nettelbeck and Tiggemann (1977) illustrate that retarded persons can require more time than non-retarded to achieve this. RTs of retarded adolescents (average IQ 50, average age 18 years) and controls of above-average intelligence were measured under different response conditions to the same two stimulus lights. Conditions included one in which responses were made with both index fingers; another required that the index and middle fingers of the preferred hand be used, thereby increasing the discrimination required between responding members.

In the retarded group, mean RT was slower and more variable for the condition requiring the more demanding response organization. Responses that were the same as the previous response were faster than responses that were not repeated, a result in line with the general finding that the likelihood of such effects increases as the relationship between stimulus and response becomes more complex (Bertelson, 1963). Neither of these results were found for the non-retarded subjects, among whom RTs remained virtually unchanged.

It is even possible that under some circumstances additional time is spent, not in central response selection, but in confirming that the response to be made is appropriate. Observations of their subjects by Brewer and Nettelbeck (1977) in an eight choice task suggested that retarded subjects were looking at the finger required by a response before making it, thereby lengthening RT. Testing this possibility, they found that when retarded subjects (mean IQ 63) were prevented from seeing the fingers while responding, RT decreased by an average of about 130 msec. Errors increased from about 6 per cent when the hands were visible to about 10 per cent when they were covered. These effects were most marked for ring and middle fingers. Among non-retarded controls, however, RT remained almost identical whether the hands were covered or not. Thus, part of the longer RTs of retarded subjects appeared to be used to check the response visually before it was made, particularly where the identification of the responding fingers was most difficult.

(D) RESPONSE PROCESSES AND RT

Findings for choice reactions by retardates may be illustrated by two experiments reported by Lally and Nettelbeck (1977). In one of these, subjects responded with the same finger regardless of the number of stimuli involved in the task. Lights were arranged in a semi-circle so that each was the same distance from a "home" key. To respond, the subject first released the home key, then moved to depress a key adjacent to the stimulus light that was on. RT was partitioned into "decision time" and "movement time".

Decision times for both groups of subjects became longer as the number of stimulus alternatives increased, the effect being significantly more marked in the retarded group. The slopes of regression lines for retarded and non-retarded groups respectively corresponded to information processing rates of 6.2 and 9.1 bits/sec. Intercept values were 230 msec in the retarded and 180 msec in the non-retarded group, this small difference perhaps reflecting the relative motor component in lifting the finger to release the home key. Slopes derived from movement times were close to zero in both groups. However, the difference between zero intercepts of the movement time functions for the two groups was 160 msec, a large difference.

In another experiment involving the same subjects the RT tasks were repeated but with response alternatives increasing with stimulus alternatives—i.e. a different finger was used for each stimulus involved. On this occasion processing rates were 3.7 bits per sec among retarded subjects, compared with 5.7 among non-retarded. The effect of complicating response selection was therefore to halve the average rate of information transmission found in the retarded group in the previous experiment, whereas in the non-retarded group it was reduced less—by about 40 per cent.

These results raise the question of how far longer RTs among retarded subjects are to be attributed to purely motor factors, and how far to decisional processes guiding action. There is anatomical and behavioural evidence that motor factors are in part responsible for the general finding that RTs of children with Down's syndrome (mongolism) are slower and more variable than those of other retardates (for a review see Johnson and Olley, 1971). Thus, the weight of the brainstem and cerebellum of such persons is on average only about two thirds of that expected from normals (Crome, Cowie and Slater, 1966). Frith and Frith (1974) have summarized observations from a variety of sources that Down's retarded persons are slower to develop ambulatory skills, clumsy throughout childhood and adolescence, and poorer at performing motor tasks involving feedback control like arm movements, finger tapping and rotary pursuit tracking.

Motor deficit also appears to be a critical aspect of Cerebral-Palsy (CP). Rees (1971) has measured RTs for affected (contralateral to the damaged hemisphere) and non-affected hands, made by CP young adults with life-long unilateral lesions, and IQ scores in the low average range (75 to 104). A special responding apparatus suited to these subjects enabled Rees to obtain separate measures of decision and movement times in situations involving 1, 2, 4 and 6 stimulus alternatives. Although overall RTs were much slower than would be found in a non-handicapped population, the slopes of RT functions were similar for the affected (8.1 bits per sec) and non-affected hand (6.6 bits per sec). These values are within the range of 5 to 8 bits per sec usually observed in normal populations (see Chapter 3). In the same way, slopes for decision and movement times separately were similar for both affected and non-affected hands, and compared favourably with research involving university students. For each function, however, the zero intercept for the affected hand was appreciably higher than that for the non-affected hand. Thus, cortical centres involved in the execution of coordinated movement may be of more importance to an understanding of CP than structures responsible for either perception or the initiation of movement.

While there is evidence to suggest that the speed of making a movement can be slowed by specific brain lesion or maldeveloped critical structures within the central nervous system, it is questionable whether this is generalizable to all cases of brain damage. Parsons and Bruhn (1973) compared brain damaged patients approaching middle age (heterogenous with respect to aetiology, extent and site of damage) with alcoholics and orthopaedic patients in a two choice task requiring a response to one alternative but not the other. Inter stimulus-interval (ISI) throughout a session was either 2.5 or 4 seconds, with conditions balanced for order. Parsons and Bruhn argued that perceptual requirements and response execution were identical in both ISI conditions and could not therefore influence RT differentially. The outcome that brain damaged subjects were not only slower but disproportionately so when the ISI was four seconds, was attributable to some factor of response initiation. What this factor was, is not clear. It might be argued that memory factors or central executive processes influencing vigilance and attention could account for the result. In any case it does not seem to have been due to motor limitation but to some more central factors.

Brewer (1978) has attempted to measure directly the contribution of motor components to RT of mildly retarded adults (mean IQ 68). In one condition of an eight choice task, young adult subjects responded to stimulus lights that were positioned immediately above the response keys. In a second condition the fingers were stimulated directly by a vibrating key, thereby minimizing stimulus discrimination and response organization factors. The apparatus was similar to that used by Smith and described in Chapters 3 and 4.

RTs in both groups were much faster, markedly less variable, and differences between fingers substantially reduced when the fingers were stimulated directly. There was substantially more improvement among retarded subjects, the average difference between the groups being reduced from about 170 msec when lights were involved to only 40 msec in the vibrotactile condition. The small remaining differences, together with more positive skewness in the RT distributions of retarded subjects, suggested possible delays in their peripheral motor system. However, the results make it clear that central decision processes antecedent to action are the major components of RT in a task of this kind, and that the speed with which a movement is actually executed is only a minor determinant of retarded RT.

Wade, Newell and Wallace (1978) have provided a complementary comparison of the influence of response complexity on the decision and movement time components of simple and choice RT among retarded adults (mean IQ 33) and non-retarded persons of the same chronological age. Response complexity was defined in terms of the amplitude and precision of movement (Fitts, 1954). Subjects lifted a stylus from a home key in response to a stimulus (decision time), moving to contact a target of varying size and distance from the starting point (movement time). Movement times became slower in retarded and non-retarded groups as response complexity increased. The slopes of regression lines in the simple and choice situations were much steeper among retarded subjects, suggesting that their slower overall RTs were largely attributable to response organization factors. It is clear, however, from studies of aimed movements (see Welford, 1976) that the slowing is unlikely to be due to motor factors, but to perceptual and decisional processes involved in guiding the response.

Four further lines of evidence regarding response factors deserve to be noted:

(i) Fleer (1972) reports that movement times initiated by retarded subjects (mean age 16, IQ 61) without an accompanying auditory signal were slower than when stimulation was involved. Furthermore, average movement time was faster when the intensity of the accompanying signal was raised. A possible interpretation is that slower ballistic movements by retarded persons may be caused in part by a lower capacity for self arousal but, since Fleer did not employ non-retarded controls, this hypothesis remains untested.

(ii) Bruininks (1974) concluded from studies of various motor abilities that retarded children are probably more impaired with regard to fine than gross motor abilities.

(iii) RT of retardates is slowed more than for normals under conditions emphasizing stimulus uncertainty (Baumeister, Wilcox and Greeson, 1969). Mulhern and Baumeister (1971) manipulated task complexity by varying the relative frequency of occurrence of four stimulus lights, while controlling compatibility between stimulus and response arrangements independently. (Compatibility was "high" when symbols identifying stimulus alternatives were consistent with those identifying response keys, and "low" when they were not.) When compared with non-retarded subjects, RTs of retarded (mean IQ 63, mean age 19) became slower as complexity increased, and showed relatively greater impairment when the stimulus-response arrangement was not compatible.

A similar study by Morelan (1976) has examined the relative effects of mental age and IQ on RT by comparing retarded with younger non-retarded children at about the same level of cognitive development. Results confirm that RT is slowed by increasing complexity, and suggest that mental age is the more important determinant. It is difficult, however, to accept Morelan's conclusion that his results raise doubts about retarded subjects being less efficient at processing information in the various situations discussed above. While one can only agree that it is essential to explore the contribution that developmental factors may make to these psychological processes (e.g. Jones and Benton, 1968), it should be borne in mind that many of the retarded participants in the research described here have been adults. It seems unlikely that such persons would ever show marked improvement in this regard as a consequence of further development.

(iv) Turning from retardates to schizophrenics, Broen (1968) has argued that schizophrenic deficit is primarily the consequence of increased competition between alternative available responses, so that an appropriate response has a lower probability of occurring. Thus, problems of "attention" are regarded as synonymous with problems of response selection, rather than stimulus selection (e.g. McGhie, 1969), or a slowed rate of information processing (Yates, 1966).

Karras (1973) has attempted to examine the distinction between input and response interference factors by manipulating stimulus-response complexity and response competition independently. Complexity was varied by using both a simple and a two choice auditory *RT* task. The subject responded either with the hand on the same side as the ear receiving the signal (low competition), or with the contralateral hand (high competition). Groups involved were acute non-paranoid schizophrenics, depressives, and non-depressive patients having neuroses or character disorders.

Although slower overall, *RT*s of schizophrenics were not disproportionately slower than those in the other groups, either in simple-choice differences, or under competition in the simple task. Karras did find that contralateral responding produced significantly slower *RT* among schizophrenics in the choice condition, so that response competition did appear to augment the overall schizophrenic deficit where stimulus-response requirements were more complex. However, taken together, the results suggested that a slower rate of stimulus processing was not involved, that response interference was not a sufficient explanation by itself, and that presumably more than one factor was responsible.

Karras's conclusion is therefore in line with an earlier and more specific proposal made by Venables (1965)—that chronic schizophrenics may be characterized by two different kinds of slowness. Venables noted that although *RT* among schizophrenics can be influenced by stimulus factors, like intensity, modality, uncertainty of occurrence, and by the complexity of the response required, differences between schizophrenic and normal populations remain remarkably constant irrespective of condition, schizophrenics always being slower (see also Sutton and Zubin, 1965; King, 1976). This suggested one speed component that can be influenced by reducing delays in the accumulation of information, but also the presence of a residual slowness in the effector system, perhaps reflecting some inherently slower periodicity in corticothalamic structures, that is therefore not amenable to change.

Marshall (1973) has also sought to resolve the issue of whether slower schizophrenic *RT* is essentially a stimulus analysing or a response selection process. Three groups comprising schizophrenics, neurotics and prison inmates (as a control for institutionalization) completed a series of continuous card-sorting tasks in which uncertainty was increased across stimulus and response values independently. Marshall argued that sorting time per card would increase with increasing stimulus uncertainty if stimulus selection was a difficulty; if, on the other hand, response selection was a problem then the relationship between sorting time and response uncertainty should reflect this.

Sorting time per card increased as a function of both increasing stimulus and increasing response uncertainty, but with the latter a much greater source of difficulty. Both outcomes were more marked in the schizophrenic group, these subjects also being considerably slower than either neurotics or prisoners, who did not differ from one another. The result could not be attributed to the effects of medication taken by the schizophrenic patients.

While this outcome appears to be inconsistent with any theory that seeks to account for slower schizophrenic RT in terms of any single defect, Nuechterlein (1977) has pointed out that this is not necessarily the case. Broen (1968) regards even initial scanning, prior to the controlled direction of attention, as reflecting a response aspect of information processing, so that in this sense his theory can account for both of Marshall's findings. It should be noted, however, that broadening the theory in this way makes it more difficult to test. The issue of the role of executive attentional processes is discussed below in the concluding section.

(E) TEMPORAL FACTORS

Baumeister and Kellas (1968a) have outlined evidence showing that the RTs of retarded subjects are changed more than those of non-retarded by the manipulation of various temporal parameters of the stimulus situation. The essential features of this approach are derived from methods pioneered by Shakow and his group when assessing schizophrenia (Huston, Shakow and Riggs, 1937), and involve varying the length of the preparatory interval (PI) between the warning signal and the reaction stimulus in a simple RT procedure. Since this work in the field of schizophrenia has been pursued systematically for a long period of time, and since the results from this area of research are complex, it is best to summarize them before proceeding to an evaluation of findings relevant to mental retardation.

As discussed in previous chapters, the RT of normal subjects is influenced in different ways depending on whether PIs of different length are presented within a regular series (e.g. a block of trials at a consistent PI, followed by a block at a different PI, and so on), or whether PI is varied randomly from trial to trial (i.e. an irregular procedure). Within a regular procedure, RT typically increases gradually as PI is lengthened. Within an irregular procedure, RTs are substantially slower at shorter PIs than is the case in a regular series, but become somewhat faster following longer PIs, providing that the subject is well practised. If RTs for regular and irregular series are plotted as a function of PI, then a "crossover" effect is sometimes found; at very long PIs, RTs in the irregular procedure can actually be faster than with regular presentations—but not with normal subjects until the PI is beyond about 15 sec, or even as long as 25 sec (Olbrich, 1972).

It is widely considered that PI effects involve a central expectancy factor (Poulton, 1973), an interpretation that owes much to the theorizing of Shakow (see, for example, Shakow, 1962). Briefly, it is thought that as the PI within the regular procedure is lengthened, it becomes increasingly difficult for the subject to focus attention, so that irrelevant distractions interfere with the maintenance of a mental set that is appropriately task-directed. Thus, RTs become longer. When the presentation series is irregular, then adequate expectancies about signal occurrence develop less effectively at shorter PIs. Again, therefore, RT is slowed.

Early work by Shakow (e.g. Rodnick and Shakow, 1940) established that chronic schizophrenics are not only much slower than normals overall; they do not respond more rapidly in a regular procedure than in an irregular one when PIs are longer than about 2 to 5 sec. In other words, a cross-over effect may be found among schizophrenic patients at very much shorter PIs than is the case for normals. Subsequent research has confirmed that this effect is most marked in the case of process schizophrenics, but less characteristic of reactive patients. The cross-over effect is not attributable to fatigue or to occasional lapses in attention (Nuechterlein, 1977), and appears resistant to contextual influences within the arrangement of trials (Bellissimo and Steffy, 1975).

Zahn, Rosenthal and Shakow (1963) have shown that within an irregular procedure schizophrenics are markedly influenced by the PI to the immediately preceding trial (termed the PPI). It seems, therefore, that the strength of the cross-over effect is, among severe schizophrenics, the consequence of inappropriate attention to prior stimulation; just as attention is not sustained in a regular series as the PI becomes longer, resulting in a slower RT, so attention is not sustained in the irregular procedure for the time required when the PPI is long. Because a very long PPI is more likely to be followed by a shorter PI, RT to the latter will be slower on average. Similarly, faster RTs will be found when PPI is less than PI.

However, why attention is affected by stimuli earlier than the imperative stimulus is not known. Uncertainty because of the irregular procedure about when a signal will occur may play some part, but this cannot be the only reason. This has been shown by Zahn (1970) who found that when advance information was provided about whether a PI in an irregular series would be short or long, RT of schizophrenics was not improved more than that of normals, although both groups did become faster. Other experiments have confirmed that reducing stimulus uncertainty regarding spatial position (Zahn, 1970), or the modality in which the stimulus is to be presented (Sutton and Zubin, 1965; Waldbaum, Sutton and Kerr, 1975) does not result in greater shortening of *RT* among schizophrenics than among normal subjects.

The picture is complicated by an additional finding, that schizophrenics benefit more than non-schizophrenics from trials within an irregular procedure when the PPI equals the PI, their *RT*s being even faster than on trials when PPI is less than PI (Nideffer, Deckner, Cromwell and Cash, 1971; Nideffer, Neale, Kopfstein and Cromwell, 1971). Although this outcome is consistent with an attentional deficiency hypothesis—in that a repetition of stimulus conditions should aid expectancy or set—it poses an awkward contradiction. Since the PPI always equals the PI in a regular series, then *RT* under these circumstances should not become slower than with an irregular procedure.

Steffy and his co-workers have addressed this problem, beginning with an experiment in which a run of four identical PIs was embedded repeatedly within a much longer irregular order of trials (Bellissimo and Steffy, 1972). Within the four regular trials *RT* at first improved but then become slower over successive trials. This effect was most marked among the more severely handicapped process schizophrenics, the groups for which the cross-over effect was found. Bellissimo and Steffy interpreted this outcome as reflecting two processes: firstly, an initial enhancement because a single repetition improves predictability; secondly, a deterioration resulting from the rapid accumulation of inhibition held to accompany continued repetitions—they termed this influence a "redundancy-associated deficit".

This interpretation differs from Shakow's (1962) position, that poorer schizophrenic performance reflects an inability to maintain set and exclude distractible aspects of the situation. It receives some support from a study by Steffy and Galbraith (1974) in which a regular sequence of four trials was again embedded within an irregular procedure, but with an intertrial interval (ITI) of either 2 or 7 sec. A greater cross-over effect was obtained for the shorter ITI, suggesting that the longer interval permitted the more effective dissipation of inhibition. This outcome would not be expected if the cross-over effect reflected an inability to maintain attention, as Shakow has argued. However, as Nuechterlein (1977) has pointed out, there are some aspects of Steffy and Galbraith's results that are not consistent with their hypothesis. For example, *RT* was actually fastest in that condition where the effect of inhibition would have been expected to be most marked. For the time being then, the question as to whether set or inhibitory constructs account satisfactorily for schizophrenic *RT* performance remains open. It is possible, of course, as Nuechterlein (1977) has recognized, that both processes may exert an influence.

These procedures have not as yet been as systematically applied to the study of mental retardation, and little attention has been paid to the cross-over effect among retarded subjects. Nevertheless, the same broad relationships outlined above have been found with retarded subjects (Baumeister and Kellas, 1968a).

When presentation is regular, RTs become slower with increasing PI. With an irregular procedure, optimum RT may follow either longer PIs, or those at the middle of the PI range, if this is extensive. Most studies before 1968 found that differences between normal and retarded groups with the irregular procedure were less when PIs were longer than when shorter; that is, the difference between the groups was least under optimum conditions. Kellas (1969a) and Gosling and Jenness (1974) have confirmed these findings. Both these papers also reported that PPI influenced RT among retardates. RT was faster following a short PPI than following a long, and fastest when the PPI–PI sequence was short-long. Similarly, RT was slowest following a long-short sequence.

Very little work of this kind has involved brain-damaged patients. Olbrich (1972) did not find any tendency for a cross-over effect using PIs up to 25 sec among RTs from twenty brain-damaged subjects. Although they responded much more slowly than normal controls, the patterns of RT obtained from the two groups were virtually identical in both regular and irregular procedures. If replicated, this finding would confirm that the cross-over effect found with chronic schizophrenics is not simply a consequence of slower performance.

RTs of children with average IQ but mild chronic cerebral dysfunction have been found to increase more than those of normal children of the same age when PI is decreased using an irregular condition (Czudner and Rourke, 1970, 1972). Although Rourke and Czudner (1972) found that the differences had largely disappeared by the time the children reached 10 to 13 years of age, it is not known whether children suffering from more severe brain damage that impaired intellectual functioning would recover to the same extent.

A few studies have compared serial RTs in retarded and non-retarded subjects. Baumeister and Kellas (1967) required retardates (average IQ about 60) and university students of the same age to identify (R_1) a figure (S_1), and then to respond to a tone (S_2) by releasing a key (R_2). S_2 followed R_1 at varying intervals. RT in both groups slowed when the R_1–S_2 interval was 200 msec; retarded participants showed marked delays at 500 msec, and some delay at up to 2 sec. Baumeister and Kellas (1967) concluded that these results were in line with those from other studies which suggested that the attentional processes of retarded persons are less efficient. They hypo-thesized that because retardates persevered in concentrating on the initial stimulus, they were less prepared to respond when a further, unexpected stimulus occurred (see Chapters 4 and 6).

Joubert and Baumeister (1970) examined the extent to which retarded (IQ about 60) and non-retarded subjects developed expectancies influencing RT from temporal cues by manipulating the probabilities with which different R_1–S_2 intervals occurred. At the shortest intervals, RTs to S_2 were faster in both groups when these intervals occurred more frequently. However, compared with non-retarded, retarded subjects had markedly slower RTs following the shorter intervals, even when the probabilities of occurrence for these were high, and the development of expectancies therefore favoured. Joubert and Baumeister concluded that retarded subjects were therefore less able to develop preparatory sets appropriate to existing temporal cues. It is possible, however, that these subjects were continuing to monitor R_1 to a more marked extent, so that less attentional capacity was available when S_2 occurred.

In both studies outlined above the demonstration of refractoriness relied on comparisons between RTs to S_2 at different R_1–S_2 intervals. RTs to S_1 and S_2 could not be compared directly, since two different kinds of response were required. However, Friedrich, Libkuman and Hawkins (1974) com-pared RT_1 and RT_2 directly, with R_1–S_2 intervals presented either in random order or in regular blocks of intervals having the same duration (250, 500 and 750 msec). While retarded subjects (IQ about 60) were slower overall, a lengthening of RT_2 was found only at the R_1–S_2 interval of 250 msec and with the irregular procedure for either retarded or non-retarded subjects. Expectancy effects in all other regular or irregular conditions were about the same for both groups. Since a regular presentation procedure reduced RT_2 among retardates, even at 250 msec, the development of appropriate expectancies can apparently overcome delay due to a limited central processing capacity. A subsequent study by Friedrich and Hawkins (1975), but using somewhat more retarded subjects (average IQ 45), found that RT_2 was slower than RT_1 with an R_1–S_2 interval of 250 msec, regardless of whether presentation was regular or irregular, suggesting that a more limited information processing capacity among the subjects in this experiment could not be compensated by gains from expectancy about the next signal presentation.

Despite differences in overall RT among chronic schizophrenic and mildly retarded participants in research involving the manipulation of PI, similar trends point to the possibility that similar attentional processes are involved—or in other words, that diverse forms of psychopathology can result in similar outcomes. Because of the many kinds of damage, injury and presumed impairment underlying these different conditions, it seems untuitively unlikely that the same structural aspects of processing, such as specific sensory storage or response systems, could be responsible in all cases. An alternative, therefore, is that diverse forms of psychopathology have similar functional effects.

Although it is difficult for many reasons to obtain homogeneous samples and equate comparison groups for severity of condition, future work should attempt to examine retarded, mentally ill and brain damaged samples under identical conditions, with a view to defining more precisely similarities and differences in the performance of different groups. An early experiment by Tizard and Venables (1956) did attempt such a comparison, including a retarded group together with chronic schizophrenics and university graduates. RTs in the retarded group fell between those of the other two, but the outcome was not satisfactory for comparison purposes. For example, no significant cross-over effect was found among retarded subjects, despite one among schizophrenics (PI 4 sec) and graduates (PI 25 sec).

The study of serial reactions introduces an aspect not present in the other research involving temporal variables, since two or more responses are required in rapid succession. Future research should examine whether differences in refractoriness between retarded and non-retarded samples are attributable to a tendency for retarded persons to spend more time monitoring the outcome of a response. If this were the case, it would demonstrate that poorer attention is not always due to distractibility by irrelevant stimulation, and that under some circumstances slower RT may reflect the manner in which attention is distributed.

(F) SENSORY AROUSAL

It has been widely suggested that variations in non-specific activity in the central nervous system should accompany changes in arousal, the relationship between arousal and performance being described by an inverted-U function (see Chapter 9, and Welford, 1976, Chapter 7). According to this model, improved performance accompanies increased central nervous activity up to an individual's optimal arousal level, but beyond this level the channel capacity of the brain is progressively reduced, so that performance deteriorates.

Berkson, Hermelin and O'Connor (1961) have established that Down's syndrome and non-mongoloid retardates register shorter periods of alpha blocking to the initial presentation of a short flash of light. In line with theories that alpha blocking is a concomitant of the "orienting reflex" towards novel stimulation (Sokolov, 1963), this result suggests lower general responsiveness among retardates.

Although many authors have postulated that mental retardation is characterized by lower than average levels of cortical arousal, few RT studies relevant to this question have included independent indices of arousal level, relying instead on the dependent variable to reflect assumed changes in maintained central activity following stimulation. As Baumeister and Forehand (1973) have pointed out, this makes the interpretation of findings difficult, since experimental results are by no means unequivocal. Only studies employing independent measures of biological activity are therefore discussed below.

Comparing six year old Down's syndrome children (IQ less than 50) with normal children of the same age, Wallace and Fehr (1970) found that evoked heart rate (HR) and skin resistance (SR) in the retarded group were less reactive to environmental events. These children also showed lower levels of non-specific cortical activity, as indicated by fewer spontaneous HR and SR fluctuations (Lacey and Lacey, 1958; a more recent review of Lacey's physiological attention theory is provided by Hahn, 1973). Wallace and Fehr found good evidence of a relationship between these measures of biological activity and RT: those persons having faster RT also registering more spontaneous HR and SR fluctuations. Thus, the subnormal children had slower and more variable RT than normals, and lower measures of arousal.

It is well established that HR falls immediately prior to the onset of expected stimulation (Lacey, 1967; Obrist, Webb, Sutterer and Howard, 1970), RT and HR being positively correlated. The extent to which HR decelerates increases with advancing age throughout childhood, as does speed of RT (Stroufe, 1971). Obrist et al (1970) have hypothesized that this relationship reflects some central attentional process arising out of the integration in both autonomic activity and somatic activity that prepares the organism to cope with environmental events.

Evidence that retarded persons may have more difficulty in preparing to respond comes from an investigation of cardiac deceleration and simple RT by Krupski (1975), using retarded young adults (mean IQ 70) with university students as controls. She found much less marked deceleration in HR of retardates when compared with non-retarded subjects prior to the occurrence of the reaction stimulus, in this case the offset of a light after a PI of either 4, 7 or 13 sec (regular procedure). In fact, following the longest PI, Krupski found a negative correlation between HR and RT in her retarded group. These results suggest that retarded subjects were less able to use the warning stimulus as a preparation for the reaction to follow.

Similar results have been obtained for adult retardates (mean IQ 57) by Runcie and O'Bannon (1975), and for brain damaged war veterans by Holloway and Parsons (1972). These studies found either no relation between HR and *RT* or a negative one. Brain damaged participants also displayed an impaired ability to habituate various components of their orienting responses, particularly alpha blocking, to novel stimuli (Holloway and Parsons, 1971). These findings suggest that retardation and brain damage may result in a lack of coordination between somatic and autonomic activity, so that while some reflexive awareness accompanies the presence of a signal, corresponding attention and preparation linked to expectancy do not occur, so that the subject is less ready to respond.

These studies raise a number of questions that require further research. The role of developmental factors in the maturation of internal readiness to respond is not yet known, since no study made so far has employed normal subjects with the same mental age as retarded participants. Although the attentional processes studied in the HR deceleration experiments might reasonably be assumed to be related to the accurate judgement of time duration, rather than to distractibility, this remains to be demonstrated. There is evidence in the literature suggesting that retarded persons are more susceptible than normals to distracting factors, and tend to distribute their attention over more possible sources of stimulation (O'Connor and Hermelin, 1971). Also, an extension of the Holloway and Parsons studies (1971, 1972) by Callan, Holloway and Bruhn (1972) seems to confirm that brain damaged patients were more distracted than either chronic alcoholics or orthopaedic patients by events irrelevant to the task in hand.

Turning to schizophrenics, Cromwell (1975) describes a recent unpublished study by Bradley, examining HR changes among process schizophrenics and normal subjects which accompany simple *RT*. The comparison was restricted to a PI of 6 sec within both regular and irregular procedures.

HR among normals slowed prior to a signal in both the regular and irregular series, deceleration being associated with faster *RT* in the regular condition and slower *RT* in the irregular condition. This suggests that HR was reflecting some preparatory tendency that resulted in faster *RT* where signal occurrence was predictable. Among schizophrenics, however, the results were different. As would be expected from studies of the cross-over effect, faster *RT* was observed for the irregular series, and this was accompanied by decelerating HR. In the regular condition, where signal onset was predictable, HR oscillated between acceleration and deceleration, this fluctuation being accompanied by slower *RT*. What this outcome means is not known. The different possible interpretations are that it reflects fluctuations in attention associated with deficient use of redundancy (Bellissimo and Steffy, 1972), or that it reflects anxiety about having to deal with relevant information (Kaplan, 1974, cited by Cromwell, 1975).

Essential procedural differences between Krupski's study of mental retardation and Bradley's study of schizophrenia preclude any useful comparison of the results. However, the methods used hold considerable promise of providing an index of momentary changes in attention that can be examined in association with *RT*.

(G) *RT* IN SHORT-TERM MEMORY: APPLICATION OF STERNBERG'S MODEL

The Sternberg paradigm for the study of *RT* in short-term memory has been discussed in Chapter 7. The subject is first required to memorize a short list of items, termed the "positive set". He then decides whether or not a test stimulus presented subsequently was a member of the positive set. The subject responds as quickly as possible, for example by pressing one of two keys, and the latency of the response is measured. In this situation, *RT* rises in approximately linear fashion as the number of items in the positive set is increased. The slope of this function is thought to reflect retrieval operations, representing the rate at which a person can compare a test stimulus with memorized material. The height of the ordinate at the intercept indicates the time required for other factors such as the perception and encoding of the test stimulus, and the formulation and execution of a response. Such processes are assumed to be constant, regardless of the number of items constituting the positive set, and can be examined separately using experimental procedures designed to manipulate various perceptual and response processes independently.

Four such investigations comparing retarded and non-retarded subjects have appeared in the literature (Dugas and Kellas, 1974; Harris and Fleer, 1974; Silverman, 1974; Maisto and Jerome, 1977). All studies have found that intercept values of choice *RT* function obtained with retarded subjects were substantially larger than those found with non-retarded subjects of the same chronological age. This outcome therefore suggests differences between populations in the perceptual encoding or response formulation or both.

Maisto and Jerome (1977) included a procedure developed by Sternberg (1967) and Bracey (1969) and described in Chapter 3, for examining time spent encoding the test stimulus prior to the central scanning process. This involved degrading the quality of the test stimulus, it being assumed that any resulting increase of encoding time would increase intercept values. They found that *RT*s in this condition were slower overall, with retarded subjects being affected more, and therefore apparently requiring substantially more time to encode the degraded stimulus material.

The validity of this conclusion has been questioned, however. Silverman (1978) and Maisto (1978) have drawn attention to significant negative correlations between slope and intercept values for retarded subjects in the available studies. Such correlations suggest that the memory search measured by the slope and other processes measured by the intercept are not independent. Although Chase (1978) has pointed out that statistical correlation between two variables does not necessarily imply processing interdependence, since separate stages may all be influenced by some other process, such correlations would be unlikely to be negative.

Other problems exist when attempting to interpret the outcome of these experiments. Harris and Fleer (1974), Dugas and Kellas (1974) and Maisto and Jerome (1977) have reported slope functions for retarded groups that were considerably steeper than those in the non-retarded groups. In the Harris and Fleer experiment an even steeper slope was found for a brain-damaged group. This is therefore evidence that central scanning processes of retarded and brain-damaged persons are less efficient than those of non-retarded. Since there is no evidence of this among younger non-retarded children of the same mental age, a permanent impairment rather than retarded development would appear responsible. This suggestion is supported by an experiment by McCauley, Kellas, Dugas and DeVellis (1976) that examined the effects of training on memory search in children. Subjects were taught to memorize a list of digits by a serial rehearsal procedure (Dugas and Kellas, 1974), whereby the contents of the list were gradually extended, previous items being rehearsed before adding a new item. Although their subjects could not be classified as retarded, half had IQ scores below 95, and these were compared with children having above average intelligence. Slope values for the two groups differed significantly. McCauley and co-workers compared these results with those of Dugas and Kellas, demonstrating a systematic, inverse relationship between the IQ scores of participants in the two experiments and both slope and intercept aspects of choice RT. They also found that training the less bright subjects to use a serial rehearsal strategy when memorizing the positive set did not shorten RT substantially. Thus, IQ related differences in choice RT in the experiments did not appear to be due to the manner in which items had been stored and presumably resulted from differences in the scanning process itself.

Once again, however, there are grounds for questioning these conclusions. In Silverman's (1974) study, the average slope among non-retarded subjects was actually somewhat steeper than that for the retarded subjects. A close scrutiny of the experiments referred to above reveals a number of awkward anomalies with respect to the results for non-retarded participants when these are compared with other studies in the literature (Cavanagh, 1972). Data published by Swinney and Taylor (1971) comparing a heterogeneous sample of middle-aged asphasics with normals of the same age and level of education suggest that the asphasics adopted strategies that were qualitatively different from those of the normals; one cannot be certain that this has not happened in other studies.

Any attempt to resolve these differences is hampered by the fact that different investigations have involved subjects from different chronological and mental age groups, and have not been even approximately uniform with respect to stimulus materials or procedure. The much slower RTs measured by Dugas and Kellas (1974) for both retarded and non-retarded groups reflect their requirement that before responding the subject move his hand from a resting position midway between the two response keys. Silverman (1974) displayed the positive set continuously, so that the task did not involve a memory scan as defined by Sternberg (1975). Slopes of RT functions in this study were uncharacteristically steep, perhaps reflecting the rate at which subjects looked back and forth between the test stimulus and the set, rather than the speed with which items stored in memory were processed. Only Harris and Fleer's (1974) experiment involved conditions comparable with the existing body of research using non-handicapped samples, and results for the three non-retarded groups included in the study were similar to those published previously for adults—intercepts between 300–400 msec slopes about 40 msec per item (Cavanagh, 1972), and for children—slopes as for adults, intercepts beyond 600 msec (Hoving, Morin and Kovick, 1970; Maisto and Baumeister, 1975). However, Harris and Fleer did not publish correlations between intercept values and slope functions, and in view of significant correlations between these variables in the other studies one cannot be confident that they were independent here.

Two other difficulties with research of this kind to date should be noted. First, with the exception of Harris and Fleer (1974) who used four different set sizes, experimenters have relied on only three points from which to derive slope functions. A close examination of available data suggests that in some instances it is at least questionable whether these should be described as linear. Second, insufficient attention has as yet been paid to the significance of errors. Error rates have been reported for groups only and there might well be considerable individual differences in this regard, especially among retarded persons. In their first experimental session Harris and Fleer (1974) found that retarded subjects made significantly more errors (11.9 %) than non-retarded samples (3.6 %), so that some doubt arises as to whether some retarded participants had memorized material as effectively as their non-retarded controls. Scott (1971) has reported that error rates and RT among retarded adolescents were not significantly correlated in a modification of Sternberg's procedure that he has applied to the study of short-term recognition memory and mental retardation. Despite a number of critical differences between Scott's methods and those followed in the four studies reviewed above, this finding is worth noting. It implies that different processes may be involved in the speed and accuracy of retarded subjects, whereas a frequent finding among non-retarded subjects is that speed and accuracy are related by way of some common process (Pachella, 1974).

Sternberg (1975) has compared results typical of his research with those from an unpublished study by Checkosky involving 48 schizophrenics and 24 alcoholics, hospitalized for an average of 15 and 8 months, respectively. Intercept values for both patient groups were considerably higher than those for normal students—at about 600 msec, schizophrenics were much slower than alcoholics or either of the retarded groups in Harris and Fleer's study. On the other hand, slope functions were virtually the same in all three groups—between 34 and 37 msec per item.

Whether these findings reflect important differences between the processes of retarded and schizophrenic populations remains to be clarified. Future research should address the difficulties discussed above before further attempts are made to apply Sternberg's procedure to the study of mental dysfunction. The limited memory span of most retarded persons clearly limits the maximum size of positive set that can be used where mental retardation is involved, and this may also be an important consideration in other areas of psychopathology. In this regard, the simple and readily discriminable cartoon-like pictures from children's books adopted as stimulus items by Scott and his associates (Scott, 1971) may prove more appropriate than stimulus material used so far. A thorough examination of accuracy and its relationship with the speed of responding must be undertaken. It is necessary to ensure that the speed-accuracy operating characteristics of different populations follow the same trends, and that, in spite of perhaps fundamental differences in the relative levels of these functions, subjects are operating in a comparable way. Pachella (1974) has discussed statistical approaches to the error problem that might provide a starting point for future research.

3. Cognitive influences

Two broad assumptions underlying RT studies of information processes are of particular importance where groups or individuals categorized as different in mental function are compared.

First, all subjects, irrespective of category, must understand what is required, and no subject should be influenced or disadvantaged by factors in the experimental situation not accounted for—for example, insufficient practice, fatigue or undetected sensory or physical disabilities. Considerations relevant to these assumptions of understanding, RT stability, and the influence of specific disabilities are discussed briefly in the first three sections to follow.

Secondly, it is assumed that RT reflects basic mental capacities, and will not be biassed in an uncontrolled way by the intentions of the subject. In other words, unless the experimental procedure is designed to examine cognitive aspects of performance determining motivation and attention, all participants should be equivalent in these respects. The usual way of achieving this is to ensure that few errors are made and that the error rates of different participants are the same. What is known about this assumption is outlined in the fourth section below, before discussing the major areas of motivation and attention.

(A) THE RT TASK IS EASILY UNDERSTOOD

Although it is usual practice that subjects meet certain learning criteria before participating in research, some persons appear to demonstrate a deeper or more complex understanding than others. Even with willing volunteers, differences between handicapped and non-handicapped persons that may affect persistence in the task situation are sometimes apparent. Thus, Brewer (1976) has emphasized that whereas his non-retarded subjects invariably realized that RT is measuring some basic ability, retarded subjects frequently did not seem to have understood the significance of what they were being asked to do. What effect this issue has upon the outcome of research is not known, and it could be argued that such a limitation is intrinsic to the psychopathological condition. It should be recognized, however, that to the extent that this is so, it becomes difficult to distinguish between alternative hypothetical influences like "understanding", "cooperation", "motivation" or "attention".

Handicapped subjects tested are often a selected group in the sense that only those able to do the task can be included. It is reasonable to assume that such selection will exclude those who are most likely to make errors due to misunderstanding. The number of retarded persons rejected is seldom included in published accounts of research. Personal experiences suggests, however, that for persons with IQ scores between 50 and 80 the rejection rate is likely to be as high as about 20 per cent, particularly if subjects are required to produce independent finger movements. Nothing is known about the rejection of psychiatric subjects, but it is probable that, as for mental retardation, research findings have underestimated average differences existing between handicapped and normal populations. For example, Shakow and his group have generally limited selection to schizophrenic patients rated as most cooperative (Nuechterlein, 1977).

(B) RT IS RELIABLE AND STABLE ACROSS TIME

After reviewing more than twenty years of visual choice RT research, Teichner and Krebs (1974) concluded that RT is not subject to marked improvement, providing the subject is practised thoroughly beforehand, and particularly when a lights-keys paradigm is employed. None of the studies examined included retarded, brain damaged or psychiatric samples and very little is known about practice effects among such subjects. Fatigue is probably not a problem, since a typical experimental session would not last for an inordinately long period. However, to the extent that subjects were not sufficiently practised when experimental sessions began, estimates of RT would be misleadingly long.

Huston *et al.* (1937) did measure RTs of 38 schizophrenic patients on three separate occasions at intervals of three months, finding a similar improvement by the third test period in each of three different types of reaction—simple visual and auditory and visual discrimination. The authors attributed this outcome to practice, but could not make comparisons with normal performance since control subjects only participated on a single occasion. It is certainly possible, however, that mentally ill patients require more sustained practice than normals in order to achieve maximum performance.

Benton and Blackburn (1957) reported little change in either simple or two-choice RTs of non-psychotic brain damaged subjects within 30 trials, although neither situation could be considered demanding, either in terms of session length or task complexity. Halbert (1976) found no evidence of change in RT among twenty mildly retarded adults (mean IQ 66), either within 30 trials in a three choice situation, or between five successive experimental sessions each of 30 trials. A preliminary analysis of unpublished research still in progress by Kirby and Nettelbeck has not found any evidence of practice effects in RT data collected from 18 institutionalized retarded subjects (mean IQ about 50) on four successive occasions, each consisting of 192 trials, in an eight choice task. However, average RT did vary considerably across sessions. Bruhn and Parsons (1971) found no significant evidence of changes within a session lasting about 40 minutes in the mean RT of either an adult group with heterogeneous neurological disorders, or a control group of orthopaedic patients. Within-subject variability decreased slightly in the latter group, remaining unchanged for the brain damaged subjects.

However, Kellas and Baumeister (1970) found that simple RT improved during the course of 75 trials when signals were of low intensity. Normals showed most improvement early in the session, whereas retarded subjects improved later. It may therefore be the case that in RT, as in other areas of performance, retarded subjects require much longer periods of practice— and perhaps practice following special training—before they achieve optimum performance. Morelan (1976) also found that RTs of both retarded and non-retarded subjects improved with practice during the course of 300 trials in a four choice task. Scott (1971) has reported a steady decline in the average *RT* of retarded subjects, beginning with the initial session and persisting throughout many subsequent sessions, even after regular and prolonged training in the task for three or four days before entering the experimental condition.

It should also be borne in mind that a decision that no change in performance has accompanied practice, depends upon the experimenter accepting a null hypothesis. If, as is usually the case, a fairly conservative significance level has been applied, this will not constitute a sufficiently stringent test, particularly where small samples are involved.

A reasonable conclusion is that the effect of practice on *RT* among various psychopathological groups has not yet been determined. A systematic examination of trends following sustained practice is required, involving not only retarded, but also brain damaged and psychiatric subjects.

(C) PARTICIPANTS WILL BE EQUIVALENT WITH RESPECT TO SPECIFIC SENSORY OR PHYSICAL MOTOR DISABILITIES

A major problem for research is that many retarded persons have handicaps of other than an intellectual nature. Cases of specific brain damage, or involving psychopharmaceutical treatment, or various sensory and physical handicaps are not uncommon and can be very difficult to detect. Frequently, the person concerned is unaware of the problem, or does not wish to relate it. Personal records maintained by schools and institutions for the retarded are notoriously inadequate in this regard. While the influence of such factors cannot be specified, it seems most likely that their presence would exacerbate differences between retarded and non-retarded samples.

Where psychosis is involved it is now frequently the case that drugs will already be being administered, especially if schizophrenia has been diagnosed. Some studies have reported improvement in *RT* among schizophrenics following medication (for example, Freedman, Deutsch and Deutsch, 1960), while others have found no significant changes (Held, Cromwell, Frank and Fann, 1970). Nuechterlein (1977) has examined the small number of investigations into drug effects on *RT* among schizophrenics, concluding that the available evidence is not sufficient to permit a conclusion at this time.

(D) ERROR RATES ARE CONSTANT BOTH WITHIN AND BETWEEN SAMPLES

To date, no systematic analysis of errors made by retarded, brain damaged or psychiatric subjects in *RT* research has appeared in the literature. The number of errors occurring is usually too small to permit separate analysis and incorrect responses are therefore omitted from RT calculations. Some authors have provided group average error data, but error rates seldom exceed 5–6 per cent. Where statistical tests have been applied, the absence of a statistically significant result has most often led to the acceptance of the null hypothesis and of the assumption that no critical difference exists.

This assumption is almost certainly not justified in many instances where psychopathology is involved. Hemsley and Hawks (1974) have reported that the time taken by both acute and chronic schizophrenic subjects to complete a sorting task influenced the number of errors associated with the correct response, as opposed to irrelevant errors. Induced speeding led to more errors and slowing to less. At least one study involving substantial samples has found that long-term psychiatric patients made *fewer* errors on average than normals in both simple and choice RT tasks (Jankowski, Grzesiuk and Markiewicz, 1970). Thus, the slower RT of psychiatric subjects may in part reflect a more strongly developed bias to avoid error, as has been noted in Chapter 9 for older people.

Many studies have found at least marginally higher error rates as well as slower RT among retarded subjects, but this is not to say that such subjects try less hard than normals. It is possible that the level of maximum accuracy attainable is lower among some retarded persons, and that this is related in some way to their lower RT. Furthermore, samples may be heterogeneous in this regard, a large proportion of errors being made by a small number of "atypical" individuals. Scott (1971) did not find a statistically significant correlation between RT and errors made by retarded subjects, and therefore suggested that separate processes may underly speed and accuracy for these subjects. This suggestion should be treated cautiously, however, since a significant correlation is difficult to demonstrate in a small sample, particularly when the range of errors made within the group is small.

Brewer and Nettelbeck (1979) have examined errors made in two conditions common to several experiments (Nettelbeck and Brewer, 1976; Brewer and Nettelbeck, 1977; Brewer, 1978). As mentioned earlier, in one condition an eight choice display was immediately adjacent to the response keys; in the other it was 2.8 m from the response keys. Combining data from the different experiments provided 816 instances of each stimulus in the close condition and 1632 occurrences of each in the distant condition.

In the close condition there were virtually no differences between error rates among retarded (3.7%) and non-retarded subjects (3.9%). The pattern of errors was the same in both groups. Most errors involved middle and ring fingers and were made with fingers next to those that should have been used. However, when the stimulus display was placed at a distance from the subject, more errors were made by retarded (5.7%) than by non-retarded subjects (4.9 %). Differences involving index and little fingers were small, but retarded subjects made considerably more errors when responding with middle and ring fingers. Once again, adjoining fingers were mainly involved, although there was more scatter in this regard in the retarded group, suggesting greater confusion between response alternatives at the selection stage.

On the basis of these data it seems likely that if comparisons between retarded and non-retarded samples were based upon a sufficiently large number of trials, differences in the accuracy of responding would become apparent. The possibility exists that research to date has actually under-estimated the problems that retarded subjects have with stimulus discrimi-nation and response selection.

A low error rate is usually accepted as indicating that the subject has understood what is required, is trying hard to comply with instructions and is concentrating on the task. Although it is almost always the case that subjects make some errors, these are assumed to be due to random fluctuations in cognitive factors influencing performance and not to sys-tematic differences between subjects or samples in this regard. However, as Pachella (1974) has pointed out, the relationship of speed to accuracy of performance is such that, when accuracy is near maximum, small differences in accuracy could reflect substantial differences in the intention of subjects.

(E) MOTIVATION

When considering motivation, it is useful to differentiate between some hypothetical drive factor that may vary in ways intrinsic to the handicap-ping condition, and the extent to which different groups, psychopathological or otherwise, respond to the presence of reward or punishment. It is likely that the influence of the former construct could never be distinguished from that of poor understanding or inadequate attention, since these various aspects of behaviour can each be regarded as reflecting some all-pervasive conceptual impairment. Thus, an experimenter could not assume that handicapped and normal populations were equivalent with respect to motivation, a difference in this regard being in effect an essential aspect of the handicapping condition.

Motivation in the second sense, however, is a more flexible factor, defined in terms of the nature of the relationship between reinforcement and change in behaviour: reinforcement is attributed to "motivation", as opposed to constructs such as "arousal", or changes in "attention" only when it is necessarily contingent upon a specified behaviour.

A number of studies have shown that retardate RT performance can be influenced by the manipulation of incentives, including praise and reprimand, sensory stimulation and money (Baumeister and Kellas, 1968a). There is also some evidence that *RT* among brain damaged persons can be reduced by motivating instructions, information about performance and mild electric shock (Hicks and Birren, 1970).

More recently, Hasazi and Allen (1973) have demonstrated that to be effective reinforcement must be contingent, i.e. linked directly to improved *RT* performance. Reinforcement can also, to some extent, offset the less effective influence of lower levels of signal intensity. Furthermore, these authors found no differences due to the effects of motivational and attentional variables between the *RT*s of a group of familial retardates (aged about 12 years, IQ about 50) and a group matched for age and IQ but diagnosed as brain damaged. However, none of these studies made comparisons with non-retarded performance, and it should therefore not be assumed that motivating factors are equally effective with retarded and non-retarded persons.

Several experiments have found that aversive stimulation, for example loud noise or electric shock, produces more improvement in *RT* of schizophrenics when compared with normals (Nuechterlein, 1977). However, the extent of improvement is related to initial performance in the absence of reinforcement, so that differential improvement between handicapped and non-handicapped samples may not reflect motivational differences so much as a reduced opportunity among normals to improve. The results of studies into the effects of social reinforcers, such as praise, encouragement and censure, have been equivocal, some suggesting more improvement among schizophrenics than normals, but others not supporting this.

Lang and Buss (1965) have argued that improvement by reinforcement of *RT* among schizophrenics is attributable to enhanced attention; stimulation is assumed to alert the subject so that critical cues in the signal are attended to more effectively. A discussion of how this might occur is to be found in Chapter 9. Results obtained by Halbert (1976) support this proposal. Choice *RT*s of retarded (mean IQ about 65) and psychiatrically disturbed persons became significantly shorter as the level of controlled exercise undertaken on a bicycle ergometer was increased, whereas *RT*s of normal subjects remained virtually unchanged throughout the study. Improvement was not attributable to practice. Furthermore, only the decision component of *RT* showed improvement, movement time being stable throughout.

Although Karras (1962, 1968) has established that improved *RT* among schizophrenics in the presence of aversive stimulation is dependent upon the opportunity to avoid such stimulation, this finding does not rule out an attentional hypothesis. It could be that unavoidable noxious stimulation increases arousal beyond some optimal level so that performance deteriorates compared with the condition in which avoidance is possible.

The issue is not whether motivation plays some part—it obviously must—but whether retarded or mentally ill persons are on the whole insufficiently motivated when compared with normals. Personal experience suggests that this is unlikely and that most subjects try very hard to meet research requirements, irrespective of whether they are handicapped or not. Jankowski *et al.* (1970) even found evidence among a large sample of chronic schizophrenics hospitalized for more than ten years that such patients can be more cooperative in *RT* tasks than normals, tending towards higher accuracy.

As Nuechterlein (1977) has pointed out, explanations for overall changes in *RT* in terms of motivational differences are not readily extended to incorporate those studies, already considered above, in which temporal and sequential variables have been found to influence *RT*. On the other hand, a theory of attentional dysfunction like that of Broen (1968) can account for both sets of findings, relating improvement in *RT* to the suppression of competing attentional processes. A recent experiment by Steffy, cited by Cromwell (1975), suggests that even if motivation is involved, an attentional factor is still critical. Steffy found that although training and verbal reinforcement reduced overall *RT* of schizophrenics to within normal range, the cross-over phenomenon established previously for these subjects remained. Improvement in *RT* following verbal urging might represent a motivational effect, but the finding that schizophrenics continued at the same time to be impaired to a much greater extent than normals at shorter PIs in an irregular procedure suggests an attentional deficit.

(F) ATTENTION

As will now be clear from the wide body of research reviewed in this chapter, no single theory yet developed can readily account for all the evidence available from *RT* studies of various psychopathological groups. Different theories of schizophrenic performance have suggested various explanations, including a defective ability to develop and maintain an appropriate set (Shakow, 1962), differences in arousability (Venables, 1965), a generally slower rate of information processing (Yates, 1966), deficient response selection resulting in greater interference between alternative responses (Broen, 1968), faulty selective processing with impaired ability to inhibit extraneous stimulation (McGhie, 1969) and the more rapid accumulation of inhibition accompanying information redundancy (Bellissimo and Steffy, 1972). Some evidence exists to support each of these explanations (Nuechterlein, 1977).

It is also the case that different explanations have been required to account for different outcomes from studies of mental retardation and brain damage. Constructs put forward include poorly developed expectancy (Baumeister and Kellas, 1968a), differences in arousal and motivation (Baumeister and Kellas, 1968a; Baumeister and Forehand, 1973), slower accumulation of information relevant to stimulus and response discrimination (Nettelbeck and Brewer, 1976), slower perceptual speed (Lally and Nettelbeck, 1977), slower stimulus encoding (Maisto and Jerome, 1977) and difficulties in response organization (Wade *et al.*, 1978). In short, every distinguishable concept relevant to attention (Moray, 1969), including orientation and selection, concentration, search, activation and preparedness has been invoked to account for the wide diversity of findings.

Taken as a whole, therefore, the evidence suggests that every component of information processing is affected in most cases where mental disorder is established, presumably because such disorder influences the executive processes responsible for directing attention to different aspects of the total process. There may be subtle differences between various disorders in the extent to which different component operations are influenced, and even fairly specific effects where specific brain damage is involved. This has not yet been established, however, and even in such cases an overall impairment also appears to be involved. Furthermore, it is possibly the case that where evidence of a deficit has not been found, the experimental task employed was either inappropriate to the aim of the research or not sufficiently complex to highlight the deficit.

This conclusion resolves conflicts about the nature and magnitude of *RT* impairment found by different researchers; if some flexible executive process is involved then an experimental outcome will largely be dependent upon aspects of the information process emphasized by the procedures employed. For example, the tasks used by Nettelbeck and Brewer (1976) required relatively complex visual discrimination but responses involving short finger movements of a predominantly ballistic nature. Since such responses are largely programmable in advance (Klapp, 1975), it could be argued that differences between retarded and non-retarded groups in Nettelbeck and Brewer's research were in stimulus discrimination. On the other hand, the task employed by Wade *et al.* (1978) involved motor responses that required progressive adjustments and control over the termination of movement. These guidance aspects of movement could not be pre-programmed, so that *RT* differences could have reflected processing difficulties in response organization.

This viewpoint draws on theorizing by Hochberg (1970), Neisser (1976) and Norman (1976), all of whom acknowledge the influence of F. C. Bartlett. Attention is controlled by active, flexible, anticipatory processes that govern search and rehearsal strategies, or encoding procedures, in a selective fashion. Selection is determined by the active construction of concepts which rely upon accumulated past experience, while incorporating new experience and influencing the interpretation of ongoing events. According to Neisser (1976) there are no separate mechanisms of "attention"; instead there are the cognitions by means of which we choose and anticipate what we will perceive. This position therefore draws a distinction between fixed aspects of processing structures, such as specific sensory storage, or response systems, and the executive processes ("schemata", "plans", "feedforward") that control their functioning.

In these terms, the essential problem of mental dysfunction, whether mental retardation, mental illness, or some more specific brain damage is involved, is regarded as a deficiency in the capacity of the individual to develop learning in new situations, rather than as impairment within particular aspects of the brain's fixed structure. O'Connor and Hermelin (1978) appear to have reached a similar conclusion, arguing that to view information processing as a sequence of stages, from sensory encoding, through decision and response organization mechanisms, to action, is misleading. Rather, theorizing must take account of the interaction that exists between all aspects of the system.

This conclusion is unpalatable for at least two reasons. First, it lacks precision and parsimony—it can account for every finding in terms of some attentional deficiency, but without clarifying the nature of the deficiency. Secondly, deficiencies related to conceptual faculties would seem likely to result in a more pervasive handicap than would a specific sensory impairment. For both reasons, the task of improving the general performance of persons suffering brain damage and mental disorder is likely to be more difficult than would be the case if specific mechanisms underlying deficiencies in information processing abilities could be identified.

Nevertheless, on the basis of available evidence the conclusion reached here seems inescapable. Before further progress can be made towards an understanding of the influence of the various psychopathologies on RT we must come to grips with the problem of how the basic mental processes of those persons concerned are organized. To this time, theories of information processing applied to the study of mental handicap have been concerned to isolate various operations intervening between stimulus and response, but without detailing the control processes involved. No adequate theory of control processes in mental handicap has yet been formulated.

Several other problems remain. For instance, it has yet to be established whether more complex RT procedures can distinguish between different psychopathological conditions for which overall measures of RT appear similar. The nature of processing difficulties that characterize the various psychopathologies is not resolved. The possibility certainly exists that impairment in RT is a consequence of some central executive function that controls all aspects of perceptual and response organization, so that performance will reflect the relative processing requirements of components within any particular task, and will vary between experimental situations rather than between different types of handicap. Nevertheless, it seems clear that various aspects of *RT* are sensitive to different handicapping conditions and certainly to severity of impairment and, if that is so, *RT* can be a useful and perhaps sometimes crucial aid to diagnosis.

References

Baumeister, A. A. (1968). Behavioural inadequacy and variability of performance. *American Journal of Mental Deficiency* **73**, 477–483.

Baumeister, A. A. and Forehand, R. (1973). Stereotyped Acts. *In* "International Review of Research in Mental Retardation" (N. R. Ellis, ed.), Vol. 6, pp. 55–96. Academic Press, New York.

Baumeister, A. A. and Kellas, G. (1967). Refractoriness in the reaction times of normals and retardates as a function of response-stimulus interval. *Journal of Experimental Psychology* **75**, 122–125.

Baumeister, A. A. and Kellas, G. (1968a). Reaction time and mental retardation. *In* "International Review of Research in Mental Retardation" (N. R. Ellis, ed.), Vol. 3, pp. 163–193. Academic Press, New York.

Baumeister, A. A. and Kellas, G. (1968b). Distribution of reaction times of retardates and normals. *American Journal of Mental Deficiency* **72**, 715–718.

Baumeister, A. A. and Kellas, G. (1968c). Intra subject response variability in relation to intelligence. *Journal of Abnormal Psychology* **73**, 421–423.

Baumeister, A. A. and Wilcox, S. J. (1969). Effect of variations in the preparatory interval on the reaction times of retardates and normals. *Journal of Abnormal Psychology* **74**, 438–442.

Baumeister, A. A., Wilcox, S. and Greeson, J. (1969). Reaction times of retardates and normals as a function of relative stimulus frequency. *American Journal of Mental Deficiency* **73**, 935–941.

Bellissimo, A. and Steffy, R. (1972). Redundancy-associated deficit in schizophrenic reaction time performance. *Journal of Abnormal Psychology* **80**, 299–307.

Bellissimo, A. and Steffy, R. A. (1975). Contextual influence on crossover in the reaction time performance of schizophrenics. *Journal of Abnormal Psychology* **84**, 210–220.

Belmont, I., Handler, A. and Karp, E. (1972). Delayed sensory motor processing following cerebral damage: II. A multisensory defect. *Journal of Nervous and Mental Disease* **155**, 345–349.

Benton, A. L. and Blackburn, H. L. (1957). Practice effects in reaction time tasks in brain injured patients. *Journal of Abnormal and Social Psychology* **54**, 109–113.

Benton, A. and Joynt, R. (1959). Reaction time in unilateral cerebral disease. *Confinia Neurologica* **19**, 247–256.

Berkson, G. (1960a). An analysis of reaction time in normal and mentally deficient young men. I. Duration threshold experiment. *Journal of Mental Deficiency Research* **4**, 51–58.

Berkson, G. (1960b). An analysis of reaction time in normal and mentally deficient young men. II. Variation of complexity in reaction time tasks. *Journal of Mental Deficiency Research* **4**, 59–67.

Berkson, G. (1960c). An analysis of reaction time in normal and mentally deficient young men. III. Variation of stimulus and response complexity. *Journal of Mental Deficiency Research* **4**, 69–77.

Berkson, G., Hermelin, B. and O'Connor, N. (1961). Physiological responses of normals and institutionalized mental defectives to repeated stimuli. *Journal of Mental Deficiency Research* **5**, 30–39.

Bertelson, P. (1963). S–R relationships and reaction times to a new versus repeated signals in a serial task. *Journal of Experimental Psychology* **65**, 478–484.

Bracey, G. W. (1969). Two operations in character recognition: a partial replication. *Perception and Psychophysics* **6**, 357–360.

Brewer, N. (1976). Intellectual retardation and parameters of choice reaction time. Unpublished Ph.D. Thesis, University of Adelaide.

Brewer, N. (1978). Motor components in the choice reaction time of mildly retarded adults. *American Journal of Mental Deficency* **82**, 565–572.

Brewer, N. and Nettelbeck, T. (1977). The influence of contextual cues on the choice reaction time of mildly retarded adults. *American Journal of Mental Deficiency* **82**, 37–43.

Brewer, N. and Nettelbeck, T. (1979). Speed and accuracy in the choice reaction time of mildly retarded adults. *American Journal of Mental Deficiency* **84**, 55–61.

Broen, W. E., Jr. (1968). "Schizophrenia: Research and Theory". Academic Press, New York.

Bruder, G. E., Sutton, S., Babkoff, H., Gurland, B. J., Yozawitz, A. and Fleiss, J. L. (1975). Auditory signal detectability and facilitation of simple reaction time in psychiatric patients and non-patients. *Psychological Medicine* **5**, 260–272.

Bruhn, P. (1970). Disturbances of vigilance in subcortical epilepsy. *Acta Neurologica Scandinavica* **46**, 442–454.

Bruhn, P. and Parsons, O. A. (1971). Continuous reaction time in brain damage. *Cortex* **7**, 278–291.

Bruininks, R. H. (1974). Physical and motor development of retarded persons. *In* "International Review of Research in Mental Retardation" (N. R. Ellis, ed.), Vol. 7, pp. 209–261. Academic Press, New York.

Caffrey, B., Jones, J. D. and Hinkle, B. R. (1971). Variability in reaction times of normal and educable mentally retarded children. *Perceptual and Motor Skills* **32**, 255–258.

Callan, J. R., Holloway, F. A. and Bruhn, P. (1972). Effects of distraction upon reaction time performance in brain-damaged and alcoholic patients. *Neuropsychologia* **10**, 363–370.

Cancro, R., Sutton, S., Kerr, J. and Sugerman, A. A. (1971). Reaction time and prognosis in acute schizophrenia. *Journal of Nervous and Mental Disease* **153**, 351–359.

Cavanagh, J. P. (1972). Relation between the immediate memory span and the memory search rate. *Psychological Review* **79**, 525–530.

Chase, W. G. (1978). Elementary information processing. *In* "Handbook of Learning and Cognitive Processes" (W. K. Estes, ed.), Vol. 5. Lawrence Erlbaum, Hillsdale, New Jersey.

Crome, L. C., Cowie, V. and Slater, E. (1966). A statistical note on cerebellar and brain stem weight in mongolism. *Journal of Mental Deficiency Research* **10**, 69–72.

Cromwell, R. L. (1975). Assessment of schizophrenia, *Annual Review of Psychology* **26**, 593–619.

Czudner, G. and Rourke, B. P. (1970). Simple reaction time in "brain-damaged" and normal children under regular and irregular preparatory interval conditions. *Perceptual and Motor Skills* **31**, 767–773.

Czudner, G. and Rourke, B. P. (1972). Age differences in visual reaction time of "brain-damaged" and normal children under regular and irregular preparatory interval conditions. *Journal of Experimental Child Psychology* **13**, 516–526.

Dee, H. L. and Van Allen, M. W. (1973). Speed of decision-making processes in patients with unilateral cerebral disease. *Archives of Neurology* **28**, 163–166.

Dingman, H. F. and Silverstein, A. B. (1964). Intelligence, motor abilities and reaction time in the mentally retarded. *Perceptual and Motor Skills* **19**, 791–794.

Dugas, J. L. and Baumeister, A. A. (1968). A comparison of intra-subject variability in auditory difference limens of normals and retardates. *American Journal of Mental Deficiency* **73**, 500–504.

Dugas, J. L. and Kellas, G. (1974). Encoding and retrieval processes in normal children and retarded adolescents. *Journal of Experimental Child Psychology* **17**, 177–185.

Finkel, N. J. (1976). "Mental Illness and Health". MacMillan, New York.

Fisher, M. A. and Zeaman, D. (1973). An attention-retention theory of retardate discrimination learning. *In* "International Review of Research in Mental Retardation" (N. R. Ellis, ed.), Vol. 6. Academic Press, New York.

Fitts, P. M. (1954). The information capacity of the human motor system in controlling the amplitude of movement. *Journal of Experimental Psychology* **47**, 381–391.

Fleer, R. E. (1972). Speed of movement under two conditions of response-initiation and retardates. *Perceptual and Motor Skills* **35**, 140–142.

Freedman, A. M., Deutsch, M. and Deutsch, C. P. (1960). The effects of hydroxyzine hydrochloride upon the reaction time performance of schizophrenic children. *Archives of General Psychiatry* **3**, 153–159.

Friedrich, D. and Hawkins, W. F. (1975). Response-stimulus interval performance of moderately retarded institutionalized subjects. *American Journal of Mental Deficiency* **80**, 281–285.

Friedrich, D., Libkuman, T. and Hawkins, W. F. (1974). Response-stimulus interval performance of non-retarded and institutionalized retarded subjects. *American Journal of Mental Deficiency* **79**, 64–69.

Frith, U. and Frith, C. D. (1974). Specific motor disabilities in Down's syndrome. *Journal of Child Psychology and Psychiatry* **15**, 293–301.

Gosling, H. and Jenness, D. (1974). Temporal variables in simple reaction times of mentally retarded boys. *American Journal of Mental Deficiency* **79**, 214–224.

Groden, G. (1969). Mental ability, reaction time, perceptual motor and motor abilities in handicapped children. *Perceptual and Motor Skills* **28**, 27–30.

Hahn, W. W. (1973). Attention and heart rate: a critical appraisal of the hypothesis of Lacey and Lacey. *Psychological Bulletin* **79**, 59–70.

Halbert, J. (1976). Effects of physical exercise on the performance of the mentally handicapped. Unpublished M.A. Thesis, University of Adelaide.

Harris, G. J. and Fleer, R. E. (1974). High speed memory scanning in mental retardates: evidence for a central processing deficit. *Journal of Experimental Child Psychology* **17**, 452–459.

Hasazi, J. E. and Allen, R. M. (1973). Signal intensity and reinforcement effects on reaction time in brain-damaged and familial retardates. *Perceptual and Motor Skills* **36**, 1227–1233.

Held, J. M., Cromwell, R. L., Frank, E. J. Jr. and Fann, W. E. (1970). Effects of phenothiazines on reaction time in schizophrenics. *Journal of Psychiatric Research* **7**, 209–213.

Hemsley, D. R. and Hawks, D. V. (1974). Speed of response and associative errors in schizophrenia. *British Journal of Social and Clinical Psychology* **13**, 293–303.

Hicks, L. H. and Birren, J. E. (1970). Aging, brain damage, and psychomotor slowing. *Psychological Bulletin* **74**, 377–396.

Hochberg, J. (1970). Attention, organization, and consciousness. *In* "Attention: Contemporary Theory and Analysis" (D. J. Mostofsky, ed.). Appleton, New York.

Holloway, F. A. and Parsons, O. A. (1971). Habituation of the orienting reflex in brain damaged patients. *Psychophysiology* **8**, 623–634.

Holloway, F. A. and Parsons, O. A. (1972). Physiological concomitants of reaction time performance in normal and brain-damaged subjects. *Psychophysiology* **9**, 189–198.

Hoving, K. L., Morin, R. E. and Konick, D. S. (1970). Recognition reaction time and size of memory set: A developmental study. *Psychonomic Science* **21**, 247–248.

Huston, P. E., Shakow, D. and Riggs, L. A. (1937). Studies of motor function in schizophrenia: II. Reaction time. *Journal of General Psychology* **16**, 39–82.

Jankowski, K., Grzesiuk, M. A. and Markiewicz, L. (1970). *Psychophysiological after-effects of prolonged stay in psychiatric hospital: a study of factors involved in rehabilitation of chronic patients: final report.* Warsaw, Poland: State Sanatorium for Nervous Diseases.

Johnson, J. T. Jr. and Olley, J. G. (1971). Behavioural comparisons of mongoloid and non-mongoloid retarded persons: A review. *American Journal of Mental Deficiency* **75**, 546–559.

Jones, D. and Benton, A. L. (1968). Reaction time and age in normal and retarded children. *American Journal of Mental Deficiency* **73**, 143–147.

Joubert, C. E. and Baumeister, A. A. (1970). Effects of varying the length and frequency of response-stimulus interval on the reaction times of normal and mentally deficient subjects. *Journal of Comparative and Physiological Psychology* **73**, 105–110.

Karp, E., Belmont, I. and Birch, H. G. (1971). Delayed sensory-motor processing following cerebral damage. *Cortex* **7**, 419–425.

Karras, A. (1962). The effects of reinforcement and arousal on the psychomotor performance of chronic schizophrenics. *Journal of Abnormal and Social Psychology* **65**, 104–111.

Karras, A. (1968). Choice reaction time of chronic and acute psychiatric patients under primary or secondary aversive stimulation. *British Journal of Social and Clinical Psychology* **7**, 270–279.

Karras, A. (1973). Effects of competing and complex responses on the reaction time of acute psychiatric groups. *Journal of Abnormal Psychology* **82**, 134–138.

Kellas, G. (1969a). Effects of preparatory intervals and stimulus intensity on reaction times of normal and retarded individuals. *Journal of Comparative and Physiological Psychology* **68**, 303–307.

Kellas, G. (1969b). Reaction time and response variability of normal and retarded individuals. *American Journal of Mental Deficiency* **74**, 409–414.

Kellas, G. and Baumeister, A. A. (1970). Effects of adaptation level on response speed of normal and retarded individuals. *American Journal of Mental Deficiency* **74**, 533–536.

King, H. E. (1962). Psychomotor indications of behaviour disorder arising from neurologic trauma and disease. *Psychiatric Communications* **5**, 31–35.

King, H. E. (1965). Psychomotor changes with age, psychopathology, and brain damage. *In* "Behavior, Aging and Nervous System" (A. T. Welford and J. E. Birren, eds.). Charles C. Thomas, Springfield, Illinois.

King, H. E. (1969). Psychomotility: A dimension of behavior disorder. *In* "Neurobiological Aspects of Psychopathology" (J. Zubin and C. Shagass, eds.). Grune and Stratton, New York.

King, H. E. (1975). Psychomotor correlates of behaviour disorder. *In* "Experimental Approaches to Psychopathology" (M. Kietzman, S. Sutton and J. Zubin, eds.). Academic Press, New York.

King, H. E. (1976). Incidental serial reaction time: normal and schizophrenic response to the onset and cessation of auditory signals. *Journal of Psychology* **93**, 299–311.

Kirby, N. H., Nettelbeck, T. and Tiggemann, M. (1977). Reaction time in normal and mentally retarded young adults: sequential effects and response organization. *American Journal of Mental Deficiency* **81**, 492–498.

Klapp, S. T. (1975). Feedback versus motor programming in the control of aimed movement. *Journal of Experimental Psychology: Human Perception and Performance* **104**, 147–153.

Krupski, A. (1975). Heart rate changes during a fixed reaction time task in normal and retarded adult males. *Psychophysiology* **12**, 262–267.

Lacey, J. I. (1967). Somatic response patterning and stress: Some revisions of activation theory. *In* "Psychological stress: Issues in Research" (M. H. Appleby and R. Turnbull, eds). Appleton-Century-Crofts, New York.

Lacey, J. I. and Lacey, B. C. (1958). The relationship of resting autonomic activity to motor impulsivity. *Proceedings of the Association for Research in Nervous and Mental Disease* **36**, 144–209.

Lally, M. and Nettelbeck, T. (1977). Intelligence, reaction time, and inspection time. *American Journal of Mental Deficiency* **82**, 273–281.

Lang, P. J. and Buss, A. H. (1965). Psychological deficit in schizophrenia: II. Interference and activation. *Journal of Abnormal Psychology* **70**, 77–106.

McCauley, C., Kellas, G., Dugas, G. and DeVellis, R. F. (1976). Effects of serial rehearsal training on memory search. *Journal of Educational Psychology* **68**, 474–481.

McGhie, A. (1969). "Pathology of Attention". Penguin, Harmondsworth.

Maisto, A. A. (1978). Comments on the use of the additive factor method with mentally retarded persons: a reply to Silverman. *American Journal of Mental Deficiency* **83**, 191–193.

Maisto, A. A. and Baumeister, A. A. (1975). A developmental study of choice reaction time: The effect of two forms of stimulus degradation on encoding. *Journal of Experimental Child Psychology* **20**, 456–464.

Maisto, A. A. and Jerome, M. A. (1977). Encoding and high-speed memory scanning of retarded and non-retarded adolescents. *American Journal of Mental Deficiency* **82**, 282–286.

Marshall, W. L. (1973). Cognitive functioning in schizophrenia; I. Stimulus analyzing and response selection processes. *British Journal of Psychiatry* **123**, 413–423.

Miller, E. (1970). Simple and choice reaction time following severe head injury. *Cortex* **6**, 121–127.

Moray, N. (1969). "Attention: Selective Processes in Vision and Hearing". Hutchinson Educational, London.

Morelan, S. J. (1976). IQ, Mental age, complexity, and trial blocks and the response latency of retarded and non-retarded children. *American Journal of Mental Deficiency* **80**, 437–441.

Mulhern, T. and Baumeister, A. A. (1971). Effects of Stimulus-Response compatibility and complexity upon reaction times of normals and retardates. *Journal of Comparative and Physiological Psychology* **75**, 459–463.

Nathan, P. E. and Harris, S. L. (1975). "Psychopathology and Society". McGraw Hill, New York.

Neisser, U. (1976). "Cognition and Reality". Freeman, San Francisco.

Nettelbeck, T. and Brewer, N. (1976). Effects of stimulus-response variables on the choice reaction time of mildly retarded adults. *American Journal of Mental Deficiency* **81**, 85–92.

Nettelbeck, T. and Lally, M. (1976). Inspection time and measured intelligence. *British Journal of Psychology* **67**, 17–22.

Nettelbeck, T. and Lally, M. (1979). Age, intelligence, and inspection time. *American Journal of Mental Deficiency* **83**, 398–401.

Nideffer, R. M., Deckner, C. W., Cromwell, R. L. and Cash, T. F. (1971). The relationship of alpha activity to attentional sets in schizophrenia. *Journal of Nervous and Mental Disease* **152**, 346–352.

Nideffer, R. M., Neale, J. M., Kopfstein, J. H. and Cromwell, R. L. (1971). The effect of previous preparatory intervals upon anticipatory responses in the reaction time of schizophrenic and non-schizophrenic patients. *Journal of Nervous and Mental Diseases* **153**, 360–365.

Norman, D. A. (1976). "Memory and Attention", second edition. Wiley, New York.

Nuechterlein, K. H. (1977). Reaction time and attention in schizophrenia: A critical evaluation of the data and theories. *Schizophrenia Bulletin* **3**, 373–428.

Obrist, P. A., Webb, R. A., Sutterer, J. R. and Howard, J. L. (1970). The cardiac-somatic relationship: some reformulations. *Psychophysiology* **6**, 569–587.

O'Connor, N. and Hermelin, B. (1971). Cognitive deficits in children. *British Medical Bulletin* **27**, 227–231.

O'Connor, N. and Hermelin, B. (1978). "Seeing and Hearing and Space and Time". Academic Press, London.

Olbrich, R. (1972). Reaction time in brain-damaged and normal subjects to variable preparatory intervals. *Journal of Nervous and Mental Disease* **155**, 356–362.

Pachella, R. G. (1974). The interpretation of reaction time in information processing research. *In* "Human Information Processing: Tutorials in Performance and Cognition" (B. H. Kantowitz, ed.). Lawrence Erlbaum, New Jersey.

Parsons, O. A. and Bruhn, P. (1973). Effects of inter-stimulus interval on continuous choice reaction time performance in brain-damaged, alcoholic and control patients. *Cortex* **9**, 176–182.

Poulton, E. C. (1973). Unwanted range effects from using within-subject experimental designs. *Psychological Bulletin* **80**, 113–121.

Rees, J. A. (1971). Simple and choice reaction time in spastic hemiplegics. *Developmental Medicine and Child Neurology* **13**, 772–778.

Rodnick, E. H. and Shakow, D. (1940). Set in the schizophrenic as measured by a composite reaction time index. *American Journal of Psychiatry* **97**, 214–225.

Rourke, B. P. and Czudner, G. (1972). Age differences in auditory reaction time of "brain-damaged" and normal children under regular and irregular preparatory interval conditions. *Journal of Experimental Child Psychology* **14**, 372–378.

Runcie, D. and O'Bannon, R. M. (1975). Relationship of reaction time to deceleration and variability of heart rate in non-retarded and retarded persons. *American Journal of Mental Deficiency* **79**, 553–558.

Scott, K. G. (1971). Recognition memory: A research strategy and a summary of initial findings. *In* "International Review of Research in Mental Retardation" (N. R. Ellis, ed.), Vol. 5, pp. 84–111. Academic Press, New York.

Scott, W. S. (1940). Reaction time of young intellectual deviates. *Archives of Psychology* No. 256 **36**, 1–64. New York.

Shakow, D. (1946). The nature of deterioration in schizophrenic conditions. *Nervous and Mental Disease Monographs*, No. 70.

Shakow, D. (1962). Segmental set: A theory of the formal psychological deficit in schizophrenia. *Archives of General Psychiatry* **6**, 1–17.

Shakow, D. (1972). The Worcester State Hospital research on schizophrenia (1927–1946). *Journal of Abnormal Psychology* **80**, 67–110.

Sharp, S. E. (1898–99). Individual psychology; a study of psychological method. *American Journal of Psychology* **10**, 329–391.

Silverman, W. P. (1974). High speed scanning of non-alphanumeric symbols in cultural-familially retarded and non-retarded children. *American Journal of Mental Deficiency* **79**, 44–51.

Silverman, W. P. (1975). Utilization of redundant information by EMR and non-retarded adults. *American Journal of Mental Deficiency* **80**, 197–201.

Silverman, W. P. (1978). Comments on 'Encoding and high-speed memory scanning . . .' by Maisto and Jerome. *American Journal of Mental Deficiency* **83**, 188–190.

Sokolov, E. N. (1963). "Perception and the Conditioned Reflex" (translation, S. W. Waydenfeld). Pergamon, Oxford.

Solis, D. H. (1974). Visual and auditory reaction times with EEG in epileptic subjects. *Biological Psychology Bulletin* **3**, 120–134.

Sroufe, L. A. (1971). Age changes in cardiac deceleration within a fixed foreperiod reaction-time task: An index of attention. *Developmental Psychology* **5**, 338–343.

Steffy, R. A. and Galbraith, K. (1974). A comparison of segmental set and inhibitory deficit explanations of the crossover pattern in process schizophrenic reaction time. *Journal of Abnormal Psychology* **83**, 227–233.

Sternberg, S. (1967). Two operations in character recognition: some evidence from reaction-time measurements. *Perception and Psychophysics* **2**, 45–53.

Sternberg, S. (1975). Memory scanning: New findings and current controversies. *Quarterly Journal of Experimental Psychology* **27**, 1–32.

Sutton, S. and Zubin, J. (1965). Effect of sequence on reaction time in schizophrenia. *In* "Behavior, Aging and the Nervous System" (A. T. Welford and J. E. Birren, eds). Charles C. Thomas, Springfield, Illinois.

Swinney, D. A. and Taylor, O. L. (1971). Short-term memory recognition search in aphasics. *Journal of Speech and Hearing Research* **14**, 578–588.

Sylvester, P. E. and Roy, R. K. (1971). Hemispherical response to fine touch in normal and mentally subnormal epileptic subjects. *Journal of Mental Deficiency Research* **15**, 303–309.

Talland, G. A. (1965). Initiation of response, and reaction time in aging, and with brain damage. *In* "Behavior, Aging and the Nervous System" (A. T. Welford and J. E. Birren, eds.). Charles C. Thomas, Springfield, Illinois.

Teichner, W. H. and Krebs, M. J. (1974). Laws of visual choice reaction time. *Psychological Review* **81**, 75–98.

Terrell, C. G. and Ellis, N. R. (1964). Reaction time in normal and defective subjects following varied warning conditions. *Journal of Abnormal and Social Psychology* **69**, 449–452.

Tizard, J. and Venables, P. H. (1956). Reaction times by schizophrenics, mental defectives and normal adults. *American Journal of Psychiatry* **112**, 803–807.

Venables, P. H. (1965). Slowness in schizophrenia. *In* "Behavior, Aging, and the Nervous System" (A. T. Welford and J. E. Birren, eds.). Charles C. Thomas, Springfield, Illinois.

Wade, M. G., Newell, K. M. and Wallace, S. A. (1978). Decision time and movement time as a function of response complexity in retarded persons. *American Journal of Mental Deficiency* **83**, 135–144.

Wagenaar, W. A. (1975). Performance of epileptic patients in continuous reaction-time situations. *American Journal of Mental Deficiency* **79**, 726–731.

Waldbaum, J. K., Sutton, S. and Kerr, J. (1975). Shifts of sensory modality and reaction time in schizophrenia. *In* "Experimental Approaches to Psychopathology" (M. L. Kietzman, S. Sutton and J. Zubin, eds.). Academic Press, New York.

Wallace, R. M. and Fehr, F. S. (1970). Heart rate, skin resistance, and reaction time of mongoloid and normal children under baseline and distraction conditions. *Psychophysiology* **6**, 722–731.

Weaver, L. A. and Ravaris, C. (1970). The distribution of reaction times in mental retardates. *Journal of Mental Deficiency Research* **14**, 295–304.

Weaver, L. A. and Ravaris, C. L. (1972). Psychomotor performance of mental retardates. *Journal of Mental Deficiency Research* **16**, 76–83.

Weaver, L. A., Jr. and Ravaris, C. L. (1974). Psychomotor test scores and rated functional impairment of mental retardates. *Perceptual and Motor Skills* **38**, 487–490.

Welford, A. T. (1976). "Skilled Performance: Perceptual and Motor Skills". Scott, Foresman, Glenview, Illinois.

Wells, F. L. and Kelley, C. M. (1922). The simple reaction time in psychosis. *American Journal of Psychiatry* **2**, 53–59.

Wickens, C. D. (1974). Temporal limits of human information processing: a developmental study. *Psychological Bulletin* **81**, 739–755.

Wissler, C. (1901). The correlation of mental and physical traits. *Psychological Monographs* **3** (6, whole No. 16).

Yates, A. J. (1966). Data processing levels and thought disorder in schizophrenia. *Australian Journal of Psychology* **18**, 103–117.

Zahn, T. P. (1970). Effects of reduction in uncertainty on reaction time in schizophrenic and normal subjects. *Journal of Experimental Research in Personality* **4**, 135–143.

Zahn, T. P., Rosenthal, D. and Shakow, D. (1963). Effects of irregular preparatory intervals on reaction time in schizophrenia. *Journal of Abnormal and Social Psychology* **67**, 44–52.

Zeaman, D. (1973). One programmatic approach to retardation. *In* "The Experimental Psychology of Mental Retardation" (D. K. Routh, ed.). Crosby Lockwood Staples, London.

Zeaman, D. and House, B. J. (1963). The role of attention in retardate discrimination learning. *In* "Handbook of Mental Deficiency" (N. R. Ellis, ed.). McGraw Hill, New York.

Author Index

Smith, P. G., 145, 153, 160, *171*, 256, 266, 284, *307*
Smith, W. A. S., 60, *68*
Smith, W. M., 220, *252*
Snodgrass, J. G., 50, *70*
Sokolov, E. N., 378, *400*
Solis, D. H., 359, *400*
Speidel, C. R., 190, *212*
Spencer, T. J., *213*
Spieth, W., 335, *349, 353*
Spiker, V. A., 175, *211*
Spotnitz, H., 3, *20*
Sroufe, L. A., 379, *400*
Stacy, E. W., Jr., 265, *304*
Standfast, Susan, 220, *248*
Stanovich, K. E., 116, *127*, 188, 189, 192, *213*
Starkes, Janet, L., 224, *251*
Steffy, R. A., 374, 375, 380, 391, *394, 400*
Stelmach, G. E., 219, *249*, 335, *353*
Sternberg, S., 113, 114, 120, *127*, 187, 188, 190, *213*, 227, 236, *252*, 253, 254, 256, 258, 259, 260, 261, 263, 267, 269, 275, 284, 285, 286, 303, *306, 307*, 381, 383, 384, *400*
Stevens, S. S., 18, *22*
Stone, G., 175, 188, 190, *213*
Stone, G. C., 103, 104, 105, *127*, 148, 154, 158, 159, 160, *170*
Stone, M., 41, *70*, 180, 181, *213*, 287, *307*
Storandt, Martha, 335, 347, 348, *349*
Stuart, A., 50, *68*
Stull, G. A., 322, *353*
Suci, G. J., 332, 333, *353*
Sugarman, A. A., 360, *395*
Sullivan, S. J., 224, *251*
Summers, J. J., 155, *171*
Surwillo, W. W., 332, 333, 335, 336, 344, *353*
Sutterer, J. R., 379, *399*
Sutton, S., 220, *248*, 360, 372, 375, *395, 400, 401*
Swanson, J. M., 54, *70*, 263, 279, *304, 307*
Swensson, R. G., 38, 42, 53, 54, 62, *70*
Swets, J. A., 28, 32, 35, 38, 54, *67, 70*
Swink, J., 243, *252*
Swinney, D. A., 382, *400*

Switzer, G., 104, *124*
Sykes, R. N., 246, *249*
Sylvester, P. E., 359, *400*
Szafran, J., 331, 332, 333, 334, 335, 336, 346, *350, 353*

T

Talbot, S. A., 6, 9, *21*
Talland, G. A., 332, 333, 339, *353, 354*, 357, *400*
Tanner, W. P., 28, 32, 35, *67, 70*, 101, *124*
Taylor, D. A., 116, *127*, 189, 192, *213*, 255, 256, 257, 260, 266, 285, 286, *307*
Taylor, D. H., 44, 50, *70*, 106, *127*
Taylor, M. M., 35, 54, *70*
Taylor, O. L., 382, *400*
Teasdall, R. D., 331, *351*
Teichner, W. H., 18, *22*, 100, 109, 115, *127*, 183, 201, *213*, 385, *400*
Telford, C. W., 215, *252*
Teplov, B. M., 311, *320*
Ter Linden, W., 41, *70*
Terrell, C. G., 362, *401*
Theios, J., 256, 266, 284, *307*
Thomas, E. A. C., 42, 54, *70, 71*
Thomas, G. B., 161, *169*, 183, *211*
Thomas, R. E., 42, 54, 62, *70*
Thompson, L. W., 331, 336, 344, 346, 347, 348, *349, 350, 352, 354*
Thomson, G. H., 35, *71*
Thorne, P. R., 347, 348, *350*
Thurmond, J. B., 36, 38, *71*
Thurstone, L. L., 28, 31, 32, 53, *71*
Tiffin, J., 12, *23*
Tiggemann, M., 164, *170*, 367, *398*
Tisseyre, F., 159, *168*
Tizard, J., 378, *401*
Todd, J. W., 6, *23*
Torgerson, W. S., 56, *71*
Townsend, J. T., 116, *127*, 189, 192, *213*, 256, 260, 285, 286, *307*
Traupmann, J., 256, 266, 284, *307*
Travis, L. E., 12, *23*
Travis, R. C., 8, 11, *19*
Treisman, Anne, 102, 103, 109, 112, *123*, 221, *252*
Treisman, M., 32, 56, *71*

Subject Index